The Ultimate Data and AI Guide

150 FAQs About Artificial Intelligence, Machine Learning and Data

Alexander Thamm,
Michael Gramlich,
Dr. Alexander Borek

Copyright © 2020 Data AI GmbH. All rights reserved.

No part of this book may be reproduced in any form or by an electronic or mechanical means, including information storage and retrieval systems, without permission in writing from the publisher, except by a reviewer who may quote brief passages in a review.

Most of the illustrations have been created by the authors and illustrators. However, some illustrations and data are the courtesy of other companies, organizations or individuals. These are explicitly marked in their figure caption and are reprinted in this book with prior written approval.

This book may be purchased for educational, business, or sales promotional use. For more information, contact the publisher at +49 89 30760880 or your@data-ai-guide.com.

ISBN 978-3-9821737-0-2 (paperback)
ISBN 978-3-9821737-1-9 (eBook)

Technical Editors:	Dr. Olav Laudy, Jörg Bienert, Stefan Sexl, Gernot Molin and Prof. Dr. Patrick Glauner
Copyeditor:	Charlie Wilson
Proofreader:	Stephanie Cohen
Cover Designer:	Jannes Lojkasek
Illustrators:	Nida Lovchev and Michael Gramlich

Published by Data AI Press.

Postal address:
Sapporobogen 6–8
80637 Munich
Germany

For any questions, inquiries or comments, contact your@data-ai-guide.com.

www.data-ai-guide.com

"The impacts of AI and ML in our lives are huge. However, there are myths and misconceptions that need to be put down right now. This book is a place to start planning your journey in this area. Concise, practical and lots of examples to guide you."

Mario Faria, VP and Program Director for CDOs, Gartner

"Read this! If you are at A = 'Slides and Stickynotes' and want to go to B = 'Real Data and Impact', this can be your travel guide. If you are a practitioner already creating impact, read this to get structure and perspective into the flow of topics you are handling."

Marcel Kling, Senior Director Data Driven Customer Journey, Lufthansa Group

"Much like a puzzle, you have to fit a lot of pieces together to succeed with AI. But how could you even know what pieces you need? This volume, by Thamm, Gramlich and Borek, provides the answers – a huge assist for anyone concerned about the future!"

Thomas C. Redman, the Data Doc, HBR Blogger and Book Author

"Alexander Thamm, Michael Gramlich and Alexander Borek have written a unique book that is the go-to reference in the AI and data space. It covers an impressive breadth and scope of topics and explains them in a highly accessible way. If you are in any way interested in the world of data and AI you owe it to yourself to read this book, there is something to learn for everyone."

Harvinder Atwal, Chief Data Officer at Moneysupermarket.com

"This book is a veritable smorgasbord of insight into the world of data and analytics, singularly lucid and accessible. Even after more than a decade spent working in analytics and AI, I found myself enjoying the clever summaries and learning a thing or two. Interesting lists of valuable examples, yet organised usefully. Terms are knowledgeably explained! Recommended to anyone with an interest in the field."

Ryan den Rooijen, Group Head of Data & Analytics, Chalhoub Group

"This book is not a novel and not an essay. This is a guide, a guide for those who are willing to feel the power of science out of academia, for those who seek for the facts, for those who find it ridiculous to repeat tasks, and for those who have fun unveiling secrets. In this guide you will find answers to the most common questions that we data practitioners have been facing in the last years in business environments. Alex, Alex and Michael did a great job sorting them out, and providing crystal-clear answers. If you are into data-transformation business on any industry, this book is a must. This book is the Hitchhiker's Guide to the Data Galaxy."

Dr. Diego Villuendas, Global Head of Data & Analytics, SEAT

"There is no artificial intelligence without data. There is no business value without people in organizations applying AI and data in production. If you found yourself asking 'what is AI?' or 'what is data?' then you'll find the exact answer in this book, together with 150 FAQs and multiple case studies as a clarifying, coherent framework for your initiative."

Stijn Christiaens, Co-founder and CTO of Collibra

*For Cordula and our unborn child –
we can't wait to welcome you.*
- Alex T.

*For my family and friends,
thank you for your patience and support.*
- Michael

For Nadine.
- Alex B.

Table of Contents

Foreword xvii
Preface xviii
Acknowledgments.. xxi
Introduction xxii

Part I | Why Do We Care: The Digital Transformation Train

1 Digital Transformation: The Role of Data and Artificial Intelligence 2

   1_1 Digital transformation 2
      1 | What is digital transformation? 2
      2 | What is the impact of digital transformation on
          companies and society?...................................... 4
      3 | What are the drivers of digital transformation?...................... 7

   1_2 The role of data and AI in digital transformation.................. 8
      4 | AI – Why is it the engine of digital transformation?............... 8
      5 | Data – why is it the fuel of digital transformation? 9
      6 | How are data and AI applied to generate value
          across industries?.. 10

   1_3 Buzzwords in digital transformation, data and AI 13
      7 | What is an overview of buzzwords in data and AI? 13
      8 | What is the IoT and what does it have to
          do with big data?.. 14
      9 | What are data lakes, data warehouses,
          data architectures, Hadoop and NoSQL databases? 15
      10 | What are data governance and data democratization? 16
      11 | What is the cloud?... 16
      12 | What are data science, data analytics, business
           intelligence, data mining and predictive analytics? 17

13 | What are machine learning, neural networks and
deep learning? 19
14 | What are AI, natural language processing,
computer vision and robotics? 20

Part II | The Fuel: Data

2 Understanding Data: The Fuel of Digital and
Artificial Intelligence Transformation... 22

    2_1 Understanding data... 22

        15 | What is data? 22
        16 | Why collect data and what are
           the different types of data analytics? 28
        17 | How is data created? 30
        18 | What are the factors that have enabled an
           era of mass data creation and storage?............................. 32
        19 | What is data quality and what kind of data
           quality issues are there? 36
        20 | How much data quality do you need?.............................. 39

    2_2 Types of data.. 41

        21 | What are unstructured, semi-structured and
           structured data? 41
        22 | What are master data and transactional data?.................... 45
        23 | What is streaming data and what is the difference
           between batch and streaming processing?........................ 46
        24 | What is big data? 48

3 Data Storage Technologies 52

    3_1 Understanding data storage... 52

        25 | Why can't a company store its structured
           data in an Excel file like we do on PCs?............................. 52
        26 | What is a database and how does it work?........................ 54
        27 | What are the advantages of storing data
           in a database?.. 56

		28 | What types of databases are there and how are they classified?	57
3_2		**Relational (SQL) databases**	59
		29 | What is a relational database system and how does it work?	59
		30 | How does the relational model work?	61
		31 | What is a key attribute and why is it indispensable?	64
		32 | How is data accessed and manipulated in a relational database system (SQL)?	68
		33 | What are the strengths of relational database systems?	72
		34 | What are the limitations of relational database systems and how were they revealed with the dawn of big data?	73
3_3		**Distributed file systems and non-relational (NoSQL) databases**	76
		35 | What are computer clusters and how did the idea of "scaling out" form the basis for storing and processing big data?	76
		36 | What are distributed file systems and how do we store data with them?	79
		37 | What are non-relational (NoSQL) databases and what does the CAP theorem have to do with them?	81
		38 | How do relational and non-relational databases compare and when is it best to use each one?	88
3_4		**Popular data storage technologies**	90
		39 | What are the types of data storage technologies?	90
		40 | What are Hadoop and the Hadoop Ecosystem (e.g. Hive, HBase, Flume, Kafka)?	91
		41 | What is Spark?	93
		42 | What are MySQL, PostgreSQL, Oracle, Microsoft SQL Server, SAP HANA, IBM Db2 and Teradata Database?	94

43 | What are MongoDB, Neo4j, Amazon DynamoDB,
   CouchDB and Redis? 95

4 Architecting Data: Data Warehouses, Data Lakes and the Cloud 96

4_1 Understanding data architectures 96
44 | What is a data architecture and why
   do companies need it? 96
45 | What are the most popular
   architectural blueprints? 99

4_2 Data warehouse architectures 100
46 | What is a data warehouse (DWH) architecture? 100
47 | How does a DWH work? 103
48 | What does a typical data pipeline in a DWH look like? 107
49 | What are the limitations of a DWH? 108
50 | What are popular ETL tools? 110

4_3 Data lakes and streaming architectures 111
51 | What is a data lake architecture? 111
52 | How does a data lake work and where should it be used? 112
53 | How do a DWH and data lake compare? 115

4_4 Cloud architectures 118
54 | What is the cloud? 118
55 | What types of cloud architectures are there? 120
56 | What types of cloud services are there? 123
57 | What are the advantages and disadvantages of
   using cloud services? 126
58 | What is a serverless architecture? 130
59 | What are the popular cloud providers and services? 132

5 Managing Data in a Company 134

5_1 People and job roles 134
60 | What does a chief data and analytics officer do? 134
61 | What does a data architect do? 135
62 | What does a database administrator do? 136

63 | What other job roles are involved in creating
and maintaining a data architecture? 136

5_2 Data governance and Democratization 137

64 | What are data governance and democratization and
why does data need to be governed and democratized? 137

65 | What are the key elements of data governance and
data democratization? 138

66 | How can we make data more findable and accessible? 139

67 | How can we make data more understandable and share
knowledge on data? 140

68 | How can we make data more trustworthy and
improve the quality of data? 141

69 | How can we empower the data user with self-service
BI and analytics? 141

70 | How can data governance and data
democratization be implemented? 142

5_3 Data security and protection (privacy) 143

71 | What is an overview of data security, data protection
and data privacy and how do they relate
to each other? 143

72 | What is data security and how can it be achieved? 145

73 | What is personal data? 148

74 | What is data protection (privacy) and why is the
distinction between non-personal and personal
data so important? 150

75 | General Data Protection Regulation (GDPR) –
who, what, where and why? 153

Part III | The Engine: Artificial Intelligence and Machine Learning

**6 Understanding Machine Learning as the Key
Driver Behind Artificial Intelligence** 160

6_1 Understanding AI and ML 160

76 | What is AI? 160

77 | Where can AI be applied and how have approaches to create AI developed over time? ... 163
78 | What is currently possible with AI and what are some top breakthroughs? ... 165
79 | Why is AI almost tantamount to ML (AI = ML + X) today? ... 168
80 | What is ML and how can it create AI? ... 170
81 | How is a machine able to learn and why is ML often considered "Software 2.0"? ... 172
82 | What is a machine able to learn – can it predict the future? ... 176

6_2 Types of ML ... 180
83 | What types of ML are there and how do they differ? ... 180
84 | What is supervised ML? ... 184
85 | What is the difference between regression and classification? ... 186
86 | What is unsupervised ML? ... 187
87 | What are the most commonly used methods in unsupervised learning? ... 189
88 | What is reinforcement learning? ... 193

6_3 Popular ML tools ... 196
89 | What types of ML tools are there? ... 196
90 | What is Python? ... 199
91 | What is R and RStudio? ... 199
92 | What is scikit-learn? ... 200
93 | What are Tensorflow and Keras? ... 200
94 | What are MLLib, PySpark and SparkR? ... 201
95 | What are some popular cloud-based ML tools? ... 201

7 Creating and Testing a ML Model with Supervised Machine Learning ... 203

7_1 Creating a machine learning model with supervised ML methods ... 203

96 | What ingredients do you need and what is
the recipe for creating an ML model?................................. 203
97 | What is an ML model? 205
98 | What is a correlation and why is it necessary for
ML models? 208
99 | What is feature engineering and why is
it considered "applied ML"? 213
100 | What is feature selection and
why is it necessary? 215
101 | Why do we need to split a dataset into
training, validation and test sets? 219
102 | What does it mean to "train an ML model" and
how do you do it?... 222

7_2 Validating, testing and using a machine learning model 227

103 | What does it mean to "validate a model", and
why is it necessary? 227
104 | What is the difference between validating and
testing a model and why is the latter necessary?............ 231
105 | What are overfitting and generalization?........................... 233
106 | Preventing overfitting: how does
cross-validation work?.. 237
107 | Preventing overfitting: how does ensemble
learning work? 238
108 | How else can overfitting be prevented?............................ 240
109 | How much data is needed to train
an ML model?.. 240

8 Popular Machine Learning Model Classes for Supervised Machine Learning 243

8_1 Some classic ML models 243

110 | What model classes are there in ML? 243
111 | How do generalized linear models work?......................... 244
112 | How do decision trees work?... 245
113 | How do ensemble methods such as
the random forest algorithm work? 246

114 | How do we choose the right ML model?........................... 247

8_2 Neural networks and deep learning.. 249

115 | What are neural networks and deep
learning and why do they matter?.................................... 249
116 | How do neural networks work?... 253
117 | What is so special about deep neural
networks compared to classic ML model classes?............ 256
118 | Why are neural networks so good at natural
language processing and computer vision?...................... 259
119 | Are neural networks a universal cure for all
ML problems or do they also have some drawbacks? 263
120 | What is transfer learning? 266
121 | Deep neural networks – why now and what
will their future look like? 268

9 Managing Machine Learning in a Company.. 271

9_1 Phases of an ML project 271

122 | How does the ML process work (an overview)?................. 271
123 | Phase 1: How can ML use cases be identified? 273
124 | Phase 2: What are data exploration and data
preparation and why are they necessary? 276
125 | Phase 3: What is model creation?..................................... 282
126 | Phase 4: What is (continuous) model deployment?........... 282

9_2 Lessons learned from machine-learning projects 285

127 | How long does a machine-learning project
take from the conception of the idea until the
model is deployed?... 285
128 | How many projects make it from the idea to
the end and where do they fail? 286
129 | What are the most common reasons
why projects fail? 287
130 | Why is model deployment the bottleneck for
most companies implementing ML projects?.................... 289

9_3 People and job roles in ML 291
- 131 | Which roles are required to implement an ML project? 291
- 132 | What does a data scientist do? 293
- 133 | What does a data engineer do? 293
- 134 | What does an ML engineer do? 294
- 135 | What does a statistician do? 294
- 136 | What does a software engineer do? 295
- 137 | What does a business analyst do? 295
- 138 | What do other roles do? 296

9_4 Agile organization and ways of working 296
- 139 | What is agile project management and why is it appropriate for ML projects? 296
- 140 | What are DevOps and DataOps? 300
- 141 | What are the popular organizational structures and best practices? 302

9_5 Data ethics in ML 306
- 142 | What is data ethics? 306
- 143 | What are the ethical considerations in data collection? 307
- 144 | What are the ethical considerations when creating ML models? 309
- 145 | What best practices and principles can ensure the ethical use of data? 312

Part IV | Where will we go?

10 The Future of Data, Machine Learning and Artificial Intelligence 316
- 146 | How are AI and its drivers going to develop? 316
- 147 | What are the implications of ML and AI for companies? 319
- 148 | We benefit a lot from AI, but will it cost me my job? 322
- 149 | Which nation will win the AI race? 325
- 150 | When are we going to see the creation of general AI? 329

Appendix

List of Abbreviations	334
List of Tables	335
List of Figures	339
List of Case Studies	343
Reference List	346
Index	365
About the Authors	371

Foreword

This book takes the overwhelming haystack of popular AI and Machine Learning terminologies and pinpoints the needle, presenting sensible details about these disruptive technologies. It distinguishes AI fact from fiction, and tips the scales back towards reality with clear, easy to absorb information revolving around critical AI topics.

With the unprecedented speed of technological advancement of the 21st century, the proliferation of intelligent technologies has led to a competition to understand and master the root of these advancements: data. This serves an informational need for guidance across the data and AI landscape, introducing and submerging readers into one of the most urgent topics of our generation.

The authors have brought AI full circle here; from the data groundwork to the ethical cornerstones. The content addresses the technological and organizational frameworks for AI, as well as conceptual drivers that provide context for digital transformation. From neural networks, deep learning, transfer learning, IoT, cloud, predictive analytics, big data, and machine learning, there is no stone left untouched when it comes to clarifying the why of AI. Real-world case studies edify the reader with useful conclusions that they can draw upon and reference for their own applicable business scenarios.

Whether you're an aspiring data practitioner, working in an organization that is planning AI adoption, or just take an interest in data or AI, this will bring you up to speed and allow you to better navigate the world of data and AI.

Ronald van Loon
Global Top 10 AI & Data Influencer

Preface

Let's be honest. It is not like there isn't any information about artificial intelligence, machine learning and data out there. In fact, the *opposite* is the case. As of December 2019, a Google search for these terms yielded around 455 million, 1,110 million and 6,100 million results respectively. On top of that there are plenty of books, vlogs and videos out there – more than enough, right?

There is a catch. We've seen it in the 500+ data projects that we have implemented and consulted for at over 100 European companies in all sectors over the past eight years. The information is either too narrow and deep (*à la* "Creating AI with deep reinforcement learning in Keras")[1] or it is too shallow and striking (*à la* "AI-fuelled technology is about to take your job")[2]. Consequently, there exists widespread fear, confusion and misconceptions about these topics. Very few are what we call *data natives*, i.e. people who have a solid understanding of AI, machine learning and data without being in-depth experts.

To empower our clients and fill that knowledge gap, we started implementing hands-on corporate trainings in 2017. Since then, we have tested, refined and honed the content of this course and shared our knowledge with hundreds of data and AI enthusiasts. This book is the result of this extensive training. Here, we pull together the essential information you need to know about artificial intelligence (AI), machine learning (ML) and data in one comprehensive, easy-to-understand text. This is the ultimate guide to data and AI.

This book is for those who want to gain an understanding that goes beyond scratching the surface, who want to know what they are talking about when playing the buzzword bingo of AI, ML and data. With this guide, you can spare yourself the minutiae of how algorithms and databases work to a level that you could program them on your own and simply learn the essentials. It's all you need to know, wrapped up in 150 easily navigable FAQs.

What you can expect from this book:

- A complete overview of the most important concepts in AI, data and ML
- Simple, hands-on explanations of complex topics, accompanied by clarifying visualizations
- Content organized into 150 FAQs that you can refer to individually or read as a whole

---

1. Don't worry – once you have worked through this book, you will understand what we are talking about.
2. Whether or not this is true is covered in Chapter 148.

Preface

- Real-world-inspired case studies based on our experience of 500+ implemented data projects
- Information from practitioners for aspiring practitioners or simply interested readers

What you won't find in this book:

- Academic discussions with lots of theory (we are practitioners, not professors)
- In-depth content on every topic covered, including mathematical formulas and algorithms (we aim to give you a solid understanding in this book, not make you an expert in all topics)

Here are some key facts and data about the book so you can see the overall picture:

Table P.1 Key facts about the content of this book

Total number of words[3]	131,502
Number of FAQs	150
Average number of words per FAQ	877
Total number of illustrations	120
Total number of tables	126
Total number of case studies	63
Average reading time per FAQ[4i]	3min 54sec
Total reading time[5ii]	9h 45min

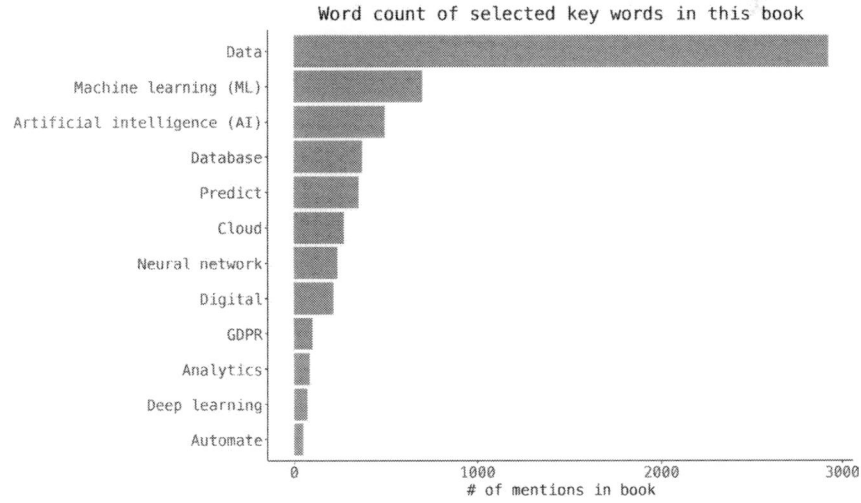

Figure P.1 Wordcount of selected key words in the book

---

3. Only counting the content from Chapter 1 until Chapter 10
4. Assuming a reading speed of 225 words/minute, which is a little under the 238 words/minute average reading speed for nonfiction books (s. reference)

xix

The Ultimate Data and AI Guide

Our promise to you

Reading this book will make you a data native. With this book, you will:

- Gain a complete overview and understanding of the most important buzzwords and topics related to AI, data and ML, so that you can delve deeper into them independently.
- Understand how AI, data and ML are used by companies to create added value and how they affect us in our daily lives.
- Be inspired by lots of real-life case studies that offer tips on how you can leverage data and AI in your company and workplace.

The book is written so that you can understand the content even if you have no previous knowledge of AI, data and ML. The book can also serve as a reference if you encounter buzzwords or unfamiliar concepts in the media or during the course of your work.

As you will see throughout this book, AI, data and ML are currently transforming our societies and economies, and they will increasingly do so, becoming even more dominant in the future. The changes brought about by these developments are huge, comparable only to previous industrial revolutions or the invention of the printing press. Being uninformed about these topics is like being illiterate when the first printed books were produced. In other words, there is no better time to delve into the world of data and AI than *right now* – and this is *the* guidebook to accompany you on your journey.

Visit our website, www.data-ai-guide.com, for answers to more fascinating FAQs. We would be grateful if you took a moment to share your feedback and comments about the book on Amazon (s. link below) – we look forward to hearing your thoughts. And don't forget to connect with us or follow us on LinkedIn to keep in touch.

Website	Amazon review link

www.data-ai-guide.com	www.rpbook.co.uk/azr/3982173701

Thank you for your interest in this book and the topics we cover here. We hope that this guide will get you as excited about AI and data as we are!

---

5. Ibid.

Acknowledgments

We would like to thank everyone who helped and supported us along the journey of writing this book. We are especially grateful to everyone who provided us with feedback, shared valuable comments or simply asked questions and listened to us and thereby helped us hone this book. Our special thanks goes to our technical editors Dr. Olav Laudy, Gernot Molin, Jörg Bienert, Stefan Sexl and Prof. Dr. Patrick Glauner – it would not have been possible without your invaluable input.

We are also deeply grateful to all institutions, companies and individuals who allowed us to reprint their illustrations.

Finally, we would like to thank our clients and partners. It is an honour to accompany you along your data journey and we are looking forward to growing and learning with you in the future.

Introduction

Artificial intelligence, big data, deep learning, relational databases, SQL, NoSQL databases, data lakes, machine learning, data warehouse, data protection, data mining, GDPR, data governance... No doubt you have encountered many of these buzzwords, but do you know what they *actually* mean and how they relate to each other? As exciting as it is to work with data, it can be extremely confusing. It truly is a buzzword jungle out there, and it is easy to get lost and fail to see the wood for the trees, especially if you are a newcomer in the field.

Why all the confusion? There are three main reasons. Firstly, many of the topics around data, artificial intelligence (AI) and machine learning (ML) are extremely hyped. Some of the hype is justified, given the enormous transformations that these developments mean for us on an individual, societal and economic level. But in some cases talk is inflated and exaggerated, especially by people who do not really know what they are talking about. Secondly, the world of data and AI is moving fast, extremely fast. We are only at the *beginning* of the transformations that will be brought about. New data-driven technologies, concepts and breakthroughs pop up constantly and it is hard to keep track of all of them. Thirdly, a lot of the concepts are rather complex and interrelated with many other topics, which makes it difficult to make sense of them.

Content and scope of this book

This book serves as a guide to the data and AI jungle, so that you can stay on top of all of these buzzwords. It covers a good deal of the data- and AI-related topics that are currently most important. You won't be an expert after reading the entire book (no one can be, because the field includes so many topics). But you *will* be a jack of all trades. You will acquire a solid understanding so that you are able to put data and AI into context and make deep dives independently.

Here is an overview of what this book covers.

Part I | Why Do We Care: The Digital Transformation Train

Chapter 1 deals with digital transformation. You will learn what digital transformation is, how it is affecting you as an individual and how it affects our societies and economies. We will see why digital transformation train is increasingly driven by data (the oil) and AI (the engine) and why you should know about them.

Part II | The Fuel: Data

Part II is made up of Chapters 2 through 5 and is dedicated to the fuel of digital transformation: *data*.

In Chapter 2, you will learn the basics about data: what it is, why it has become so important, how it is collected, what types of data there are and how we have entered the era of big data.

Chapter 3 deals with how different kinds of data can be stored. We look into the most prevalent technologies, such as relational database systems, NoSQL databases and distributed file systems. The chapter closes with an overview of the most important data storage providers.

As opposed to Chapter 3, which looks at data storage from a technical point of view (i.e. the physical hardware and software that store data), Chapter 4 looks at data storage from a logical and organizational point of view. We explore data architectures, i.e. how data flows within companies: how are the hardware and software that store data such as databases orchestrated and connected within a company? We look at two commonly used blueprint architectures: the data warehouse and the data lake. The chapter closes with a peek into how the cloud works and why it has been a true game-changer for every company.

Chapter 5 walks you through the organizational, legal and security aspects of managing data in a company. We look at data governance, the discipline that is concerned with managing data, to ensure it is findable, of high quality and ready for use within a company. We consider the job roles that are required to collect, store and manage data. Finally, we take a brief look at data security (how data can be shielded from unwanted access or manipulation) and data protection (what legal regulations govern the use of personal data), including a peek into the General Data Protection Regulation (GDPR).

Part III | The Engine: Artificial Intelligence and Machine Learning

Part III of the book is dedicated to the engine of digital transformation: *artificial intelligence*, or rather machine learning (ML). As you will see, right now AI is mostly driven by ML, the discipline that is concerned with creating algorithms to make computers perform tasks without being explicitly programmed to do so. The vast majority of recent breakthroughs in the field of AI have been achieved through the application of ML techniques.

In Chapter 6, we explain exactly why ML has become so crucial for AI, so that today $AI = ML + x$. We explore types of ML and tools to create ML models.

Chapter 7 uses an example to walk you through the process of how an AI system is created with supervised ML methods.

In Chapter 8, we look at some relevant ML model classes. First, we consider the classical ML model class. Then we look at a model class that has been heavily employed and has led to a number of breakthroughs in various fields: artificial neural networks. We look into why the use of such neural networks, especially in the form of deep learning, is becoming increasingly prevalent.

The Ultimate Data and AI Guide

Chapter 9 is dedicated to how ML is (and should be) managed within a company. How is a ML project implemented? What job roles are necessary to successfully implement an ML project? We share tips based on our consulting experience, and we also look at the ethical considerations when creating an AI system.

Part IV | Where Will We Go?

Part IV consists of Chapter 10, which gives an outlook on how data, ML and AI are going to develop in the future as they continue to drive the digital transformation. What will the consequences be for us?

A guide to the guide: How this book is structured and how to read it

We know your time is precious, so we have tried to make navigating this book as easy as possible for you.

All of the content is broken down into answers to questions that we hear frequently as data consultants. These are grouped into ten Chapters. Table I-1 provides an overview of these chapters.

Table I.1 Summary statistics and overview of chapters

	Chapter	Total number of words	Number of FAQs	Total reading time[6][iii]
1	Digital transformation: the role of data and AI	6,935	14	30min
2	Understanding data: the fuel of digital and AI transformation	11,960	10	53min
3	Data storage technologies	16,174	19	1h 12min
4	Architecting data: data warehouses, data lakes and the cloud	14,890	16	1h 6min
5	Managing data in a company	11,026	16	49min
6	Understanding ML as the key driver behind AI	17,691	20	1h 19min
7	Creating and testing models with supervised ML	15,368	14	1h 8min
8	Popular ML model classes for supervised ML	11,686	12	52min
9	Managing ML in a company	18,059	24	1h 20min
10	The future of data, ML and AI	7,713	5	34min
	Total	131,502	150	9h 45min

---

6. Assuming a reading speed of 225 words/minute, which is a little under the 238 words/minute average reading speed for nonfiction books (s. reference)

Introduction

You can read the FAQs individually and customize your own journey through the data and AI universe. However, each chapter builds on the preceding one, so there is a natural flow in the content that you can follow if you want to read the book from start to end. Assuming that you have an average reading speed of 225 words per minute, reading the entire book will take you approximately 9 hours and 40 minutes.

If you prefer not to read the whole book, you can follow one of these suggested routes that we have tailored for different interests. The estimated reading time for every route assumes a reading speed of 225 words per minute.

Route 1: Data and AI in a nutshell for busy people and managers

Figure I.1 Route 1: Data and AI in a nutshell for busy people and managers

Table I.2 Route 1: Data and AI in a nutshell for busy people and managers

Ch. 1	Ch. 2	Ch. 3	Ch. 4	Ch. 5	Ch. 6	Ch. 7	Ch. 8	Ch. 9	Ch. 10
1–6	15, 21, 24	26, 28, 37, 38 29, 35,	44, 46, 51, 53, 54	64, 71	76, 78–81, 83	96	110, 115	122, 131	146

Route 2: Technical trip into data for (aspiring) practitioners

Figure I.2 Route 2: Technical trip into data for (aspiring) practitioners

The Ultimate Data and AI Guide

Table I.3 Route 2: Technical trip into data for (aspiring) practitioners

Ch. 1	Ch. 2	Ch. 3	Ch. 4	Ch. 5	Ch. 6	Ch. 7	Ch. 8	Ch. 9	Ch. 10
15–25	26–43	44–59	60–63						

Route 3: Technical Trip into AI and ML for (aspiring) practitioners

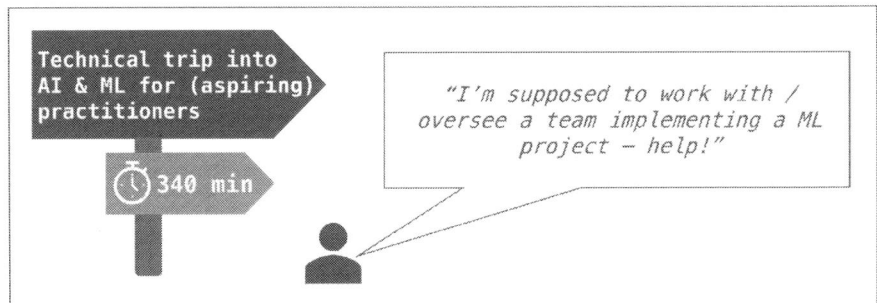

Figure I.3 Route 3: Technical Trip into AI and ML for (aspiring) practitioners

Table I.4 Route 3: Technical Trip into AI and ML for (aspiring) practitioners

Ch. 1	Ch. 2	Ch. 3	Ch. 4	Ch. 5	Ch. 6	Ch. 7	Ch. 8	Ch. 9	Ch. 10
15–24	39–43				76–95	96–109	110–121	122–145	

Route 4: "Why should I care route?" for the average person

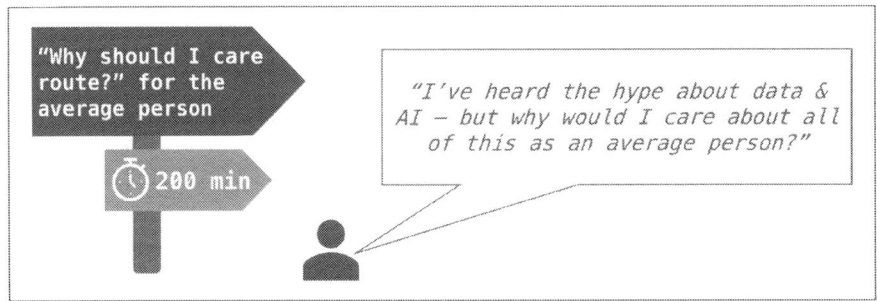

Figure I.4 Route 4: "Why should I care route?" for the average person

Introduction

Table I.5 Route 4 "Why should I care route?" for the average person

Ch. 1	Ch. 2	Ch. 3	Ch. 4	Ch. 5	Ch. 6	Ch. 7	Ch. 8	Ch. 9	Ch. 10
1–14	15, 18, 24		54	71–75	76–82		115, 121	142–145	146–150

Route 5: The impress-me route for people looking to be entertained

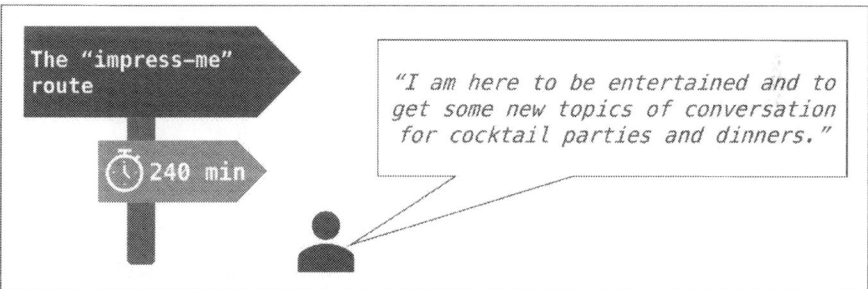

Figure I.5 Route 5: The impress-me route for people looking to be entertained

Table I.6 Route 5: The impress-me route for people looking to be entertained

Ch. 1	Ch. 2	Ch. 3	Ch. 4	Ch. 5	Ch. 6	Ch. 7	Ch. 8	Ch. 9	Ch. 10
1–14	15, 18, 24		54	71–75	76–82, 88, 89	96	115–118, 121	131, 139, 142–145	146–150

The book touches upon a lot of topics, many of which are rather complex. To break the content down and make it more digestible, we have incorporated three key elements throughout the book: an ongoing fictional case study; "What is it and why does it matter?" boxes; and real case studies.

Fictional case study

We often illustrate theory by means of a fictional case study that centres on you being the CEO of an online shop for model cars. A lot of the theoretical concepts are put into the context of this case study to make them more accessible and easier to understand.

The Ultimate Data and AI Guide

Our fictional case study: Your Model Car

Imagine you are the CEO of an online shop that you founded a couple of years ago. This online shop is called "Your Model Car" and it specializes in retailing both second-hand and new model vehicles, i.e. miniature toy cars, ships, airplanes, etc.

Customers search and order model vehicles through the Your Model Car website, https://www.your-model-car.com. Shipment is worldwide, and the company is headquartered at a hip start-up tech-hub in Berlin.

Your business has been going pretty well. By now you have gained a reputation in the model-vehicle lovers' community and you regularly attract new customers to your website. In fact, to your customers you essentially *are* your website. Most people do not know that behind this website is an entire machine. Your several dozen employees ensure that everything from IT to HR to logistics is working smoothly. This is a screenshot of your website:

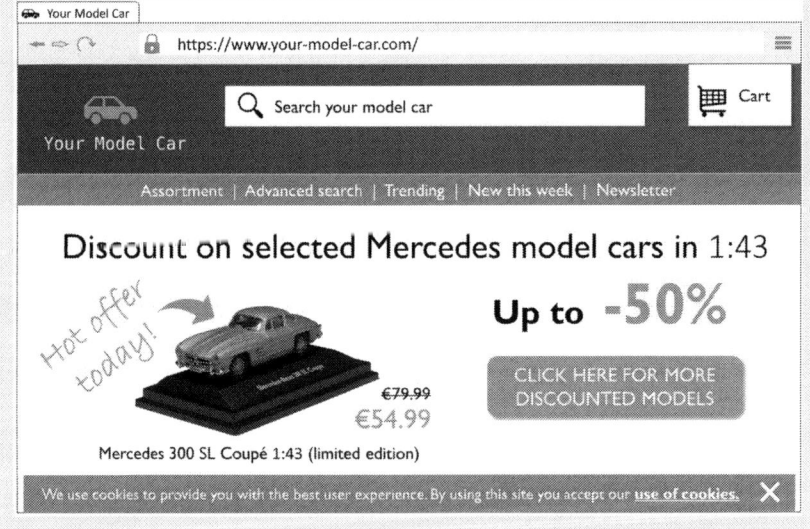

Figure I.6 Screenshot of fictional website of Your Model Car

"What is it and why does it matter?" boxes

You will encounter these in many chapters. These boxes act as quick reference guides that tell you what a certain concept is and why it is important to know about it. The boxes also summarize the chapter and capture the essence of the topic covered.

Real case studies

We include actual case studies that are inspired by our daily work as data consultants. These case studies show you how a certain topic works in real life and why it matters. One of the coolest things about data is that it truly is *everywhere*. Therefore, these case studies cover a wide range of industries.

Part I
Why Do We Care: The Digital Transformation Train

"It is not the strongest of the species that survives, nor the most intelligent that survives. It is the one that is most adaptable to change."

Charles Darwin

1 Digital Transformation

The Role of Data and Artificial Intelligence

1_1 Digital transformation

1 | What is digital transformation?

We are living in an age where humankind is experiencing some of the most profound changes in the history of our species. Just compare what the world looked like when you were born and what it will look like by the time you die (which hopefully won't be any time soon). Regardless of whether you are a teenager or close to retirement, the difference will be immense. There has barely been a generation for which changes have been as manifold and far-reaching as ours. A lot of these changes relate to one of the biggest developments that we are living through at the moment: *digital transformation*.

Digital transformation refers to the changes associated with digital technologies and the process of using them in all aspects of our lives. The term is often used interchangeably with *digitization* and *digitalization*. However, they mean slightly different things.

Table 1.1 What is digital transformation and why does it matter?

What is digital transformation?
Digital transformation refers to the overall process of, and effects brought about by, the use of novel digital technologies to solve problems. Digital transformation can occur at a company, sector or even societal level.
Both digitization (turning analogue information into digital form) and digitalization (restructuring processes around new digital technologies) are prerequisites for digital transformation.
As we shall see, novel innovations and technologies to push digital transformation are increasingly *data-driven*. A lot of these innovations are based on machine learning (ML) models and AI.

Digital Transformation

Why does it matter?

Digital transformation is bringing about fundamental changes to our societies and economies, and it will continue to do so. For example, companies will have to digitally transform in order to remain competitive.

The innovations that come with digital transformation will also affect us as individuals. For example, increasingly sophisticated AI systems and technologies will equip humanity with *mind power*, i.e. the ability to automate tasks that require human intelligence and perception. Therefore, the innovations and novel technologies that are ushering in digital transformation have the potential to replace us, or at least tasks and jobs that we carry out.

It is safe to say, therefore, that no one will be unaffected by the innovations and changes that digital transformation is washing to our shores now and in the (near) future.

Digitization refers to *changing analogue information into digital form*, i.e. creating digital versions of analogue or physical things, such as paper documents or cassettes. Essentially, digitization means we are turning "things" into bits and bytes to store them digitally. Digitization is a process that has already been happening for a couple of decades. For example, we used to store pictures in analogue form in physical photo albums. Today, we store them on our phones, computers and in the cloud.

Digitalization is very closely related to digitization and refers to *the restructuring of processes and other domains of our lives around digital technologies and digitized information*. Digitalization is therefore enabled through digitization. For example, a hospital may digitize its information about patients, such as their personal data, medical reports, lab results and X-ray images, from paper to digital form. Based on that, the hospital may digitalize the process for how patients receive their medical results. Back in the day, the process may have been as follows: the doctor wrote their diagnosis by hand, a secretary typed it up on a typewriter and it was posted in the mail along with the lab results. Digitalizing this process would mean simply sending the digitized medical report and lab results via email. The reason why organizations and companies are increasingly digitalizing their processes is because it is more cost efficient and quicker for them and more comfortable for customers.

Here are a couple more examples of things that have been digitized, which has led to the digitalization of related processes:

Table 1.2 Examples of digitization, digitalization and digital transformation

Digitization of	Digitalization	Digital transformation of
Texts in written form	We used to write letters and postcards to people. Today this has given way to emails, text messages and social media. Do you even remember when you last sent a letter (or if you are a younger reader, have you ever written a letter)?	The way we communicate

Digitization of	Digitalization	Digital transformation of
Audiovisual storage forms (e.g. VHS, cassettes)	We used to record an episode of our favourite TV series on VHS when we weren't at home in order to watch it later. Or we would buy an audio cassette of our favourite band. Today we can watch and listen to any movie, song or podcast at any time through streaming services, or we can download and store them on our computer or smartphone.	The entertainment industry and the way we engage with entertainment
Product and service information	We used to go to travel agencies and ticket counters to buy a train or plane ticket, and we used to go to stores to buy products. Today we purchase most of our services and products online – the digitalization of purchasing processes or products and services.	The retail industry

Digital transformation goes beyond that and is an even more profound concept. It refers to the overall *changes associated with the use of novel digital technologies*. We like to think of it as the sum of all digitalization processes and the effects brought about by that. While processes may be digitalized, digital transformation applies to entire companies, economic sectors or even societies. For example, the digitization of text has enabled the digitalization of our written communication. But more importantly, this has transformed our lives in countless ways. Today, we do not catch up with friends over the phone, but instead we send a chat message. Companies do not have to hire customer-support employees, but instead use chatbots that help customers with their problems. We do not send postcards anymore, but instead send pictures and holiday greetings digitally. These are all changes that have transformed how we communicate as a society.

2 | What is the impact of digital transformation on companies and society?

Digital transformation affects us as individuals who are part of society and it affects companies. Depending on who you talk to, these effects can make "the physical world better, worse, or just different", as businessmen Eric Schmidt and Jared Cohen describe it.[iv]

While the effects of digital transformation on companies differ from case to case, there is one central consequence for companies across all sectors and of all sizes: an increased pressure to innovate and "disrupt themselves". When we talk to top executives or incumbent leaders in traditional industries such as banking, insurance, consumer products and manufacturing, they all admit that the biggest threats to their companies' futures are data-driven tech companies like Google, Facebook, Amazon and Apple and new technology start-ups from Silicon Valley and other innovation hubs. CEOs have carefully observed how new digital players have exiled established players in the retail, music and TV industries and they fear that the same will happen to them.

This fear is not ill-founded. Just consider how the composition of the top ten companies with the highest market capitalization worldwide has changed. In 2010, the top ten was mostly dominated by oil giants. In 2020, several new players, such as Amazon, Alphabet and Tencent, have taken over the dancefloor. What they have in common is that they are all data-driven tech companies whose immense capability to innovate has disrupted traditional players.

Table 2.1 Publicly traded companies with highest market value in 2010 and 2020 (data-driven tech companies in blue)

Rank	2010[v]	2020[7]
1	Exxon (US$ 369 billion)	Apple (US$ 1,315 billion)[vi]
2	PetroChina (US$ 303 billion)	Microsoft (US$ 1,213 billion)[vii]
3	Apple (US$ 295 billion)	Alphabet (US$ 928 billion)[viii]
4	BHP Billiton (US$ 244 billion)	Amazon (US$ 926 billion)[ix]
5	Microsoft (US$ 239 billion)	Facebook (US$ 590 billion)[x]
6	ICBC (US$ 233 billion)	Alibaba (US$ 580 billion)[xi]
7	Petrobras (US$ 229 billion)	Berkshire Hathaway (US$ 554 billion)[xii]
8	China Construction Bank (US$ 222 billion)	Tencent (US$ 461 billion)[xiii]
9	Royal Dutch Shell (US$ 209 billion)	JPMorgan Chase (US$ 439 billion)[xiv]
10	Nestle (US$ 204 billion)	Visa (US$ 420 billion)[xv]

The pressure to innovate in order to remain competitive is not only felt at the top of the pyramid, but for companies of all sizes across all sectors. In 1958, the average age of an S&P 500 company stood at around 60 years. By 2012, this number had decreased to under 20 years.[xvi] It is forecasted that the average tenure of companies on the S&P 500 will shrink to just 12 years by 2027.[xvii] The creative destruction, which is a direct result of digital transformation, means that within the next ten years about half of the S&P 500-listed companies could be replaced.[xviii] Digital transformation is therefore changing the rules of the game for companies. It used to be enough for companies to be just a little more cost

---

7. The 2020 numbers disregard the Saudi Arabian Oil Company, which went public in December 2019. Raising a significant amount of money in its IPO, it was valued at US$ 1,700 billion in its first days and would therefore be on the first place in the 2020 rankings.

efficient or reliable or better than their competitors. Today, what counts is the ability to adapt to changes and new environments as quickly as possible – so there is a constant pressure for companies to engage in their own transformation and tap into new business models for their mere survival. The story of Netflix and Blockbuster in Case Study 1 is an illustrating example.

Digital transformation also affects us as individuals in a myriad of ways. On the one hand, we are benefiting tremendously from novel and improved products and services at lower prices. Just think back to when we had to go to a travel agency to buy a plane ticket instead of buying it via an online search engine. There are all sorts of apps and digital technologies that have made life a *lot* easier for us. On the other hand, there are also some drawbacks. For example, the latest data breach scandals have shown that the digital age has made our privacy vulnerable.

Arguably the biggest consequence for us as individuals, however, is the fact that we will be competing for jobs with ever more intelligent machines. Digital transformation and the waves of innovation it is delivering to our doorsteps have reignited a debate around technological unemployment, i.e. the unemployment caused by technological innovation. We will discuss whether the fear held by many of losing their job to a computer is justified in 📖 148.

Case study 1

How the Blockbuster night was replaced by Netflix binge watching

Netflix, founded in 1997, initially competed with Blockbuster using a similar business model: selling and renting DVDs to customers. However, in 2007 Netflix decided to augment its traditional business model with a subscription-based, on-demand streaming service. This was not perceived as a threat by Blockbuster, which continued to stick to its tried-and-true business model.

This complacency would turn out to doom the once-popular movie-rental company because the rules of the game changed. With increased bandwidth and an ensuing cultural change in customers' media consumption, Netflix's new business model helped it rise to the top and prevail in the competition against Blockbuster. Digital transformation has changed the way we consume media: our preference for on-demand streaming has made DVDs obsolete. If Netflix hadn't disrupted itself but had stuck to its traditional business model, it would probably not exist today.

Netflix continuously gained market shares and rose in value, while Blockbuster wasn't able to regain an edge and eventually went bankrupt in 2013. The concept of a "Blockbuster night" was crushed by the digital transformation train, making way for the nowadays ubiquitous "Netflix binge watching".

Today, Netflix has a net worth of around US$141[xix] billion and serves more than 100 million customers worldwide.[xx] The digital transformation it brought about has not only disrupted its direct competitor but is also worrying the traditional TV network industry. Today, Netflix' business model has been emulated by many other companies such as Apple TV+ and Disney+.

3 | What are the drivers of digital transformation?

Digital transformation causes changes in a myriad of fields. But there are just as many factors that have been driving the digital transformation train so fast. We can group these into two major blocks that have been mutually reinforcing each other: altered customer behaviour and a whole range of technological innovations.

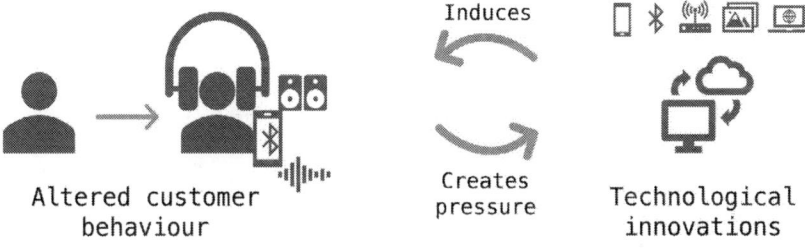

Figure 3.1 Mutually reinforcing drivers of digital transformation "altered customer behaviour" and "technological innovation"

Altered customer behaviour refers to the changes of our behaviour, expectation and preferences as customers and consumers. These have been unfolding over the past few decades, and companies have had to adapt. We want to order taxis and food with an app, stream media on demand, buy plane and train tickets on the internet, rent cars on demand rather than buying our own ones, and shop online rather than going to physical stores. Having gotten used to digital technologies, we want companies to live up to our expectations and provide us with a pleasant customer experience. Companies need to cater to these new customer expectations, which puts a lot of pressure on them to transform themselves digitally in order to remain competitive. Furthermore, we want these products and services to be as cheap as possible, which in turns forces companies to adopt digital technologies to save costs and operate their business more efficiently. All of this creates pressure for companies and thus drives technological innovation.

At the same time, new technological innovations that we are confronted with change our behaviour. And so the second set of factors driving digital transformation falls under the category of technological innovation and progress. This includes a whole range of innovations such as the World Wide Web, increased bandwidth enabled by broadband cables, the spread of increasingly fast mobile internet, smartphones, sensors, an increased computational power and many more. A lot of these innovations are based on digitization and the digitalization.

The changes in customer behaviour, technological innovations and their mutually reinforcing interplay taken together have been the driving forces behind digital transformation train so far. While this has got the digital transformation train running in the past couple of years, increasingly, it is and will be driven by another major factor of digital transformation: data and AI.

1_2 The role of data and AI in digital transformation

4 | AI – Why is it the engine of digital transformation?

For a long time, digital transformation has been driven mostly by digitization and the digitalization of processes in our lives. Increasingly, the possibilities that these developments enable will be exhausted. That does not mean that the digital transformation train is about to stop. The opposite is the case, since digitization and digitalization provide us with the resource that drives the engine of the next wave of digital transformation: data, which in turn is the fuel for *artificial intelligence* (AI).

So far, digital transformation has been mostly focused on equipping us with technology that simplifies our lives in many ways. Yet we still have to do a lot of work ourselves. Even though we are able to buy a train ticket online now, rather than going to a counter, we still have to go through the process of buying the ticket.

The dawn of AI will provide us with intelligent systems and algorithms that take such work off our shoulders. It is often said that previous industrial revolutions have equipped us with *muscle power*. The invention of the steam engine saved us a lot of elbow grease. Just think about all the heavy machinery involved in the building and mining industries.

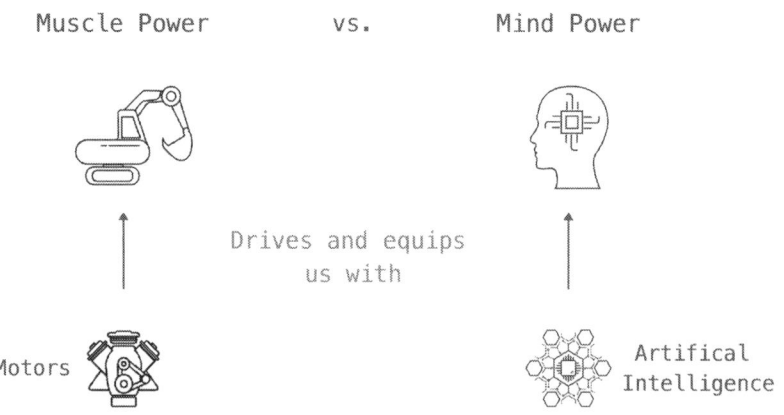

Figure 4.1 Muscle versus mind power

The progression and increasing availability of AI systems are equipping us with *mind power*. These systems display intelligent behaviour: they can arrive at decisions autonomously, make predictions about the future, communicate with us in natural language and ultimately automate certain tasks that presently require human intelligence. There are endless potential applications for such technologies, which is why AI is often regarded as a general purpose technology (📖 76).

These intelligent systems will do more and more tasks for us. Business processes will become increasingly efficient through automation, and we will benefit from products and services being augmented with smart algorithms. Instead of buying a ticket online, in the future we will simply be able to tell our virtual assistant to buy the ticket for us. Such AI systems will be the main driving force of digital transformation in the time to come.

Here are some more examples that illustrate how the next wave of digital transformation will be driven by AI.

Table 4.1 Examples of digital transformation driven by digitization and digitalization versus driven by AI

Area	Digital transformation driven by digitization and digitalization	Digital transformation driven by AI
Retail	Buy products online rather than going to a physical store.	Anticipate customer needs and preferences to show relevant product recommendations to the customer as soon as they visit an online shop – or even before that.
Insurance	Apply for an insurance policy online rather than sending in a printed form.	Automate the process by having an AI system assess insurance applications and yield results within seconds.
Production	Monitor the state or production level of a machine with a dashboard visualized on a tablet rather than paper report.	Not only show the state of a machine, but also have an intelligent algorithm that predicts when it will break down.
Medicine	Store and receive medical and lab results from screenings (MRI, X-ray and CT) digitally rather than in analogue.	Have an AI system aid and eventually replace the doctor in diagnosing patients based on such results.
Transportation	Use a rear-view camera rather than side mirrors to park a car.	Have the car park and drive autonomously.
Marketing	Send out marketing campaigns via email rather than posting hardcopy brochures.	Send customer-tailored marketing materials via email.

5 | Data – why is it the fuel of digital transformation?

All digital technologies that have been adopted in the context of digitization and digitalization have one crucial output: they produce a massive amount of data.

This data is the fuel for the AI engine that is driving the digital transformation train in the time to come.

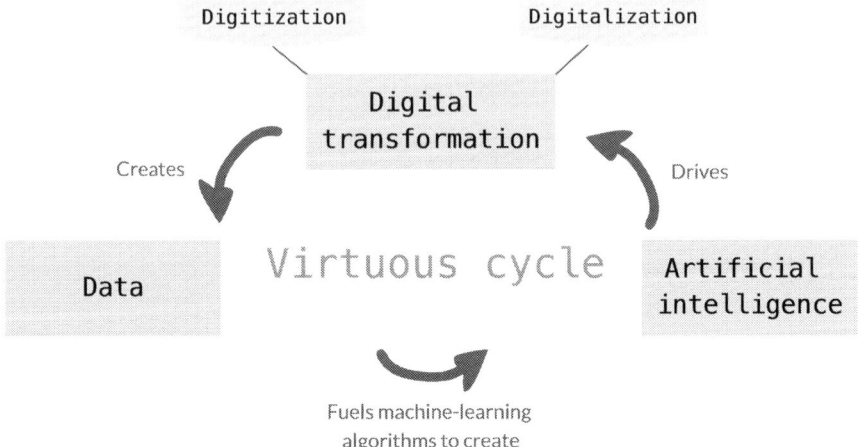

Figure 5.1 Virtuous cycle of data, AI and digital transformation

Much like how fossil fuels have propelled the machines that equip us with muscle power, data propels the AI systems that are equipping us with mind power. Unlike oil, however, data is a resource that cannot be depleted. And unlike oil, the amount of data that we have at our disposal will massively grow rather than decline. In fact, with the turn of the century we have entered an era of mass data storage and availability (📑 18).

The creation of data, the use of it to fuel AI systems and digital transformation driven by such intelligent algorithms – these form a virtuous cycle, and it is going to accelerate. Digitization and digitalization, which got the digital transformation train rolling, have started to produce massive amounts of data. This data can be used to create AI systems. As we will explain, this happens mostly with ML methods (📑 79). Increasingly, these AI systems lie at the heart of digital transformation. As digital transformation advances, more data is created, and the cycle continues.

6 | How are data and AI applied to generate value across industries?

AI fuelled by data can be used in many different ways to create value across industries. The tables that follow provide examples of some standard ML-based AI systems that are already being employed by companies to drive their digital transformation. Also take a look at 📑 78, where we include a list of some current top-notch AI breakthroughs that illustrate where our boundaries for creating AI currently lie.

Digital Transformation

Manufacturing

Table 6.1 Examples of ML-based AI systems in manufacturing

Example	Data collected	AI system to...	Value generation
Failure prediction and preventive maintenance for machines	Machine sensor data, Data on past failures, Machine specifications	Predict faults and machine failures	Schedule maintenance at right time
Demand forecasting and inventory management	Order data, Inventory data	Predict future demand and corresponding levels of inventory	Optimize logistics and supply chain management
Product warranty analysis	Past warranty cases	Predict future warranty cases	Improve parts to reduce warranty cases

Banking and insurance

Table 6.2 Examples of ML-based AI systems in banking and insurance

Example	Data collected	AI system to...	Value generation
Fraud detection of transactions	Fraudulent activities from the past	Automatically identify fraudulent transactions	Prevent fraud
Insurance applicant assessment	Insurance claims from the past	Predict probability that an insurance applicant will file a claim	Better product pricing and selecting profitable applicants
Automated customer service	Frequently asked questions, customer data	Predict to which FAQ the customer question best maps	Provide 24/7 support to customers via chatbot

Healthcare

Table 6.3 Examples of ML-based AI systems in healthcare

Example	Data collected	AI system to...	Value generation
Drug development	Antibodies, genes and active compounds and their effects	Identify prognostic biomarkers and investigate effect of the potential drug	Reduce failure rates in drug discovery and development
Patient monitoring and care	Electronic health records of patient	Filter out false alarms and detect true critically important alarms	Precise patient monitoring
Improved and automated diagnoses	Diagnostic medical images	Automatically analyse patterns in images to diagnose diseases, e.g. cancer	Reduce misdiagnoses

The Ultimate Data and AI Guide

Telecoms

Table 6.4 Examples of ML-based AI systems in telecoms

Example	Data collected	AI system to...	Value generation
Customer churn of mobile phone subscribers	Customer profiles, transactions, past churns	Predict customers who are likely to churn and sources of dissatisfaction	Reduce churn by engaging with at-risk customers
Customer lifetime value management	Customer profiles, transactions	Predict future profits and revenues of customer	Ensure that highly profitable customers are valued

Energy and utilities

Table 6.5 Examples of ML-based AI systems in energy and utilities

Example	Data collected	AI system to...	Value generation
Failure detection in grid	Weather data, sensor data, past outage events	Predict possible failures and their potential impact	Prevent blackouts and prepare for failure events
Equipment maintenance	Sensor data, weather data, past machine failures	Predict likely equipment breakdowns	Schedule preventive equipment maintenance
Energy management optimization	Energy production data, energy consumption data	Forecast production, in particular for renewables, and usage by time	Save energy and manage temporary loads more efficiently

Travel

Table 6.6 Examples of ML-based AI systems in travel

Example	Data collected	Machine learning	Value generation
Next-best-action marketing	Customer behaviours, customer profiles	Predict which marketing messages best fit which customer at what time	Increased revenue through personalized marketing and engagement
Product offer recommendation engines	Customer behaviours, customer profiles, past transactions	Predict which customers would like to get which offers	Cross- and upsell matching hotels, flights, car rental, etc.
Dynamic pricing of flight tickets	Customer demand data, price data of competitors	Predict optimal price to maximize revenue	Increased sales and utilized capacity

E-commerce

Table 6.7 Examples of ML-based AI systems in e-commerce

Example	Data collected	Machine learning	Value generation
Product recommendation	Visitor behaviours, customer profiles	Predict which product has highest probability of being bought	Increase sales, cross- and upselling
A|B testing of websites	Visitor behaviour	Predict which website set up works best for a visitor	Increase visitor engagement, increase sales
Personalization of ads on website	Cookies, visitor data	Automatically choose ad most likely to be clicked on	Increased conversion

> **Case study 2**
>
> **Next-best-action marketing by a software company**
>
> A multinational IT-company sells both software and hardware solutions such as customer relationship management software (CRM) in the business-to-business sector. To increase customer satisfaction, optimize its marketing efforts and increase its cross- and upselling rates it decides to implement a next best action (NBA) marketing program.
>
> NBA is a customer-centric marketing approach. The goal is to contact the right customer through the right channel with the right message at the right time in order to maximize customer experience and sales. The company has various touchpoints and engagement channels with its customers, e.g. website visits, email newsletters, social media, phone consultation centres and sales force.
>
> By using historical customer engagement data, it creates an intelligent system, which suggests what would be the next best action for a given customer. The system aids the marketing and sales department in its operations. For example, the system would suggest how many days after a customer has purchased a product, they should be contacted via phone with personalized offers for complementary products.

1_3 Buzzwords in digital transformation, data and AI

7 | What is an overview of buzzwords in data and AI?

One of the great things about working in the field of data and AI is that it touches so many other fields. Given that AI is often considered a general purpose technology, it can be applied in many fields, as the previous section shows.

On the one hand, this is extremely exciting, because it means the data and AI sector is tremendously dynamic and will expand even more in the future. On the other hand, it can be quite frustrating, because the hype around these topics often renders newcomers and practitioners alike utterly confused. It is a downright buzzword jungle out there in the sphere of AI and data.

Figure 7.1 maps out some of the most widely used buzzwords relating to AI and data. Going into all of these areas in detail is beyond the scope of this book, but the following sections offer brief descriptions and contextualizations, and for the crucial terms we refer you to the chapters where we explore them further.

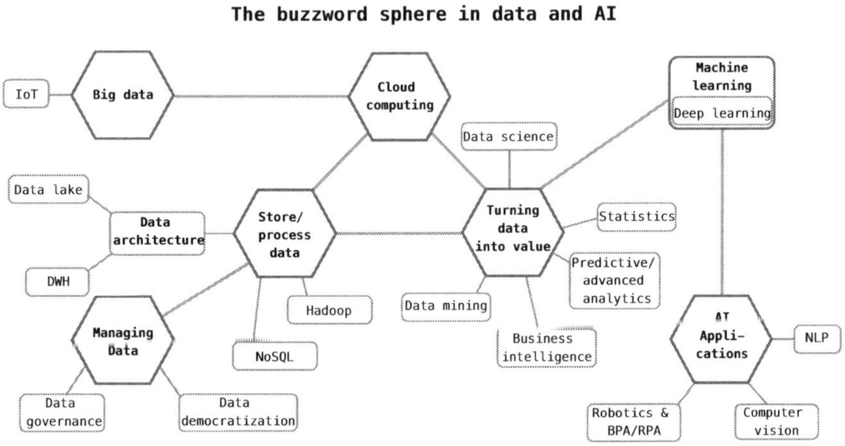

The buzzword sphere in data and AI

Figure 7.1 Overview of buzzwords in the data and AI sphere

8 | What is the IoT and what does it have to do with big data?

Data is information stored in digital form. The amount of information stored digitally used to be comparatively low compared to the amount stored on/in analogue devices such as books, cassettes and tapes. This has been changing since the end of the 1990s, which was when exponential growth of data creation and storage took off. In 2002, we entered the "digital age". From this point onwards, more information was stored in digital rather than analogue formats globally.[xxi] Today, we are witnessing the continued exponential growth of data (📑 146).

This development of mass data creation, storage and processing is commonly referred to as *big data*. There are several reasons why this growth came about. These are the subject of 📑 18.

One of the main factors contributing to this development is the *Internet of Things (IoT)*. IoT refers to the concept of an increasing number of (computing) devices being connected to the internet and/or other connected devices. The IoT is thus a giant network of connected devices that are able to exchange data and thereby communicate among themselves. Given that the IoT has the potential to make human input superfluous in certain processes, it is a cornerstone of automation.

Connected devices can be used just about everywhere. By the end of 2018, some 22 billion devices had been connected into the IoT. This number is expected to grow to some 50 billion by 2030.[xxii] Some of these devices are only able to collect and transmit data (sensors), some are able to receive data and take an action (actuators) and some are able to do both.

We often distinguish between devices being used in the private realm and in the industrial sector. The consumer IoT (CIoT) consists of devices such as wearables, connected fridges, smart thermostats, connected toys and, in the future, self-driving cars. The industrial IoT (IIoT) is closely related to the concept of industry 4.0 and refers to the use of connected devices in the industrial realm, above all in manufacturing and production processes.

The promise of the IoT both in the private and industrial sectors is to make processes "smart". This entails a lot of use cases in a wide range of fields, such as smart cities, smart manufacturing halls, smart homes, smart traffic via self-driving vehicles, etc. The underlying goal of all these use cases of the IoT is to increase the efficiency of a given process or provide a new type of service. For example, in the sector of logistics, connected devices enable the monitoring of events across the entire supply chain. Therefore, the inventory can be traced globally on an item level, so that deviations or anomalies in the chain can be detected and dealt with in good time.

As exciting as the possibilities created by connected devices are, in this book we do not go into the depths of the IoT. Instead, we focus on the resource that it provides: i.e. data.

9 | What are data lakes, data warehouses, data architectures, Hadoop and NoSQL databases?

Big data has been putting massive pressure on data storage and processing technologies, leading to numerous innovations.

Traditionally, most of the data in companies was stored in so-called relational database systems (Chapter 3_2). Invented in the early 1970s, they were able to fulfil the vast majority of data storage requirements for decades. However, the rise of big data from the 2000s onwards exceeded what traditional relational database systems could provide.

Consequently, since the mid-2000s onwards, a plethora of new data storage technologies have emerged. Among these are numerous NoSQL databases (📄 37) as well as the rise and commercialization of computer clusters (📄 35), which refers to a network of computers connected into a single system. Special software is required to coordinate the workload within a computer cluster, and one prominent example of this software is Apache Hadoop (📄 40).

Besides the technological side, data storage also requires a logical setup for how data as an asset is collected, stored and processed within a company. How does data flow within the company? How does data end up at the place where it is consumed? The field concerned with these questions is data architecture (Chapter 4). Two blueprint data architectures are the data warehouse (Chapter 4_2) and the data lake (Chapter 4_3).

10 | What are data governance and data democratization?

Closely related to the data architecture within a company is the field of data governance (Chapter 5_2). Data governance is concerned with the setup of processes, workflows and roles within a company. Where is data located? Who owns it? Who should get access to it and how? These are just a few questions that require proper data management. The goal of data governance is to ensure that the data is trustworthy, findable, usable and consistent within a company.

Data governance can also help to enable data democratization, which refers to making data available to a wide base of users within a company. The goal of widening the user base for data within a company is to make its culture more data-driven and have everyone harness the power of data. Traditionally, data has been located in silos pertaining to a certain department in a company, which makes cross-departmental access of data difficult. Furthermore, with data being stored in databases, access is difficult for the average layperson from a technical point of view. By setting up clear guidelines and procedures for how data is to be accessed, data governance can alleviate these barriers to data democratization.

11 | What is the cloud?

Cloud computing refers to using remote computer systems and infrastructure on demand. The cloud is therefore nothing more than an extensive network of server farms that can be rented whenever needed. Who owns the cloud's infrastructure and who has access to it determines the type of cloud: public, private, hybrid or virtual private cloud. For example, "public cloud" refers to third-party providers that rent out such computer resources that are accessible from the world wide web, e.g. Amazon Web Services (AWS).

The number of services and the infrastructures offered by such cloud providers is immense. In general, these are grouped into three categories: infrastructure as a service (IaaS), platform as a service (PaaS) and software as a service (SaaS). The services offered by cloud providers therefore range from bare infrastructure to store (large amounts of) data through to sophisticated software able to perform extremely complex tasks, e.g. chatbot services.

Enabled by a number of factors – first and foremost, an increased bandwidth – the rise of the cloud has turned out to be a real game changer for every industry. Being able to rent unlimited computational power at the click of a mouse for a relatively cheap price has relieved companies of the burden of setting up and maintaining their own IT infrastructure and enabled a lot of use cases. There are, however, also some drawbacks of making use of cloud services.

These and other topics relating to the cloud are the subject of Chapter 4_4.

12 | What are data science, data analytics, business intelligence, data mining and predictive analytics?

There are a number of disciplines that share one underlying goal: to use data and turn it into insights or added value; for example, by visualizing or analysing it. These are business intelligence (BI), data analytics, predictive/advanced analytics, data mining, data science, statistics and ML.

They are all interrelated and overlap greatly, so it can be difficult to demarcate them. Therefore, different people define them in different ways. Figure 12-1 shows how we think of these disciplines.

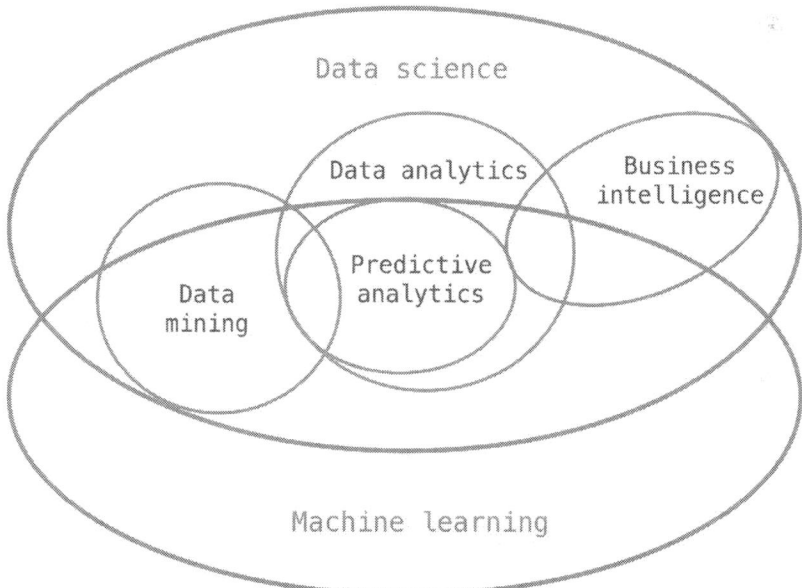

Figure 12.1 Overview and relationship between data science, data mining, data analytics, predictive analytics, business intelligence and ML

Data analytics and predictive/advanced analytics

Data analytics refers to the process of inspecting data to extract useful information. There are different types of data analytics and they differ in their goal.

Descriptive analytics tries to describe *what* has happened. For example, we would use descriptive analytics to answer the question: "How many parcels did Your Model Car ship last month?"

Predictive analytics tries to predict what is going to happen in the future, e.g. when a customer receives a parcel. It is therefore another type of data analytics, which usually involves the use of ML methods to create models capable of making predictions.

The types of data analytics typically also differ in their degree of complexity. Those analytics cases that use more involved methods are referred to as advanced analytics.

The types of analytics, along with examples, are further explained in 📑 16.

Business intelligence

Business intelligence (BI) is the application of data analytics to business information and data. The goal of BI is to provide historical, current and future snapshots of a company and its operations. The methodologies it employs to do that are manifold and include, for example, data visualization, sometimes ML methods, interactive dashboards, and descriptive analytics in the form of reports. For example, a standard BI measure would be to create weekly reports of how many parcels Your Model Car has shipped and how many were returned.

Business intelligence has been practised by many companies for decades already. It became really popular during the 1980s and 1990s. Back then most of the data in companies was stored in relational databases and data warehouses, which store structured data (📑 21). That is why BI is usually associated with the analysis of structured data.

Today, BI is still popular. However, the term (and discipline) is starting to become somewhat out of vogue, and is being superseded by other buzzwords, notably data science. In fact, data science is often viewed as having evolved from BI because it has the same goal of creating value from company data, but it uses a wider range of methodologies, including more sophisticated ones that also take on unstructured data (📑 21).

Data mining

Data mining is somewhat of a misnomer. The goal of data mining is to mine for patterns within data, rather than mine for data itself. This is done with methods from statistics, computer science and ML. Like BI, data mining employs descriptive and diagnostic analytics, but it also draws on predictive analytic methods.

The concept of data mining appeared sometime around the 1990s and stemmed from the idea of mining for useful information in companies' (relational) databases. Today, the term is used less and has been superseded by the term "data science". One could argue that there is a difference between the two, but by and large they are similar.

Data science

Data science is arguably the blurriest concept of them all and it has developed into a kind of umbrella concept that subsumes all others. This shouldn't come as a surprise, since it refers to the use of scientific methods to extract knowledge and create added value from data. Typically, data science methods are applied in companies.

Data science draws on a number of disciplines, notably statistics, mathematics, business analytics, computer science and ML.

Given the broad definition, the methodologies employed in data science span a wide range. These include all types of analytics methods and ML, but also extend to data visualization of both structured and unstructured data. Within companies, the application of data science methods also encompasses the analyses of business processes and data preparation.

Data science really took off in 2012, when *Harvard Business Review* magazine named data scientist "the sexiest job of the 21st century".[xxiii]

Some regard data science as having evolved from BI or data mining, since it is based on a similar idea, but it employs a wider and more progressive range of methods, such as ML. Others with a more critical stance claim that data science is just a rebranding of statistics, BI or data mining.

Statistics

Statistics is like the mother of all the previously mentioned concepts and disciplines. While all of them are phenomena of the 20th and 21st centuries and are associated with data in digital form, statistics has been around for centuries already. Generally put, statistics is the discipline that deals with the collection, analysis, interpretation and presentation of numerical data.

Statistics itself draws heavily on mathematical methods such as calculus. Statistical methods are central to all of the aforementioned concepts and disciplines. In fact, ML draws so heavily on statistical methods that a popular saying goes: "Machine learning is essentially a form of applied statistics."

13 | What are machine learning, neural networks and deep learning?

ML is a field of study concerned with algorithms, statistical models and computer systems (📖 80). The goal of ML is to give computers the ability to learn to do tasks without being explicitly programmed to do so. This happens by creating ML models (Chapter 7) that are trained to identify patterns in historical data in order to make predictions about the future.

One of the ML model classes that has led to major breakthroughs in the creation of AI since the 2010s is artificial neural networks (ANNs), or simply neural networks for short (Chapter 8_2). Neural networks that have a complex form are called deep neural networks. Creating deep neural networks is called deep learning, and this has proven to be extremely powerful in a number of fields. For example, the vast majority of intelligent machine translation systems such as Google Translate[xxiv] have a neural network running as their engine.

14 | What are AI, natural language processing, computer vision and robotics?

Artificial intelligence refers to two things (📑 76). Firstly, it is an academic discipline that studies the intelligence of machines. The creation of AI has been a dream of humankind for centuries, but the academic and goal-oriented research to create it has existed since 1956. Secondly, AI refers to machines or computer systems that display intelligent behaviour.

Intelligent machines and systems are already used in a number of fields. Recently, the vast majority of such intelligent machines and systems have been created through ML methods, so that today essentially $AI = ML + x$.

There are some areas where the use and progress of AI has garnered special attention and these have evolved into important subfields of AI.

Natural language processing

Natural language processing (NLP) is concerned with how to program computers to analyse, understand and create large amounts of human natural language. This field of study is a mix of computer science, linguistics and AI, and is vital in the development of, for example, personal virtual assistants or chatbots.

Computer vision

Computer vision studies how computers can be programmed to understand digital videos or images. Computer vision is vital in areas such as object recognition and autonomous driving.

In both NLP and computer vision, deep learning approaches have proved to be extremely powerful. We look into both NLP and computer vision in the context of deep learning in 📑 118.

Robotics

This field of study is concerned with the design, construction and operation of robots. It is thus a mix of various engineering fields including mechanical, electronic and information engineering and AI. Such robots are used, for example, for robotic process automation (RPA), which is a form of business process automation (BPA).

The junction of robotics and AI is already bearing impressive fruits. For example, researchers from NVIDIA have developed a deep-learning-based system that enables a robot to complete a task simply by observing a human doing it. This could ultimately be used to teach robots to perform a task alongside humans, e.g. in a production hall.[xxv]

We will likely see further breakthroughs like this one in the field of robotics fuelled by advancements in AI. As exciting as these developments are, going into further detail on robotics is beyond the scope of this book, and we are limiting ourselves to the AI part of it.

Part II
The Fuel: Data

"Data is the oil, some say the gold, of the 21st century – the raw material that our economies, societies and democracies are increasingly being built on."

Joe Kaeser, CEO Siemens AG[xxvi]

2 Understanding Data

The Fuel of Digital and Artificial Intelligence Transformation

2_1 Understanding data

15 | What is data?

It's an ordinary Wednesday. At 7 a.m. your alarm rings to wake you up. As usual, you get ready in the bathroom. Today you leave the house earlier, because you have a doctor's appointment before work. Your working day is packed, but fortunately you make it out of the office just in time to grocery shop. Back home, you cook yourself dinner and relax in front of your favourite comedy series.

Question: How much data have you created during this average day?

A lot. This is an estimate of how you might have gone about your day:

Table 15.1 How much data do you generate on an average day?

Time	Activity	Data you created/ have revealed	Who has access to/owns the data?	What is the data (potentially) used for?
07:05	Unlock phone to answer WhatsApp/ Messenger/ Viber/ WeChat messages	▶ You are active on your smartphone ▶ You have sent messages	▶ Depends how many apps you *denied* permission to collect that data ▶ Text messaging app	▶ Understand you as an app user to improve app service, e.g. optimise time to send you a push notification
07:10	Skim through the breaking news and read one article of interest	▶ What news article you are interested in	▶ Your news app	▶ Tailor suggested articles for you to read and target you with ads
07:15	Like a song to include in your Spotify shower list (or other streaming app)	▶ That you like the song in a shower context	▶ Spotify	▶ Improve suggestions for songs to listen to

Understanding Data

Time	Activity	Data you created/have revealed	Who has access to/owns the data?	What is the data (potentially) used for?
08:00	Drive to the doctor's in your car	• Various data collected by sensors in the car (e.g. location, engine temperature, tyre pressure etc.)	• Car producer	• A number of use cases, e.g. predictive maintenance or traffic jam prediction
08:30	Fill in a form with your personal data at the doctor's	• Your personal data	• The doctor, maybe the insurance company	
09:00	Use GoogleMaps to navigate to your office	• Your location and travel speed	• Google	• A whole range of use cases, e.g. fastest route calculation and traffic jam indication
09:00 – 19:00	Browse the internet to do research for a project Write emails	• Cookies • What websites you visited, how you behaved on websites, etc. • With whom you had what sort of contact	• Website hosting companies • Your browser • Your email hosting provider	• Personalize websites based on your profile in order to increase click-through rate or personalize advertisements on website
14:00	Fill in a feedback form during your appraisal interview	• Information on how you assess your boss, your satisfaction within the company, etc.		
19:30	Do the grocery shopping, use your loyalty card to get a discount and pay with your credit card	• Money transfer data • What you have bought	• Bank • Supermarket	• Send you personalized advertisements of products on sale
20:30	Post a picture of your cooked dinner on Instagram	• Where you are, what you have been doing	• Potentially everyone (depends on account settings)	• Personalize ads and recommend people to follow
21:00	Order new shoes on Amazon	• What type of shoes you like	• Amazon	• Product recommendations
22:00	Watch a new series that's recommended to you on Netflix	• What type of series you are interested in	• Netflix	• Personalized movie and series recommendations
All the time	Location (through your smartphone GPS sensor)	• Your location	• All apps that have permission to access your GPS sensor	• A whole lot of use cases

The Ultimate Data and AI Guide

That's quite something, right? The sheer amount of data about a person that is being collected by companies can be daunting. Looking at Table 16-1, it is clear that data is really ubiquitous and you contribute to creating it every day, fuelling companies to develop and run their data-driven technologies.

Two items on the list may make you say, "Hold on a second, is this really data, though?" While it is clear that the forms filled out by hand, at the doctor's and during the interview, contain (highly valuable) *information*, is this data? What is the difference between data, information and facts in the first place? These terms are often used interchangeably. Discerning the differences between these concepts can easily result in a philosophical debate that could fill a book in itself. Instead of going down this avenue, we offer simple ways to distinguish between facts and data, and information and data.

Facts versus data

Considering validity can allow us to differentiate facts from data. *Facts are assertions of the truth*. In the words of the famous philosopher Wittgenstein, "The world is everything that is the case"[xxvii] – i.e. the totality of all facts. What data is trying to do is *depict and represent these facts* and thereby the real world. Therefore:

Data/information = a representation of facts.
This representation may or may not be valid and accurate.

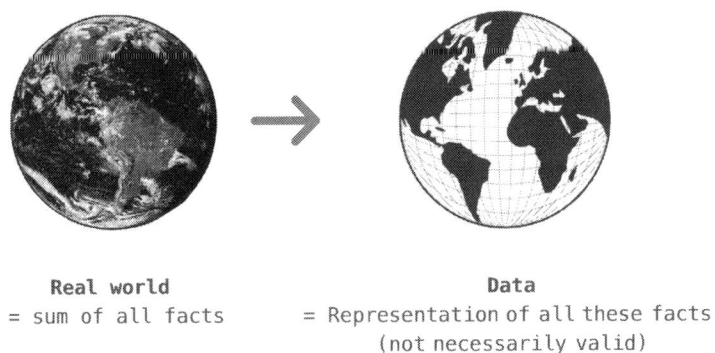

```
          Real world                          Data
        = sum of all facts         = Representation of all these facts
                                         (not necessarily valid)
```

Figure 15.1 Data as a representation of facts

To clarify this point, consider these five examples:

- A customer of Your Model Car is providing personal data on the website when she orders one of the products.
- A phone's GPS sensor is trying to provide the geo-coordinates and thereby the true position of the device.
- By writing a report about how I slipped and dropped my friend's camera in order to claim money from my liability insurance, I am providing information that is meant to describe the events of the accident.
- News is meant to inform us about the state of the world.
- Most illustratively, a photo tries to capture the real world visually.

Understanding Data

All of these are examples of how data is trying to depict an aspect of the real world. However, the picture the data draws of that real world is not necessarily *valid*, i.e. in accordance with the facts:

- Customers entering their personal data on the Your Model Car website might enter the wrong data – unknowingly, or maybe even intentionally.
- Everyone knows the problems that occur when a phone's GPS sensor is not working properly (or is just not sufficiently accurate).
- My description of how I slipped is based on my subjective perception of the accident and I might not have sensed all of the things that were happening. So the picture I draw with the description is subjective at best, or may even be wrong.
- News might be deliberately manipulated to influence its audience (fake news).
- I might edit a picture I took to make it look prettier, thereby distorting the representation of the real world. This is what happens every millisecond when somebody uploads an image on Instagram or Facebook after altering it with a filter or other effects.

All of the above are data. But the data is not necessarily valid and therefore these might not be facts.

Information versus data

We can make two clear distinctions between information and data. The first relates to the degree of consumability and meaning, and the second to how they are stored.

Consumability and meaning

Data can be any sequence of values, numbers, text, picture, files and so on. All of these things do not necessarily have to be informative to a consumer of that data. In most cases, data needs to be processed and put into context to make it informative for the consumer. Consider the following example:

Table 15.2 Cryptic sensor data

	PK_ID	PK_SEN_TI	OBJ_LO	OBJ_LAT	OBJ_ST	OBJ_TEM	OBJ_PRES	FK_C_U
1	213806	19.12.19 15:42	0.037758	51.507351	2	80.7	26.2	6300461
2	214704	19.12.19 15:42	0.037758	51.487323	3	73.4	23.47	6300178
3	214722	19.12.19 15:42	-0.06078	51.349050	4	60.4		6300259
4	21522	19.12.19 15:44	0.037758	51.600023	1		13.4	6300222
5	215345	19.12.19 15:44	0.13623	51.499983	2	23.8	19.53	6300653
6	323532	19.12.19 15:44			2	90.4		6300835
7	214532	19.12.19 15:45	0.200623	51.507351	4			6300789
8	214343	19.12.19 15:46			4	95.2	22.2	6300738
9	212133	19.12.19 15:46	-0.07075		3	40.2	30.13	6300555

The Ultimate Data and AI Guide

This is an example of *raw data*, i.e. data that has not been processed yet. It is not informative to you as a reader. To understand this as information, you would need some context and probably also some processing of the data. For example, knowing that "OBJ_TEM" is data from the temperature sensor in a production machine engine gives you some context. Or you could turn this data into valuable information by visualizing it.

Because processing raw data and making it informative for a recipient is usually time consuming, information can be regarded as something that is more refined and valuable than data. In fact, (former) business students will probably be familiar with the so-called Data-Information-Knowledge-Wisdom (DIKW) pyramid, as shown in Figure 15-2. In a nutshell, this model states that "information is defined in terms of data, knowledge in terms of information, and wisdom in terms of knowledge".[xxviii]

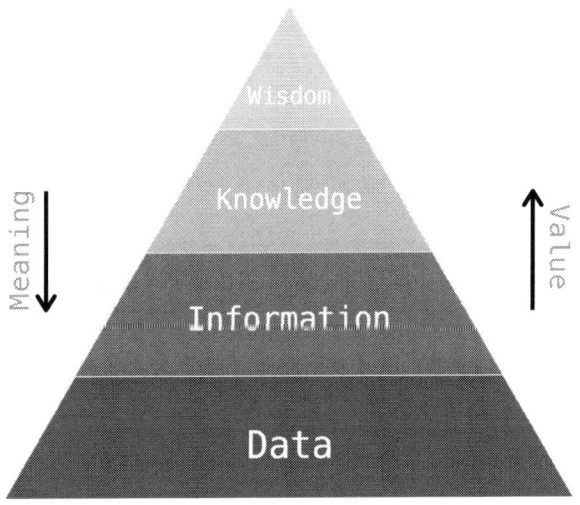

Figure 15.2 DIKW pyramid

Storage format

The second distinction to make between information and data is the way in which they are stored. In the example of your average daily routine, you created highly valuable information in an analogue form by filling in a form by hand with your personal data. Furthermore, you took important notes in the interview. These things are highly informative and valuable. Yet most of us would not consider what we've handwritten to be data, because it is not stored in a digital form. Information can be stored in a multitude of ways: on paper, in music, in paintings, on signs, on videotape, on vinyl and perhaps most efficiently in DNA (the latter is currently being researched with a view to using it as a data storage medium).[xxix] However, if the information is stored in *digital form*, we can harness the power of computers to store, process and analyse it with unprecedented speed and efficiency. The switch from analogue to digital data storage was therefore a real game changer.

Understanding Data

Definition of data

Given the two ways in which information and data differ, our definition of data in this book is as follows:

Table 15.3 What is data and why does it matter?

What is data?
(Typically unprocessed) representations of facts that are stored in digital form. Data can take many forms; that is why it helps to distinguish between the different types of data (📑 21).
Why does it matter?
You can think of data as information stored in digital form. Information has always been important ("information is knowledge, and knowledge is power"), but the rise of data has revolutionary. Storing data in digital rather than analogue form has enabled humankind to harness the power of computers and algorithms. With these we can collect, store and process information on unprecedented scales. This has enabled a whole new range of innovations and technologies, like artificial intelligence (AI).
Data is often called the fuel of the 21st century. Much like oil and electricity have powered innovations and economies in the past, data will be the (not so natural) resource that fuels these in the present and future.

Case study 3

Digitalizing business processes in a hospital

A hospital conducts most of its activities in an analogue way. Patients fill in their personal data by hand upon arrival. Doctors and nurses document patient records that contain diagnoses in analogue files. Patients are given test results such as X-ray images in a printed form – and so forth.

All of this is highly valuable and extremely sensitive information. However, there is plenty of scope for the hospital to increase its operational efficiency by conducting parts of its processes digitally and storing the information in digital form, i.e. data. For example, patients' personal data could be collected by reading their health insurance cards. Doctors could record patients' diagnoses verbally and have these audio files transcribed into text by speech-to-text algorithms so that patients' records can be stored digitally in text form. Lab results could be stored and shared with patients digitally. All of this would turn the highly valuable information of the hospital's operations into *data*.

In some cases, this will even increase the validity of the information. For example, obtaining a patient's personal data from their insurance card is much less likely to produce errors than having the patient fill out a form by hand, as illegible handwriting could lead to inaccuracies.

16 | Why collect data and what are the different types of data analytics?

By collecting data, we obtain information about the world we live in – we take a snapshot of some aspect of reality. Often, collecting data and having such a snapshot of reality are necessary for conducting business. For example, Your Model Car *has* to collect customer data in order to process payments and ship its products. If we didn't have the addresses of our customers, then how would we know where to ship our products?

However, with data increasingly driving smart algorithms and thereby also digital transformation, companies are collecting more and more data that goes beyond the "bare necessities". And with more data comes more possibilities. For example, Your Model Car might collect web log data to draw a picture of how the website is being used, e.g. how are customers coming to the website and for how long do they stay? And, of course, as an online retailer the company cares about its sales. So on top of collecting data about how many products are sold, Your Model Car might also collect data about factors that influence the sales, e.g. how many visitors came to the website and bought a product as a result of an online advertisement. All of this data reflects an aspect of the real world that Your Model Car navigates.

It is like the data is giving us a picture of an aspect of the world. This is the basis for data analytics, which is concerned with *analysing* this picture to draw valuable insights from it. The powerful thing about data analytics is that it is not confined to just looking at the picture itself, but it also enables us to infer the future from data. There are four different types of data analytics that we can distinguish. These are shown in Figure 16-1.

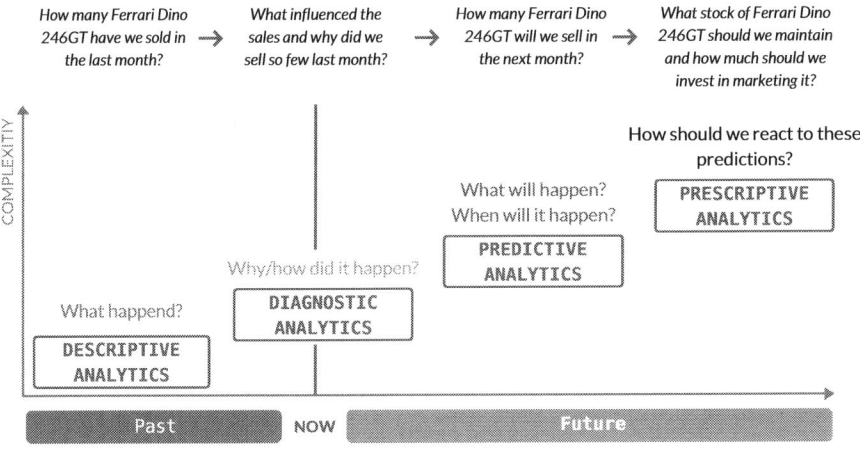

Figure 16.1 Different types of data analytics

- **Descriptive analytics:** Describe what has happened in the past and monitor how something has developed.
- **Diagnostic analytics:** Explain why something happened.

- **Predictive analytics:** Predict what is going to happen.
- **Prescriptive analytics:** Predict what is going to happen and give a recommendation for how best to react to the predicted outcome.

Let's see what each of these could look like in the Your Model Car context.

An example of descriptive data analytics would be to look at how many model cars of a specific brand or type we have sold in the past day, week, month or year. Implementing such a descriptive analytics use case is comparatively easy.

Things get a little more complicated if we go a step further into diagnostic data analytics. So instead of only describing what happened in the past, we could be asking what influenced the sales numbers of a given model car type and why the sales in the past developed the way they did. To answer these kinds of questions we typically need to resort to statistical and mathematical models. Therefore, diagnostic use cases are more challenging to implement than "simple" descriptive use cases and consequently require higher level of expertise to implement.

Another layer of complexity is added when we do not only want to explain why or how something happened, but we also want to predict what will happen in the future. These two items are typically closely related, because we predict the future by looking at and understanding the past. In our use case, one field of application could be to predict how many model cars we are going to sell on a given day. Predictive analytics typically draws heavily on ML and statistical methods.

Prescriptive analytics adds yet another layer on top of predicting the future. In a prescriptive data analytics case, we would take into account the predictions and ask ourselves how we should react to these predicted outcomes. In our example this could be a use case like how many model cars we should order to avoid an out-of-stock situation given the predicted sales. Or it could be a use case where we prescribe how much of the marketing funds we should allocate to promoting a model car in order to raise the sales numbers to a certain level. Prescriptive data analytics use cases are usually the most involved ones to implement and typically have the goal of automating a certain business process. For example, an algorithm that will predict how much we sell and at the same time prescribe how much we should order could be used to automate the stock-purchasing process.

> **Case study 4**
>
> **How an airline can use data to employ different types of data analytics**
>
> To operate its business, an airline *has* to collect, process and store a lot of data – ticket orders, customer details, baggage details, money transactions, employee data, etc. This data can be used to monitor its operations. For example, it could create monthly reports about the number of passengers on its various routes (descriptive analytics). This data could also be used

to analyse factors that have an influence on the number of passengers such as ticket pricing, marketing expenses, and the time of the year (diagnostic analytics). However, to remain competitive in a market that is almost exclusively conducted online, this airline should also go beyond collecting the standard data.

For example, the airline will certainly want to implement dynamic pricing for its tickets sold online. Dynamic pricing refers to adjusting prices of tickets according to the real-time competitive offering and the market demand, in order to maximize profit. So on top of collecting all of the standard data, the airline might want to collect data about how many people are looking for a given ticket on a given day on its website as an indicator of demand. Using this data, the airline might predict how high the demand for a given route will be on a specific day (predictive analytics). Furthermore, the airline might monitor the prices of competitors and try to predict these as well. With this data at hand, it could develop an algorithm to adjust its prices in order to maximize sales and profit (prescriptive analytics).

17 | How is data created?

Given the power that comes with having data available, it shouldn't come as a surprise that companies are increasingly collecting more and more of it. But how is all of this data created? How does information about a real-world process end up in a database, in an Excel sheet or on some server? The foundation of it all is what is called the *data generating process*.

Table 17.1 What is the data generating process and why does it matter?

What is the data generating process?
The data generating process, also called data collection, is the way in which data about a given real-world process or entity is collected.
There are countless ways to collect data. Some processes are based on human-generated data (e.g. somebody entering data manually on a computer or taking a picture with a camera) and others are machine based (e.g. a sensor transmitting the temperature every couple of seconds).

Why does it matter?
The data generating process lies at the very heart of the creation of data. It is where data is born. Designing this data generating process carefully is the key to obtaining high-quality data, which is the basis for doing anything really with data.
If data quality issues exist in a dataset, very often they can be traced back to flaws or problems in the data generating process.

Given that the data generating process lies at the very heart of the creation of data, it is important for everything that builds upon this data. The design of the data generating process can have huge effects on the data quality and therefore on the results of any data visualization, analysis, ML model, etc. We have seen projects fail that we have consulted on because the data was inadequate for a given use case. In most cases, the root cause can be traced back to how the data generating process was set up. A lot of companies have rich data sources already, but their data generating processes were designed and implemented years or maybe even decades ago. When they were conceived, they were not intended to be used for data analytics, let alone ML or AI projects, which is why they often lack the necessary data quality or structure to be used in such projects.

For example, we worked with a leading utilities company on predictive maintenance for wind turbines. Our client assured us that plenty of data was available. And indeed, a glance at the databases revealed that the company had enormous amounts of data – but it was useless. How come? In order to optimize data volumes, the sensor data was aggregated in five-minute intervals. This was fine for monitoring the wind turbines but not granular enough to implement a predictive maintenance use case, because this aggregation filtered out the necessary data points. The company's data collection process was good enough for condition monitoring but not detailed enough for predicting upcoming failures.

So, just because a company has plenty of data that does not necessarily mean that this data is fit for applying ML algorithms. Often companies have to redesign, update or augment their data generating processes in order to collect the data that is necessary for advanced analytics.

There are numerous ways to collect data. In general, data and its generation can be separated into human and machine generated data, though the distinction is not always clear-cut.

Table 17.2 Human versus machine generated data

	Human generated data	**Machine generated data**
What is it?	Data that is created through the active action of a human being.	Data that is produced by machines without significant input from humans.
Examples	▶ Manually written text: 　❏ Word documents 　❏ Emails 　❏ Posts or chats on social media (e.g. Facebook) 　❏ SMS 　❏ Messages via apps (e.g. WhatsApp) 　❏ Etc. ▶ Manually collected and entered data (e.g. in Excel sheets) ▶ Manually collected pictographic data (e.g. videos, photos, voice recordings)	▶ All kinds of sensor data: 　❏ Barcode scans 　❏ Weather sensors 　❏ GPS sensors 　❏ Etc. ▶ Web server logs ▶ Video surveillance cameras ▶ Machine generated scans and images ▶ All sorts of apps that constantly create and collect data about your phone and the way you use it

Machine generated data is the backbone of the Internet of Things (IoT) and industry 4.0 trends and is largely responsible for the skyrocketing of data creation. This will also hold true in the future. The ability of humans to actively produce data is limited and population growth is relatively slow compared to the development of machines. The data collection capabilities of machines, on the other hand, are bound only by computational and storage capacity. Between 1971 and 2017 the human population has almost doubled from 3.8 billion to about 7.5 billion,[xxx] which is a growth of around 97%. This is dwarfed by the growth of the number of transistors on a microprocessor which has grown from 2,308 in 1971 to around 19.2 billion in 2017,[xxxi] which is a growth of around 831,888,981%. Therefore, machine generated data essentially decouples data growth from population growth, enabling the collection of data on unprecedented scales.

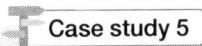

Case study 5

Human and machine generated data in the production process

In order to monitor its production process, an automotive supplier that produces car engines tags every engine part with a barcode. As soon as a part runs through a certain production step – for example, it is connected to another engine part – the barcode is scanned and the time at which it entered this production step is stored. In this way, every part can be tracked across the entire production process, so that bottlenecks that cause jams can be identified. Because it is a machine that scans the barcode in an automated manner, this is an example of machine generated data.

At the end of the production process, every assembled engine is assessed in an end-of-line test, where an employee tags the engine as "OK" or "NOK". This is an example of human generated data, which, for instance, can later be used to identify factors that led to the production of NOK parts.

18 | What are the factors that have enabled an era of mass data creation and storage?

Until a couple of years ago, the wisdom and knowledge of humankind was stored on paper in libraries. Today, it is stored digitally in the form of data on computers. In 1986 the global information storage capacity stood at 2.8 exabytes[8]. Back then, the share of information stored in analogue form (paper, analogue videotapes, vinyl etc.) was 93%, the remaining 7% were stored in digital format. The year 2002 marks the point in time when we entered the "digital age". From that point onwards more information was stored digitally than in analogue form. In 2007 the global information storage capacity had increased to some 299 exabytes. However, the percentage of information stored in

---

8. 1 exabyte = 1,000,000 terabyte = 1,000,000,000 gigabyte

analogue form fell to a mere 6%. The other 94% of information were already stored digitally on hard drives, DVDs and other digital storage technologies.[xxxii]

That was more than a decade ago, so just imagine how low the percentage is now.[9] But how did this shift happen? The factors that helped usher us into the era of mass data creation and storage can be divided into two types: data creators and data enablers.

Data creators

The first significant factor that contributed to the increased creation of data was the invention, development and commercialization of all sorts of electronic data-logging devices (e.g. sensors and barcodes, but also computers themselves). This laid the foundation for machine generated data, which enabled the creation and collection of data on a scale that humans could not possibly match. Machine generated data decoupled data growth from population growth, allowing for a much steeper trajectory and the skyrocketing of data volumes. Aside from sensors, all sorts of connected devices, first and foremost our smartphones, are the big contributors to the vast amounts of data created today. They are also the basis for the Internet of Things (IoT). The number of connected devices is expected to grow to some 50 billion by 2030.[xxxiii]

A second factor is the transition in our lives from analogue to digital. We used to phone each other on landlines, go shopping in malls, and look up things in books and on physical maps. Today, we send emails, order products online and google all sorts of things on the World Wide Web. All of this online activity leaves digital footprints and so creates data that previously did not exist.

Related to that is another factor: the growth of social media and other platforms that have equipped us with the means to communicate. Today, everyone produces plenty of data, sharing pictures, videos and text with friends, family and strangers. The King James version of the bible counts around 0.79 million words.[xxxiv] Today, Twitter produces around 4,172 million words – every day.[10][xxxv][xxxvi]

Data enablers

The exponential growth of data generating devices had to be accompanied by several *data enabling developments* that allowed for the storage and processing of such vast amounts of data. Most of these developments where slow evolutions rather than sudden revolutions. Notably, the prices to store a gigabyte

---

9. Unfortunately, similar up-to-date studies do not exist, to our knowledge, but the percentage of information in analogue form will certainly have been dwarfed, approaching 0%.
10. There is no data on the average Tweet length. However, the mode Tweet length is at 28 characters (Panzarino, 2012). The average character length of a word in this book is 4.94. The daily number of Tweets is around 736 million (Domo, 2019). Therefore, the total number of words created by Twitter users daily is around 736,000,000 x 28 / 4.94 = 4,172 million.

(GB) of data have decreased dramatically. In fact, the decline of prices per gigabyte of storage has been following an exponential path. While digitally storing 1 GB of data back in 1981 would have cost around US $47,549[11,xxxvii], the price dropped to less than $0.02 per gigabyte in 2019.[xxxviii] In 1981, the Ferrari 308 sold for around $49,403.[xxxix] If the price of Ferraris had dropped at the same rate as the price of gigabyte storage, a Ferrari today would cost you less than $0.02. This is the reason why almost everyone owns a computer today, but not a Ferrari.

But a steep decline in storage costs wasn't enough. The data had to be transported, which posed a challenge to connectivity and bandwidth. Nielsen's Law states that the network connection speed for high-end home users will increase by about 50% every year. Over the past 35 years or so, this prediction has turned out to be rather accurate.[xl]

Older readers might remember struggling to hook their computer up to the internet through their digital subscriber line (DSL) modem, which would transmit digital data via telephone lines. This technology was gradually superseded by broadband internet widths with copper cables, and most recently by fibre-optic cables. Thanks to the latter, bandwidth has significantly increased compared to the 56 kilobytes per second (kbps) that was standard for most consumers throughout the 1990s.

Obviously, another key development in that regard was the expansion and evolution of cellular networks. Today, the vast majority of densely inhabited land across the world is covered by these cellular networks, which provide for mobile internet. The latest breakthrough in that field is the fifth-generation cellular-network technology 5G, which is being rolled out in various countries across the globe. With a bandwidth up to ten times bigger than 4G[xli], the fifth-generation cellular network will not only give IoT another boost but will also enable entirely different use cases.

Finally, computational power has increased, which was necessary to process all of the data. Much like Nielsen's Law on the growth of bandwidth, Moore's Law proposes that the number of transistors in a computer circuit will roughly double every two years. This prediction has proven to be rather accurate for several decades. In 1971 the number of transistors per microprocessor stood at 2,308. Since then, it has experienced exponential growth. In 1995 it had increased to 9.65 million, by 2017 it was around 19,200 million.[xlii] Other aspects of technological progress, such as processing speed and the price of electronic products, are closely linked to Moore's Law.

While it is difficult to pinpoint which is the egg and which is the chicken in this case, the data growth had to go in step with innovations in data storage capacities, data transmission (i.e. increased bandwidth) and computational power. All of these, along with other technological inventions, helped usher us into the age of big data.

---

11. The IBM 3380, released in 1980 and shipped in 1981, had a price tag of $97,650 to $142,200 and a storage capacity of 2.52 GB. We took the mean of the price range.

But we have by no means "arrived". The ride continues by the second. The collection and creation of data will likely continue on its exponential path, which will continue to put pressure on data collection, storage and processing technologies. Just take one field where humans are likely to be replaced by machines soon: autonomous driving. While driving comes easy to us as human beings, discerning visual objects and correctly reacting to them is actually an enormously complex task. For a computer to complete such a task, it needs a lot of data and computational power. It is estimated that every self-driving car will create some 4 TB of data every day.[xliii] More than one billion cars are on the roads in the world today.[12][xliv] Even if only a small fraction of 1% of these are self-driving, this would equate to 10,000,000 x 4 TB = 40,000,000 TB per day. All of that data would need to be processed and even stored and transmitted among cars. Think about the storage and bandwidth that would be necessary for that. For such technologies to work, even more innovation will have to happen in the field of data storage and processing technologies. It remains to be seen if, or rather how, we will be able to cope with such challenges.

Table 18.1 The scales of data size

	Name	Number of bytes[13]	One unit is (roughly) equal to
B	Bit		A single binary digit, i.e. one "yes" or "no"
B	Byte	1	8 bits The combination of values of the bits in one byte is equal to one single character on a computer, e.g. a letter, so the letter "A" will be stored as the byte with a value of "01100001" in a computer.
kB	Kilobyte	1,000	1,000 characters, which is around 162 words of plain text in English
MB	Megabyte	1,000,000	162,000 words of plain text, which is a few more words than the total length of this book (c. 141,000). The DNA information contained in one sperm is roughly equal to 37.5 MB.[xlv]
GB	Gigabyte	1,000,000,000	162,000,000 words of plain text, which is roughly 324,000 DIN A4 pages of plain text.[14] 250 pictures (with 4 MB average file size)

---

12. In 2015 there was a total of 947 million passenger cars in use worldwide, a number which is constantly growing.
13. These numbers are not exactly accurate and are actually slightly higher, e.g. one kB is actually 1.024 bytes.
14. Assuming we fit around 500 words per page.

Name	Number of bytes[13]	One unit is (roughly) equal to
TB Terabyte	1,000,000,000,000	162,000 books[15] The size of the entire internet in 1997 was roughly equal to 88 TB.[xlvi]
PB Petabyte	1,000,000,000,000,000	162,000,000 books The Large Hadron Collider at CERN produces around 100 PB of data per minute.[xlvii] The brains memory capacity is estimated to be around 2.5 PB[xlviii]
EB Exabyte	1,000,000,000,000,000,000	162,000,000,000 books

The difference between bits and bytes

Especially when talking about bandwidth, the speed at which data is transferred is usually denoted in bit units, rather than byte units. The difference is that a byte consists of 8 bits. So one megabit (Mb) is roughly equal to one-eighth of one megabyte (MB), i.e. 125 KB.

For example, the country with the highest average mobile (cellular) download bandwidth in May 2019 was South Korea,[xlix] with an average bandwidth of 52.4 megabits per second (Mbps). That means that on average 52.4/8 = 6.55 MB per second were transferred.

The reason why we use a different metric when talking about bandwidth as opposed to storage capacity is that across the internet data is transferred one bit rather than byte at a time. Since these bits can come from various sources and might be reshuffled before being formatted into bytes again, measuring bandwidth in bits is simply more intuitive and sensible.

19 | What is data quality and what kind of data quality issues are there?

For companies and people working with data arguably the biggest bugbear is data quality. In the vast majority of projects involving data that do not deliver the expected results, fail or have to be suspended, the underlying reason is either a lack of data or insufficient data quality.

Table 19.1 What is data quality and why does it matter?

What is data quality?

The condition of data with regard to its ability to serve its purpose in an intended use.

---

15. Assuming that an average book has around 100,000 words

Understanding Data

> **Why does it matter?**
>
> Remember that data is essentially a fuel. If the quality is bad, then no matter how strong the engine, the result will always be bad. Even a Ferrari won't get you anywhere if you fuel it with water- and dirt-contaminated fuel.
>
> So if data is used to create an ML algorithm or some sort of AI, the result will only be as good as the data – no matter how good the model and how smart the people working on it. This fact is often referred to as the "garbage in, garbage out" principle. Data is the basis for everything that follows from it, so if this foundation is shaky then everything built on top will be too.
>
> In practice, an ML project can fail for a lot of reasons. But by far the most frequent reasons are insufficient data and poor data quality.

Data quality has many aspects, a lot of which we can illustrate with an example. Let's assume Your Model Car is collecting data about customer satisfaction. A couple of days after a customer receives their order, you send an email with a link to a survey that they can fill in with their feedback. Your data might look something like this:

Table 19.2 Example of data quality issues

CUSTOMER_ID	ORDER_ID	ORDER_DATE	DELIVERY_DATE	RATING_Q1	RATING_Q2	COMMENT
US733847			18.12.2018	5	5	
US648202	75938375	20.12.2018	23.12.2018	0	0	Please stop sending me these emails
FR007492	77774948	23.12.2018	N/A	4	3	Je suis tr☐s content. Merci
UK849372	78883745	02.01.2019	05/01/2019	4	5	
DE334839	11396723	03.01.2019	08-01-2019	5	5	
DE334839	11396723	03.01.2019	08-01-2019	1	1	V☐llig Unzufrieden!
CN223475	44637948	03.01.2019	2019-01-15	4	0	☐☐☐☐☐☐☐☐☐☐☐
CN223475	44637948	03.01.2019	2019-01-15	4	0	☐☐☐☐☐☐☐☐☐☐☐

Question 1: "Did you find what you were looking for on our website?"
Question 2: "Did the product meet your expectations?"
Answers: 1 = Not at all, 2 = Not really, 3 = Kind of, 4 = Yes, somewhat, 5 = Yes, totally

Even someone who hasn't worked with data before will see that there are a couple of problems with this dataset, and these are the most common data quality issues that we encounter.

37

Table 19.3 Types of data quality issues

Data quality aspect	What is the issue?	In the example above...
Missing values	Values are not available for every field.	First line
Consistency	The data within and across datasets is not consistent (or there are contradicting values for the same entity or process).	Data of customer "DE334839"
Implausible value	A variable takes on values that are out of its allowed range (e.g. a negative age).	In line two, the rating for the questions is zero, whereas the range given is 1 (= Not at all) to 5 (= Yes, totally).
Encoding errors	Characters, especially special characters, are not correctly displayed due to encoding errors.	Umlauts in the Comments column
Accuracy	Data does not accurately reflect the true value of the fact (e.g. how accurately does a GPS sensor measure the current location?).	
Duplicate data	There are multiple identical entries for the same record.	The last two lines are identical.
Integrity	Linked data that is stored in different tables can't be integrated, i.e. relationships are not valid and traceable (e.g. can all orders be linked to the customer who placed the order?).	In the first line, the order that the customer has placed is unknown.
Conformity	Entries of the same variable are not in a standard format.	The format of the delivery date varies.

The reasons data quality issues arise are manifold and are difficult to generalize. A lot of them, however, originate from how the data generating process is set up. For instance, when collecting customers' personal data, a company might make the state/province of the address a mandatory field in order to prevent missing values. But what if in some countries such provinces do not exist? This might force the customer to make implausible data entries. Or production machines might be retroactively equipped with movement sensors, but in order not to compromise the functionality of the machines, the sensors might be installed in such a way that they cannot produce perfectly accurate results.

> **Case study 6**
>
> **A flawed data generating process in the production line, Part I**
>
> A supplier of heavy-machinery components tracks the progress of its products across the production line. Every component part gets a QR code, which is scanned at every production step by an assembly-line worker. The goal is to be able to track single component parts and eventually improve the logistics chain with this data.
>
> Unfortunately, there are some flaws in the data generating process. The data produced has a lot of missing values, because the assembly-line

> workers sometimes forget to scan the barcode on a component part. There are also implausible values and consistency issues, because workers may catch up later if they realize they forgot to scan a part, so the data suggests that a part is going in reverse order through the production line. Furthermore, there are data integrity issues, because if two or more components are assembled, there are no guidelines for which of the barcodes to scan in the production process.

20 | How much data quality do you need?

Given that a lot of ML projects fail due to poor data quality, a question we often get asked is just how "good" the quality needs to be. Unfortunately, the answer is, "It depends." Obviously, the general rule of thumb is the more consistent, accurate and complete the data is, the better. But the point at which poor data quality jeopardizes a project's implementation or functionality of an AI system depends on the details of the project. You need to consider how the data will be used, the amount of data you have and whether issues can be fixed ex-post (after the event).

Use for the data

The most important question to establish data quality requirements is: "What exactly will the data to be used for?" Let's suppose you want to have an image-recognition algorithm that analyses X-ray pictures of checked-in baggage at the airport in order to determine whether or not a given piece of luggage contains a bomb. Given that lives are at stake in this use case, the correctness of the algorithm should be as close to fail-safe as possible. But the algorithm will only be as good as the data it is provided with. This in turn means that the X-ray pictures will have to be highly accurate and contain no blurs or other errors – the quality requirements are high in this case. If the data will be used for less critical projects, however, then data quality standards will naturally be lower.

Amount of data

Let's suppose you don't have the above image-recognition algorithm yet but want to create it with supervised ML methods (Chapter 7). For that you will need data, so let's suppose you have a dataset of image scans to train an ML model. How good the data quality has to be also depends on the amount of data you have. The reason is simple: the more data you have available, the more you can afford to ignore and leave out certain data points to train your ML model and still have enough data to train the necessary algorithms and models.[16]

---

16. This should be done with care, though, as it might lead to a so-called "biased sample" which is no longer representative of reality.

Ability to fix issues ex-post

Your data quality requirements will also depend on the nature of the underlying problems, because this will determine how far data quality issues are fixable ex-post. Depending on the type of issue and where it came from, some errors can be fixed more easily than others. In the Your Model Car example, say the date entries don't conform because the date variable of the product delivery is provided by the package delivery companies, and they use different date formats. This can easily be fixed retroactively. On the other hand, things like implausible values, inconsistencies in the data and a lack of integrity are much more cumbersome to fix. Typically, these cases require close cooperation with the business unit in which the data generating process is located, because such errors can usually only be fixed from a business point of view.

In other cases, there are some methods that can remedy certain data quality issues ex-post. The most prominent example is missing data values. Sometimes missing data can be "recreated" with data imputation methods. (In statistics, *imputation* is the practice of replacing missing data with substitute data.) This is only possible under certain circumstances, which are determined by the underlying reason the data values are missing. For example, it might be the case that some objects in a dataset tend to have a higher probability of missing data values – like in online surveys where men might be less patient and skip more questions than women, resulting in more missing values for men. In other cases, missing values might occur completely at random. Trained statisticians know in which of these circumstances missing data values can be sensibly imputed for a given use case and how to do so.

Another area which may require data quality issues to be fixed ex-post is data integration. To integrate datasets from different sources, an explicit connection between the data sources must be present. This connection is realized with so called *key variables*, which are typically some sort of unique ID (📑 31). Since the integration of different datasets is essential in order to paint a comprehensive picture of the real world, the key variables are crucial. Let's assume that Your Model Car has acquired a competitor and we would like to integrate our customer data and the competitor's customer data to create one consolidated dataset. Since the two companies had no previous connection, we lack the information that a given person was or was not a customer of both companies. In cases like these, all is not automatically lost, because under certain circumstances such errors can be circumnavigated. In this case we could, for example, try to relate the names, birthday and/or address of the customer in order to integrate the two datasets.

Therefore, data quality issues can be fixed, to varying degrees, ex-post. So even if data might not seem to meet the quality standards in order to implement a given project, there may be ways to improve the quality. How far it is possible and necessary to make the quality "good enough" depends on how the data will be used.

Understanding Data

The better and more comprehensive approach to ensuring data quality standards, however, is to take a forward-looking approach and actively manage your data. Preventing data errors is always better than trying to fix them ex-post. We will look into the field of data governance that is concerned with this task in Chapter 5_2.

> **Case study 7**
>
> **A flawed data generating process in the production line, Part II (Case Study 6 continued)**
>
> In order to optimize its logistic chain, the heavy-machinery component supplier wants to create an algorithm to predict how many products it will produce on a given day and how many components it will need for that.
>
> Initially, the data quality was not good enough due to various data quality issues (📑 19). The resulting ML algorithms made poor predictions, because they lacked sufficient high-quality, accurate data. However, the most detrimental quality issues could be fixed ex-post, so that the quality of the algorithm's predictions improved. For example, missing values from components "jumping" a production step because a worker forgot to scan the code could be recreated from the subsequent data points and scans.

2_2 Types of data

21 | What are unstructured, semi-structured and structured data?

Data can be differentiated using various criteria. The most important distinction is its *degree of organization*. From this perspective, we typically distinguish between three types of data:

Table 21.1 Structured, semi-structured and unstructured data

	Structured data	**Semi-structured data**	**Unstructured data**
What is it?	Data with a high degree of organization, typically stored in a spreadsheet-like manner	Data with some degree of organization	Data with no predefined organizational form and no specific format
To put it simply	Think of an Excel table or data in a tabular format	Think of a TXT file with text that has some structure (headers, paragraphs, etc.)	Essentially anything that is not structured or semi-structured data (which is a lot)

The Ultimate Data and AI Guide

	Structured data	Semi-structured data	Unstructured data
Example formats	• Excel spreadsheets • Comma-separated value file (.csv) • Relational database tables	• Hypertext Markup Language (HTML) files • JavaScript Object Notation (JSON) files • Extensible Markup Language (XML) files	• Images such as .jpeg or .png files • Videos such as .mp4 or m4a files • Sound files such as .mp3 or .wav files • Plain text files • Word files • PDF files
Characteristics	• Data is structured in a spreadsheet-like manner (e.g. in a table) • Within that table, entries have the same format and a predefined length and follow the same order • Is easily machine-readable and can therefore be analysed without major pre-processing of the data • It is commonly said that around 20% of the world's data is structured[17]	• Data is stored in files that have some degree of organization and structure • Tags or other markers separate elements and enforce hierarchies, but the size of elements can vary and their order is not important • Needs some pre-processing before it can be analysed by a computer • Has gained importance with the emergence of the World Wide Web	• Data that can take any form and thus be stored as any kind of file (formless) • Within that file, there is no structure of content • Typically needs major pre-processing before it can be analysed by a computer, but often easily consumable for humans (e.g. pictures, videos, plain texts) • Most of the data that is created today is unstructured

The following tables and figures show examples of the three types of data. Table 21-2 shows customer data of Your Model Car, using a spreadsheet as an example of structured data. The tabular form and inherent structure make this type of data analysis-ready, e.g. we could use a computer to filter the table for customers living in the USA (the data is machine-readable).

Figure 21-1 shows a JSON file containing employee data. As you can see, JSON files have an inherent tree-like structure that gives some degree of organization, but it is less strong than in a table. Therefore, analysing the data by using simple filter options is partly possible, but more cumbersome than with structured data.

Figure 21-2 shows an example of unstructured data, a product image and description text. Even though this type of data might be easy to consume for us humans, it has no degree of organization and is therefore difficult for machines to analyse and interpret. In Table 21-2 we could use a computer to filter the data to customers living in a certain country, but we cannot filter the image in this figure according to the brand of the car (data is not easily machine-readable, instead we would have to look manually).

---

17. But there is no actual data to back up that claim.

Table 21.2 Example of structured data (customer data)
CUSTOMER

CUSTOMER_ID	LAST_NAME	FIRST_NAME	STREET	CITY	ZIP_CODE	COUNTRY
10302	Boucher	Peter	54, rue Royale	Nantes	44000	France
11244	Smith	Maryam	8489 StrongSt	LasVegas	83030	USA
11405	Han	Sun-Hee	636 St Kilda Road	Sydney	3004	Australia
11993	Mueller	Gisela	Tillystrasse15	Tamm	71732	Germany
12111	Carter	Cynthia	5 Tomahawk Dr	Los Angeles	90006	USA
14121	Cortez	Martin	Av. Grande, 86	Madrid	28034	Spain
14400	Brown	Beata	165 S 7th St	Chester	33134	USA
14578	Wilson	Stephanie	Seestreet 6101	Emory	1734	USA
14622	Jones	Eddy	71 San Diego Ave	Arlington	69004	USA

```
1   {
2       "EMPLOYEES": {
3           "SALES": {
4               "648229": {
5                   "NAME" : "Olivia Johnson"
6                   "DOB" : "1989-08-08"
7               },
8               "648666": {
9                   "NAME" : "Frank Mueller"
10                  "DOB" : "1985-05-11"
11                  "MISC" : "On paternal leave from 2019-01-01 until 2020-01-01"
12              }
13          }
14      }
15  }
```

Figure 21.1 Example of semi-structured data (employee data)

Mercedes 300 SL Coupe

The commercial version of the Mercedes 300SL was first unveiled in 1954. This successful model then went into mass production soon after. With only 1,400 manufactured coupés in total, the gullwing was not an economical success, however.

Figure 21.2 Example of unstructured data (product data)

Comprehending this distinction is crucial, because the type of data will have implications on how the data can be stored and how it has to be processed before it can be analysed. Yet there is often confusion about the three types of data. This is partly because different people use different definitions (e.g. some reckon that structured data follows a specific data model; see 30). More importantly, however, the confusion arises because the difference between the types is far from clear-cut. Consider the following Your Model Car example:

Table 21.3 Unstructured structured data

	PRODUCT_ID	PRODUCT_NAME	PRODUCT_LINE	SPECIFICATIONS	PRICE	IMAGE
1	S6374	Mercedes Benz 300SL Coupé	Classic Cars / Sports Cars	Scale 1:35 Availability: there are currently 30 items in stock (09.10.2019). UPDATE: stock has decreased to 23 (01.11.2019).	€89.90 (but a 10% discount is given for orders with >5 items)	
2	D7483	Ferrari 360 red (1999)	Sports Cars	NOT IN PORTFOLIO ANYMORE	N/A	
3	D7848	1988 Harley Davidson	Motorbikes	Scale 1:15, or 1:20 (old version) This replica features kickstand, gear-shift lever and drive chain. This product is extremely delicate and so is shipped with special materials.		Not available (currently being revised)

This data about products looks familiar to most of us. While Excel is meant to store data in a structured way, it is often butchered so that data is consumable by humans but not computers. In Table 21-3, we are still able to make sense of the mess that's been made of the structured format. We understand that there are different buy prices for our products, we can conceive what the product looks like, we see what scales the products have, etc. But for a computer, obtaining information on, say, the scale from this file, is extremely difficult. So if someone browsing on the Your Model Car website wanted to filter or sort the products according to scale, having such a dataset would be useless, since a computer would not be able to retrieve and handle that kind of request. Therefore, even if data is stored in a format that is meant to hold structured data, it does not mean that the data in it is actually structured data. The lines between the data types are thus blurry.

> **Case study 8**
>
> **Collecting structured and unstructured data from insurance claims**
>
> A car insurance company collects data about claims that it receives via an online form that customers fill in when they file a claim.
>
> This online form consists of a number of standardized questions, such as "When was the damage incurred?" and "What part of the car was damaged?". Customers choose the answers to these questions from a drop-down menu. This creates structured data.

> The online form also allows customers to upload additional information in order to specify the damage and how it occurred. This could be videos from dash-cams, pictures of the damage, police documents or witness reports. These are all examples of unstructured data.

22 | What are master data and transactional data?

Another distinction that is made in types of data is between master and transactional data.

Master data describes an object that is shared across a company. Companies collect all sorts of data in all sorts of fields across their various departments. Consider Your Model Car, where we have a number of departments ranging from marketing to sales to logistics and so on. A lot of the data in, say, marketing (e.g. customer value, landing-page conversion rates) will be irrelevant in, for example, the logistics department.

There is data about certain objects, however, that is relevant across most departments – for example, the personal data of customers (name, address, contact details, etc.) and data on the products (product specifications, description, picture). These are examples of master data because they describe business entities that are shared across various departments. This data rarely changes and is rather static (typically, customers don't often change their personal data and products aren't often altered).

Table 22.1 Master versus transactional data

Master data	Transactional data

▶ Data about business objects that are shared across a company
▶ Usually static data that rarely changes
▶ Examples:
  ❏ Customer data (name, address, phone number, etc.)
  ❏ Product data (description, specifications such as size etc.)
  ❏ Employee data (name, address, emergency contact, etc.)
	▶ Data that describes events and transactions
	▶ Not static, typically has a temporal dimension
	▶ Examples:
	  ❏ Orders of online retailer (order data and time, ordered product)
	  ❏ Website logs (access date and time, IP address of computer that requested access, etc.)
	  ❏ Sensor data from a car (measurement time, temperature of engine etc.)
	  ❏ Workload of a machine or power grid at given points

Table 22.2 Example of master data
CUSTOMER

CUSTOMER_ID	FAMILY_NAME	GIVEN_NAME	EMAIL
DE00120	Schmidt	Justin	j.schmidt@web.de
UK00439	Bennon	Lara	l.bennon@yahoo.co.uk
...			

Table 22.3 Example of transactional data
WEBLOG

TIMESTAMP	IP	REQUEST
07.02.2019 15:42:02	65.55.53.29	/order.html
07.02.2019 15:42:03	216.129.13.4	/faq.html
...		

Transactional data is data that describes or collects data about an event rather than a business object. It therefore typically features a temporal dimension, i.e. some information on when the event happened. Examples of transactional data are the records of all orders of products in a company and the log data of a website.

Both master and transactional data are often structured (as in Tables 22-2 and 22-3) but they can also be unstructured. For example, Your Model Car is likely to have master data in the form of pictures or videos of its products (unstructured data), along with product specifications such as the width, length, height, weight and colour (structured data). As far as transactional data goes, unstructured data could come in the form of sound files, videos or pictures. Consider a manufacturing line where all parts have to undergo an end-of-line test to assess their quality. This test could consist of taking a picture of the part to look for visual flaws, or it could consist of checking the quality through noise and vibration tests in which sound data is stored and analysed.

> **Case study 9**
>
> **How master data management can save costs**
>
> A beverage manufacturer wants to standardize master data across its factories. It notices that different factories source raw materials from the same suppliers but use different notations. As a result, different factories pay different prices for raw materials from the same suppliers.
>
> To improve the situation, the manufacturer runs a master-data-management project to identify and harmonize the supplied items across all factories. With this master data, the manufacturer is able to identify suppliers that deliver their products to various factories at different prices. It can therefore renegotiate the terms and set a standardized, cheaper price for all the supplied items.

23 | What is streaming data and what is the difference between batch and streaming processing?

Data needs to be processed in different ways depending on how it is generated and what it is used for. When data is continuously generated by a large number of data sources and is collected in small sizes on a frequent basis, this is streaming data. A good example of streaming data is web-server-log data and log files of customers' mobile and web applications. Collecting the

Understanding Data

web-server-log data about the customers visiting the website of Your Model Car would be a prime example of streaming data. Another example would be any connected device or sensor that continuously collects data on the transactions of customers of a bank. Due to its high velocity and volume, streaming data is often associated with big-data use cases (📄 24).

Table 23.1 What is streaming data and why does it matter?

What is streaming data?
Streaming data forms the basis for (near) real-time use cases. For example, a bank can analyse streaming data on transactions conducted by customers every second to check for fraudulent activities in (near) real time. This analysis could be used to deny money withdrawals at an ATM, for instance.
Why does it matter?
Streaming data forms the basis for (near) real-time use cases. For example, a bank can analyse streaming data on transactions conducted by customers every second to check for fraudulent activities in (near) real time. This analysis could be used to deny money withdrawals at an ATM, for instance.

Irrespective of how data is created, it is processed through either batch processing or stream processing.

Batch processing refers to processing blocks of data that have already been stored over a period of time. These blocks are large batches of data. For example, say in Your Model Car we want to create a daily report on the revenue we generated the previous day. To create this report, we would need to process the entire block of all transactions and payments the previous day. Rather than analysing each order and payment, we store all the data and process it all at once on a daily basis.

Stream processing refers to analysing data as it arrives, rather than storing it and processing it in a block. As opposed to batch processing, where large batches are processed at once, in stream processing data is processed on an individual-record or micro-batch level. For example, with Your Model Car we could analyse the data of a customer visiting our website in order to personalize the advertisements for them. If cookies in their browser reveal that they have already visited our website and looked for vintage model cars, we could specifically advertise those to the customer. If we do that for every customer as they visit our website (in real time), this is an example of stream processing the streaming data "website visits".

> **Case study 10**
>
> **Streaming data of bank customers withdrawing money**
>
> A bank wants to improve its fraud-detection algorithm on customer transactions. In order to train its algorithm, it uses the historic data of its customers. That is, an algorithm is created by learning from a large block

of historic data. Since this large block of data is processed at once, the processing of the data for the model is an example of batch processing.

Once the algorithm is trained, it can be deployed for use in real life. Every transaction request of a customer of the bank goes through this algorithm, which either declares it valid or fraudulent. Since every record is being fed into the algorithm individually, the result is a stream of data that is continuously being processed by the algorithm. This is an example of stream processing.

24 | What is big data?

We have seen in 18 that we have entered an era of mass data creation and storage. People like to refer to this as "big data", a buzzword that has been trending so much that it has found its way into everyday vernacular. We have seen departments and projects renamed to contain the words "big data" because otherwise they wouldn't get funding for implementation. For example, we implemented one project in which we were urged to include social media data in our analysis. We knew it wouldn't bring any added value in terms of our model accuracy or anything else. But given that social media counts as unstructured data, we were able to brand the project as a "big data" project instead of "just data". And *voilà*, we received the necessary funding to get the project started.

Yet behind closed doors we are often asked: what is the difference between big and normal data, and just how big does the data have to be for it to be considered "big"? As Professor Dan Ariely at Duke University succinctly put it: "Big data is like teenage sex; everyone talks about it, nobody really knows how to do it, everyone thinks everyone else is doing it, so everyone claims they are doing it."[1] Big data is one of those buzzwords that has been so overused it seems to be occluded by a big blur. Despite this blur, the business world has found a common definition for big data:

Table 24.1 What is big data and why does it matter?

What is big data?
Data that is too large or complex to be stored or processed with traditional technologies. This will typically arise due to the 3 Vs that big data is associated with:[18] ▶ **Volume:** The quantity of data that is collected, stored and processed. Big data = a lot of data. ▶ **Velocity:** The speed at which data needs to be collected, stored and processed for a given use case, often in (near) real-time. Big data = data needs to be processed fast. ▶ **Variety:** The type and structure of the data. Big data = data taking any form including unstructured data (previously data was almost exclusively structured).

---

18. Depending on the source, the number of 'V' words varies from three to ten, or even more.

Understanding Data

> **Why does it matter?**
>
> Regardless of how exactly you define big data, the skyrocketing in the creation, storage and processing of data has had profound consequences in a number of fields.
>
> On the one hand, the availability of so much data has opened up completely new avenues for putting this data to use, e.g. with ML methodologies to create AI. Thus, big data has enabled a whole new range of data use cases.
>
> On the other hand, it has also put a lot of pressure on data storage and processing technologies. Since traditional technologies were not able to deal with big data, the pressure to innovate and improve has led to an entire new range of technologies.

Let's look at what big data means in practice. As we saw in 📑 18, we entered the digital age sometime in the 2000s. This is when the trajectory of data growth took off on an exponential path which ultimately led to where we are today. By 2015 already, 90% of all data ever produced had been create in the previous two years. This is worth a reread, because the brain has difficulty conceiving of exponential growth: *90% of all <u>data</u> on this planet had been created in the previous two years.* That year, around 2.5 quintillion bytes of data were created *every day*. That is 2,500,000 terabytes.[ii]

It is hard to wrap your head around just how much that is. Today, the situation is even more mind-blowing. Figure 24-1 provides some examples of what is happening every minute on the internet to make big data more graspable.

While most people associate big data with examples like those in Figure 24-1, the definition relating to the 3 Vs (Table 24-1) has some inherent flaws that tend to lead to confusion and lack of clarity.

First, if you classify big data like this, then by definition it is an evolutionary concept. What would be considered big data 20 years ago – i.e. too complex to be processed with the traditional technologies back then – is peanuts today. Likewise, everything that falls under the big data label today will be peanuts in a few years from now. So according to the definition, we have been in an age of big data for several decades because data storage and processing requirements have always been bigger than what was possible at a given point in time – this lies at the very heart of the pressure to innovate and improve existing technologies.

This definition is also completely case-specific. When is data large enough or unstructured enough to be classified as big data? It will always depend on the underlying goal of a given project and the available technology. It might be that a couple of gigabytes of data could already be a "big data" problem, because they have to be processed so fast, or that the data is so complex to process and analyse that it is not possible with traditional technologies or would be very challenging.

Likewise, we have often been approached by clients who claim that they have terabytes of data for a given project – clearly "big". Now, it often turns out that while there might be *a lot of raw data at first*, we will not need all of it for a

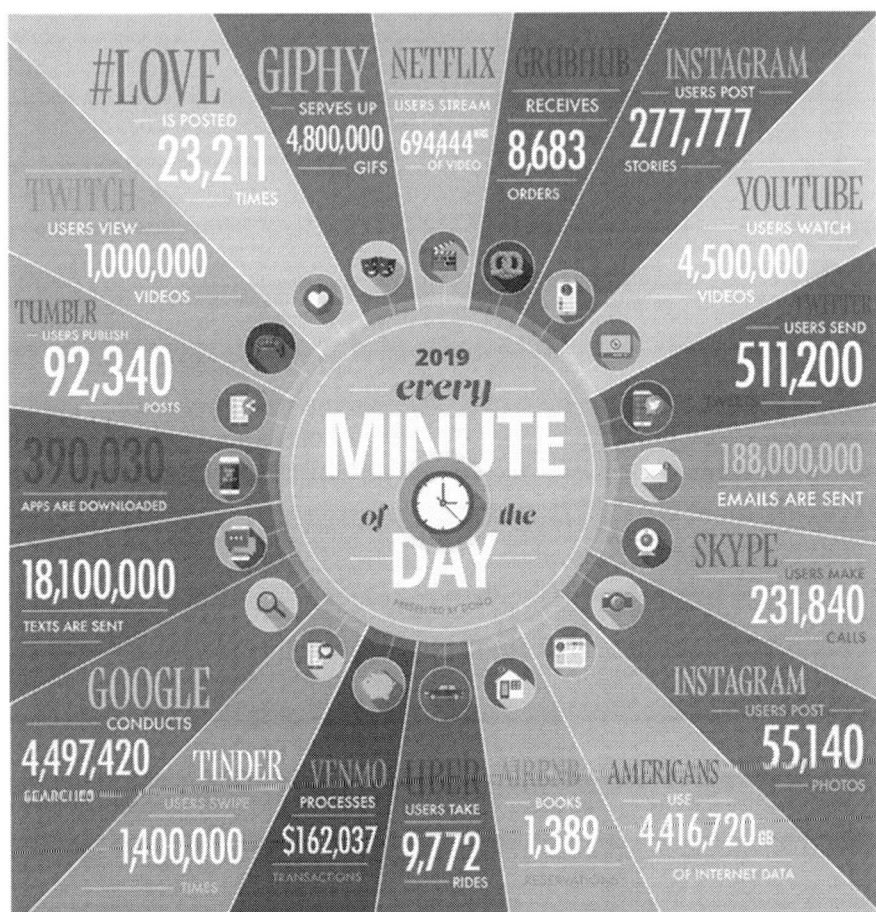

Figure 24.1 What happens in 60 seconds on the internet?
From "Data Never Sleeps 7.0," by Domo Inc., 2019 (https://www.domo.com/learn/data-never-sleeps-7). Copyright 2019 by Domo Inc. Reprinted with permission.[lii]

given use case. When pre-processing data for a given use case, you often aggregate it or just throw away the unnecessary rubbish, leaving a very limited fraction of the original raw data for the analysis. This is often the case with sensor data, where data might be too granular and only certain measurements from a collecting device are relevant. For example, if you want to predict the remaining lifetime of a production machine at a week or maybe even month level, sensor data on a millisecond level will simply be too granular.

For these reasons we like to avoid classifying data as big or small; the boundaries in terms of the 3 Vs are just too blurry. Instead, when we need to estimate the work and complexity of a given project, we typically ask ourselves whether or not the project will have to be implemented on what is called *distributed systems with parallel processing* (computer clusters) or whether it can be implemented on single servers. This makes a real difference in terms of

Understanding Data

the feasibility, difficulty and expertise required. Working with a system of parallel computing is much more complex than working on a single server or computer. (We look into why this is the case in detail in 📄 35. Basically, working with a computer cluster and using parallel computing is like working in a big team as opposed to working alone. You can achieve much more, but you also have to coordinate with the rest of the team over who is doing what and when. This can create a lot of overhead costs.)

Since it is quite clear-cut whether a given use case or project requires the use of parallel computing, this is also a good indicator of whether or not a project is a big data project. Therefore, we like to think of big data projects as follows:

Table 24.2 An alternative definition of big data

What is a better definition of big data?
Data storage and processing use cases that require the use of parallel computing on computer clusters to store, process or analyse data.
Why does it matter?
Having to work with computer clusters rather than single-node servers or computers typically makes data analysis and processing much more complex.

3 Data Storage Technologies

3_1 Understanding data storage

25 | Why can't a company store its structured data in an Excel file like we do on PCs?

On an individual level, storing data has never been easier than today. We can create and directly store photos and videos on our smartphones. We can send and receive emails and collect them in our inboxes. We can download terabytes of books, games, videos and pictures from the internet in an instant and store them on our computers.

But what do things look like for companies? How does a car manufacturer store the millions of measurements that its sensors in the production hall produce every day? How does a hotel store and manage the bookings of thousands of guests? How does a bank or stock exchange store millions of money transactions every split second?

Let's go back to our online retailer example. Suppose you are the CEO of Your Model Car and you have a list of all the products with their product specifications (product master data): ID, name, brand, price, size, weight, etc. Because the data is pretty structured (no videos or unstructured text or anything of that sort involved), it lends itself to being saved as an Excel file, right? Suppose you actually have an Excel file with all the product data stored in the "Products" folder of your server, which is running in the company's basement. It might look something like this:

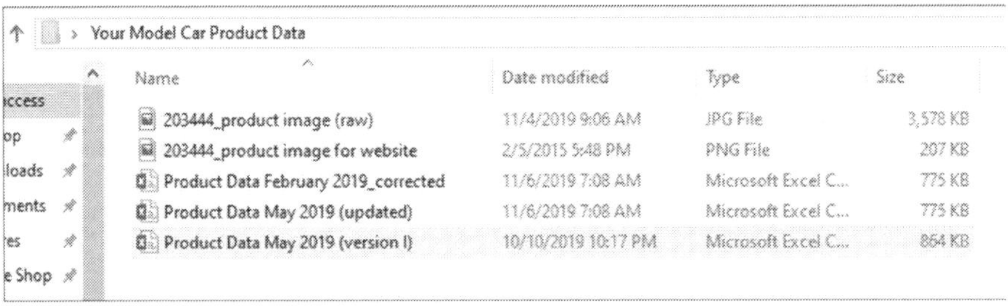

Name	Date modified	Type	Size
203444_product image (raw)	11/4/2019 9:06 AM	JPG File	3,578 KB
203444_product image for website	2/5/2015 5:48 PM	PNG File	207 KB
Product Data February 2019_corrected	11/6/2019 7:08 AM	Microsoft Excel C...	775 KB
Product Data May 2019 (updated)	11/6/2019 7:08 AM	Microsoft Excel C...	775 KB
Product Data May 2019 (version I)	10/10/2019 10:17 PM	Microsoft Excel C...	864 KB

Figure 25.1 Screenshot of a file system containing product data

This is not the smartest way to store that kind of data for a lot of reasons:

- Product data is something that your customers might want to view on a regular basis through your website. If the data is stored as an Excel file on

your server, then making this information available to customers browsing your website will be difficult and impractical.
- Since product information is one of your core data assets, many users will probably want to view and edit the data at the same time; i.e. you want to provide multi-access to the data. This multi-access should come with different rights, so while your customers are only allowed to view the data through your website, your employees can edit the product information. Such identity and access management is difficult in Excel.
- Over time, products will be added to and deleted from your portfolio. Furthermore, since product information is truly a crucial data asset, you will want to protect yourself against malicious edits of the data and unforeseen loss of data. Therefore, you need a versioning and a backup system for it. Excel does not offer these functionalities, so it is not the ideal solution here.
- Someone might make a local copy of the Excel file on their computer, edit some of the entries and upload this revised version of the Excel file to the central server. This would create inconsistencies and redundancies in your data. If there are various Excel files with differing data entries, how can you tell which is the correct file?

There are plenty more reasons why Excel is not the ideal solution for storing your product data. Some readers might say that it is a no-brainer that data should not be stored like this, especially if the data plays a vital role in the company's business. You are right. The reality witnessing on the ground, however, is that for a lot of companies Excel is still the go-to solution. This is especially true for very small businesses, which often lack the time and financial resources to put in place a proper data storage system. But even in the departments of big, internationally renowned companies, we have seen data being entered, edited and versioned manually in Excel files because going through the process of setting up and maintaining a more sophisticated IT infrastructure is too cumbersome.

> **Case study 11**
>
> **Setting up a database to replace Excel**
>
> A premium luxury goods manufacturer that specializes in jewellery and lifestyle accessories has outlets across the world. Data within these outlets is stored in various data formats, including Excel files. This data includes the number of customers on a given day, the number of items sold, the number of items delivered, the work plan with employees' shifts, etc.
>
> The headquarters, which are located in Paris, receive this data on a regular basis. The incoherence with regard to the storage format and the structure within the files has led to a lot of inefficiencies and confusion.
>
> To remedy these inefficiencies, the systems of all outlets are linked to a central database located at the headquarters. So instead of entering data

> in an Excel file which is then sent to HQ, staff use a dedicated software tool that is linked to the central database. That way the data is stored directly in the central database, some of it automatically (e.g. sales) and some of it manually by the employees (e.g. the work plan).

26 | What is a database and how does it work?

Everyone has heard the term "database" before, but few actually know what one is, let alone how one works. This should not come as a surprise, given that storing data on a computer is a rather complex and multi-layered process.

Every bit of data or information is stored as an array of 0s and 1s. This sequences of 0s and 1s could, for example, be stored on magnetic storage (traditional hard-disk drives, HDD) or integrated circuits (solid-state drives, SSD) or on Blu-ray discs. But on top of that, there are countless abstraction layers, software and interfaces that make storing data feasible in the first place. If you want to store a picture, you are not going to type a sequence of 0s and 1s into your computer for each pixel. Instead, you just store a file in a folder on your file system and the computer takes care of the rest. Or you might store the picture in the cloud, which adds another abstraction layer on top. Having all of these abstraction layers can make the topic of storage somewhat confusing.

A database is one layer of abstraction from 0s and 1s and one way to store data. Just like we can store a document in the file system on a PC, data can be stored in a database system on the PC. It is important to note that a database is *not* the same thing as a server. The notion that a database is some big, bulky server in a basement is not quite correct. The database might *run and reside* on such a server, but it is not the actual hardware. Instead, the database runs on a computer, just like other pieces of software and files. It is also important to note that often when people speak of a database what they actually mean is the sum of the database and the database management system (DBMS) related to it. These two things are defined as follows:

Table 26.1 What is a database and why does it matter?

What is database?
A collection of data organized in a certain way, typically stored on a server, that allows for easy access, retrieval and updating of data.
The DBMS is a piece of software that runs on the server to act as an interface and enables end-users to communicate with and manipulate the database.
Note that the database as such is nothing but a collection of data. However, often when people speak of databases, what they are referring to is the database *and* the corresponding DBMS used to access it.

Data Storage Technologies

> **Why does it matter?**
>
> In most cases, database systems are the most efficient and practical way to store data, and so they are used by companies and organizations around the globe. If there were no database systems, we would not be able to store the masses of data we are generating today. If data is the oil of the 21st century, then databases are something like the tanks used to store that oil.

A database in itself is nothing but the actual data organized in a specific way. In contrast, the DBMS is the intermediary between the user and this database. It is a piece of software that runs on a computer just like other software does. If you have an Excel sheet with some data in it, then you can think of the content of this Excel sheet as a database (i.e. the actual numbers and data entries) and the software Excel as the DBMS that manipulates and provides access to this database. Both reside and run on a computer. Unlike Excel, though, a dedicated database system offers a multitude of advantages (see 📄 27).

The user of a database system could be you, but it could also be another application or machine, or a combination thereof. For example, Your Model Car stores most of its product data in a database. Customers visiting our website and browsing products – say, filtering all of our products by a certain brand – communicate with our database via our website.

All of the data in a database is accessed and manipulated through the DBMS. The DBMS receives all manipulation requests from the user (for example "display all Ferrari cars") and translates them into operations in the database itself. The DBMS therefore hides as much of the complexity of the database from the user as possible. Prominent examples of DBMSs are SQL Server, Oracle Database and SAP HANA.

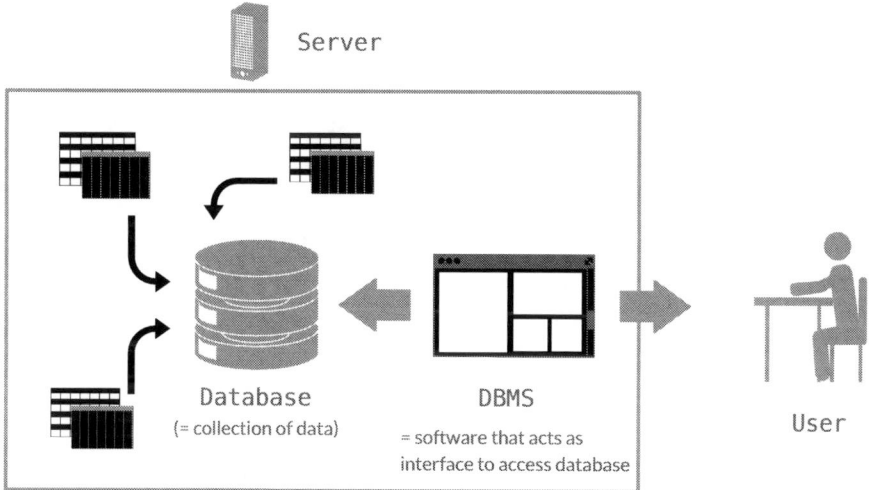

Figure 26.1 Visualization of a database system

We differentiate between various types of database based on how data is structured in the database.

27 | What are the advantages of storing data in a database?

Our world would look very different if we had no database systems at our disposal – essentially, they enable the operation of any business process that relies on data collection and/or data storage. This is because storing and organizing data in a database system has several advantages compared to storing data in other ways, such as in an Excel file.

- Databases and, more importantly, their respective DBMSs are sophisticated software that is specifically designed to store and process data in an efficient way and make it available to users. They allow for multi-access – that is, multiple users can access and manipulate the database at the same time. Those users could be humans or other machines or tools to which the database is connected.
- Database systems allow you to restrict and manage the rights that a certain user has on a database. This is called *identity and access management* (IAM).
- When set up correctly, a database alleviates data redundancies and inconsistencies, because instead of having data residing across several scattered files and possibly even various computers, you have all the data in one centralized repository.
- Since databases are specifically designed to store and process data, they do so in a highly efficient way and can read, write and store however much data companies require.
- Most DBMSs have built-in backup and recovery systems that make sure data in the database is secure.
- With most DBMSs you can *query* the database, which means you make a request for specific information. For example, say a database stores product data. Very simple queries would be to display all the products above a certain price and to display the total number of products in the database. (You can think of queries as the filter option in an Excel sheet.)

There are plenty of other advantages of database systems, but these ones certainly suffice to show that when it comes to storing and making available *company data*, database systems are the go-to solution in the vast majority of cases.

> **Case study 12**
>
> **Setting up a database to digitalize business processes**
>
> With its customer base increasing and demand exceeding class capacities, a fitness and yoga studio is expanding by opening up a second and third branch. So far, the data has been collected and stored in a mix of analogue

forms (e.g. customers buy stamp cards for ten yoga sessions) and Excel (e.g. customer data has been recorded in Excel sheets).

With three branches in operation, there is a need to have a centralized view of all the data. For example, all branches will need access to the customer data in order to check the membership status of a customer upon entry. Furthermore, the yoga studio wants to offer its customers the functionality to access their personal data and membership status (e.g. number of remaining classes) via its website and an app.

To create one consistent and up-to-date view of the data, the yoga studio buys dedicated membership software which is connected to a database. Access to the database is managed and regulated. For example, employees have a full view of the data, whereas customers can only see their respective data. The database also enables simple queries, such as the total number of customers and the number of customers per given yoga class.

28 | What types of databases are there and how are they classified?

Database systems can be classified in a number of ways. In the business world, for example, databases are often classified by their application area and by the type of data they hold. For example, in the Your Model Car context, we might refer to the database that contains information about our customers as "the customer database".

While a content-based distinction might be useful within companies, a more technical distinction helps us understand the workings, advantages and limitations of certain types of databases. We classify database systems according to the *database model* they follow. The database model stipulates how data is logically organized in a database. Remember that a database is merely some data organized in a certain manner. This *manner* is the database model.

Numerous database models exist. Choosing the right database model for a given situation – i.e. choosing how you want to organize and structure the data that you store – depends on the underlying real-world process and entities you want to model. Data is meant to serve as a representation of the real world, so you need a database model that best depicts the real-world aspects.

Table 28.1 What is a database model and why does it matter?

What is database model?
The database model is the way in which a database is logically structured. It determines how data is stored, organized and manipulated.
There are a number of different database models that exist, e.g. the relational database model.

The Ultimate Data and AI Guide

> **Why does it matter?**
>
> The database model determines the type of a database, which in turn determines for what kind of use case the database is appropriate. You can think of the database model as the roadmap and key to understanding the structure of a database.

For example, one type of database model is the flat model. Database that follow a flat model are called flat-file databases. This is arguably the simplest data model there is. The basic idea is to just store all the desired data in one two-dimensional table, i.e. a classic spreadsheet. If our real-world process is extremely simple, this works fine. For example, if we just want to model our very basic employee data, a flat file like the one below is adequate because it contains all the relevant information.

Table 28.2 A flat-file data model of employees
EMPLOYEE

EMPLOYEE_ID	LAST_NAME	FIRST_NAME	AGE
2537	Beck	Fabian	34
1433	Wilson	Tina	45
2231	Mayer	Holger	60
...			

However, just imagine we do not want to limit ourselves to storing only this employee data. There is plenty more data we should collect. Who is using what equipment (computer, phone, keyboard, etc.)? What are the relationships between employees (who reports to whom)? What are the emergency contacts for our employees? What department is a given employee working in? What are employees' salaries? And so forth.

Extending the data that we collect about our employees and other entities and processes around them would be extremely impractical with the flat model. Just imagine all of the above information cramped into this single flat file: it would be very messy and difficult to navigate. One solution is to store the data in different tables that have some sort of connection – and this lies at the heart of many other database models. As we will see, if the real-world process that we want to depict with our data is too complex to fit comfortably in one table, then other database models are more appropriate.

The choice of how we should structure, organize and eventually store our data in a database – in other words, which database model is appropriate – fundamentally depends on what process we are trying to depict with our data. Apart from the flat model, there are plenty of other database models. For example, the hierarchical model is great when we have nested structures, such as the table of contents in books (part → chapters → sections → subsections → paragraphs).

However, by far the most important data model is the relational model.

3_2 Relational (SQL) databases

29 | What is a relational database system and how does it work?

The vast majority of databases are relational databases. That means that the data they hold is organized based on the relational model. In the relational model, a given real-world process is described through data that is organized in interrelated tables (called relations).[19] Note that unlike in the flat model, the data is distributed across several tables rather than just one. Each table contains data on a certain entity or process and is structured like a spreadsheet, i.e. in rows and columns. You can think of a relational model as a bunch of Excel tables, each of which contains data on a certain entity (e.g. customers or products), that are connected via the "VLOOKUP" command.

Table 29.1 What is a relational database system and why does it matter?

What is a relational model and what is a relational database system?
The relational model is one type of database model, i.e. one way to organize structured data (📄 21) in a database. In a relational model a real-world process is depicted with data organized in interconnected tables (also called *relations*), each of which stores data on a certain entity or process.
Databases in which data is organized according to a relational data model are called relational databases. Since data is stored in tables, relational databases are not appropriate for storing unstructured data.
Why does it matter?
The relational model is an extremely versatile and powerful yet simple way to organize data in a database. It can therefore be used to model a lot of real-life situations. As a result, it is the most commonly employed database model today – and has been so for the past couple of decades.
Relational database are the workhorses of the industry and are used in the vast majority of data storage situations. These databases have several advantages over other types of database, such as being very versatile and enabling complex queries (📄 33).

---

19. A "relation" in the relational model refers to a table, not to the connection between tables.

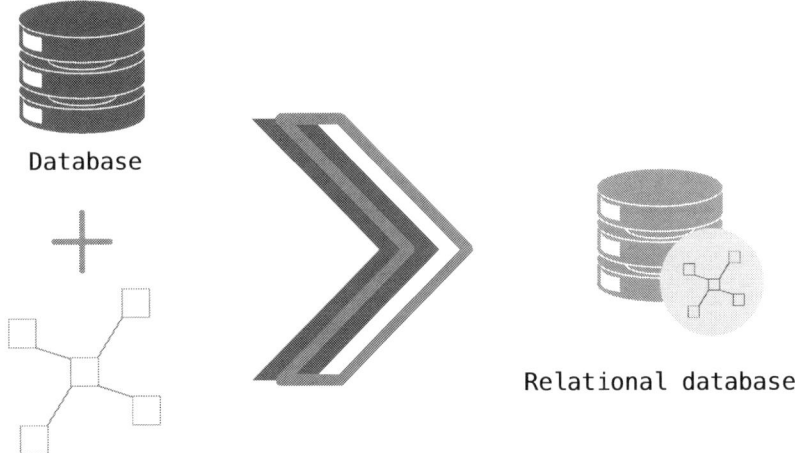

Figure 29.1 Visualization of a relational database system

The relational model has proven to be very powerful in modelling a lot of real-world processes. It is extremely versatile and rigorously defined, yet pretty easy to understand and intuitive. As a result of that, databases that follow a relational model are by far the most widely used ones in all industries today – and have been so for the past couple of decades.

For almost half a century, the answer to the question "Where and how should we store data?" has been: with a *relational database system*. You have thousands of financial transactions of banking customers to store and process? You need to store data on customers, data from your production process or data from the checkout at a supermarket? You need to obtain analytical information from your database on a regular basis? As long as the underlying problem and aspect of the real world could be modelled with structured data in interrelated tables – and a lot can be done with that! – then for a long time the answer to these questions has been "just use a relational database".

The relational model dates back to 1969, when it was first described by Edgar F. Codd, a computer scientist who was working at IBM at the time. Fast-forward half a century and relational databases are still the workhorses for storing data in the vast majority of companies, as can be seen in Table 29-2, which ranks various databases according to their popularity (note: today, many relational databases also support other data models). In the information technology world, surviving and outcompeting other technologies for 50 years is close to impossible. Think back to technological capabilities 50 years ago – how many of them have survived? Back then if you went to a tech store, you would buy music cassettes, Walkmans and ultra-heavy CRT TVs; today, these things seem a Stone Age away. Yet relational database systems have survived. Therefore, when dealing with data, knowing the basics of relational database systems is a must.

Table 29.2 Ranking of database systems according to popularity.[20]
From "DB-Engines Ranking," by solid IT gmbh, 2019 (https://db-engines.com/en/ranking). Copyright 2019 by solid IT gmbh. Reprinted with permission.[liii]

Rank			DBMS	Database model	Score		
Dec 2019	Nov 2019	Dec 2018			Dec 2019	Nov 2019	Dec 2018
1	1	1	Oracle	Relational, multi-model	1346.39	+10.33	+63.17
2	2	2	MySQL	Relational, multi-model	1275.67	+9.38	+114.42
3	3	3	Microsoft SQL Server	Relational, multi-model	1096.20	+14.29	+55.86
4	4	4	PostreSQL	Relational, multi-model	503.37	+12.30	+42.74
5	5	5	MongoDB	Document, multi-model	421.12	+7.94	+42.50
6	6	6	IBM Db2	Relational, multi-model	171.35	-1.25	-9.40
7	7	8	Elasticsearch	Search engine, multi-model	150.25	+1.85	+5.55
8	8	7	Redis	Key-value, multi-model	146.23	+1.00	-0.59
9	9	9	Microsoft Access	Relational	129.47	-0.60	-10.04
10	10	11	Cassandra	Wide column	120.71	-2.52	-1.10

30 | How does the relational model work?

The basic idea is that a real-world process is broken down into entities and processes about which data is collected in the form of interconnected tables. Typically, each table contains data on a certain entity; for example, the entity "customer" or "employee". Within the table, the data is structured in a two-dimensional spreadsheet, where each row represents one instance of the entity (e.g. one specific customer) and each column represents an attribute of that instance (e.g. the customer's age). Since data is organized in tables, relational databases hold structured data by definition.

---

20. Most relational databases support other data models today (hence multi-model). For methodology on score calculation see source.

The Ultimate Data and AI Guide

Let's look at a very simple relational model of the real-world process "customer makes order" for Your Model Car. This is a very simple process in which there are only two relevant entities, "customers" and "orders". Let's assume that the data we collect on a customer is their internal customer ID, last name, first name and shipping address. The table containing the customer data in a relational model would look like this:

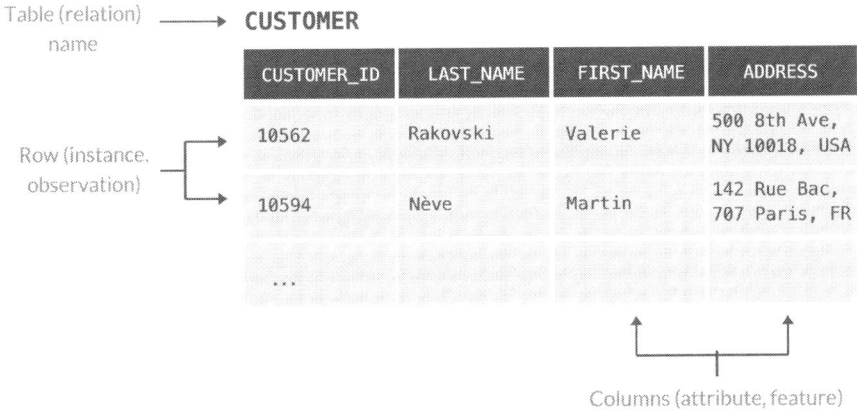

Figure 30.1 Simple table in the relational model with terminology explained

When dealing with a relational model or with data stored in spreadsheets in general, it is important to be clear on the notation. The name of the table, which is typically the name of the entity about which the table contains data, is called the *table* or *relation name*. The table consists of a number of *instances*, which are also called *observations* or simply *rows*. Since our table here contains data on customers, every row is equal to one customer. The data that we collect about each customer is called *attributes*, *features* or *columns*. In this case, the attributes are the customer ID, last name, first name and shipping address.

The second set of entities that is relevant in our real-world process is the orders. Let's assume that the data we collect about the orders is the date on which an order was placed along with the amount due. What is the relationship between our two entities in the real world? In this case it is rather straightforward: "a customer makes orders". Therefore, every given order has to belong to a certain customer.

How can we depict this relationship in our database? On top of the aforementioned attributes that we collect about every order, we also have to collect the information "to which customer a given order belongs". We can do that by simply including another column in the table ORDER that contains the information about who placed the order: "CUSTOMER_ID". This yields the connection between the two entities (see 📖 31).

CUSTOMER

CUSTOMER_ID	LAST_NAME	FIRST_NAME	ADDRESS
10562	Rakovski	Valerie	500 8th Ave, NY 10018, USA
10594	Nève	Martin	142 Rue Bac, 707 Paris, FR
...			

ORDER

ORDER_ID	DATE_TIME	AMOUNT	CUSTOMER_ID
0627334	2019-09-16 15:33:24	69.90	10562
0949301	2019-09-16 15:50:13	126.90	10594
...			

Figure 30.2 Example of two interconnected tables

In this way, the (admittedly rather simple) process of customers placing orders on the website can be perfectly modelled with our simple relational model. It provides both the necessary information on the entities and the connection that exists between them.

The vast majority of relationships between entities and processes in the real world can be depicted like in this example. This makes the relational model extremely powerful and apt for a lot of real-life situations, which explains the great success of relational databases.

Obviously, in reality the processes will be much more complex: they will typically contain many more entities, and these will have more involved relationships with each other. The relational model can also model such complex situations. It is not uncommon for the underlying relational model of a database to model tens or hundreds of interrelated entities and processes, yielding a relational model with many tables. Relational models can occupy entire walls in a project room to serve as a "data map".

However, to keep things in order – especially in large relational models – we often refrain from displaying a table in its *detailed form* with sample data, and instead denote the relations in a relational model in their *compact form*. That is, we only display the name of the relation, the attributes that it contains and the relationship it has to other entities in the model, like in Figure 30-3.

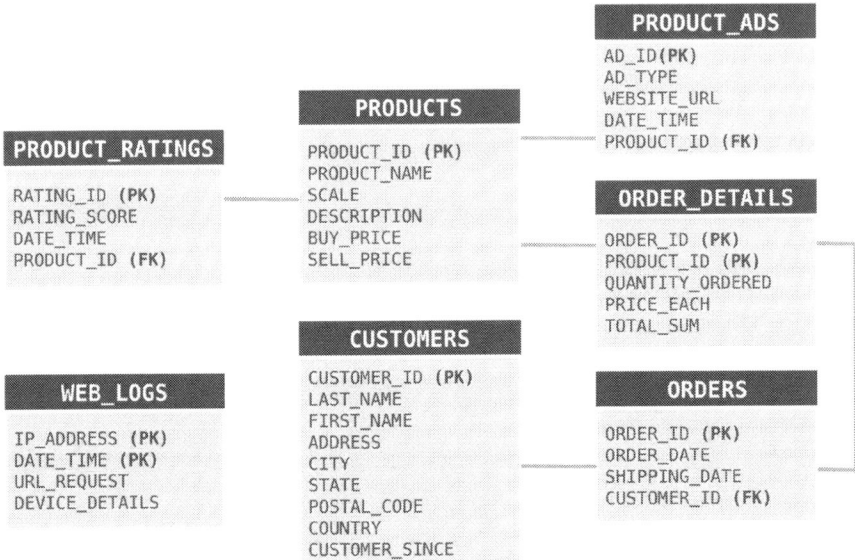

Figure 30.3 Example of relational data model of Your Model Car

Case study 13

Digitizing the certification process with a relational database, Part I

A product inspection and certification company is certifying elevators for safe use. For that, they send out technicians that inspect elevators and certify them as permissible or in need of maintenance and repair. The technicians record the state of elevators in handwritten reports. Not only does this take a long time, but the reports also have some significant quality issues, like undecipherable handwriting.

The company starts storing this data digitally. It identifies the relevant entities in the process – e.g. technicians, reports, elevators and invoices – in order to set up a relational database system and model this process with data. Technicians enter the data on tablets, which transmit the data directly to the relational database.

31 | What is a key attribute and why is it indispensable?

In a relational database, real-world processes and situations are broken down into their entities and processes. Information about these is stored in various tables. To fully model the real-world process, it is necessary to also depict how such entities are connected. In relational models, such logical connections are

Data Storage Technologies

modelled with *key attributes*. (These are also called *key variables*, but for simplicity we stick with the term *key attributes* throughout).

Remember that attributes are characteristics of the entity that we collect data about. In a table containing structured data, each column depicts one attribute. For example, the column "LAST_NAME" is the attribute indicating the last name of a given customer. *Key attributes* are a special type of attribute of an entity that play an indispensable role in relational models – firstly, because they enable you to identify one given instance in a table, and secondly, because they enable you to interrelate the various tables (hence entities) in a relational model. Typically, key attributes are some sort of ID that is artificially created.

Table 31.1 What is a key attribute and why does it matter?

What is a key attribute?

The attributes (also called variables or features) of a table are the characteristics of an entity or process that we collect data about. For example, a table containing data about the entity "PRODUCT" would probably contain such attributes as type of product, price, size, weight etc. In the table, each column is equivalent to one attribute.

Key attributes (also called key variables or simply keys) are a special type of attribute in a table. Typically, keys will be some sort of artificially created ID, e.g. a product ID or transaction ID.

There are two types of key attributes that fulfil indispensable functions in the relational model:

- *Primary keys* uniquely identify each row in a table. For example, every customer in the Customer table is uniquely identified in the column (attribute) "CUSTOMER_ID".
- *Foreign keys* are attributes in a table that act as a link to another table, and so they enable tables to be interrelated in a database.

Key attributes thus enable the database to model the relationships that entities have in the real world.

Why does it matter?

Attributes lie at the heart of any sort of database because they describe the characteristics of a certain entity or process.

Key attributes are crucial for the functioning of a relational database. Without keys we would not be able to relate the various tables of a relational database. (Just imagine not being able to know which product comes from which producers or which payment was received from which customer.) The more tables can be interrelated, the more pieces of the real world can be put together to give a picture as a whole, which opens up a range of use cases (see Case Study 14).

So how do key attributes work? First, each table in a relational model has at least one key attribute by means of which every row in the table can be uniquely identified. This key attribute is called the *primary key* and it is typically an artificially created ID, e.g. customer ID, order ID, social security number, etc. One key attribute that is used a lot on the World Wide Web is your email address. The important thing about the key attribute is that it is unique to every row in the table and no two rows in a table should have the same ID. Only then can the key attribute fulfil its purpose of uniquely identifying each row in the table.

If two entities have some sort of connection in the real world that is supposed to be depicted in the data as well, then another type of key attribute is necessary: the foreign key.

Let's look at the example of customers and orders from 📘 30. Both the Customer and Order tables have a primary key attribute: the customer ID and the order ID. However, if we stored the two tables with only their primary key attributes and their attributes, we would not be able to relate these two entities, even though they have the connection "customer places orders" in real life – because how would we know which order belongs to which customer and vice versa?

To model this aspect of the real world it is necessary to include the information "which order was placed by which customer". We can do that by including the column "CUSTOMER_ID" in the Order table and thereby collecting the corresponding customer ID for every given order. Note that customer ID, which is the primary key in the Customer table, is also in the Order table. However, in that table it does not serve as a unique identifier for a given order, because that role is fulfilled by the order ID attribute. Instead, its only function is to create the link between orders and customers. Attributes that fulfil this function in a given table and at the same time are the primary key in another table are called *foreign key attributes*.

With these primary keys and the foreign key, every order can be related to its customer so that the two tables can be connected. We can thus create one big table that contains the combined information on which customer made which order. Combining information from two or more tables is called *join* in a relational database.

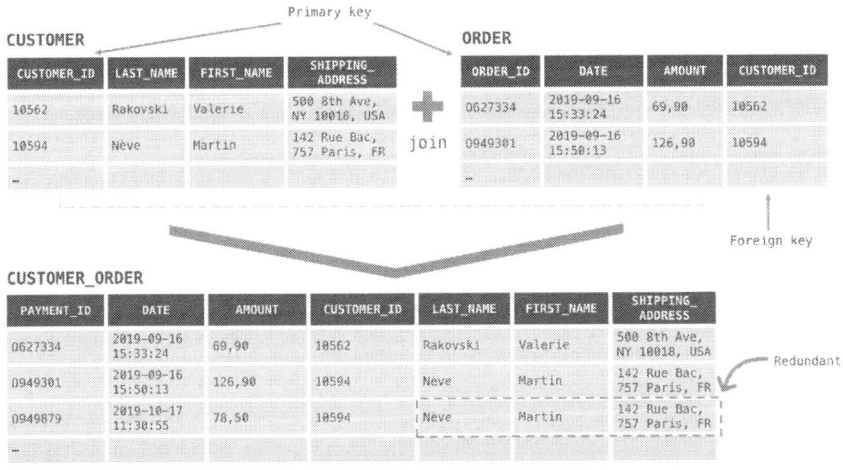

Figure 31.1 An example of a join operation

Why not store data directly in one big table like in the flat model (📄 28) and instead split it up into several smaller tables that have to be joined again? Look at rows two and three in Figure 31-1. Since there are two different orders placed by the same customer, a lot of the fields in the table are redundant. The last name, first name and shipping address could be inferred by just knowing the customer ID and looking up the data in the other order made by the customer.

This redundancy in data means a loss of storage efficiency. By splitting data up into several interconnected tables, relational databases gain storage and perform better – plus they are easier to navigate and more structured. But because of the join functionality, relational databases don't have to compromise, giving a comprehensive, integrated picture when needed. This, however, requires there to be key attributes.

Case study 14

The power of key attributes in creating a comprehensive picture

The more tables can be related to each other, the bigger and more comprehensive the picture that a database paints of the real world is. One use case where this is extremely valuable is in customer understanding. For a lot of companies, the goal is to have a 360-degree customer view.

Just imagine you are a global car manufacturer. There are plenty of customer touchpoints, like customers coming into your shops, using your car, searching for your products online, using your app and following you on social media. Imagine you have one centralized customer ID that the customer uses across all these platforms. That way you know when, where and how the customer is engaging with you. This is incredibly powerful information that can ultimately be used not only to understand your customers but also to target them better.

Some companies have shown how formidable the power of key attributes can be in creating a 360-degree customer view. The Chinese company Tencent has been following a smart strategy by essentially offering a one-stop app: WeChat. WeChat enables users to make payments, book taxis, chat and engage on a social media platform. You don't have to leave the app, because almost everything in China (and increasingly beyond the borders) works with WeChat. By collecting data on all sorts of activities, WeChat is able to paint a close-to-360-degree picture of its almost one billion users. It knows where users have been, what they ate, whom they like, what they think, etc. This is incredibly valuable information that can be used in countless use cases.

Another example is the tech giants of Silicon Valley. Through the countless platforms and apps that use Google or Facebook accounts to sign up and verify users, these companies are able to relate a lot of activity on different apps to one specific user. Just think about the picture you can paint about a person by knowing what apps and services they have signed up to – all thanks to the fact that you have one Google or Facebook user ID that you use across multiple platforms.

In fact, this Silicon Valley dominance has grown so strong that as a reaction a conglomerate of German companies, including Allianz, Daimler and Deutsche Bank, are currently cooperating to create an opposite European pole.[liv]

Thus, the important role of key attributes on the level of database implementation extends to higher levels, to the point where key attributes are the foundation of entire business models.

32 | How is data accessed and manipulated in a relational database system (SQL)?

In order to access, manipulate and store data in Excel, a user has to know how to use Excel. In order to do the same things in a database, a user has to know how to use the database management system that is used to access the database. This also holds true for relational databases that are accessed through *relational database management systems* (RDBMSs). There are countless providers of RDBMSs, some of which are open source while others are proprietary. Some examples are Oracle, Microsoft SQL server and MySQL.

Fortunately, while each RDBMS differs somewhat depending on the provider, there is no need to learn the workings of all providers in order to communicate with relational database systems. The reason is that regardless of the provider or brand of the RDBMS, virtually all RDBMSs speak the same language: *structured query language (SQL)*. SQL is therefore a basic and standard requirement for everyone who deals in one form or another with structured data and relational databases. This is one of the reasons why SQL is such a widely used programming language required in many job profiles (see Figure 32-1). While each provider might have some nuances in its implementation of SQL and might have some extra commands, SQL is understood by virtually every RDBMS. In that sense, SQL is somewhat like English: it is spoken in every English-speaking country, but different regions might have slightly different dialectic idiosyncrasies.

SQL is a computer language that was specifically designed to manipulate and manage data held in relational database systems. Since one of its purposes was to open the world of data storage to an audience beyond trained computer scientists, it is a rather simple language that almost reads like normal English. It was designed to reflect the logic of the relational database model (📑 30). Because most of the database systems in use have been and still are relational database systems, and because all of these relational database systems work with SQL, it is used extremely widely across the globe. This makes it an essential language to learn when working with data.

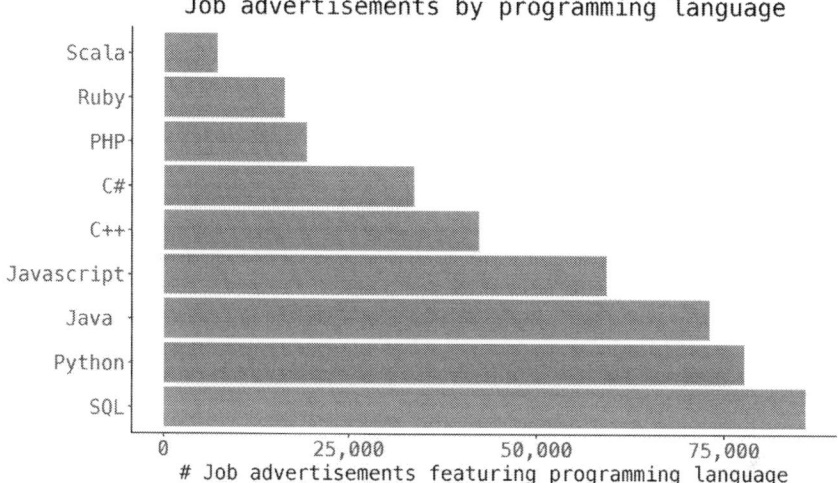

Figure 32.1 Popularity of programming languages measured in number of job advertisements in the US market featuring SQL in their job description[21][iv]

Table 32.1 What is SQL and why does it matter?

What is SQL?
Structured query language (SQL) is a computer language used to manage data held in relational database systems, i.e. to communicate with relational databases.

Why does it matter?
SQL is a universal language for all relational database systems. That means that if you speak SQL, you can essentially communicate with every relational database system there is – regardless of the provider or brand of the database system.

By using SQL to communicate with a relational database system, it is possible to manipulate data in the database (insert, update or delete entries), control access to certain tables, define and design tables in the database and, most importantly, query the database.

A database *query* is a request for information from a database – to put it simply, it asks the database a question. A simple query would be to view some data. An example of a query expressed in English could be "show me all customers of Your Model Car in Ireland". In order to retrieve this kind of

---

21. Data retrieved 2020-02-29 from the job portal www.indeed.com by looking for programming languages as key word (e.g. "SQL") in the search engine and counting the number of total results for the entire US market. This list disregards the programming languages R and C, because searches for these keywords also yielded undesired results.

information, such a query would need to be translated into the language that a relational database system speaks, i.e. SQL.

One of the most important and powerful features of relational database systems and SQL is that they support rather complex queries. Let's look at an example of what such a query would look like when expressed in SQL. Suppose we have our Customer table and we are interested in getting a list of all customers located in Ireland. SQL queries are built following a very specific structure in which you have to specify:

- How you want to manipulate data (e.g. view, delete, insert, change, etc.)
- What data you want to manipulate (which columns in which tables)
- Extra requests (e.g. filtering by viewing only observations that fulfil a certain criteria)

If we typed in the following query, we would create a view of the Customer table in which all displayed customers are based in Ireland.

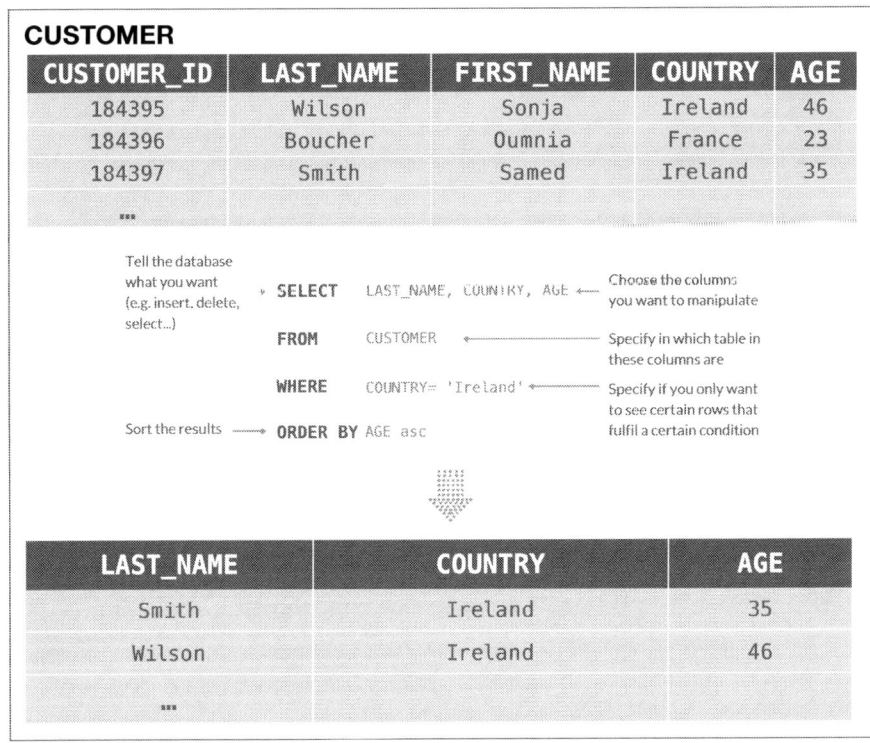

Figure 32.2 Example of an SQL query which selects only certain columns and rows from the Customer table, i.e. customers located in Ireland sorted by their age

Even if you have not used SQL to interact with a relational database system, you have certainly communicated with several ones before. A lot of websites store some of their data in relational databases in their backend. For example, we might store product information data at Your Model Car in a relational database system and enable visitors to our website to access this data. Of course, we will not require visitors to enter SQL commands themselves, but instead we will provide them with some sort of user-friendly online mask that allows them to search for products and filters for them. For example, we might offer filters for the product category and price range. The queries that are made by a website visitor in an online mask are then translated into SQL code. This code is passed on to the RDBMS working in the backend, which then gives out its results. Thus, the end-users of a relational database system can be other machines or software systems and humans directly.

Despite its simplicity, SQL enables you to create complex queries that can be used for data analysis. This query functionality is one of the key assets of relational database systems.

Case study 15

Digitizing the certification process with a relational database, Part II (Case Study 13 continued)

Weeks after the relational database system has been set up, the product inspection company has gathered enough data to start creating value from it.

The company creates various reports to answer analytical questions, such as how many elevators were inspected in a period of time and what the most common reasons for a rejection of certification were. One of the tables in the database, Inspection, contains data on which elevator was inspected by which technician with which result. The following SQL statement reports how many inspections led to certifications and how many did not fulfil the certification criteria.

INSPECTION

INSPECT_ID	ELEVAT_ID	TECHN_ID	DATE	RESULT	...
73632	CH_847242	ts-42321	2019-09-29	cert	
75939	FR_645253	ts-65261	2019-09-29	reject	
75786	DE_736351	ts-66563	2019-09-30	other	
...					

Request the number of rows that fulfil the following criteria → `SELECT count(RESULT)`

`FROM INSPECTION` ← Data is is the Inspection table

Only count the inspections that led to a certification → `WHERE RESULT = 'cert'`

Figure 32.3 Another example of an SQL query

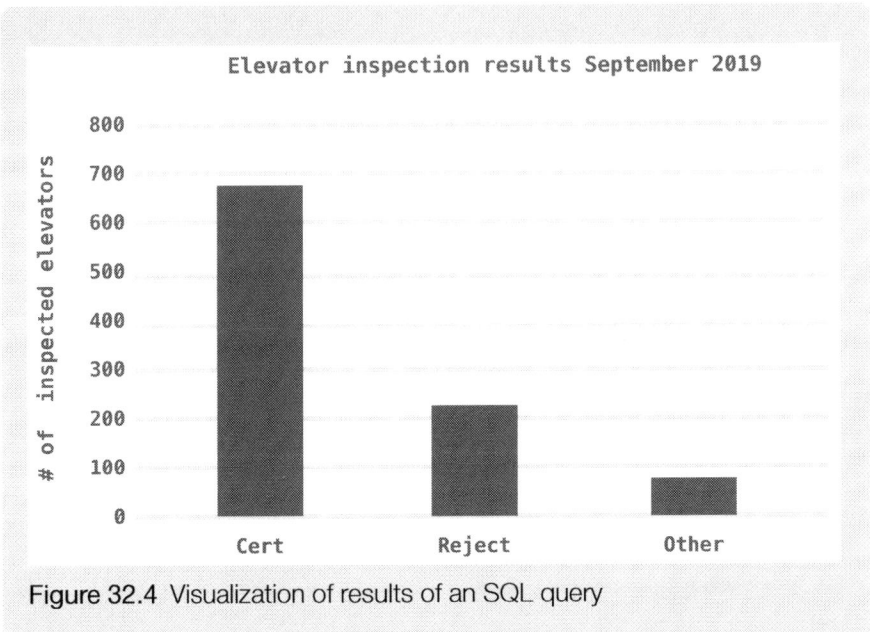

Figure 32.4 Visualization of results of an SQL query

33 | What are the strengths of relational database systems?

Relational database systems have been the go-to solution for storing structured data for decades. This should not come as a surprise, given that they have some extremely powerful features. The following sections explore the most important strengths of relational database systems. There are other strengths, but these important ones should give you a sense of why relational database systems have been used across industries worldwide.

Versatility of the relational model

One of the core strengths of relational database systems is the data model that they are based on. The relational model is easy to understand and intuitive, yet rigorously defined. Most importantly, it is extremely versatile and does a marvellous job of modelling the vast majority of real-life situations and processes across industries. Breaking down real-life processes into different entities and modelling them with interconnected tables works well in a lot of cases. And the relational database system does this in a highly efficient way when it comes to storage space.

Complex queries

Another core strength of relational database systems is that they allow you to do complex queries. Even though in large relational databases data is spread across tens or hundreds of tables (which makes storage very efficient), information from all of these tables can be joined in complex queries to give a comprehensive picture of the data and answer analytical questions.

With Your Model Car, for example, it would be no problem to answer questions like "How many products of a certain product line did we sell to female customers in the United States under the age of 35 between the 15th and 24th of December 2019?" and "How many sales have we had in Australia in the past month as compared to one year ago?". Such answers require the integration and manipulation of data from a number of tables in a relational database. Even such complex queries can easily be expressed in SQL and thus retrieved from relational database systems.

Reliability

Relational databases have certain properties that make them extremely reliable. This is essential in a lot of situations, such as banking transactions and other crucial business processes, where minor errors in writing, reading or storing data can have disastrous consequences. Just imagine you want to make a money transfer from your bank account and the database is showing you a wrong balance of your account. The properties that make relational databases so reliable relate to how transactions of data are handled, e.g. how data entries and retrievals in the database happen. We use the acronym *ACID* for these properties: atomicity, consistency, isolation and durability.

We provide an example that highlights the advantages and power of such ACID properties in 📑37, where we compare relational and non-relational databases.

Standardized language

Even though there are countless providers of RDBMSs, virtually all of them are based on SQL. This unified standard has contributed to the popularity of relational database systems. SQL was invented way before personal computers became popular. Before that, dealing with data meant learning complex programming languages. SQL was introduced as a computer language that is extremely easy to understand and learn (since it almost reads like normal English language), and thus it opened up dealing with data to people who were not trained computer scientists.

There are other strengths that relational database systems have, but these few important ones should give you a sense why relational database systems have been used across industries worldwide.

34 | What are the limitations of relational database systems and how were they revealed with the dawn of big data?

For decades, relational databases solved most of the data storage needs of companies. Store and process payment transactions? Use a relational database. Store customer data? Use a relational database. There was no question of how to store data. The simplicity, efficiency and versatility of the relational data model along with the query functionality that RDBMSs offer made the relational database system the foundation of data storage across the globe.

Enter big data, and we have a problem. Why? While relational databases can be applied for a lot of use cases, they are not ideal for *every* situation. And the advent of big data revealed the shortcomings outlined in the following sections.

Hard to scale

The first of the 3 Vs of big data is the volume of data. Traditionally, relational databases ran on single servers. As a consequence, more data meant needing to buy a bigger and more powerful server. This approach worked for a while, because the capacity of servers grew at an enormous rate. But at some point, data simply outgrew the computational power of single servers, so companies started hitting the limits of data volumes they could store. And so too did relational databases, since they were limited to the capacity of the server they ran on.

Many relational database system providers have sought solutions to alleviate this problem. And in fact, it has partly been solved by the use of massive parallel processing (MPP) for relational database systems. Through MPP, a relational database system can be distributed to several computers to harness their combined power in certain situations. However, even though MPP overcomes the scalability limitations to some extent, other weaknesses exist that, combined with this scalability issue, make relational database systems unsuitable for certain situations.

Structured data only

Variety is another of the 3 Vs of big data. Relational databases model the real world in a tabular form and are therefore a great fit for structured data. But especially in the wake of big data, more and more unstructured data is being created. Storing unstructured data, like pictures, videos and emails, is a challenge for relational databases.[22] They are simply not designed to store such unstructured data. It turns out there are better ways to deal with this kind of data (Chapter 3_3).

Limits of the relational model

While the relational database model is extremely powerful and versatile, it is not the best way to describe *every* real-world process. For example, the relational model falls short with social networks and situations where instances of one type of entity can have a lot of interconnections with other instances of the same entity. Think of a social network. At its heart there is only one basic type of entity, namely the users, and there are a lot of interconnections between users (they are friends, they are family, they "like" and react to each other, etc.). Modelling this with a relational data model is extremely cumbersome and inefficient. To solve this problem, another type of database was developed, called a graph database.

---

22. We are not saying it is impossible, because with any technology you can find ways to solve a given problem. Like you could certainly store your pictures and emails in Excel, but would that make sense? Probably not, because Excel was not designed for it.

Data Storage Technologies

Need to define a schema before data can be stored

Lastly, and probably most importantly, before you can store data in a relational database system you have to define the schema, i.e. the structure of the data and the tables. With Excel you can just open a file and type in any kind of data (numbers, currencies, text etc.) in any form (two-digit numbers, text of unlimited length, date in any format etc.) in any cell, but you have to do more work in relational databases.

Before you can store any data in a relational database, you have to create a table and meticulously specify the exact structure of that table. That means you have to indicate a name, the number and names of the columns you want to store, the format of the columns (number, text, date etc.), how long each entry in a cell is allowed to be and so on. In order to rigorously define the structure in this way you have to know what questions you want to ask the data before you store it in the database. If at the point of setting up the database you don't know what questions you want to ask the database later, this can make things very complicated.

If you want to store data that does not fit with this exact structure, it will not be possible to store it without changing the structure. Data structures may change over time because, for example, the underlying real-world process changes or evolves. Suppose that in Your Model Car we want to offer a new warranty service for the products that we ship to customers. In order to provide this service, we have to adjust and extend the data that we collect. We need to record the production and shipping date, and we need to store the data provided by the customer in the case of a warranty claim (which product is broken, why it is broken etc.). These altered data storage requirements that arise from an altered real-world process force us to update the structure of our database. Doing this every now and then for minor changes is feasible. However, given that data storage requirements evolve and change constantly because real-world processes change constantly, accommodating such changes can be quite cumbersome.

The need for change

These are exactly the challenges that a lot of companies, especially the ones that increasingly relied on data as one of their core assets, were facing by the turn of the century. Just put yourself in the shoes of Google. Larry Page and Sergey Brin, still graduate students at Stanford University at that time, came up with a novel way to design a search engine for the growing World Wide Web. The 24 million indexed web pages that their search engine contained in their initial setup amounted to some 14 GB of data.[lvi] This was still manageable with a lean setup of (mostly donated and sponsored) computers and existing data storage technologies including relational database systems.

However, the growth of the internet entailed data storage requirements that these traditional technologies – both on a soft- and hardware level – were simply not able to fulfil. By 2016 the number of individual web pages that the index of Google spanned stood at some 130 trillion (that is 130,000,000,000,000).[lvii] The technologies including relational database systems of the "old world" – that is, the world before the dawn of big data – were being put in their place and revealed to be limited.

It was time for some fundamental innovations to deal with the increasing and ever-changing flood of data.

> **Case study 16**
>
> **Digitizing the certification process with a relational database, Part III (Case Study 15 continued)**
>
> The product inspection and certification company wants to extend its digitization to the certification process for all the products it inspects (engines, production machines, tools, cars, etc.).
>
> However, some of these products come with further data requirements. For some of the products, inspections must include images, audio-test reports, videos etc. Furthermore, the business units are still uncertain what kind of questions they expect to answer with the data gathered, so it is not yet clear what data should be collected in what form.
>
> The relational database system of the company is not designed for this increased volume and the unstructured/semi-structured format of the data. Furthermore, the uncertainty with regard to the exact data storage requirements make the relational database system a bad choice for this use case. Since the schema of the database will often have to be adapted in line with new data storage requirements, this will lead to a lot of work.

3_3 Distributed file systems and non-relational (NoSQL) databases

35 | What are computer clusters and how did the idea of "scaling out" form the basis for storing and processing big data?

While relational databases satisfied a lot of data storage needs for decades, things changed with the dawn of big data. Suddenly, data storage requirements exceeded what traditional technologies were able to satisfy. A novel way to store and process data was needed.

Data volumes and with them storage requirements had been growing since the first bit of information was stored in digital format. But so were the capacities of data storage and processing technologies, so that things never "got out of control". If there was more data to be stored or some data to be processed faster, most of the time it was possible to just buy a bigger and more powerful computer that was able to deal with it. This concept of simply buying a "better" computer is called *scaling up* or *vertical scaling*.

Data Storage Technologies

By the turn of the century, a lot of companies found themselves unable to source technologies that would satisfy their data storage and processing requirements, especially the tech companies such as Google, Yahoo and later also Facebook. Their needs were just so big that simply buying a bigger computer, i.e. scaling up, didn't work anymore.

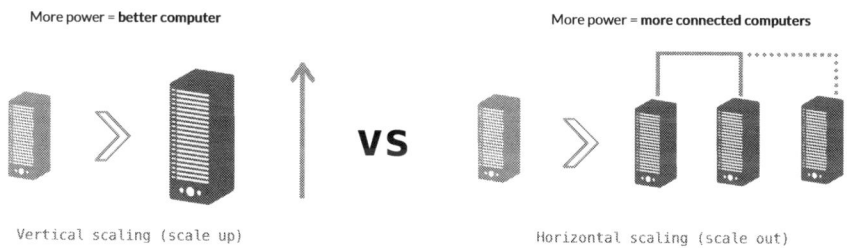

Figure 35.1 Horizontal versus vertical scaling

This mismatch gave rise to the evolution and commercialization of an idea that would overcome the limits of single computer servers: the use of *computer clusters*.

Table 35.1 What is a computer cluster and horizontal scaling and why do they matter?

What is a computer cluster and what is horizontal scaling (scaling out)?
A *computer cluster* is a network of connected computers (nodes). While resources and tasks are shared within the network of computers, the user is provided with just a single point of access.
The great thing about a computer cluster is that it enables *horizontal scaling (scaling out)*. This refers to increasing the computational power of a cluster by adding more nodes to it. This is in contrast to scaling up, where the computational power is increased by buying a more powerful computer.
Why does it matter?
Computer clusters make use of the principle of scaling out (horizontal scaling). This bypasses computational power limits that exist with single-node computers, because the size of a computer cluster can be increased deliberately just by adding additional nodes.
Due to their scalability, computer clusters have enabled the storage, processing and analysis of big data. If it weren't for computer clusters, our computational power would largely be bound to what single-node servers could provide – which is a joke when you consider the requirements created by the masses of data out there.

The idea of computer clusters is simple. Instead of processing data and running applications on just one computer, we use lots of them and connect them, so that they share the workload and we harness their combined capacities. With such a network of computers, we can easily overcome the limits of what one computer can perform. Instead of *scaling up*, we just *scale out* (scale horizontally). That is, if the capacity of our computer cluster is not sufficient, we just add another computer (also called a *node*) to the network and thereby increase the computing and storage power of the computer cluster. The beautiful thing is that there are ways to set up such computer clusters so that a user is presented with only a single point of access. That means that as a user you don't have to communicate with and configure an entire network of computers; you just have one single point of access to a "supercomputer" consisting of several nodes.

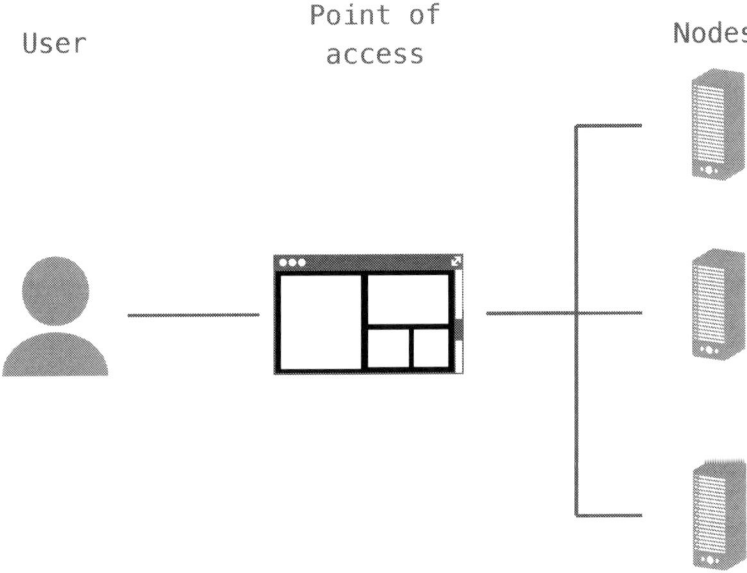

Figure 35.2 A computer cluster

Today, such computer clusters are ubiquitous and used in all big-data use cases. In fact, you probably use computer clusters on a daily basis because a lot of the cloud services are run on such computer clusters. You might have seen pictures of data centres that consists of thousands of computers stacked on top of each other and organized in racks. Such data centres are essentially big computer clusters consisting of thousands of interconnected commodity computers, i.e. off-the-shelf, relatively inexpensive computers.

Why didn't we use computer clusters before now?

The idea of computer clusters seems so simple that you may wonder why they didn't come about before, at least not in commercial and widespread use. There are three reasons for that:

- The prices of normal commodity computers had to fall to a certain level before adding more such computers to a cluster would be economically viable. The increase in computing capacity and simultaneous fall in prices of data storage was a gradual evolution that happened over several

Data Storage Technologies

decades. By the turn of the century, prices for commodity hardware were low enough to make it economically viable to connect such commodity hardware in computer clusters.

- To operate a computer cluster, you need the necessary bandwidth to transport the information between the nodes. This meant that network speed had to be at a certain level for the cluster to be viable. This too was an evolution that took some years.
- Distributing tasks and sharing resources among several nodes requires a lot of coordination. Running clusters requires sophisticated software that enables the coordination of the respective nodes. It turns out that such software is enormously complex, and it wasn't until the 2000s that it had matured enough to be used commercially.

36 | What are distributed file systems and how do we store data with them?

Computers need operating systems (OSs) to function. Operating systems are the fundamental level of software that support a computer's basic functions and makes it work and workable in the first place. Everyone knows the most famous operating systems for personal computers, such as Microsoft Windows, MAC OS and Linux.

One of the most fundamental functionalities that comes with an operating system is the file system. For example, everyone knows the Windows file system, which provides Microsoft users with a folder hierarchy in which they can store data in any form, such as documents, music and images.

Just like normal computers, computer clusters need software that takes care of their fundamental tasks, such as the coordination between the nodes in the cluster. One such software framework for operating a computer cluster is Apache Hadoop (📄 40).

Frameworks for operating computer clusters must provide for a *distributed file system*. Just like with normal computers, users need a way to store data in computer clusters. Implementing a file system is easy on a single computer compared to implementing one on a distributed system. The reason is that if you want to store files and documents across computers, they have to be split up and stored in parallel on several nodes – all seamlessly for the user. This is an extremely difficult thing to do (just think of how hard it is to keep track of what you have packed in small boxes when you move house).

Some examples of distributed file systems are the Google File System (GFS) and the Hadoop Distributed File System (HDFS).

How is data stored and processed on a computer cluster with a distributed file system?

This is an extremely complex process, but to give you a basic understanding let's look at an example. Imagine that the product portfolio of Your Model Car has expanded so immensely that storing the data in a relational database

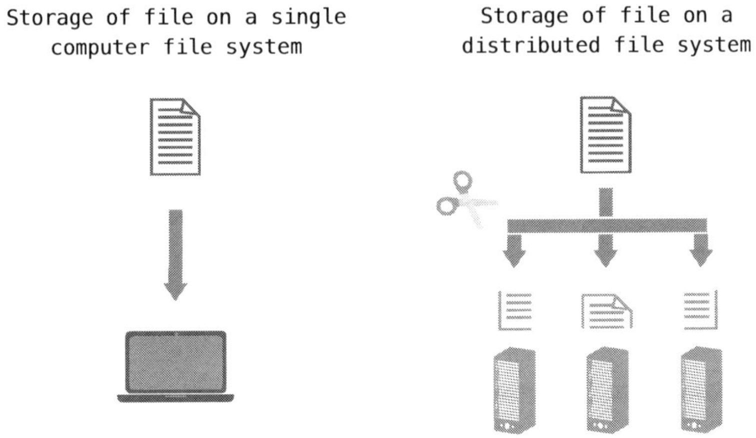

Storage of file on a single computer file system

Storage of file on a distributed file system

Figure 36.1 Schematic view of how a file is stored on a distributed file system

system on a single server has become unviable. Instead, the table containing the product data is stored on a computer cluster.

As soon as we give this data to the computer cluster, the framework that administers the cluster – for example, Hadoop –takes care of slicing the data up into chunks and storing these chunks on the several nodes of the cluster. You can imagine storing the first 1,000 lines on Node 1, the second 1,000 rows on Node 2 and so forth.[23]

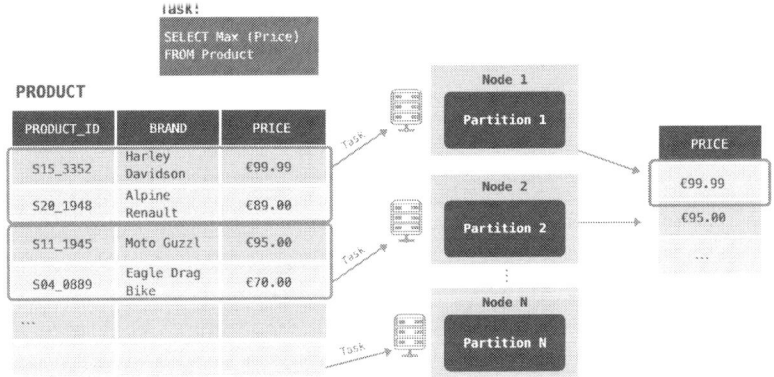

Figure 36.2 Schematic overview of how data is processed on a computer cluster

This is how data is stored on the distributed file system – but how is it processed? Let's say we want to find the most expensive product in our

---

23. In reality a table, just like any other file, would be split up on a bit level rather than along its rows or columns, but we thought envisioning a table being split up into rows was more intuitive. The chunk size of the parts that Hadoop creates can be adjusted but is typically 128 MB. Also, in reality every chunk will be replicated on several nodes to back up the data in case one node fails.

Data Storage Technologies

portfolio. This would require looking through all the chunks of the split-up table.

We could simply reassemble the chunks into one big table and look for the most expensive product there. However, remember that the data is so big that it can't be held in one single computer, so there is simply no space to do that. The genius idea of computer clusters and how they process data is that we invert the flow. Instead of bringing the data to one centralized place to perform a certain job on it, we *bring the job to the data* on every single node. That is, instead of combining the data to calculate the most expensive product, we send the task "find the most expensive product in your part of the table" to every node. Each node then performs the task and the *results* are combined to yield the most expensive product in the entire table.

In reality, the way in which a computer cluster stores and processes data on a distributed file system is much more complex, but conceptually this is more or less how it works. Data is split between the various nodes of a computer cluster for storage and is worked on in parallel for data processing. Through this parallelism, the computational load is distributed, and the power of *all nodes* is harnessed.

The great advantage of distributed file systems is that since they are implemented on computer clusters, there are virtually no limits to scalability. Need to store terabytes or even petabytes of data that would fit on no single-server system? Just set up a computer cluster and store it there. Is the cluster running out of capacity? Just scale out and add a couple more nodes to the cluster.

> **Case study 17**
>
> **Telemetric automotive data**
>
> A car manufacturer equips its newest series of cars with plenty of sensors. Some of these sensors produce structured data, e.g. temperature and pressure measurements. However, some sensors also produce unstructured data that is stored in proprietary file formats, e.g. acoustic sensors that measure the sounds of the car engine and the tyres. Since this data is not suitable for storage in a relational database system due to its size and structure, it is loaded into a horizontally scalable distributed file system.

37 | What are non-relational (NoSQL) databases and what does the CAP theorem have to do with them?

Along with the rise of computer clusters, another trend over the past two decades or so in the world of (big) data has been the *NoSQL database* (also called *non-relational database*).

Any database that is not based on the relational data model is referred to as a NoSQL database. NoSQL refers to "non-SQL" – or more recently also to "not only SQL", since a lot of the NoSQL databases today support SQL language. Such databases have been around since the 1960s. However, the term "NoSQL database" only really caught on during the 2000s with the rise of big data, as a lot of companies had to find alternative databases in order to handle their specific data storage requirements that were not being met by their relational database system anymore. The fact that all databases that are not relational databases are subsumed under one umbrella highlights the importance of the relational database, while making the term "NoSQL database" pretty unspecific.

Table 37.1 What is a NoSQL database and why does it matter?

What is a NoSQL database?

All NoSQL (meaning "non-SQL" or "not only SQL") databases are those that are implemented with a database model other than the relational one.

There are hundreds of different NoSQL databases and they may be grouped into a handful of different types. What they have in common is that they typically trade off consistency, one of the most important features of relational databases, for higher performance in one way or another.

They are often referred to as "not only SQL" databases to emphasize that a lot of them also support SQL-like languages.

Why does it matter?

NoSQL databases have been around for decades already, but they really only took off with the rise of big data, when a lot of tech companies were confronted with data storage and processing requirements that their traditional relational databases could not cope with.

NoSQL databases can be implemented on computer clusters and can therefore be scaled horizontally. That means there is virtually no limit to their capacity in terms of storage and processing. This scalability is comparatively cheap, so their price-to-performance ratio is one of their main selling points. Furthermore, they offer a great deal of flexibility with regard to their schema, which typically does not need to be as meticulously worked out as in relational databases.

Because of that, NoSQL databases are increasingly used in big data use cases.

The majority of NoSQL databases were invented due to situations where the relational database system fell short of data storage requirements. As a result, unlike relational databases, which are extremely versatile and thus widely employed in countless use cases, most NoSQL database systems are rather specialized and designed to serve in very specific data storage use cases. Consequently, there are several hundred different NoSQL database systems, each of which is unique and specially designed for a given data storage and processing requirement. It is difficult, therefore, to categorize the plethora of NoSQL databases, but in general they are grouped into four different types: key-value stores, document databases, graph databases and column-oriented databases.

Data Storage Technologies

Key-value stores

Key-value stores are an extremely simple form of database. The main idea is that every item (or observation) in the database gets a unique identifier (the key) and just one value associated with it. Unlike in relational databases, where data entries have to adhere to the pre-specified conditions (e.g. only numeric values are allowed in the "age" column in the Customer table), this value could take any form – i.e. it could be text, numbers, images, documents or a combination of these. With regard to what form a value can take, a key-value store is thus much more flexible.

EMPLOYEE

KEY	VALUE
10531	Name: Noah Jean DOB: 19-05-1963 Office: Works 50% in HQ and 50% off-site Degree: MA Economics Comments: Will take a gap year starting 01-01-2020
10534	Name: Dina Cantini DOB: 07-08-1985 Office: - Status: Currently on leave
...	

Figure 37.1 Example of a key-value store

Key-value stores are extremely performant; that is, in certain use cases they are very fast. Furthermore, they scale extremely well. However, unlike relational database systems, they lack the functionality of sophisticated queries that allow for analysis, since their operations are limited to the basic functions such as insert, get and delete a key-value pair. Examples of key-value stores are Amazon DynamoDB and Redis.

Document databases

Document databases are a subclass of key-value stores. The defining feature of document databases is that the value associated with a key is documents, typically XML or JSON documents. These files contain information organized in a tree-like hierarchical structure. They are considered semi-structured data: they have some inherent structure that is less "strict" than in a relational data model but still enables you to query them to look for and retrieve information.

Popular document databases are MongoDB, CouchDB and CosmosDB.

Graph databases

Graph databases implement a data model (i.e. a way to model the real world) based on graphs. In this context, "graph" is used in the sense of graph theory, a subfield of mathematics, and has nothing to do with images or drawings. Graphs are structures that model the pairwise relationship between two entities.

The basic components of graphs are nodes (instances of entities), edge (the relationship that exists between them) and properties (information about nodes). With these components, graph models do a great job of modelling situations in which there are a lot of interrelations between instances of the same entity.

The best example of where graph databases are the go-to solution is social networks. Graph databases are used to model the relationships between members of the social network because there is essentially only one entity, "user", but the single users have a lot of interrelations between them (likes, friends, followers, etc.)

Column-oriented databases

In traditional relational databases, data is stored row-wise. That means to retrieve data the database will read row-by-row. Column-oriented databases aren't that different from relational database systems. However, rather than row-wise, data is read column-wise in column-oriented databases. In certain situations, this can significantly increase the performance of the database for queries. The reason is that in certain queries many rows need to be scanned only to be discarded afterwards, which lowers performance. In such situations, storing and scanning a table column-wise can increase the speed at which queries are executed.

What is the CAP theorem?

Even though all the NoSQL databases have their own idiosyncrasies, the vast majority of them address two major shortcomings of relational databases: their limitations in (affordable) scaling and performance. Most of the NoSQL databases can be implemented on computer clusters and so they can be scaled horizontally. That means that, unlike with relational database systems, there are virtually no limits to their scale and capacity.

Relational databases have certain properties that are extremely important in a lot of situations and relate to how transactions of data are handled. These properties are atomicity, consistency, isolation and durability (ACID). To explain the importance of these properties in detail would go beyond the scope of this book. However, we will examine consistency here, because it is extremely important and helps us to understand the sacrifices that a lot of NoSQL databases make for increased performance.

Relational databases are said to have *strong consistency*, whereas NoSQL databases usually only have *eventual consistency*. Consistency in this case refers to the fact that if two users request information from a database system at the same point in time, they get the exact same answer. This is the case for relational database systems with ACID properties at any given point in time (strong consistency).

However, things look different for a lot of NoSQL databases when they are implemented on computer clusters. There, depending on which node in the cluster you request information from, you might get different answers. The reason is that storing information across an entire cluster with many nodes, rather than just one single computer, is challenging and can lead to situations where the nodes are unable or too slow to keep each other updated at any given point in time.

This is similar to working in a team. If you just have one chef cooking a meal in the kitchen and he is asked by several people when the food will be ready, these people will get the same answer. However, if there is an entire team cooking in the kitchen and you ask when the food will be ready, you might get different answers because people won't have an overview of the state and progress of their colleagues' work. You would get inconsistent information – unless, of course, the person you ask confers with the rest of the team to give you a cross-checked answer, but this takes time.

Cross-checking is essentially what a lot of NoSQL databases do. But since it takes time, they are not consistent at every given point in time. So the nodes across which the NoSQL databases is distributed need some time to update each other in order to converge into one consistent state (eventual consistency).

Therefore, the power that comes with being able to scale out and use a computer cluster often comes at the cost of sacrificing some desirable property that relational database systems have – above all, strong consistency. The fact that there is no free lunch is theorized with the CAP theorem. CAP stands for consistency, availability and partition tolerance.

The CAP theorem states that a database system distributed across several nodes can only have two of these three features:

- *Consistency* refers to the fact that all nodes of the database have the exact same data, so that it does not matter which node we read data from, we will get the same answer.
- *Availability* refers to the fact that no matter when we request information from the database, we will always get the data.
- *Partition tolerance* refers to the database system continuing to operate in the case of network failures (if the connection between two nodes is cut or extremely slow).

The Ultimate Data and AI Guide

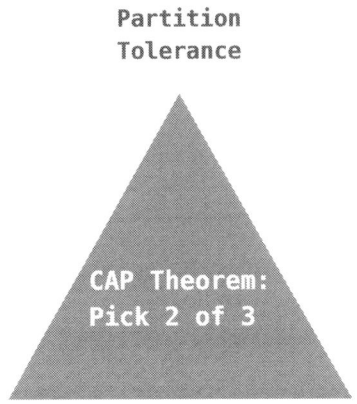

Figure 37.2 Visualization of the CAP theorem

While in relational databases the emphasis is on consistency, NoSQL databases typically compromise their consistency for increased availability and partition tolerance.

To see the CAP theorem at work, let's look at a Your Model Car example (see Figure 37-3). We hold the data on the remaining stock of our products in a non-relational database system distributed across a multi-node computer cluster. Two customers, John and Francois, want to order a product, but only one item is left in stock. John communicates with Node 1 of the distributed database and Francois communicates with Node 2. John orders a couple of milliseconds before Francois. However, it takes a couple of moments until the information that the stock has decreased from one to zero is updated from Node 1 to Node 2. This is equivalent to a network failure (because it takes so much time to update). If we want to keep the database system operating, we essentially have two options: compromise the consistency of the system or its availability.

If we want to keep the database available to the users, then we have to put up with inconsistency. That means that the time window required to update the nodes in the system creates an inconsistency in the database. In our example, there is no item left in stock, but Francois is shown that he can still order the product. So if Francois orders exactly in that time window, we will run into problems, because he's ordering a product that is not in stock anymore.

If we do not want to put up with inconsistencies in the database, we have to accept unavailability. That means that Francois receives an error message when he tries to buy the product. If he tries again a few moments later after the nodes have had time to update each other, he will find that the product he wanted to order is now out of stock.

Whether we prioritize availability or consistency depends on the underlying use case. Both can cause severe problems. In many cases, strong consistency is preferred and considered the more important feature. Just think of things like money transactions where strong consistency is absolutely crucial. This is why relational database systems are and will continue to be used in a lot of cases.

Data Storage Technologies

In contrast, in cases that are less critical, eventual consistency is sufficient and is a sacrifice that we are willing to make for increased performance of the database system. One such example is the transmission and storage of chats, e.g. on WhatsApp or Facebook. We don't really care if in a group chat *all* users see the exact same chat history at the same time or if the delivery of a message to one person takes a few milliseconds longer than to another, leading to temporary inconsistencies. In return for eventual consistency, companies such as Facebook and Tencent are able to process the billions of messages sent by their users each minute, which would be unimaginable with a relational database system.

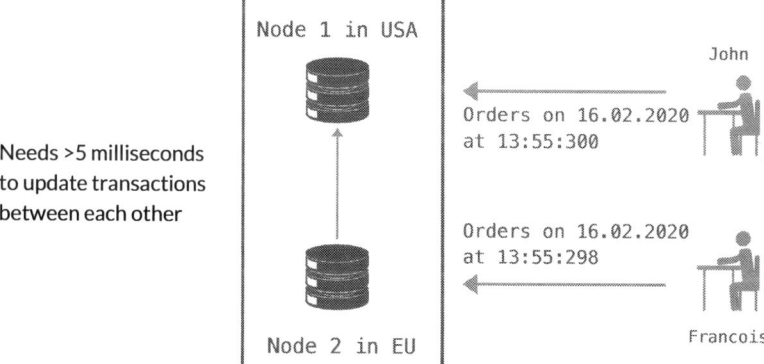

Figure 37.3 The CAP theorem in practice

Apart from the limits to performance and scale, certain NoSQL databases also address and overcome other limitations of relational databases, such as where the relational model is not the optimal way to model the real world. An example of this is situations where a lot of interrelations between instances of the same entity exist. This is the case when modelling social networks of friends, for example, where essentially the only entities are persons or members of this network, but the core information is the relationships between them. Another example is creating a database to store all movies, their actors and the relationships between the actors. Cases like these could theoretically be modelled with the relational model, but it would be extremely difficult and cumbersome. A database based on a *graph data model*, which models the real world as a graph structure with nodes and edges, would do a much better job.

> **Case study 18**
>
> **Spotify uses Apache Cassandra (NoSQL database) to store user-profile data**
>
> By 2019, Spotify had more than 200 million users streaming their music content across the globe.[lviii] The storage technologies that support this massive data flood are interwoven in a complex data architecture consisting of numerous tools.

> One of these tools is Apache Cassandra, an open-source, distributed wide-column store. Spotify stores user-profile data as well as metadata about central entities such as playlists and artists in this non-relational database. Two of the primary reasons for choosing Apache Cassandra as the central technology in the data architecture of Spotify were its performance and its ability to scale horizontally.[lix]

38 | How do relational and non-relational databases compare and when is it best to use each one?

When NoSQL databases became a thing sometime during the 2000s, the hype around them was immense. They were praised as a new form of data storage that would make relational database systems obsolete – increased performance, no limits to scale and ability to handle unstructured data were just some of the promises that proponents of NoSQL databases emphasized.

Things have turned out very differently, however. Relational database systems are still here to stay. Today, they have barely lost any significance, and they not only coexist but are even complemented by NoSQL databases rather than being replaced by them. The reason is that there is no one-size-fits-all solution when it comes to data storage. Every situation in which data needs to be stored is unique.

At the end of the day, whether we are talking about relational databases, non-relational databases, file systems or any other type of data storage technology, all of them are simply tools to fulfil a certain need or requirement. So the choice of the right tool depends on what the underlying problem is. Just like a drill is the wrong tool to hammer a nail into a wall, some databases are inadequate for storing data with the goal of modelling a certain real-life situation.

Therefore, comparing relational and non-relational databases is a bit like comparing a hammer to a drill – they both exist as tools for different types of jobs, but they are used in different situations. Nevertheless, here are some areas in which the two types of database can be contrasted:

Table 38.1 Comparison of relational and non-relational databases

	Relational databases	Non-relational databases
Data	▸ Designed to handle structured data.	▸ Designed to handle data forms beyond structured data, i.e. semi-structured data (e.g. JSON files) and even unstructured data.
Scalability and performance	▸ Traditionally implemented on single servers and thus designed to scale vertically, which is more difficult. ▸ However, today there are various providers that offer relational databases harnessing massive parallel processing (MPP) by being implemented on computer clusters	▸ Designed to scale horizontally and be implemented on computer clusters, so they are extremely scalable at a rather low cost. ▸ In certain situations they perform better, e.g. reading and writing data faster.

Data Storage Technologies

	Relational databases	**Non-relational databases**
Versatility	- Extremely versatile and can be used in a lot of situations. - All relational database systems speak SQL.	- Usually designed for rather specific problems and use cases. - While a lot of NoSQL databases support SQL, each one tends to have its own way of working, so there is no commonly shared standard to work with.
Flexibility	- Before data can be stored, the schema of the database has to be meticulously and rigorously defined. - If data storage requirements change, the schema has to be adjusted accordingly, which can be cumbersome. For example, if we want to store additional data about our products, we need to redesign and adapt the data model and schema.	- The data models tend to be somewhat more flexible: their schema is not as rigid, so changes in data storage requirements can more easily be accommodated. For example, if we want to store additional data about our products and we are using a document store, we can just include the additional information in the relevant document (e.g. JSON file) without having to make changes to the overall schema of the database.
Queries and analytics	- Support complex and ample queries, which enables (simple) data analytics.	- Limited query possibilities.
Maturity	- Established, well-known and well-understood technology. - Easy to find experts and help.	- Newer technologies that continue to evolve, and since NoSQL databases are often rather specific and specialized, it might be hard to find experts for support.
Consistency	- Strong consistency.	- Often sacrifice strong consistency for eventual consistency in order to gain performance and scalability.

In what situation would you use which type of database? Unfortunately, there are no specific guidelines. Unless you are dealing with big data – i.e. immoderate data storage and processing requirements – you are probably doing just fine with a relational database. If Your Model Car is a niche online retailer with just a couple of thousand customers and orders not exceeding a couple of hundred products per day, then a relational database system will support most of the business processes just fine.

The situations in which relational databases fall short of data storage and processing requirements are typically the ones where their limits to scale and performance are exceeded. If Your Model Car serves millions of customers worldwide, with several thousand visitors viewing and ordering products through the website on a daily basis, then at least some business processes will have to be supported with solutions other than a relational database. Likewise, if an app or digital service is used by millions of users and needs to support storage, access and processing of data on a scale that simply cannot be handled by a single-node computer, then technologies of the "new world" such as NoSQL databases are needed.

Relational databases are also not an option when we are dealing with semi-structured or unstructured data. By definition these types of data require other storage technologies, since relational databases are designed to handle structured data only.

3_4 Popular data storage technologies

39 | What are the types of data storage technologies?

Working in the world of data, it can be really hard to keep up with the pace of innovation and new technologies entering the market. It seems that on a weekly basis some new technology to store or process data pops up claiming to be the holy grail of data storage. This has led to a plethora of technologies, brands and products that can be quite confusing to navigate, especially if you don't know how to classify them.

In the following sections we give you a brief overview of some popular data storage technologies. First, it is helpful to classify the different layers involved in data storage.

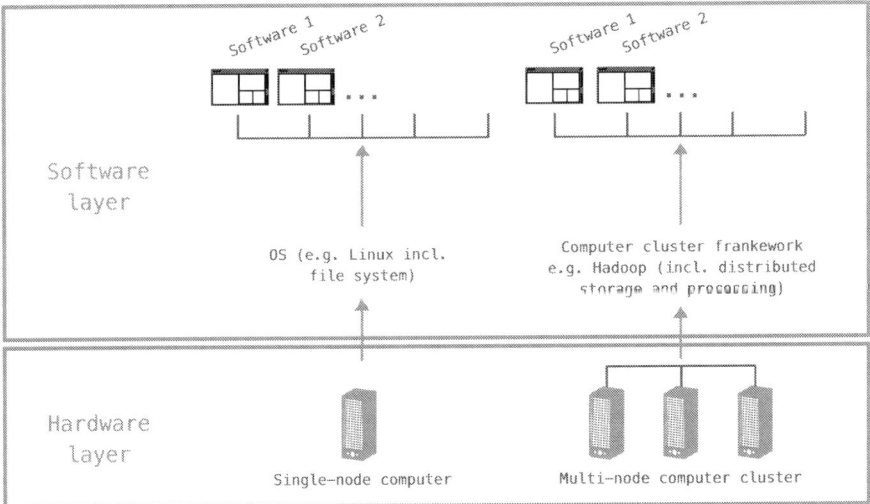

Figure 39.1 Overview of data storage technologies

On a hardware level, some software is designed to run on single computers, but with the rise of big data, computer clusters (i.e. networks of computers) have gained popularity because they are easier to scale (horizontal scaling) and thus more performant.

On a software level, the most basic component at single-computer level is the operating system (OS) of a computer (e.g. Linux). The basic components of the OS are to manage computing resources within the computer and the provision of a file or data storage system. Things look similar with computer clusters. However, as well as every single computer in the cluster needing its own OS, computer clusters also need an overarching software framework that acts as the "OS" for the *cluster*. The basic function of this framework is to allocate and manage computer resources between the different nodes of the cluster and to handle the distributed data storage and processing to the nodes in the cluster. Just like we store files on our computer directly in the file system, we can do the same with a computer cluster, and the software framework will take care of distributing the file to the nodes in the cluster.

We can also add another layer of abstraction on top of the OS and use software such as database management systems to store data. Some software is specially designed to be implemented on computer clusters to harness the power of several nodes, whereas other software is designed to run on single-node computers only. For example, most relational database management systems (RDBMSs) are designed to run on single computers and cannot simply be "installed" on a computer cluster so that they can be scaled out.

40 | What are Hadoop and the Hadoop Ecosystem (e.g. Hive, HBase, Flume, Kafka)?

Hadoop

Table 40.1 An overview of Apache Hadoop

What is Hadoop?
Apache Hadoop is a framework for operate computer clusters. It enables distributed data storage (a distributed file system) and parallel data processing across the nodes of a cluster.
You can think of Hadoop as an OS for computer clusters. Like a normal OS, it consists of several components. The most important ones are: ▶ Hadoop Distributed File System (HDFS), enabling the distributed data storage   ▶ YARN, the platform that manages and distributes the computer resources among the nodes   ▶ MapReduce, the programming model that enables the parallel processing of data within the computer cluster
Hadoop is open-source software that is managed and licensed by the Apache Software Foundation. Nonetheless, several proprietary adaptations of it are sold and rented by companies, and these come with support. Examples of proprietary providers of computer-cluster frameworks are MapR and Hortonworks.
Why does it matter?
When Hadoop was first released in 2006, it was a real game-changer for the big data world. Before that some top-notch tech companies had proprietary solutions that operated computer clusters to handle their requirements for storing and processing big data, but these were out of reach for the rest of the world. Then along came Hadoop, an open-source framework that made it economically viable for a wide range of organizations to operate computer clusters.
When is it used?
Hadoop is used when you are dealing with "big data" – i.e. data storage and processing requirements that exceed traditional, single-computer capacities and require you to operate a computer cluster – and if you want to go open-source rather than paying for the software.

Hadoop Ecosystem

Table 40.2 An overview of the Apache Hadoop Ecosystem

> **What is the Hadoop Ecosystem?**
>
> The Hadoop Ecosystem refers to a number of software frameworks that run on top of Hadoop and that are used to store, manage and process data on computer clusters. Because many of them bear the name or logo of an animal, they are also referred to as Hadoop Zoo. All of these tools are licensed under the Apache Software Foundation and are open source.
>
> Just like MS Windows has an ecosystem of software programs related to it (e.g. MS Office with Word, Excel etc.), Hadoop has some tools that are designed to run on top of Hadoop. Some popular tools of the Hadoop Ecosystem are:
>
> - **Apache Spark:** Analytics engine for large-scale data processing. Spark is arguably the most important tool in the Hadoop Ecosystem and is used in the vast majority of cases where data needs to be stored and processed across multiple nodes. In fact, it has become so important that Spark has turned into its own ecosystem with several components.
> - **Apache Hive:** Data warehouse software that enables writing SQL-like queries (HiveQL) to access and manage data residing in the underlying distributed file system.
> - **Apache HBase:** Non-relational (column-oriented) distributed database.
> - **Apache Flume:** Tool used to collect, aggregate and move large amounts of streaming data such as log files.
> - **Apache Kafka:** A distributed, horizontally scalable streaming platform used to build real-time data pipelines and streaming apps.
> - **Apache Cassandra:** Distributed, non-relational database management system (wide-column store).
> - **Apache Accumulo:** Distributed, non-relational database (key-value store).
>
> Most of these software tools can also run on other frameworks than Hadoop. There are a number of other tools in the Hadoop Ecosystem, but mentioning each would go beyond the scope of this book.

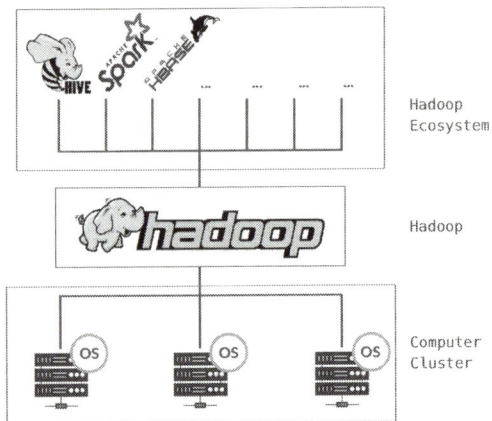

Figure 40.1 Overview of a Hadoop-based computer cluster

Data Storage Technologies

Why does it matter?

The Hadoop Ecosystem provides a comprehensive and powerful toolstack for storing, processing, analysing and managing data on computer clusters. The tools are distributed as open-source software, so they are accessible for everyone.

When is it used?

Since the Hadoop Ecosystem provides such a comprehensive set of tools, they can be used in almost any case where data needs to be stored, processed, analysed or managed on a computer cluster.

41 | What is Spark?

Table 41.1 An overview of Apache Spark

What is Spark?

Spark is an open-source cluster-computing framework for processing big data on computer clusters. Spark usually sits on top of a distributed file system such as HDFS.

While its core functionality is processing big data on computer clusters, Spark is increasingly offering further functionalities, like its MLlib package, which allows you to implement machine learning (ML) models in Spark. In fact, Spark has become so important for big data processing that it is developing its own ecosystem with related tools. For example, Spark Streaming extends the functionalities to be able to handle streaming data.

Why does it matter?

Spark has developed into the most important big data tool. It enables the processing and increasingly also analysis of big data on computer clusters, including the implementation of ML algorithms.

One great thing about Spark is that it offers various programming interfaces that allow you to use it with different programming languages, e.g. Python and R. To put this in non-technical terms, you do not need to learn another language but can just give Spark commands in, say, Python language. Nevertheless, using Spark requires a profound knowledge of how distributed systems work.

When is it used?

You can use Spark in almost any big data use case for data preparation, processing and increasingly also machine learning.

42 | What are MySQL, PostgreSQL, Oracle, Microsoft SQL Server, SAP HANA, IBM Db2 and Teradata Database?

Table 42.1 An overview of relational database providers

What is MySQL, PostgreSQL, Oracle, Microsoft SQL Server, SAP HANA, IBM Db2 and Teradata Database?

There is a plethora of providers of RDBMSs out there. Among these, some popular and widely used ones are:

- Oracle Database (proprietary)
- MySQL (open source)
- Microsoft SQL Server (proprietary)
- PostgreSQL (open source)
- SAP HANA (proprietary)
- Teradata database (proprietary)
- IBM Db2 (proprietary)

Some of these database management systems offer functionalities that go beyond those that relational database systems could traditionally provide. For example, SAP HANA is mostly used as a performant relational database, but it also supports other data models (e.g. column-oriented store).

These database systems used to run on single-node computers. However, providers have been working on overcoming this. For example, the Teradata database, produced by the Teradata Corporation, offers full scalability to various nodes, making use of massive parallel processing (MPP), where workloads are distributed to several nodes.[ix] Today, most of the proprietary RDBMSs offer such scalability.

Traditionally, these RDBMSs could be purchased as software to be installed on proprietary computing resources. That meant having to buy the software or their licenses and running it on local computers. However, with cloud services becoming more and more popular, these RDBMSs can increasingly also be rented on demand as cloud services.

Why does it matter?

RDBMSs are still the most widely used systems. If you work with data, you are bound to come across one of the RDBMS providers listed in this table.

When is it used?

Relational database systems still do an excellent job of storing data in the majority of cases (see Chapter 3_2). Given that some products offer idiosyncratic benefits and additional functions, the exact choice of RDBMS provider depends on the specific use case.

43 | What are MongoDB, Neo4j, Amazon DynamoDB, CouchDB and Redis?

Table 43.1 An overview of NoSQL database providers

What are MongoDB, Neo4j, Amazon DynamoDB, CouchDB and Redis?

Even though there are several hundred non-relational database systems, a few pop up quite frequently and have gone beyond being hyper-specialized niche products for specific problems. Some popular ones are:

- **MongoDB:** Arguably the most popular document-oriented database (open source but with the option of a paid edition).
- **CouchDB:** Another popular document-oriented store, using JSON documents to store data; licensed as open source through the Apache Software Foundation.
- **Neo4J:** A widely used graph database.
- **Amazon DynamoDB:** A cloud service of Amazon Web Services that supports both key-value as well as document data models.
- **Redis:** Open-source key-value store.

All of these non-relational database systems scale horizontally.

Why does it matter?

In some situations, traditional relational database systems are unable to satisfy data storage and processing requirements. This might, for example, be due to their limits in scalability, because the data is semi- unstructured or unstructured, or because the relational data model is a poor fit to model the situation at hand. In this case, non-relational database systems offer an alternative. While compared to relational databases their use is still limited (see Table 29-2), they have gained popularity and have become indispensable in certain use cases.

When are they used?

Use non-relational database systems where relational database systems are not able to fulfil all storage and processing needs and where strong consistency is not required, e.g. in cases where the database requires an extreme storage, read or write capacity.

4 Architecting Data

Data Warehouses, Data Lakes and the Cloud

4_1 Understanding data architectures

44 | What is a data architecture and why do companies need it?

In Chapter 3 we look at the technical side of storing data and explain that for a long time, relational database systems have been the go-to solution for storing data for a number of reasons. In reality, though, one relational database system is not enough for most companies. Usually, companies have *several* relational database systems to manage, store and process their data. Just think of Your Model Car and all of the different types of data that could (and should) be stored: employee data, web log data, customer data, social media data, product data, etc. This is too much data to store in one single database. This wealth of information and data requires the use of several databases.

But if a company is to use several databases, it also requires ample management concerning where, how and when data is stored and by whom it can be accessed. This is much like organizing a grocery store. If you have a small corner shop, you can just put all of your products in one small room. But if you grow your shop and provide more products, you have to think about how to organize things efficiently. How should the products in your shop be placed, and what sort of storage equipment do you need? You will probably sell frozen products, so you will need freezers in which you consolidate all the frozen products. How do you organize the flow of customers within your store? You will want to place the products in your store strategically to make it easy for your customers to find them. You might also have a section of products such as spirits and cigarettes to which access is restricted. How do products get to your store? On an hourly, daily, weekly basis? How many products do you want to have in your product portfolio in the first place? You might also open a second or third outlet and you will want to ensure that the product portfolio and the prices across these different stores is identical and consistent.

Architecting Data

Similar challenges apply for data. If you have a small company, then your data requirements are easy to satisfy and it is easy to consolidate and store all of the necessary data in one centralized database. But as you grow and collect more data in different fields, you need to think about how you want to organize the flow of this data in your organization. What data do you want to collect and how? What technology and types of database should be used to store and process this data? How does the data flow through the organization? What does the data life cycle look like? How can access to the right data be made as easy as possible for the end-user groups? What data should be analysed and how? Where several databases contain similar or identical data, how do you ensure that this data is consistent and can be exchanged between systems? What format should the data be in? And so forth.

Dealing with all of these questions falls under the discipline of designing the *data architecture* of a company. The data architecture refers to the way data is collected, stored and managed within an organization – or to put it simply, how data flows within an organization.

This is a rather broad definition, but a data architecture can be broken down conceptually into (at least) two layers:

- The logical architecture, which is the logical layout or ground view of the architecture. It is therefore not something tangible, but rather a logical concept.
- The technical implementation of that logical layout. This is the sum of all physical hardware and software that is used to realize the logical layer.

Typically, the technologies that are used to implement a data architecture are (distributed) file systems, (non-)relational database systems, and other processing and storage technologies. This can be likened to a city. A city is merely a logical concept; it is not tangible. The city consists of (and is thereby realized by means of) things like houses, streets, pavements, parks etc. Like the physical hardware and software to implement a data architecture, it is these things that are tangible, as opposed to the logical concept.

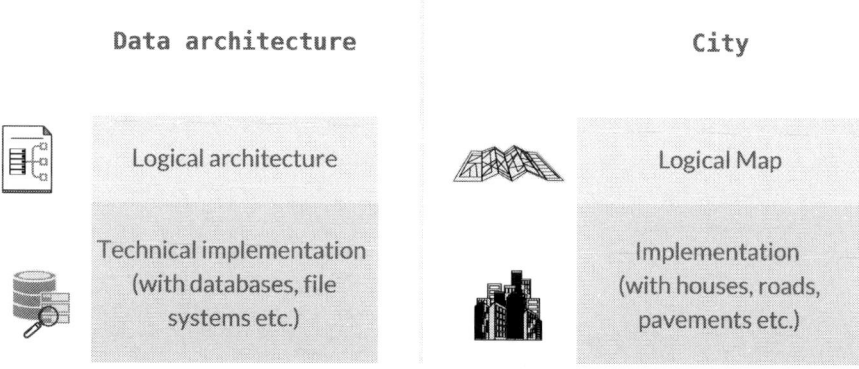

Figure 44.1 Data architectures compared to cities

Table 44.1 What is a data architecture and why does it matter?

What is a data architecture?

The data architecture is the way in which data flows in an organization, i.e. how it is collected, processed, stored and consumed. This includes:
 	
▸ *The logical architecture (conceptual design):* On a logical level, how should data in a company move around? This means asking questions like:
   ❏ What data should be collected and what form does it have (structure, unstructured etc.)?
   ❏ Who should have access to what kind of data?
   ❏ How are the various database systems in a company linked to each other?
 	
▸ *The technical implementation of that conceptual design:* With what technologies can the target state of the architectural design be realized? Questions include:
   ❏ What types of database, file systems or other storage technologies are necessary to fulfil the data storage requirements?
   ❏ How many database systems are necessary?
   ❏ Can they be linked technically, and if so, how?

Why does it matter?
One database is used to depict one real-world or business process. The data architecture is the sum and the interplay of a number of such databases, file systems and other storage technologies. The goal of a data architecture is to capture and model *all* of the processes of a company with data. The architecture stipulates: ▸ What data is collected ▸ What form it has ▸ Who has access to it ▸ How it is stored ▸ How it is processed etc.

The data architecture is an important part of an organization or company. To understand just how significant it is, remember that the purpose of collecting data is to model and depict the real world. Thus, the data architecture of a company essentially defines how the entirety of a company with all its business processes can be modelled with data. This will also determine how data is then used for analytics, and to augment and improve business models and tap into new ones. Ideally, the data architecture – which is designed and implemented by *data architects* – should help a company pursue its overall business strategy.

Architecting Data

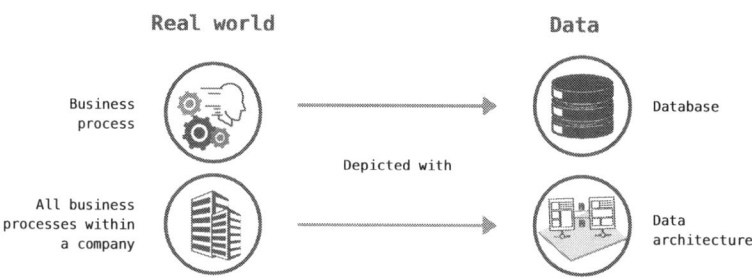

Figure 44.2 Data architecture versus database

The data architecture of a company is one of the essential pillars of the overarching enterprise architecture, and it is closely linked to the data governance discipline. Data governance is concerned with the proper management of data to ensure its quality, availability, usability and security. While the data architecture is concerned with the technical implementation and infrastructure design, data governance is concerned with the people in a company and it stipulates how processes have to be designed to ensure the proper management of data.

> **Case study 19**
>
> **Connected multi-cooker kitchen machine**
>
> A producer of kitchen machines wants to enter the Internet of Things (IoT) market by equipping its newest series of multi-cooker kitchen machines with several sensors, turning them into connected devices. The goal is to collect user data and based on that, offer various services through a newly developed app, e.g. recipe and diet recommendations.
>
> The sensors are expected to collect vast amounts of data. The kitchen machine company needs to analyse this data and make it available to users via the app. Furthermore, the new data needs to be integrated with existing data relating to the website, customers, sales, HR, procurement, marketing, etc.
>
> This requires the design and implementation of a comprehensive data architecture to support the business goals of the company. What data exactly should be collected? What data should/can be stored and for how long? Who should have access to what data?

45 | What are the most popular architectural blueprints?

The field of data architecture is extremely wide and touches on a lot of concepts. Going into all of these concepts in detail is beyond the scope of this book. We focus on two architectural blueprints that have been adopted by a lot of companies: the data warehouse (4_2) and the data lake (4_3). Given that data architectures are increasingly implemented with cloud services rather than on-premises IT resources, we also delve into the topic of cloud architectures (4_4).

Every company varies in how it is set up and organized. Naturally, then, data architectures – whose aim it is to model these companies – vary across companies, too. The data architecture of Amazon looks nothing like the data architecture of the yoga studio next door (if it has one). Still, over the past few decades a blueprint for a data architectural design has emerged that a lot of companies have adopted: the data warehouse (DWH).

Just like many cities follow a certain blueprint or structural model, the same holds true for data architectures. For example, in urban planning a city may follow a concentric-ring model. In that blueprint, the city is organized into concentric circles, with the central business district at the core, surrounded by several other zones, such as factory or residential zones. While each city is different, a lot of them follow such a blueprint, e.g. Chicago. The same holds true for data architectures. Each company may be different, but the DWH is commonly used to implement a data architecture. For decades, much like the answer to the question "How should we store data for a certain business process?" has been "Relational database systems", the answer to the question "How should various relational database systems in a company be organized and architected?" has been "In a data warehouse".

And data warehouses have been doing a great job of organizing the data flow within a company for a long time. But in recent years, in large part as a response to the rise of big data, a new concept has emerged: the data lake. On a technical level, NoSQL databases have been hailed as the next-generation database systems that will bury traditional relational database systems, and the same has happened on an architectural level. Proponents of data lakes promised no limits to scale, storage and processing of any type of data, more flexibility and ultimately more value. Data lakes were hailed as the holy grail and one-size-fits-all solution to designing a data architecture.

But a lot of confusion has emerged around these data lakes – partly because data architecture is such a complex topic touching on so many other fields, but also because data lakes fell prey to hype and a lot of people started talking about them without speaking the same language. As a result, the odds are that if you ask two people what a data lake is and how it works, you are not going to get the same answers.

4_2 Data warehouse architectures

46 | What is a data warehouse (DWH) architecture?

We have seen in 📑 44 what sort of questions the field of data architecture is concerned with. For decades, DWHs have offered a lot of answers to these questions.

To understand the emergence and benefits of a DWH, it helps to see why a single relational database system is not sufficient to meet a company's data needs.

Suppose that with Your Model Car we store all our data – products, transactions, employees etc. – in one centralized relational database system. Shortcomings will cause us to run into problems:

- The load to be carried by the database and the underlying single-node computer is too large and the capacity of the database is not sufficient for everything. Just imagine some of the jobs a single, company-wide database would have to fulfil:
    - ❑ Serve all the requests from customers who are looking for products on the website (stock, price, delivery time etc.).
    - ❑ Write and store new data (orders, payments, web logs, etc.).
    - ❑ Answer analytical queries from employees (e.g. How many products have we sold in the last month? What was the total sales volume last week?).
- Because the database is accessed from outside the company by customers, all of the company data, including sensitive internal data, is exposed to the public and might be at risk of unauthorized access.

The solution to these problems is to have several databases and integrate them into a comprehensive data architecture. That way we can overcome:

- *A single database lacking the power to complete all the different required tasks:* With several database systems we can dedicate databases exclusively to:
    - ❑ Answer customer requests on the website (available stock of product, product price etc.).
    - ❑ Write and store new incoming data (completed orders, ingoing and outgoing payments, number of web logs, etc.).
    - ❑ Analyse already existing data (answer queries such as "How many products have we sold in France last week?").
- *Unauthorized access to a central database:* By having several separated databases, we have better control over who can access which data.

Having several independently operating database systems solves a lot of problems. The main challenge in this setup, however, is to orchestrate the interrelations between all of these databases. With the rise of relational database systems, companies found themselves having several relational database systems in use across their various departments. But with a scattered data landscape came inevitable problems. The various databases lacked the interconnections to enable management of the data across the company.

This gave rise to a concept of how data and databases should be connected, i.e. how data should flow in a company: the DWH architecture.

The blueprint architecture DWH organizes the data flow of a company in a certain way. Like houses, streets and gardens make up a city, the tangible technologies with which a DWH is implemented are mostly various kinds of relational database systems. With these interconnected databases the goal is to create a comprehensive and consolidated single version of the truth of the company-wide data landscape, which is used to collect, store and process data and ultimately make it available to end-users.

William Inmon, an American computer scientist who is often hailed as the father of the DWH, defined the DWH as follows:

Table 46.1 What is a DWH and why does it matter?

What is a DWH?

A data warehouse is a centralized data storage system that is meant to integrate company-wide data. It is a subject-oriented, integrated, time-variant and non-volatile collection of data. By providing a consolidated view of company wide data, its goal is to support management's decision-making process. It is an architectural blueprint, i.e. a logical concept (not tangible).

The DWH architecture is usually implemented and realized with several relational database systems.

The goal of DWH is to centralize all data of a company in one system. However, it is not unusual for companies to maintain several DWHs, depending on their size.

The characteristics of a DWH are that it is:

- **Integrated:** A DWH integrates data from multiple data sources that might be scattered across an organization (and beyond).
- **Subject-oriented:** The goal of a DWH is to provide its users with a view of specific subject areas, e.g. "sales", and allow them to analyse them.
- **Time-variant:** DWHs store historical data permanently. This contrasts with transactional systems (22), which only store the most recent records temporarily.
- **Non-volatile:** The goal of a DWH is to store historical data to paint a picture of what happened, not to change that picture. Therefore, once stored in the DWH, data typically will not change.

Why does it matter?

For decades, DWHs have been the go-to architectural solution for how data is supposed to flow and be stored in a company. The goal of DWHs is to manage the flow of data in a company from its collection to its consumption, and by way of that it is meant to serve as a one-stop, centralized data store that contains all company data.

Case study 20

Centralized view of insurance claims

An insurance company insures buildings around the world against damage. As soon as a claim is filed by a customer, the insurance company has to put aside sufficient reserve funds in order to cover the future costs of the claim.

So as soon as a claim is filed, the employee responsible for handling the claim looks to see whether there have been similar claims in the past, in order to create an estimate of the expected costs for the accounting department.

The problem is that this data is not consolidated, but is instead spread across the various national IT systems of the company. The employee has to sift through all the national databases to see whether similar damage has been incurred in other buildings, and this can take days.

To save employees this effort and increase productivity, the company centralizes the data of all building damage recorded in the various countries in one DWH. So instead of having to search all national systems, employees now have one centralized access point for all data.

47 | How does a DWH work?

DWHs break down and organize the flow of data within a company into several layers. One of the core ideas of the DWH is to logically separate these layers and assign dedicated databases to them. Figure 47-1 shows a DWH architecture with its various layers, from where the data is generated (data sources) through to when it is consumed (data access). The separation of layers and respective tasks makes the architecture robust and performant.

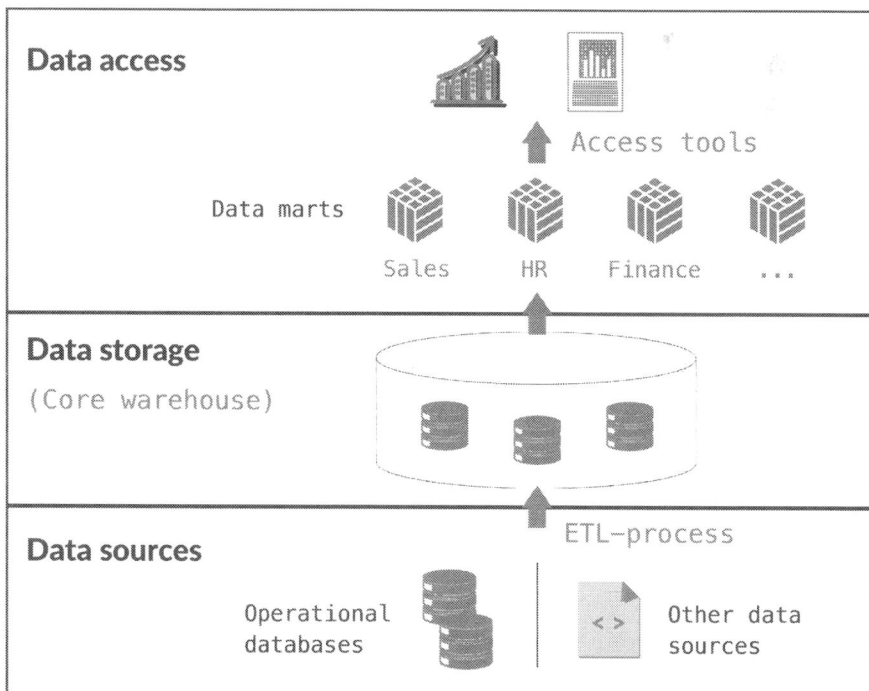

Figure 47.1 Schematic overview of a DWH

Data sources

The first layer consists of the data sources of the DWH, which is where the data life cycle begins. The data sources of a DWH are typically the *operational systems* of the company, i.e. transactional databases that are designed to record the day-to-day business of a company. In Your Model Car, for example, this would be the database that records the orders and the database that records the web logs on our website.

These databases record transactional data. The data is retrieved on a regular basis, e.g. daily or weekly, through the extract-transform-load process (see the next section), to be loaded into the DWH. After it has been loaded into the DWH, it is deleted from the operational databases, which then collect the next round of data.

Data sources can also be external. We might, for example, draw marketing or weather data from a third-party provider.

Info box

What is the operational system of a company?

The *operational system* of a company refers to the IT infrastructure and system that supports the day-to-day operations and business processes of the company. The operational system is essentially the backbone of the IT infrastructure – it is what keeps the company operating. Much like for a car manufacturer the operational system is its production line, in Your Model Car the database that records the transactions and orders of customers is part of the operational system of the company.

Data staging layer

The staging layer is where the *extraction*, *transformation* and eventually *loading* of data takes place. (This process is often abbreviated to its acronym, ETL.) Data is extracted from the data sources, e.g. various operational databases. But rather than loading all of the data directly into the DWH in its raw form, it is transformed. This transformation can, for example, consist of an actual change of format, data aggregation (if it is too granular), cleansing data or discarding unnecessary data.

Why is this transformation necessary? Why is data not directly loaded into the DWH as it is? There are several reasons:

- *Data collected by operational databases is too detailed:* In many cases operational databases collect data that does not need to be stored permanently and would take up too much storage space in the DWH. One option is to simply discard data. Another option is to aggregate data if it is too granular. For example, say the operational database records our web logs precisely on a millisecond basis, but for our later analysis it will suffice to know how many visitors our website had per minute.

Architecting Data

- *Different databases have different data formats:* Various operational database systems differ in the way they collect data. For example, if we have several web servers that store web logs, the format in which they store the date might differ. The US server might store the date in the YYYY-MM-DD format, while the European system might follow the DD.MM.YY format.
- *Data needs to be cleansed or otherwise transformed:* In many cases the data might not be in the right format for us. For example, we might want to know how long a website visitor spent on a given web page. This information might be implicit, because we know when the visitor visited the page and when they clicked on a directing link to visit another web page. We want to store the time window between the two and load that data into the DWH.

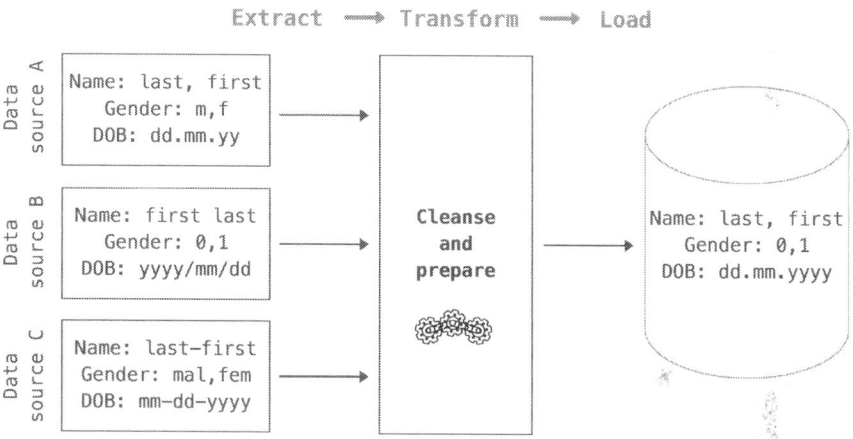

Figure 47.2 Example of an ETL process

Data storage (core warehouse)

This layer is the core of the DWH architecture. Having undergone the ETL process, all the data from the data sources is *integrated* and stored *permanently* in the DWH. *Integrated* means that the DWH's purpose is to provide a single version of truth of the data, i.e. there should be no inconsistencies or redundancies in the data and the entirety of the DWH should paint a consolidated picture of the company. *Permanently* means that data in here is stored for months/years/decades and should not be changed after it has entered the DWH. The purpose is to record the history of the company, not to alter it.

Data access

Once the data is in the DWH, it can be accessed by the end-users to aid them in their business operations and decisions. For instance, the sales department might want to visualize data of the daily ordered products, or the HR department might want to view the number of applications for a job opening or perhaps employee satisfaction.

This access is provided by means of *data marts*: subsets of the core warehouse that provide users with partial views of the entire DWH. The purpose of such partial views is to ensure that the right group of people gets access to the data that is relevant for them – and only this data. For example, the marketing department should probably have a view of all the web logs as well as customer data. On the other hand, they should not have access to the data on employees, which should be designated for the HR department only.

Unlike the transactional database in the data source layer, the data marts are implemented on databases that are designed for answering queries and read requests (fast response times).

The access to the data could happen with various technologies. For example, end-users might just create CSV or Excel exports of the data in the data marts. Or they might directly access the data in the data mart through an RDBMS or analytical/visualization tools such as Tableau, Qlik, and SAS.

Integrated view despite separation of functional layers

The separation of functional layers in a DWH and the implementation thereof with various relational database systems effectively takes the load of all the users accessing the data off the operational database in the data source layer. Thus, the operational databases are free to focus exclusively on writing new data entries while only being accessed sporadically to retrieve their data and load it in the permanent data storage layer.

Also notice that a given data mart provides an integrated and consolidated view of company-wide data. The data in the "marketing" data mart will probably contain data from operational databases that are located in departments other than the marketing department, e.g. web logs, customer data, transaction data, etc.

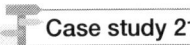
Case study 21

How the Your Model Car DWH works

Your Model Car is an online retailer, and so our operational systems have an operational database that records all the orders that are placed through the website. We also have an operational database that keeps track of who accesses the website, when and from where.

In order not to strain these operational systems with the data analysis or visualization that we might do, we transfer the data from the operational databases to our core warehouse every day at 4 a.m., which is when we have least the traffic on our website (1). That way, the operational databases can focus on writing new data without having to deal with being accessed for analysis or visualization.

Once the data is in the core warehouse, where it is stored permanently (2), it can be accessed by the relevant users that need it for their business operations. For example, the sales department might visualize the daily

Architecting Data

sales data to monitor the development of sales (3). Obviously, there are access restrictions. For example, only the HR department has access to the employee and salary data.

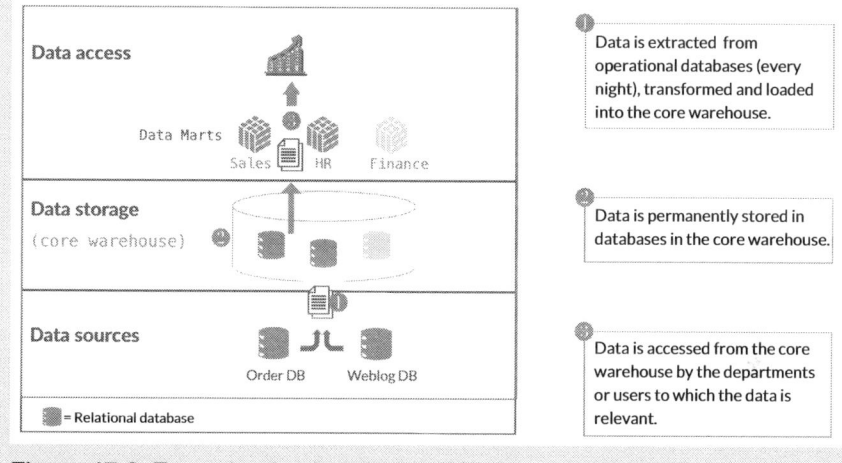

Figure 47.3 Example of a data flow in a DWH

48 | What does a typical data pipeline in a DWH look like?

There is an entire data life cycle in a DWH (or rather, since data is not reborn, it is a life history). Before a piece of information is consumed by its end-users, it passes through several layers and stages. In a DWH the life cycle that a certain piece of data goes through is called a *data pipeline*, which is a set of actions to extract, store, move, transform and process data.

Table 48.1 What is a data pipeline and why does it matter?

What is a data pipeline?

A set of actions to extract, store, move, transform and process data in a system, typically in an automated way.

For example, one data pipeline in a DWH might be extracting order data from the operational systems, cleansing it and transforming it into an analysis-ready form for the sales department. This data pipeline might be executed every night. The pipeline leads through various relational database systems in the DWH and is like a number of SQL commands to execute the manipulations in the databases.

Why does it matter?

Data pipelines structure, organize and automate the different data flow streams in a system such as a DWH. Through such pipelines data is transformed and transported to where it is needed and used, much like with real pipelines – in an automated way.

You can think of a data pipeline as a number of SQL commands that are combined to retrieve the raw data from the data sources, transform it and finally provide access to the transformed data to the end-users in a company. A DWH therefore consists of a number of data pipelines.

Data pipelines are usually an automated process that are executed on a regular basis (e.g. every night) to update applications, analyses or dashboards of data end-users. Just like real pipelines, they require maintenance and have to be updated regularly, such as when new data sources are integrated into the DWH or when end-users require the data to be provisioned in a different manner (e.g. sales data on an hourly basis rather than a daily basis).

The ETL process in a DWH is one example of a data pipeline.

Case study 22

Data pipeline in food retail

A food retailer owns various supermarkets. Product sales are one of its central core data assets and they steer the procurement and logistics of products.

Every supermarket outlet stores the sales data that is being collected at the checkouts with operational systems on-premise. During the night, when the shops are closed, the data is extracted, transformed and loaded into the central DWH, which is located in the HQ of the company.

From there it is accessed by multiple users, including the branch managers of the respective outlets, who use the data in the DWH to create reports and steer the procurement.

49 | What are the limitations of a DWH?

Much like relational database systems have been the go-to solution for data storage for years, the DWH architecture has been the go-to blueprint for organizing the flow of data and interconnecting the various database systems in a company. During the 1990s most companies whose data storage and processing requirements exceeded a single database set up a DWH.

The advent of big data revealed the shortcomings of relational database systems as storage technology, and so did it reveal the limitation of DWHs. Since DWHs are usually implemented with relational database systems, the capabilities of DWH architectures are naturally bound to the capabilities of relational database systems, as follows.

Structured data only

DWHs were developed before the dawn of big data, i.e. when the integration of various data sources was limited to structured data. They were implemented with relational database systems and were designed to store structured data, not semi-structured or unstructured data.

Lack of agility (schema-on-write)

Before a single bit of data can be stored in a relational database system, the entire structure (schema) has to be meticulously defined (📖 34). This is also referred to as *schema-on-write*: the tables have to be created, all columns have to be named, the data type has to be defined (date, number, text, etc.), the viable length for each column in each table has to be set, and so forth. And as soon as something changes in the data storage requirements, this schema has to be adapted to the new requirements.

It is quite some work to that for one database, yet it is usually still manageable. But it's another matter doing that for a number of databases that are interconnected in a DWH that is supposed to capture the entirety of a company and its processes. And since data requirements and real-world business processes tend to change over time, this is a task that has to be done repeatedly. And each time the schema changes, the structure and organization of the DWH have to be adjusted. Agile measures – such as quickly collecting new data for a prototype to implement a machine learning (ML) model – are therefore cumbersome with a DWH.

Limits to (economically viable) scalability

DWHs are usually implemented on relational database systems. That means their performance is bound to the limits of relational database systems. Scaling out (horizontally) is therefore difficult. Some vendors have specialized in horizontally scaling DWH to the terabyte and petabyte range by making use of massive parallel processing (MPP) just like computer clusters. Prominent examples of such technology providers are Teradata, Netezza and various cloud

---

Case study 23

Enhanced data storage requirements of a logistics provider

A logistic company maintains several storage plants which act as redistribution centres. Containers arrive via train or truck, are stored temporarily and then are shipped to their target destinations.

There has been quite some data collected in these redistribution centres already. However, in the course of modernization efforts, the company plans to collect even more data. For example, it plans to install sensors and to use drones to monitor the processes better. The data of the latter will help the company to better track the location of containers within the plant, as their exact location is often unknown.

The exact usage and storage requirements of the data are still unknown and there are likely to be several changes to what data is collected in what format. In other words, a flexible architecture is needed – and it also needs to able to store and process unstructured data such as the drone footage. A DWH is therefore not ideal.

service providers who offer scalable DWH at a mouse click. But in the majority of companies, the DWH is implemented on "normal" relational database systems and therefore is difficult to scale. Furthermore, while such MPP based databases overcome the limits to scale from a technical point of view, limits to economically viable scale remain, as these solutions tend to be rather expensive.

50 | What are popular ETL tools?

A core component of a DWH architecture is the extract-load-transform process (ETL), in which data from various data sources such as operational databases is integrated and consolidated. In a lot of cases, this process is still customized and programmed manually in SQL.

However, there are several tools on the market that are designed to facilitate ETL so that there is less work to do manually.

Table 50.1 An overview of ETL tools

What are ETL tools?	ETL tools are pieces of software designed to implement and facilitate the ETL processes so that they do not need to be set up manually.
	ETL tools are able to collect, migrate and integrate from multiple data sources. They usually provide the user with a graphical interface to manipulate data. They offer ample functionalities, such as filtering, merging and reformatting data.
	They also enable building and automating data pipelines with task scheduling and monitoring functions.
	Most vendors of ETL tools provide the option to run their software on-premise or in the cloud.
Why do they matter?	ETL tools can increase productivity, because they save DWH administrators and data architects from having to code and create data pipelines and ETL processes manually from scratch.
	Most of the ETL tools also offer extra functionalities too, such as metadata management, data profiling and data cleansing. So they also touch on other fields such as data governance.
When are they used?	ETL tools can be used to structure and implement data architectures in which data from various sources needs to be integrated and consolidated – above all in DWHs.
What are some popular ETL tools?	There are countless providers of ETL tools. While they all offer very similar core functionalities, they differ in terms of the additional features they provide as well as their pricing models. Here are some popular vendors of ETL tools: • **Informatica:** Arguably the most widely adopted vendor of ETL tools, it sells a whole suite of ETL (Informatica PowerCenter) and related software. • **IBM:** The InfoSphere Information Server is the ETL tool by tech giant IBM. • **SAS Data Management Platform:** Next to its wide range of other data-related products, SAS offers its Data Management Platform as ETL tool. • **Talend:** Talend's Data Management Platform offers various data governance functionalities on top of the basic ETL components. The major cloud providers also offer specifically designed ETL tools as cloud services, e.g. Amazon Web Services (AWS) Glue and Microsoft Azure's Data Factory services.

… Architecting Data

4_3 Data lakes and streaming architectures

51 | What is a data lake architecture?

For decades, DWHs were the standard for how to organize the flow of data in a company. But as the data landscape became more heterogeneous and voluminous, data storage and processing requirements began to change, and shortcomings of the traditional DWH architecture were revealed. A new way to organize the data flow was needed – a more agile and flexible architecture to accommodate the need to store heterogeneous data and the altered data storage requirements, and to scale more easily.

Table 51.1 What is a data lake and why does it matter?

What is a data lake?
A data lake is a centralized repository that stores and processes company-wide data in its raw format. Like a DWH, it is an architectural blueprint, i.e. a logical concept rather than a tangible entity. While its purpose, to centralize company-wide data, is identical to that of a DWH, it fundamentally differs in the way it does so in a number of ways.
Most importantly, data in a data lake is stored in its raw format and processed upon request, unlike in a DWH, where it is transformed before being stored.
This is enabled because a data lake is implemented with various data storage technologies including relational database systems, non-relational database systems and distributed file systems (unlike a DWH, which is mostly implemented with relational database systems).
Most of these technologies can be scaled horizontally, so data lakes are easier to scale.

Why does it matter?
With the rise of big data, DWHs were increasingly unable to fulfil the data requirements of companies, especially data-driven ones. These requirements included storing and processing large amounts of data in varied formats, including raw and unstructured data, and being able to react swiftly to changing data storage requirements.
As a result, the data lake has emerged as another architectural blueprint for use cases that require data to be stored or processed in ways that the DWH cannot fulfil.

As a result, the concept of the data lake was established by the mid-2010s. The data lake depicts one blueprint for how to organize the flow of data from its creation until its consumption. It is often mistakenly considered as just a rebranded DWH architecture. While both are architectural blueprints, there are some significant differences in how they organize the data flow within a company.

A well-designed data lake can alleviate the limitations of DWHs. This is achieved by using storage technologies other than relational database systems (e.g. NoSQL databases and distributed file systems), which can be scaled horizontally and so can be implemented on computer clusters. Furthermore, in the data lake architecture the flow of data in a company is fundamentally different from the flow of data in a DWH.

As a result, a data lake offers the following advantages.

Storage of both structured and unstructured data in raw format

Parts of the data lake can be implemented with relational database systems, just like in DWHs. However, the majority of a data lake will technically be realized with distributed file systems (e.g. Hadoop) and non-relational database systems. This enables the storage and processing of structured, semi-structured and unstructured data.

Agility and flexibility of data storage (schema-on-read)

Because data is stored in a distributed file system or non-relational database system, it does not need to be processed before it can be loaded into and stored in a data lake. Instead, data is stored in its raw format and only processed upon request. This gives the data lake architecture a great deal of flexibility and agility.

In a DWH the schema and structure of the various relational database systems have to be rigorously defined before any data can be stored. In other words, you have to know what kind of data you want to collect in what format in a DWH before you even set it up. The reverse is true for a data lake, where the idea is to collect the data in its raw format and *afterwards* structure and process it for a specific use case.

This essentially reverses the data flow of a data lake as compared to a DWH. Data is extracted and directly loaded into the data lake and only transformed for a given use case if so needed. Therefore, in a data lake the process is extract-load-transform (ELT) instead of ETL.

Easy and economically viable scalability

Data lakes are largely implemented with technologies that run on computer clusters, which makes them easy and cost-efficient to scale.

Increased data processing capabilities

DWHs are traditionally designed and used for business intelligence purposes, e.g. to create daily or weekly reports of sales of a certain product. Implementing more involved use cases with the data, e.g. making use of ML algorithms, often requires a higher computational capacity and data in its raw format. While a DWH has difficulties providing for that, a data lake is able to accommodate such requirements.

52 | How does a data lake work and where should it be used?

Before you can store data in a DWH, you have to collect all the requirements and think of all eventualities for the use of the data. (Remember schema-on-write, i.e. no data can be stored before the schema is meticulously defined, because DWHs are implemented with relational database systems.) You need to think about the format you want to store data in, and in order to determine the storage format, you have to consider the goal of the data. Who will consume the data and what will they use it for?

A typical use case of a data lake is a situation where you know that data will be valuable at some point, but you have not yet defined all the requirements and therefore don't know the format you ultimately want to have the data in. Because you don't have to define a schema to write data in your data lake, you can just store the data in its raw format first. From its raw format it can be processed into the form that is required by a specific use case or user *upon request*. Other use cases are where you are dealing with unstructured data or extremely large volumes of data.

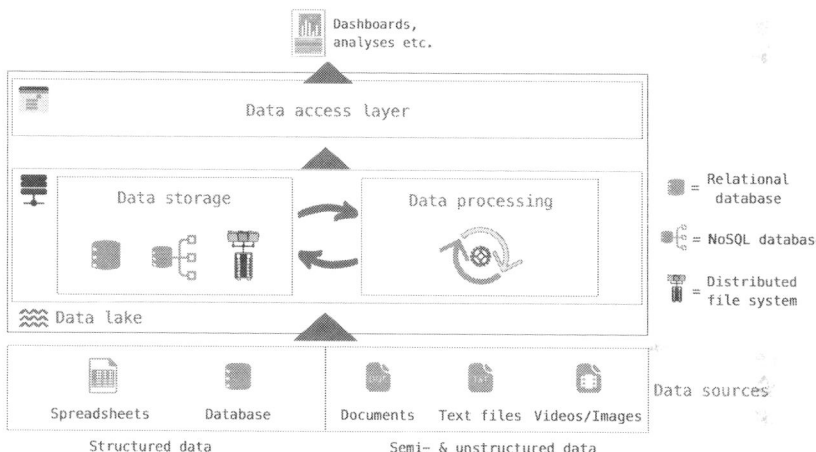

Figure 52.1 Schematic view of a data lake

So how does a data lake work? Like the DWH, the data lake consists of several logically separated layers. These might, however, all be physically implemented on the same computer cluster. The various layers logically take care of the following tasks in the flow of data in a data lake.

Data sources

Like in a DWH, the first layer consists of the data sources and is where the data life cycle begins. In contrast to a DWH, however, the data sources can consist of both structured and unstructured data including videos, images, text and documents.

Data storage

One of the main differences from a DWH is that in a data lake the data goes from its source *directly* into the storage layer. That is, data is *stored in its raw format*. Consequently, there is no staging or transformation layer. In a DWH we have to go through the process of extracting and transforming data before we can load it into the core warehouse (ETL). The opposite is the case for a data lake: we can extract and load the data directly – regardless of its form and whether it is structured or unstructured data – without having to transform it.

The storage layer is typically implemented by means of a distributed file system running on a computer cluster. It is usually complemented by non-relational and relational database systems (running on the same computer cluster).

Because the storage layer is implemented on a computer cluster, the storage capacities can be scaled easily.

Data processing layer

Once a use for the data is clear, the stored raw data can be processed *upon request* to fulfil the respective data needs. Therefore, data lakes are often said to follow a process of ELT rather than ETL: data is extracted (E) and loaded (L) directly into the data lake, and only transformed (T) and processed upon request when it is needed for a certain use case.

The data processing layer will probably be physically running on the same computer cluster as the data storage layer. The processing of data can be implemented with various data processing technologies and software, including SQL, other programming languages and big-data processing technologies such as Spark and Hive.

Data access

Once the data is processed, it can be stored in that processed format in the storage layer again and accessed via the respective access tools.

> **Case study 24**
>
> **Implementing a data lake at Your Model Car**
>
> At Your Model Car, we care about our public image and brand, and so we assume that there is a lot of information to be drawn from what people say about us and our products on social media. Because we are not entirely certain yet in what way we would like to use such social media data, we cannot extract and transform it into a DWH. Therefore, we start to collect and store tweets that feature the hashtag of our company, YourModelCar, in raw format in a non-relational database system in our lake (1).
>
> After a while, it turns out that the marketing department is interested in social listening, i.e. monitoring public sentiment on social media platforms over time. The tweets are analysed to assign a sentiment score to each tweet, e.g. 0 for a very negative tweet about our company, 10 for a highly positive tweet (2). This ultimately yields a new (tabular) dataset consisting of the tweet ID along with the date and sentiment score of that tweet. The

dataset is then stored in a relational database system again (3) and the sentiment is visualized in a chart so as to monitor its development over time (4).

Now the marketing department is interested in monitoring the *number* of tweets shared per day to analyse whether or not their marketing campaign is effective or not. Again, the raw data is processed so as to fulfil the requirements for that use case, and the processed data is stored in the storage layer.

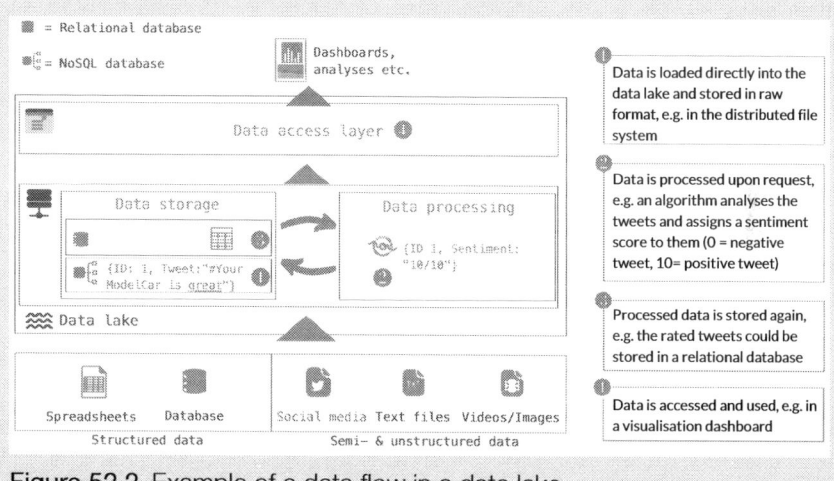

Figure 52.2 Example of a data flow in a data lake

53 | How do a DWH and data lake compare?

Both the data lake and the DWH are data architectural blueprints that have the same goal: integrate and consolidate company-wide data in one centralized system to provide data to its end-users. However, the two architectures differ in the way they do so.

Table 53.1 Comparison of a data lake and DWH

	Data warehouse (DWH)	**Data lake**
Use case	▶ Business intelligence (dashboards, visualizations etc.) ▶ Rather simple data analytics use cases (descriptive or maybe diagnostic) involving structured data	▶ Advanced data analytics use Cases (e.g. uses cases involving unstructured data such as text or image data, etc.) requiring raw data
Data	▶ Store structured data only ▶ Traditionally medium-sized amounts of data (although some providers now provide high scalability)	▶ Structured & unstructured data ▶ Large volumes of data

The Ultimate Data and AI Guide

	Data warehouse (DWH)	Data lake
Agility	▶ No storage of raw data ▶ Data needs to be transformed and cleaned before it can be stored → ETL ▶ Schema needs to be defined (which requires knowing what the database is used for)	▶ Storage of raw data without the need to define schema beforehand (danger of data swamp) → ELT ▶ Transformation of data still necessary for analysis (but only upon request for a given Use Case)
Set-up	▶ Mature architecture ▶ Expertise is more readily available	▶ Requires up-to-date experts for configuration who are harder to find

At first glance it might seem like the data lake is the superior system because it overcomes a lot of the limitations of the DWH. However, both architectures have their pros and cons and neither is necessarily better. In fact, companies increasingly maintain a data architecture that contains both of them working in tandem.

Pros and cons of the data lake

It is true that to deal with big data, i.e. vast amounts of data in various formats, a data lake is the ideal solution. That is why a lot of companies have got on the data lake train. The data lake is often implemented on a system that scales horizontally and so its computational power can easily be enhanced. Furthermore, in a data lake you store any kind of data in its raw format and are not limited to data that fits into a relational database system. This ultimately makes you more flexible: if the data you want to store or its format alters over time, you do not need to adjust the schema in a data lake like in a DWH. Instead, you can just store the data in its raw format and worry about the shape you want to bring it into when it is actually needed.

But a data lake also has several disadvantages. In many cases, data lakes end up being *data swamps*. In a data swamp data is not administered, stored and processed properly, so it fails to deliver its purpose. This can happen more easily than you may think. A data lake gives you the freedom to just chuck anything in it (which is one of its main selling points), but that also puts the burden on you to manage it well. Managing the data in a data lake and administering its resources to its users (e.g. who gets how much computing power of the computer cluster at what time) requires a lot of effort and resources.

In practice, a lot of companies underestimate the effort and resources required, neglect the proper management of their data lake and end up with a swamp. In that sense a data lake is a bit like a wardrobe with just one big storage space. Unlike with a wardrobe with many small drawers, you do not have to fold your clothes into the right shape and put them into the right drawer to store them – you just chuck them in. But the freedom and flexibility that comes with that comes at the risk or creating a mess. In contrast, a compartmentalized wardrobe deprives you of your freedom and flexibility, but automatically makes you put your clothes in order.

Architecting Data

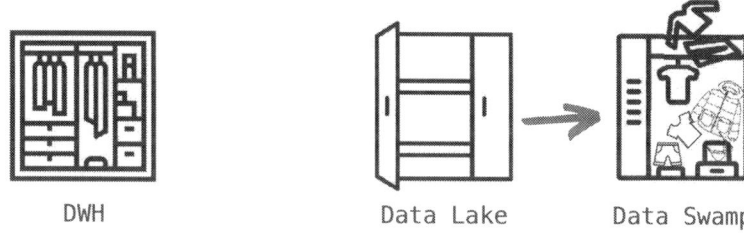

```
      DWH                  Data Lake        Data Swamp

= compartmentalized wardrobe        = open-spaced wardrobe
```

Figure 53.1 A wardrobe as a metaphor for a data lake

Pros and cons of the DWH

In a DWH you have to define the schema before you can store anything. This can be tedious, especially if your data changes on a frequent basis and you have to adjust the schema accordingly. However, it forces you to think about the structure and the order of your central repository beforehand. By definition all the data in a DWH is well-curated, clean and ordered. A lot of companies underestimate the work or do not have the necessary self-discipline to manage their central repository with a data lake, but a DWH forces them into a clear structure.

What is more, since a DWH has been the go-to solution for decades now, it is a well-established concept and there are a lot of experts in the field out there.

Choosing between the data lake and DWH – or using both

For many companies the DWH still serves its purpose, because their data requirements can be satisfied by means of a DWH. As long as this is the case – and for a lot of use cases it is – a DWH will usually do its job.

However, companies whose data storage and processing requirements go beyond the capacities of relational database systems and a DWH have to resort to alternative data architectures such as the data lake. In the world of big data, storage and processing requirements for a lot of use cases have changed and the data lake is designed to handle these requirements from the new big-data world.

Ultimately, the right data storage technologies along with the architecture in which they are embedded depend on the overarching data strategy. Once the data strategy (what data is collected, why and how) is defined, the use cases that need to be implemented to realize this strategy follow naturally. And from the use cases, the requirements for the data storage and processing technologies follow too.

Moreover, for many companies the question of their data architecture is not a question of X or Y, but rather X *and* Y. Ideally, both the DWH and data lake should be central repositories of company-wide data. In practice, however, companies tend to have several such central repositories that coexist and are interconnected (some to a greater degree than others). As a result, we have witnessed a lot of companies setting up data lakes to deal with more involved data use cases involving big data, while at the same time keeping their DWH for the applications and processing that are already in place. Or they integrate a DWH and data lake, e.g. by chucking all data in its raw form into the data lake and processing some of it from there to load it into a DWH, or by turning the existing DWH into a data source that feeds into a data lake.

At the end of the day, whether your data architecture looks more like a DWH or a data lake matters less than what requirements it is actually supposed to fulfil.

4_4 Cloud architectures

54 | What is the cloud?

The previous sections in this chapter focus mostly on the logical side of an architecture. Such logical architectures are implemented with various physical technologies. Traditionally, all these technologies had to be bought by companies in the form of both software and hardware.

Today, things look very different. Whether we are talking about a sophisticated and comprehensive data architecture or only single servers, technologies or even just software, the increased bandwidth that we enjoy has enabled an entirely new business model in the IT world: *cloud computing*, or *cloud* for short.

Cloud computing refers to using a pool of configurable computer resources and higher-level services such as software. These resources can be rented and configured on demand with minimal effort, are hosted remotely on a server farm and can be accessed via the internet or a specifically dedicated intranet.

Cloud services can range from simply renting basic hardware to sophisticated higher-level services. Instead of having to buy and set up both hardware and software by yourself on local computers, cloud computing enables you to borrow these resources remotely on demand. Today, more and more companies implement their data architecture in the cloud rather than on-premise with their own IT infrastructure.

Table 54.1 What is the cloud and why does it matter?

What is the cloud (computing)?
Cloud computing refers to utilizing remote computer resources on demand. Put simply, it means you are using somebody else's computer. There are different cloud computing models that differ according to which components of these remote resources are used: ▶ Infrastructure as a Service (IaaS) ▶ Platform as a Service (PaaS) ▶ Software as a Service (SaaS) The famous "cloud" is therefore nothing more than thousands of computers in data centres that are connected into big computer clusters. Depending on who owns these computing resources and how they can be accessed, there are different types of clouds:

- Private or enterprise cloud
- Public cloud
- Virtual private cloud

Why does it matter?

Cloud computing has become increasingly popular since it was made viable through increased bandwidth and computing power.

Cloud computing has changed the game of data storage and processing. Enabled through its economies of scale, you can now rent limitless computing power on demand – for incredibly low prices.

Need to process hundreds of terabytes of data? Before cloud computing that meant setting up your own IT infrastructure, which came with high upfront costs, effort and time. With cloud services, you can just rent these services for as long as you need them and pay only for what you use. High upfront investment costs can therefore be avoided.

Given this on-demand pricing model, the cloud also enables agility and flexibility. For example, if during peak times of a certain process (say a website visitor peak on our web page before Christmas) additional resources are needed, they can just be rented to cover such peaks.

The benefits that the use of cloud services bring are remarkable and have helped the cloud market grow quite significantly. One of the most attractive features is the immense flexibility. In the cloud, on demand and with just a few mouse clicks you can set up a sophisticated data architecture that is able to handle petabytes of data. And if the demand is gone, you can simply discard the computing resources and stop renting the services, and you only pay for what you have used.

In recent years, companies have increasingly realized the benefits of cloud services, which have enjoyed an enormous boost in popularity as a result. This is reflected in the steady growth of the public cloud market. The global market size of public cloud services stood at around US$5.8 billion in 2008.[lxi] By 2018, it had grown by more than 3000% to some US$182.4 billion[lxii] and it is expected to reach a market size of US$236 billion in 2020.[lxiii]

So why has the cloud only become popular now? While the hype around the cloud has been surging in recent years, the concept has been around and in use for decades. What has changed is that the increased bandwidth has enabled the motion of data between local and remote computers on an unprecedented scale, which has enabled a lot of new use cases.

Consider most of the applications on your smartphone. These kind of applications *run* on your smartphone, but in a lot of cases the data or processing is *hosted on remote servers*. Spotify is a good example. With this music streaming app, you don't have the songs or the algorithms to create new song recommendations for you on your smartphone. Instead, they reside on some server farm pertaining to Spotify (or Spotify might in turn use cloud services from third-party providers). The services Spotify "provides" (listening to songs, getting new song recommendations, etc.) are only sourced on demand by the user. The same holds true for your email account and most other apps you use.

The increased bandwidth has above all boosted the market for public cloud provision. Today, cloud providers offer services that allow you to access virtually unlimited computing power and technologies without having to buy them. Want to implement a data lake on a computer cluster with 1,000 nodes, or maybe just set up a relational database for a couple of minutes? There is no need to physically buy such hardware or software anymore and pay the high upfront costs of buying IT infrastructure. Instead you can rent these resources by the minute and on demand from one of the several cloud providers with just a few mouse clicks (it really is that easy and doesn't take more than a couple of minutes).

Case study 25

Netflix migration into the AWS cloud

In 2008, when Netflix was still following a business model of shipping DVDs to its customers, a database in its data centre broke down. The result was that for three days Netflix was unable to ship DVDs and serve its customers.

This was the moment when Netflix took the decision to change its data architecture and move away from a vertically scaled system in their own data centres to a horizontally scaled, distributed system – in the AWS cloud.[lxiv]

The migration into the cloud was completed in 2016. Today, Netflix maintains an extremely complex and sophisticated data architecture in the AWS cloud to fulfil all its data storage and processing needs, including big-data analytics, recommendation algorithms and other services that are part of the Netflix software. Key reasons for moving into the cloud were that it enabled Netflix to adjust and pay only for the computing power it needs and to accommodate peaks. Furthermore, maintaining its data architecture in the cloud has led to a significant cost reduction compared to maintaining its own data centres.[lxv]

55 | What types of cloud architectures are there?

By considering who provides these remote computing resources and how they can be accessed, we can differentiate between four different cloud models: private, hybrid, public cloud and virtual private cloud.

Private clouds

If a company is using a private cloud, it means it is using proprietary computing resources. These are hosted *within* the company, also called *on-premise*, and are made available to its end-users such as employees of that company. So, for example, with Your Model Car we might have set up our own IT centre including a server farm at a strategically important location, say in Ireland, but

Architecting Data

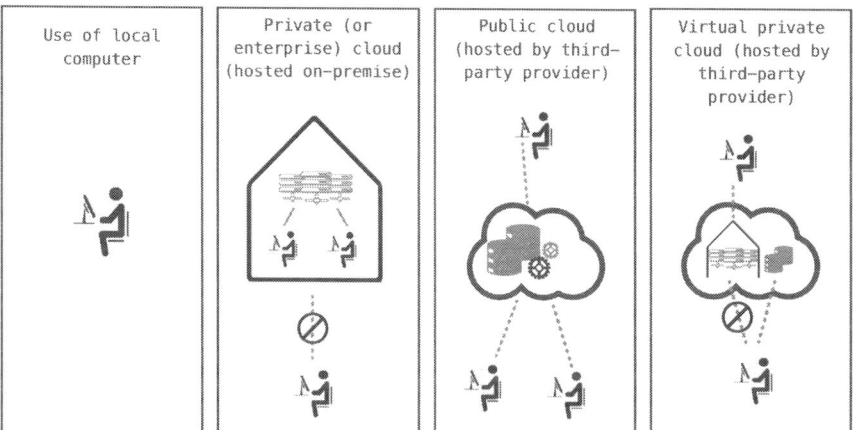

Figure 55.1 Types of cloud architectures

employees from all offices around the world can make use of these computing resources. Some internal applications might run on these servers and be accessed by employees around the world. For example, we might store our sales data on these servers and also run visualization software on them to visualize the latest sales trends in a dashboard. Typically, such an application would be accessed through a regular web browser by the employees. Note that in this case no additional software would have to be installed on the local computers of the employees. Instead, all they would need is a functioning web browser and a connection to the servers by means of the *intranet*. As opposed to the *internet*, an intranet is a network of connected computers that are not accessible to the public but only to a dedicated user group. That means they do not have a public but a private IP address.

Public clouds

A public cloud differs from a private cloud in two ways:

- The access to the remote servers does not happen through a dedicated *intranet* but through the public *internet*. That means that the servers have a public IP address that can in principle be accessed from any computer that is connected to the World Wide Web. Actually, "addressed" is more accurate here than "accessed". Even though the servers can be *addressed* worldwide from the public internet, the *actual access* will typically be subject to an *identity and access management* (IAM) system, i.e. you have to log in using certain credentials. In this way access is restricted to a specific user group that has valid accounts and the right password.
- The computer resources are not owned by the company itself but by a third-party provider. These third-party providers own large server farms from which resources can be rented. That means that if you rent, say, a database system from a public cloud provider, this database system runs on a computer cluster or server that might be used by another user at the

same time. The fact that a given computer resource is physically shared and accessed by various customers makes a lot of companies feel uneasy.

Virtual private clouds

Some companies want the perks of a private cloud without having to buy their own servers. That is, they want to have their own intranet of computing resources that is not accessible by the public internet and that runs on servers dedicated to the company so it is shielded from unwanted access. But they shy away from the costs of buying and maintaining their own computer resources. Public cloud providers have developed solutions to satisfy exactly this need: *virtual private clouds* (VPCs).

If a company rents a VPC from a third-party cloud provider, the computer resources are the same as for public cloud services, i.e. they are located in the public cloud. However, a certain level of separation between the VPC and the public cloud servers is provided. This is usually achieved by physically dedicating specific servers to the user of the VPC and allocating to them a specific IP-subnet that is only addressable by a specific user group, i.e. the company renting the VPC. While the physical servers of a VPC belong to the same hardware pool as the computers of the public cloud, there is a level of isolation from the hardware that is used for the public cloud.

Hybrid clouds

Companies using *hybrid cloud* architectures mix private and public cloud concepts. That means they have their own on-premise private cloud infrastructure that is augmented by services from the public cloud. The divide could be set up in any conceivable way. Often, companies want their sensitive data to be kept on their proprietary IT infrastructure, while applications that are less sensitive or are even meant to be accessed by the public run on the public cloud infrastructure.

In Your Model Car, for example, we might have a database containing employee data (name, contact data, position, etc.) running on an internal server which is only accessible through the intranet by employees. This database could be used by employees to find the contact details of their colleagues (like an internal LinkedIn). On the other hand, we might host the Your Model Car app on the public cloud.

> **Case study 26**
>
> **Hybrid cloud architecture to reduce storage costs**
>
> A pharmaceutical company maintains its data architecture and entire IT infrastructure on-premise. It increasingly engages in the analysis of big data with ML methods to create artificial intelligence (AI) systems to improve its business processes in a wide range of fields.

> Some of these analyses are extremely computationally demanding, and the developers complain that if they use the computer resources to develop their models, the internal IT resources are not potent enough to maintain the daily operations at the same time.
>
> To solve this problem, the company sets up a hybrid cloud architecture. Its normal operations are run on its own IT infrastructure on-premise, and the developers of the data science and AI department are allocated their own IT resources in the cloud which they can use on demand.

56 | What types of cloud services are there?

Irrespective of the cloud model used, there are different *cloud services*. Cloud service refers to which part of the remote computing resources is rented. To understand what exactly is meant by that and distinguish between the different types of cloud services, it helps to look at the concept of a *client–server model*.

The client–server model

Running a software program on your computer or an app on your smartphone requires a lot of components. Let's consider what is needed for you to display an Excel spreadsheet containing sales data on your computer:

- Hardware:
  - ❏ Disk storage and a file system
  - ❏ Monitor
  - ❏ Processor and other hardware components
- Software:
  - ❏ Operating system
  - ❏ A file system where the software and the data it uses is stored
  - ❏ The software itself
  - ❏ The data you want to display

Traditionally, we would execute a given piece of software or application on our local computer. That means that the entire workload and all the necessary components would run on this local computer, i.e. you have the hardware, the operating system, the software and so forth.

In a client–server model, this workload to execute a given piece of software or program is *shared* between a local computer (client) and a remote server (server). Traditionally, transferring data between a local client and a remote server was simply not viable due to insufficient bandwidth. However, with the spread of broadband and fibre optics the workload could easily be distributed across several computers.

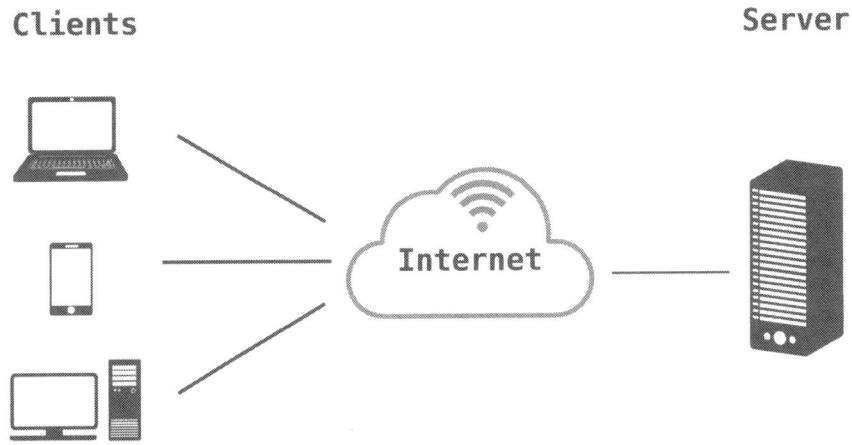

Figure 56.1 Client–server model

The main idea behind the client-server model is that the client is relieved from some of the workload to run an application or software. The division of the workload between the client and server can be cut along all conceivable dimensions. We classify the different cloud services depending on how this division of the workload is set up. They are commonly classified into three groups that are defined by what workload is borne by the client and server respectively:

Table 56.1 Types of cloud services

Type	Description	Example and use case
Infrastructure as a Service (IaaS)	Rent physical computing infrastructure (hardware); also referred to as bare metal cloud.	You want to gain access to hardware only temporarily and hence do not want to buy this hardware, e.g. entire server, computer clusters, storage, etc.
Platform as a Service (PaaS)	Rent the necessary hardware and software components to provide a platform to develop, run and manage applications.	You want to rent an environment to develop and deploy applications and software. Mostly used by developers.
Software as a Service (SaaS)	Deliver entire applications and software to users; also known as cloud application services.	Gmail Suite (including Drive, Documents etc.), Dropbox, Salesforce, Cisco WebEx conferences.

Arguably, the most tangible and understandable concept is SaaS, where the entirety of the workload is on the side of the server. An example is an email service such as Google Mail. With this service, the only thing that a client needs is a functioning web browser. The application along with its data (the emails), the operating system and all the hardware run on servers of the third-party provider. (However, Google also provides its Gmail app for mobile devices, where the application runs on the smartphone while the server provides

Architecting Data

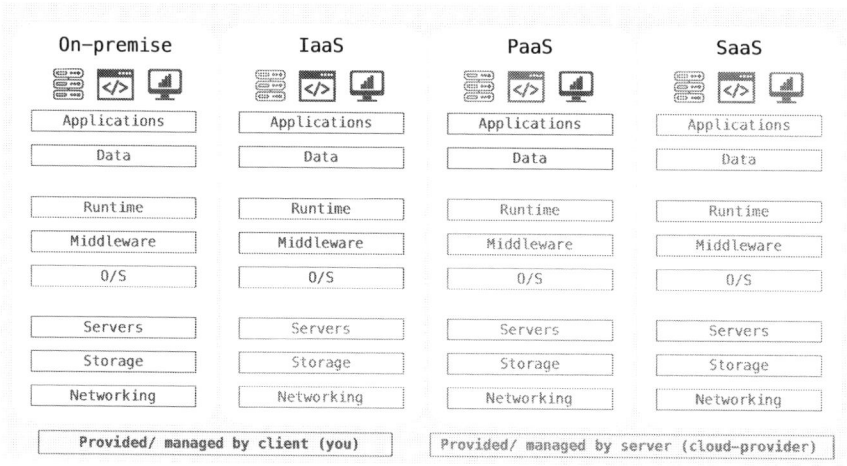

Figure 56.2 IaaS, PaaS and SaaS

everything else, though it also offers the functionality to store some of the data locally.) A lot of online services, apps and software that we use today follow an SaaS model.

At the other extreme is the IaaS model, where only the hardware is provided. This is also referred to as a bare metal cloud service. IaaS is usually used by companies, rather than end customers. It allows companies to rent hardware and infrastructure and set up and customize the hardware to meet their unique requirements. In IaaS the user is responsible for the entire software environment, including the setup of the operating system for the computers.

PaaS is the middle ground between these two extremes. In the PaaS model you rent the hardware along with some basic software, notably the operating system and usually some databases. This model is mostly used by developers to develop, maintain and run software, applications or websites.

The pricing systems (if the services come with costs) for all of these cloud services follow a pay-as-you-use model. That means you pay for the service only by the minute or by the gigabyte (GB). For example, renting a simple computer resource with two central processing units (CPUs) and 8 GB of RAM will typically cost less than a few cents per hour.

Case study 27

Data visualization as SaaS

Technology and software providers increasingly offer their services and products via the cloud. A facility management company makes use of data visualization software hosted in the cloud as SaaS. Its technicians are equipped with tablets with which they can access dashboards that visualize data about buildings, such as the energy and electricity consumption.

57 | What are the advantages and disadvantages of using cloud services?

Advantages of cloud services

A lot of us decide to rent an apartment instead of buying it because doing so offers a lot of advantages. For example, some people might be unable to handle the high upfront costs of buying their home, others might shy away from the effort of having to maintain and renovate an apartment, and yet others want to have the flexibility to move at any time.

The same principles apply to renting an IT infrastructure versus buying it. Renting it on demand with cloud services has several advantages.

Scalability without upfront costs

You have access to unlimited computing resources at the click of a mouse without having to invest in expensive hardware or software with upfront costs. Furthermore, you do not need to go through the hassle of setting up your own IT infrastructure, which tends to be time- and resource-consuming.

The convenience of not having to acquire, maintain and design your own IT system should not be underestimated. It has led to even digitally driven companies using the cloud. Consider Netflix. You would think that making the investment to acquire its own IT infrastructure would be worth it for such a digital player whose business model is based on providing a streaming service. But no, today Netflix implements the majority of its IT architecture in the cloud (see Case Study 25).

Flexibility

You have an enormous degree of flexibility with the cloud. Because you typically pay by the minute (or user, or volume transferred), you can start renting resources now and stop renting them the next minute.

This allows you to avoid short-lived shortcomings of your computational capacity. For example, let's assume that in Your Model Car we offer our customers the service to track their customized model car order through the production, packaging and shipment processes. This service will likely be subject to strong fluctuations. For instance, in the weeks leading up to Christmas the service will probably be used a lot more than during quieter times. Such peaks in computational resource demand can easily be satisfied with cloud services by just renting the required resources on demand.

The flexibility also avoids resources standing idle. Let's assume that to deal with such peaks we upgraded our proprietary IT infrastructure. While we would have been able to deal with the peak, afterwards the additional resources would stand idle (see figure 57-4) – a waste of investment.

In short: the extreme flexibility of cloud services enables you to match and satisfy your computational needs perfectly at any given point in time.

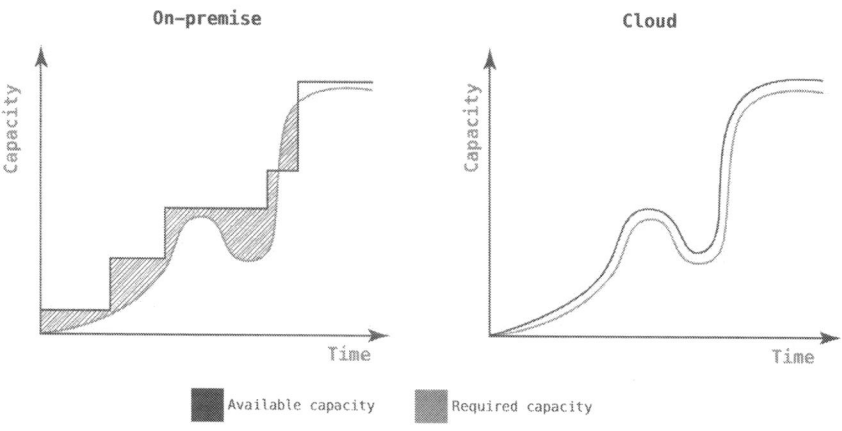

Figure 57.1 Flexibility of the cloud

Maintenance

If you rent an apartment and repair or renovation work is needed, the landlord is responsible, not you. In the same way, you do not need to worry about the maintenance and upgrading of IT systems if you make use of cloud services. Maintaining and upgrading systems to the latest standards is included in the price and happens seamlessly in the background, so that you do not need to deal with servers breaking down, problems arising due to outdated software versions or the like.

Security

Security is not your responsibility with the cloud. A lot of companies regard this as a reason not to make use of cloud services, or at least it causes them some concern – especially in Germany, where companies and people in general are very cautious about data privacy and security. Yet in our experience the fact that security is the responsibility of the cloud provider is mostly an advantage.

It is true that by storing data in the cloud you physically give away this data to be stored on some server that is owned by the cloud provider. That seems scary at first, because you give away the responsibility to protect this data. However, you typically put the data in good hands and you still remain in control of how it is processed, encrypted and stored. Furthermore, virtually all cloud providers offer the option to choose on which of their server farms the data is held. And all their networks are global, so there are abundant choices.

Concerning the security of the data, the cloud providers do their utmost to guarantee the highest standards to keep their customers' data secure and shield it from unauthorized access or unwanted loss. Given that these companies have been specializing in these kinds of services for years and employ the world's most talented engineers, the data is likely in better hands in the cloud than on your own premises.

The Ultimate Data and AI Guide

Disadvantages of cloud services

While making use of cloud services offers a lot of benefits, there are some disadvantages that should not be underestimated.

Security

This is the flipside of the last advantage. While cloud providers invest millions of dollars in security, it is true that when storing or processing data in the public cloud, you physically give away the data to be stored on the computers of another company, and this always comes with a certain level of risk.

Lock-in

Arguably, the biggest disadvantage of using cloud services is the danger of a lock-in with a given provider.

You would not believe just how easy it is to set up your infrastructure in the cloud and get into the cloud. There are dedicated solution and data architects and all sorts of support from the cloud providers. Amazon even provides its so-called Snow Mobile, a truck that picks up physical hard drives from customers whose data is too voluminous (in the exabyte range) to load into the cloud via the internet.[lxvi]

Thus, getting your data into the cloud is incredibly easy and is facilitated by the cloud provider, because they will do anything to get you into their systems as a customer. However, the way out of the cloud is far more cumbersome. The more you commit yourself to a certain cloud service provider, the higher the danger and costs of lock-in. This lock-in can happen in two ways:

- Getting data out again is difficult. As helpful as cloud providers are with getting your data into their systems, they are not helpful with getting it out of there again. The higher your involvement with a cloud provider, the higher your degree of path-dependency, and therefore the higher the costs to migrate your data and resources out of the premises of the cloud provider.
- Unless you have the weight to negotiate your own specific contracts with a cloud provider, you are subject to changes in their prices and rates over time.

Price

The pricing model of cloud providers might not work in your favour. While using the cloud saves you the high upfront costs of IT infrastructure, in the long run the pay-as-use model may end up costing more than having your own servers and software, especially if a cloud provider increases its prices.

Data storage locations

Every major cloud provider has a global network of data centres at its disposal. You can choose in which of these data centres you want your data to physically reside. While it is great to have this control, when you choose to store your data in different countries across the globe, you have the added complexity of the rules and regulations that apply to the flow of data between countries and the data storage laws in each country. For example, China has a completely different set of regulations governing the collection, processing and storage of data than the EU. While something might be perfectly fine in one jurisdiction, it might be illegal in another one.

Should a company go into the cloud or not?

Given these advantages and disadvantages of making use of cloud services, the answer to whether or not a company should go into the cloud is (as always): it depends. It depends on what the requirements and needs of the company are, which should be part of the overarching data strategy and architecture.

There are some strong selling points for the cloud, and these become even more pronounced when using the data in a company to implement sophisticated use cases including ML and the creation of AI systems. But even if the requirements are clear, each company has to weigh up the benefits versus shortcomings in dependency, flexibility, pricing, security etc. – not only on a company-wide level, but from one use case to another.

In practice, for most companies the answer lies somewhere in the middle between an on-premise infrastructure and fully cloud-based architecture. They want to have some of their architecture implemented with proprietary systems and then augment and complement other parts, e.g. certain applications or use cases, in the cloud on demand. The trend of setting up hybrid architectures will likely continue.

Case study 28

The way into the cloud for a global insurance company

A global insurance company offers products in its three business units: health, life and property insurance. The chief IT architect is charged with the task of examining which cloud technologies could be adopted, and how. Quite quickly, they realize that a hybrid cloud architecture is the way forward. They want to establish criteria for when to move an application that is currently running on the on-premise infrastructure into the public cloud and when to leave it in the private on-premise cloud.

After a first round of research, it is clear that some applications need to stay on-premise permanently due to either regulatory requirements or the complexity of lifting and shifting legacy, mainframe-based applications into the cloud. Other applications are based on proprietary software and are thus also difficult to move.

In contrast to that, younger applications or applications with low complexity and based on newer technologies are adequate to run to the public cloud because they can be lifted and migrated into the public cloud without too much effort. Moreover, it is advantageous to do the development of new applications, especially ML- and AI-driven ones, in the cloud because it requires software packages, computing power, flexible massive storage possibilities and architecture elements that are not available on-premise.

Another decisive factor is the cost structure. For some applications it is cheaper both in the short and long run to use cloud services, while for others existing IT-infrastructure can be used with barely any additional cost except maintenance.

For supporting application building in the public cloud in a hybrid cloud architecture, a performant and secure connection needs to be established between the on-premise cloud and the public cloud. As a next step, each system in each of the business units will be reviewed and classified to be run on-premise or in the cloud according to set criteria and guidelines, and a new target architecture in a hybrid environment will be designed.

58 | What is a serverless architecture?

The range of services that cloud providers offer continues to grow to satisfy all possible needs that cloud users might have. One of the services that a lot of companies have increasingly turned to is *serverless architectures*. In serverless architectures, a cloud user provides only an application or function (i.e. a piece of code) and outsources the entire backend and management thereof to the cloud provider.

For example, in Your Model Car we might offer our customers a service to predict when an order will be delivered. This requires tracking the product and an algorithm or model to predict the remaining delivery time. We could host these things on our own IT infrastructure. But this involves maintaining, patching and updating our own servers and making sure that in the event of a failure it is debugged as soon as possible. In short: there is a whole lot of complexity and work that comes with using your own backend.

The idea of serverless architectures is to save yourself all the complexity that maintaining a backend brings with it: "Focus on your application, not the infrastructure." This is achieved by simply giving the cloud provider a container that contains the relevant application and code. This container is then executed by the cloud provider, which takes care of setting up and maintaining the entire backend.

This provisioning of the backend happens dynamically and on request, and it is usually event driven. That means that in the Your Model Car example, the container and service are only executed when a customer makes a request via our website to get an estimate of the delivery time.

Architecting Data

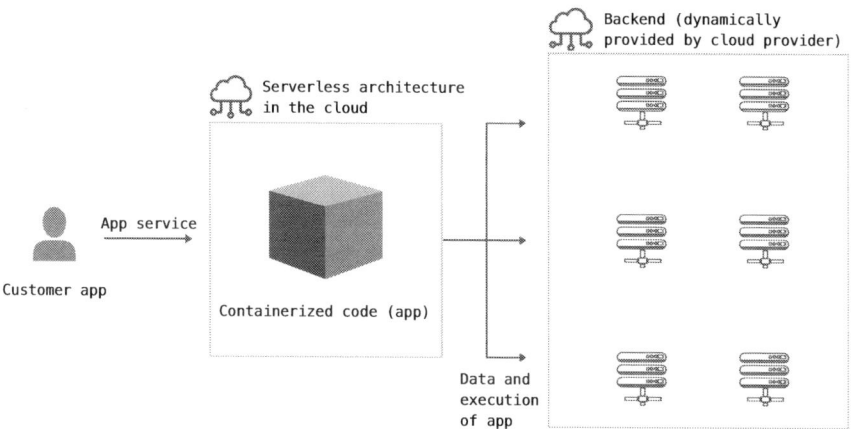

Figure 58.1 Schematic overview of a serverless architecture

Table 58.1 What is a serverless architecture and why does it matter?

What is a serverless architecture?

A serverless architecture is a cloud model in which the cloud provider essentially takes care of the entire backend, i.e. dynamically allocating and provisioning computing resources to run an app or program.

That means that the customer only has to provide a container with a certain application, a piece of code or function, which is then executed on request.

The cloud provider takes care of managing and scaling the computer resources dynamically. If no execution requests are present, no resources are provided and the customer pays nothing. Likewise, if there is a surge in execution requests, the cloud provider automatically takes care of providing the necessary resources.

Why does it matter?

Just like other cloud services, serverless architectures are convenient in certain situations. They save users having to administer and maintain their own backend, so that developers can focus on the app.

Furthermore, their pricing model is very attractive. Unlike in PaaS, where computer resources are rented and paid for by the minute, in serverless architectures you pay per execution. Thus, if there are no executions, there are no costs – so no resources stand idle.

At first glance, serverless architectures resemble PaaS models, but there is a difference: with serverless architectures the execution of an application or a piece of code is ephemeral and event-triggered. Code is only run if a certain event happens, and if the event doesn't happen, you don't have to pay. Rather than paying to rent servers as hardware and paying for computing power per minute, in a serverless architecture you pay per execution of your code, e.g. every time a customer requests an estimate of the delivery time.

One of the great benefits of serverless architectures is that the cloud provider takes care of scaling. If there is a sudden surge in requests, the cloud provider automatically scales and provides the necessary resources to handle the requests.

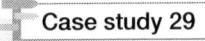

Case study 29

Completely serverless backend

The email-campaign service provider MoonMail has been using serverless architecture as a service to the fullest. Its backend architecture is fully event driven and uses AWS Lambda as its only computing service. The roughly 70 functions allow MoonMail to conduct and manage email campaigns. Whenever a user wants to start a campaign through the MoonMail website, this triggers a series of events and functions in the backend so that the necessary computational components in the cloud execute the campaign.[xvii]

59 | What are the popular cloud providers and services?

Today, there are numerous cloud providers, ranging from small niche providers to a few global tech giants. While it is difficult to pin down exact shares in the public cloud market, it is clear that the lion's share of the market is dominated by Amazon, Microsoft, Google, IBM, Oracle and Alibaba. It is estimated that in 2018, AWS alone owned some 47.8% of the IaaS public cloud market, whereas the market share of the second biggest player, Microsoft Azure, stood at some 15.5%.[lxviii] Each of these companies owns a global network of data centres that are strategically located in different regions around the globe.

Amazon entered the cloud market first and gained an edge that competitors have not been able to beat yet. However, Microsoft's Azure cloud has been catching up in terms of market share, which has been the goal of Microsoft CEO Satya Nadella and his "cloud first" strategy.[lxix]

All of these key players offer a largely similar range of cloud services, ranging from renting small computers (e.g. single-core CPU, 8 GB RAM) to full-fledged computer clusters with all sorts of software and services included. Likewise, all of them have invested heavily in compliance with country-specific laws (e.g. the GDPR) and in security. The big cloud providers' services are also within a similar price range (an exact comparison of costs is difficult, though, because of different pricing models, discounts and price cuts). Therefore, the choice of cloud provider comes down to the individual desires and needs of a given customer.

Table 59-1 overviews some selected services offered by the biggest cloud providers, AWS, Microsoft Azure and Google Cloud Platform. While there are differences in the extent, types and pricing of their services, all of them offer basic standard services that are comparable. We had to limit ourselves to the most basic ones, given that their portfolios contain hundreds of services.

Architecting Data

Table 59.1 Popular cloud providers and services

What are some popular AWS cloud services?

Amazon holds the biggest market share of the cloud services. As of 2019, AWS offers a comprehensive set of tools spanning over 150 cloud services[lxx] – and still counting.

The services that AWS offers range from simple IaaS to comprehensive and sophisticated SaaS for which tutorials and certifications are offered.

Here are some of the most widely used AWS services:

- **AWS EC2:** Elastic Compute Cloud, the most basic IaaS service; provides resizable computer capacity.
- **AWS S3:** Simple Storage Service; another very basic feature for easily scalable storage space.
- **AWS DynamoDB:** Scalable non-relational database.
- **AWS Relational Database Service:** Enables users to set up, operate and scale all sorts of relational database systems.
- **AWS Lambda:** Provides users with serverless architectures.
- **AWS VPC:** Enables users to set up their own virtual private cloud.
- **AWS SageMaker:** Service for building, training and deploying ML models.

What are some popular MS Azure cloud services?

Microsoft Azure has been trying to catch up with AWS in terms of market share since entering the cloud market in 2010. MS Azure offers a similarly wide portfolio of services. Here are some popular ones:

- **Virtual machines:** Provision of virtual Windows or Linux servers.
- **Azure SQL Database:** Relational database system.
- **Azure Cosmos DB:** Distributed non-relational database that supports various data models.
- **Azure Functions:** Serverless architecture service.
- **ML:** Service for building, training and deploying ML models.
- **Azure Bot Service:** Service for creating bots for various use cases, such as virtual assistants or Q&A bots.

What are some popular Google Cloud Platform cloud services?

Since the Google Cloud Platform launched in 2008, Google has been sharing the computing resources that it uses to run its internal operations such as its search engine and YouTube. These are employed to provide a portfolio spanning close to 100 services, including:

- **Compute Engine:** The equivalent of EC2's and Azure's virtual machines provides computing capacity.
- **Cloud Storage:** Scalable storage.
- **BigQuery:** Provides a serverless, highly scalable DWH architecture.
- **Datastore:** Distributed, non-relational database.
- **Cloud SQL:** Fully managed, relational database.
- **Cloud Functions:** Serverless architecture service.

5 Managing Data in a Company

5_1 People and job roles

60 | What does a chief data and analytics officer do?

The chief data and analytics officer (CDAO) is the highest role with regard to data, analytics and AI. Depending on the industry and the strategic importance and maturity of data and analytics in a given company, this role can be a board member, or a senior vice president, vice president or director level. Usually, the role of a chief data officer (CDO) and of a chief analytics officer (CAO) is combined into a single role, as there are many synergies and overlaps. There can be regional versions of a CDAO that report to a global CDAO. As analytics includes machine learning (ML), artificial intelligence (AI) usually also falls within the realm of the CDAO.

Table 60.1 Role of a chief data and analytics officer

What is the CDAO's role?	The CDAO is the head of data, analytics and AI in the company. They are responsible for the overall governance of how data is managed and utilized within the organization. Responsibilities can include: ▸ Developing a data, analytics and AI strategy and roadmap ▸ Setting data governance policies ▸ Developing the data organization ▸ Managing overarching data and analytics capabilities ▸ Managing the data, analytics and AI product and project portfolio ▸ Managing and steering the data, analytics and AI budget ▸ Managing and steering the data, analytics and AI platform ▸ Owning the data architecture ▸ Determining the toolstack for data, analytics and AI projects
What tools should they know?	▸ PowerPoint and Excel ▸ Jira and Confluence
What skills/ experience/ knowledge should they have?	▸ Strong experience in developing and executing a data, analytics and AI strategy and roadmap ▸ Deep understanding of the business model of the company ▸ Strong experience in data governance ▸ Strong experience in data architecture ▸ Strong experience in steering data projects and budgets ▸ Good understanding of ML and business intelligence (BI) ▸ Convincing and assertive personality ▸ Strong leadership skills

Managing Data in a Company

A typical CDAO...	<ul><li>Has previous leadership experience as a senior decision maker</li><li>Is experienced in creating tangible value with data and analytics</li><li>Is experienced in managing data assets</li></ul>
Average salary	US$181,323[lxxi]

Case study 30

Usama Fayyad – the first chief data officer

Usama Fayyad became the world's first chief data officer when he was appointed as Yahoo's chief data officer and executive vice president in 2004. The title of chief data officer actually started off as a joke. Back then, Yahoo had a culture of irrelevant titles. During an initial meeting with the executive team including Jerry Yang, co-founder of Yahoo, he was asked what he should be called in the company and the title of "chief data officer" came up, causing much laughter of the meeting participants.[lxxii]

Today, the role of the chief data officer is well established and the vast majority of major companies have hired and appointed CDOs.

61 | What does a data architect do?

Table 61.1 Role of a data architect

What is the data architect's role?	A data architect is responsible for devising, drafting and realizing the data architecture of a department or company. That means they are in close contact with the relevant stakeholders of the business department to find out the business objectives and the resulting data requirements. Their job is then to translate the business requirements into an architecture that is able to fulfil all of these requirements. In designing the target state of a data architecture they have to consider what data should be collected and how it should be stored, processed, accessed, etc. They are also responsible for implementing this architecture, which involves answering questions such as what technology stack should be used, whether the architecture should be (partially) implemented in the cloud or on-premise, and how data security can be guaranteed. Furthermore, they are responsible for maintaining this architecture and adjusting it if the data requirements of the company change.
What tools should they know?	<ul><li>All sorts of data storage and processing technologies, including (non-) relational databases, distributed systems and big-data tools.</li><li>Solid knowledge of cloud services and technologies, e.g. Amazon Web Services (AWS), Google Cloud Platform and Microsoft Azure.</li></ul>
What skills/ experience/ knowledge should they have?	<ul><li>Ability to identify the data requirements of a company or department and create an architecture that meets these requirements</li><li>Profound knowledge of all sorts of data storage and processing technologies</li><li>Knowledge of cloud services, including the ability to design architectures involving cloud technologies</li><li>Application design and basic knowledge of software development</li><li>Knowledge of computer clusters and distributed systems</li></ul>

A typical data architect...	▶ Has a degree in computer science or IT ▶ Is experienced in designing and setting up data infrastructure and architectures
Average salary	US$115,799[lxxiii]

62 | What does a database administrator do?

Table 62.1 Role of a database administrator

What is the database administrator's role?	A database administrator is responsible for maintaining a database to make sure that it is available to the users and performing properly, and that the data has integrity. They serve as the point of contact if somebody wants to access data in the database.
What tools should they know?	▶ All sorts of relational and non-relational databases, e.g. SQL databases, MongoDB, Neo4J, etc. ▶ Hadoop and related technologies, e.g. Hive and Pig ▶ Knowledge of data processing tools, e.g. Spark
What skills/experience/knowledge should they have?	▶ Implementing and maintaining all sorts of database systems ▶ Knowledge of cloud technologies
A typical database administrator...	Has a degree in computer science or IT
Average salary	US$72,874[lxxiv]

63 | What other job roles are involved in creating and maintaining a data architecture?

In order to build, develop and maintain a data architecture at a company many more roles are required. Going into the details of all of them would go beyond the scope of this book. But here a few more relevant job roles with a brief description of their responsibilities:

Table 63.1 Role of an ETL developer, data quality specialist and data artist

Job role	Responsibilities
Data integration expert / ETL developer	This role is closely related to the database administrator. A data integration expert / ETL developer builds the data loading, pre-processing and integration scripts for a BI solution. They take care of creating and implementing the path from the data sources into the relevant database systems. This is especially relevant in the implementation of data warehouses, where data needs to be extracted, transformed and loaded into the relevant database systems. Once the data storage technologies are set up, they are maintained by the database administrator.
Data quality specialist	A data quality specialist profiles data to assess and monitor its quality and defines improvement measures to make data more fit for use.
Data artist / visualization expert	The data artist / virtualization expert builds dashboards, reports and other visual artefacts. Their job is to make the data accessible and understandable to the relevant business departments through appropriate data visualizations. This requires expertise in statistics and design, and on top of that some creativity. Data artists thus bridge the gap between the IT, business and analytics departments.

5_2 Data governance and Democratization

64 | What are data governance and democratization and why does data need to be governed and democratized?

If you have read the preceding chapters in this book, you should understand why data is a key asset in any organization.

Imagine you run your own company and you are the only employee. In this case, all data is produced, managed and used by the same person – you. Hence, when you use the data, you know where it came from, what quality you can expect and what it contains. Now imagine you work for a company with thousands or even hundreds of thousands of employees. That means most of the data is produced, managed and used by other people who work with you. Finding the right data, getting access to it and understanding its meaning, its quality and how it can be used compliantly can be a huge challenge – particularly when you want to use data that you have not used before. It logically follows, then, that somebody needs to take care of the data to ensure that it is usable for others in the organization. This is where data governance and data democratization come into play.

Table 64.1 What are data governance and data democratization and why do they matter?

What are data governance and data democratization?
Data governance is the discipline of managing data to ensure it can be (re)used by people in the organization in an effective and compliant way. It is a combination of processes, roles, tools and policies.
Data democratization is the idea that organizations perform better when data can be used by as many employees as possible. It strongly draws on training all staff and giving them the right tools to apply self-service analytics.

Why do they matter?
Data governance makes data more protected, trustworthy, findable, usable and understandable, while data democratization ensures that value creation out of data is widespread across the organization. Both disciplines can strongly support each other and increase the value of data exponentially.

Data governance

Data governance is the discipline of managing data to ensure that it can be (re)used by people in the organization in an effective and compliant way. Although the goal of data governance is pretty clear and definitions of data governance are similar across organizations, how to implement data governance to achieve the goal is much less obvious. So the way data governance is implemented can vary significantly across different companies. Lightweight implementations can involve some basic rules for how data is documented, managed and shared that are followed organization-wide. More heavyweight data governance programmes can include setting up new roles and responsibilities within the organization, establishing governance committees or steering councils, training people across the organization, and implementing new processes and tools that support data governance.

The benefits of data governance can be manifold. They typically include:

- The reduction of negative business impacts resulting from poor data quality
- Increased trust in using data from other departments for innovation and process improvement
- Higher data compliance through better controls
- Some significant efficiency gains when using data, as the user can find and understand the data more quickly

Without data governance, however, there is a risk of chaos, as nobody really knows what is inside the data and synergies between data users are difficult to realize. Each user has to deal with data quality separately and cannot trust other people's data.

Data democratization

In a data-driven organization, employees use data from across business departments to improve their daily work. *Data democratization* is the idea that an organization performs better when as many employees as possible can use data from across the organization.

One element of data democratization is ensuring that data is ready for others to use, and here data governance can help. Another element is giving non-expert data users tools to easily process, combine, transform and visualize data; for example, with self-service BI and dashboarding tools and easy-to-use data science tools that work on a drag-and-drop basis.

65 | What are the key elements of data governance and data democratization?

Table 65-1 outlines the key elements of data governance and democratization. We go through each of them in the next sections.

Table 65.1 What are the key elements of data governance and data democratization?

What?	How?	Why?
Making data more findable and accessible	Registering data in a central data catalogue and providing data via standardized repositories	So employees do not have to ask around anymore to find the data they need

What?	How?	Why?
Making data understandable and sharing knowledge on data	Describing data fields and tables with the help of definitions and guidelines in a central business glossary and/or data dictionary as part of the data catalogue	So employees do not have to ask around anymore to understand what a data field actually means or how it is calculated
Making data more trustworthy and improving the quality of data	Assessing and documenting the quality of data and identified problems in a central business glossary and/or data dictionary, and establishing processes for reporting and improving data quality problems, e.g. by using data quality tools	So employees know about potential quality problems within the data before they use it and have clear paths to better data quality
Empowering the data user with self-service BI and analytics	Providing tools and guidelines for working with data to the average user, e.g. for agile data processing, self-service BI and creating dashboards and visuals	So employees can create more value out of data
Ensuring data privacy, security and compliance (see 5_3)	Establishing processes to ensure data protection, security and compliance	So your company does not have to pay penalties and employees do not end up in prison

66 | How can we make data more findable and accessible?

The biggest challenge when using data in an organization is actually finding the data in the first place. Most organizations are quite complex and data is scattered across business departments and IT systems. If you shop for furniture, there is one central place where you can find the current selection of products on offer: the catalogue of the furniture store. The idea of the *data catalogue* is similar. You want to make all available items easy to find for your customers, here the data users.

To achieve this, you need to set up processes that require each data source to register which data is available to others in the organization. There are many software tools for managing an enterprise data catalogue in an effective way. These tools offer many functionalities to describe which data is available and what it actually contains. For example, such information can be extracted directly from the existing table structures in the data sources. Moreover, digital workflows can be managed to support data stewards entering further knowledge about the characteristics and the content of the data in the data catalogue.

After finding the data in the data catalogue, the next big challenge for the data user is getting access to the data. Providing data via standardized repositories can be a good solution; for example, by loading the most frequently used data items into an enterprise data lake. When a lot of data is made available via a data lake, access approval processes need to be established for applying and getting the rights granted for data access to these central repositories. Digital workflows for data access can support the data user in applying for such data access rights in a standardized way, while ensuring that data is used in a compliant and secure way.

67 | How can we make data more understandable and share knowledge on data?

Data can be very complex and there are lots of data sets throughout an organization. Every data field can have a very particular meaning and format that we need to understand in order to work with the data. As a data scientist or business analyst, there are datasets we work with very frequently and know well – but when we work with a new dataset for the first time, it can be like a puzzle. Which tables does it contain? What does each data field contain? What format does it need to follow? Is the data field a primary or foreign key (📑 31)? How is it related to other datasets? When was the data last changed or updated? What we essentially need is data about the data we work with, which is called metadata.

Table 67.1 What are data dictionaries and data catalogues?

What are data dictionaries and data catalogues
A data dictionary is defined by the *IBM Dictionary of Computing* as a "centralized repository of information about data such as meaning, relationships to other data, origin, usage, and format".[lxxv] In simple terms, a data dictionary contains technical data about data (also known as metadata). You can think of it as a Wikipedia for company-wide data. A data catalogue usually contains a data dictionary, but it also contains other descriptions of the data – for example, how a data field is calculated and what the business meaning of the data is – often in the form of a business glossary.
Why do they matter?
If organizations have a multitude of data sources, it is easy to get lost in the complexities of the data landscape. Data dictionaries and data catalogues tell you what the data actually means, where it comes from and where to find it.

People in your organization who have knowledge of various datasets can contribute this knowledge to a data dictionary or data catalogue, which is a central repository that holds metadata. For example, take the data field "Customer Lifetime Value", which follows a certain definition and formula to compute the customer lifetime value. This is very valuable business information, but it is difficult to determine the definition and formula – unless they are documented by the business department that is responsible for them.

If everyone contributes, it is fairly easy to fill a data catalogue with very useful information and bring it to life. In return, everyone benefits if they have to work with datasets they have not worked with before. In addition, it is possible to automatically derive more technical metadata using some tools available on the market, e.g. table structures and data field formats. Contributors can then focus more on the business meaning of these data fields, which are usually stored in a business glossary.

In the best case, when properly set up, we can enter a business term in the data catalogue and business glossary tool and it will directly point us to the right data fields and the right data sets, so we can avoid searching for the data that we need for our analysis across the organization.

68 | How can we make data more trustworthy and improve the quality of data?

Once we find new data to work with and want to use it for our analysis, we are naturally concerned about the quality of the data. The "garbage in, garbage out" principle applies to data science and ML. In some cases, it is very obvious when data quality is poor; for instance, when a lot of fields are not filled at all. In other cases, it is harder to assess the quality of a dataset; for instance, when postcodes do not match addresses, which might not be visible at a first glance.

It would help if somebody specialized in assessing and improving the most frequently used and most important data sets in the company. Luckily, there is such a role: the Data Quality Manager or Data Quality Specialist. This person's main job is to ensure that the quality of the most important data assets is regularly checked and problems are reported back to the data producers.

There are many tools for data quality profiling that can assist in assessing the quality of data. Other tools focus on handling specific types of data quality problems. Tools and services for address validation, for instance, can correct spelling errors in addresses and incorrect postcodes. Entity resolution tools can remove customer records and merge those that refer to the same customer.

69 | How can we empower the data user with self-service BI and analytics?

As discussed in 📓 64, the idea of data democratization is that organizations perform better when data can be used by as many employees as possible. The central goal is to empower users by providing them with data so that they can draw insights from it; for example, by using BI methods such as reports.

These are the key steps that an organization needs to take in order to achieve data democratization:

- Make data findable and accessible. Here the data catalogue and standardized data access processes are essential.
- Ensure the meaning of particular data fields is understandable to the data user. A business glossary and data dictionary are important in order to achieve this.

- Give data users tools that help them to make use of the data in a smart way. This is where self-service BI and analytics tools come into play; for example, Tableau, Qlik and Dataiku. They make it easy for non-expert users to connect to different databases and merge and transform different datasets, in order to create powerful dashboards and conduct insightful analyses using the data.
- Provide training opportunities that equip the average employee with an understanding of how best to work with the new tools provided.

70 | How can data governance and data democratization be implemented?

This is a simple question, but unfortunately it is extremely difficult to answer. There are not many data governance success stories out there.

The biggest challenge of implementing data governance is to convince management that a data governance initiative will provide value for the business. Many business departments need to participate to make it a successful initiative, as data usually crosses departmental borders. Communicating the value of data governance to all important stakeholders in the organization is therefore a critical success factor. It is key to convince a very senior businessperson to become a sponsor early on.

Table 70.1 Data governance zones

Data Governance Zone	Zone 1, Governed Data	Zone 2, Semi-governed Data	Zone 3, Non-governed Data
Implemented data governance measures	• Data steward • Data catalogue • Data access • Data standards • Data dictionary and business glossary • Data quality	• Data steward • Data catalogue • Data access • Data standards	• No requirements

Data governance is difficult to implement in a big bang. It is much better to focus on one business function or one data asset at a time. The scope of data governance can explode quickly if you do not narrow it down to a particular data asset. The best way to start is with a clear focus on a scope that supports the most important business and compliance initiatives at that point in time.

When implementing data governance, we recommend dividing data into three different zones (see Table 70-1):

- *Zone 1, Governed Data:* This is where the most essential data items are located, those that require the most attention and care by the Data Steward who is assigned to this data. In this zone, data needs to be registered in a data catalogue and described properly in the data

dictionary and business glossary. Furthermore, the Data Steward needs to ensure that data quality is monitored and improved and complies with certain data standards.
- *Zone 2, Semi-governed Data:* Data in this zone does not need to be monitored and improved, and nor does it need to be described in the data dictionary or business glossary. But the data steward still needs to create and maintain an entry in the data catalogue about this dataset in order to make it findable and accessible via a standardized process. In some cases, data standards are defined that need to be complied with.
- *Zone 3, Non-governed Data:* All other data is put in this zone, in which there are no formal requirements for how the data is managed.

A great way to start implementing the three data governance zones is to first put all data into Zone 3. Then the data governance workgroup can suggest to the data steering council at each council meeting which data should be added to Zone 1 or Zone 2 – which would require the business department that manages the data to name a Data Steward for this piece of data. Every time a data asset is moved to a higher zone, a very strong reason needs to be presented for why exactly *this* data should be governed more strictly. We should focus on the importance of the data in creating value in the business, and potentially even create a business case for the data moving up into a stricter governance zone.

Using the data governance zone model, the scope of data governance is small at first, but can then be expanded gradually, piece by piece and one dataset at a time, in a way that keeps a strong focus on delivering direct and tangible business value through the data governance programme.

5_3 Data security and protection (privacy)

71 | What is an overview of data security, data protection and data privacy and how do they relate to each other?

Two extremely wide and complex fields relating to data are data security and data protection. Unfortunately, what we see in practice is that among ML and AI practitioners the legal and security sphere surrounding the use of data is often overlooked (or consciously neglected) even though they can be a real obstacle when implementing ML-projects. This might be in part because these are rather involved topics that are related on many levels and therefore are often difficult to separate.

So what are these concepts and how are they related? Data privacy, data protection and data security are difficult to discern, because they touch upon the same concepts and because they mean different things in the languages of different countries. In Figure 71-1 we have tried to untangle, unify and relate these concepts to each other based on a commonly shared understanding of them.

The Ultimate Data and AI Guide

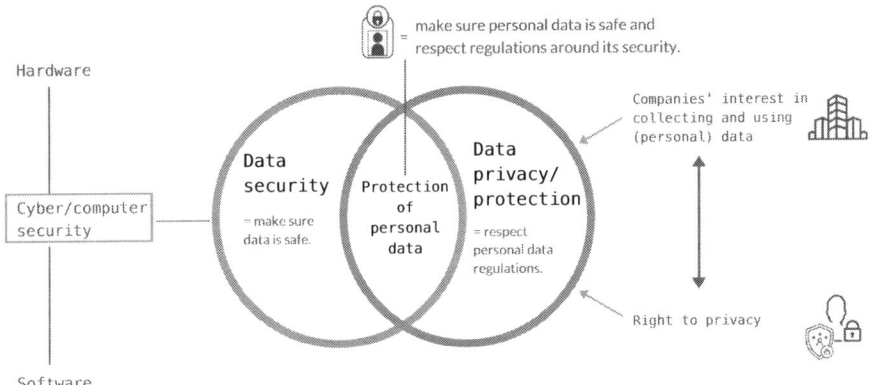

Figure 71.1 Overview of data security and privacy/protection

Data security can be considered a subfield of computer security (also called cybersecurity or IT security), which refers to the protection of computer systems. Computer systems are made up of hardware, software and data, and so data security refers to the protection of data from destructive forces and unwanted access from unauthorized users. This is a sophisticated task both on a technical and organizational level into which companies invest millions of dollars.

Data protection and *data privacy* (also called *information privacy*) essentially mean the same thing: regulations and practices for protecting the privacy rights of individuals with respect to the collection, storage and processing of personal data. In the US the term "data privacy" is established, while Europeans prefer the term "data protection". In this book we use the term "data protection".

The rules governing the handling of personal data differ from country to country. Data protection laws are often a pain for data-driven companies that are trying to collect, process and use as much data as possible (including personal data) – but at the same time the laws are the result of the actions of these companies. Some countries have laxer laws and regulations than others that impose strict rules in order to uphold what is often considered a fundamental human right: the right of an individual to privacy. For example, the Charter of Fundamental Rights of the European Union stipulates that "everyone has the right to the protection of personal data concerning him or her" (Article 8).[lxxvi]

Such data protection laws put a lot of responsibility and burden on entities that collect personal data. Some of these laws aim to ensure the proper collection, storage and processing of personal data, which puts certain requirements on data security. This is where there is an overlap between data security and data protection. While it is in the interests of every company to keep its data secure, there are specific laws that force a company to uphold certain security standards when dealing with *personal data*.

We look into each of these topics in the following sections. Exploring them all in detail would go way beyond the scope of this book, so we keep to the basics you need to get by and give you an overview of the most important concepts.

72 | What is data security and how can it be achieved?

Computer security (also referred to as IT security or cybersecurity[24]) refers to the protection of the assets of a computer system.[lxxvii] There are many assets, but we can distinguish between:

- Hardware (computer, devices etc.)
- Software (applications etc.)
- Data

The hardware and software that a company owns is usually considered to be replaceable. They are commercially available and we can simply rebuy them if they are broken or lost. So while the purchase of certain IT systems or licences to use certain software products can incur significant costs, there is no unique value attached to them because they can usually be replaced.

This is in contrast to the data assets of a computer system or company. These assets are usually unique and therefore irreplaceable. If a computer breaks down, we can easily replace the hardware but its content, the data, is impossible to recreate which is why it deserves special protection. Data security is the field concerned with adequately protecting such data assets. Given that the data often is one of the core assets for a company (especially if a data pool contains sensitive data), its value is critical and so the protection of this data is crucial.

Table 72.1 What is data security and why does it matter?

What is data security?
Data security is the protection of data from destructive forces and the undesired actions of unauthorized users. Unlike other IT assets that a company holds, such as hardware and software, the data assets of a company are typically unique and so the security of data is of paramount importance.
Given that data security is a wide field, the toolbox to ensure that data is secure is rather big. Some popular and widely adopted tools to ensure data security are: • Authentication • Access control • Encryption

Why does it matter?
Data security has an intrinsic value. Everyone who collects and stores data has a vested interest in keeping it safe and preventing it from being destroyed or falling into the hands of an unauthorized user.
Furthermore, companies that cannot 100% guarantee that they keep their data safe or that have been subject to data leaks have a hard time establishing trust with customers so that they will share their data.
Most importantly, there are legal regulations that force companies to keep a certain level of data security, notably when dealing with personal data.

---

24. Note: For many, these two terms denote different things, but for simplicity reasons we will just use them interchangeably

Threats for a computer system, above all its data, can arise from destructive forces such as unauthorized access and manipulation of the data, but also the loss of data. It is a complex field and experts have a wide range of measures in their toolbox to make sure that the data on a computer system or in a company is safe. The following sections give a brief overview of the tools most commonly used to secure data and make sure that it is only accessed by authorized users.[lxxviii]

Authentication

This term is often used synonymously with *identification*. However, there is a difference between the two. *Identification* refers to the process of asserting who a person is, e.g. if somebody wants to log in to an account or access some data. *Authentication* refers to the process of proving that the asserted identity is true, i.e. making sure that the person is who they say they are. This could for example b achieved through the use of passwords, which are only known to a specific person so that their identity can be confirmed. Identities are often well known and public (e.g. if you work at a company then it's a safe bet that your email address is something like firstname.lastname@company.com). In contrast, the authentication should be something private and secret. For example, while your email address might be easy for me to find, the passwords that are associated with its use should be known only to you. If the latter is not the case, it can pose severe security threats.

For example, in 2008 the email account of US vice presidential candidate Sarah Palin was hacked by a college student. Her email address (identity) was publicly known to be gov.palin@yahoo.com. Obviously, she had kept her password for that account to herself. However, everyone knows that companies offer other ways of authentication as a backup in case a user forgets their password. The college student made use of this to log in to Palin's account. He went through the "forgot my password" procedure and answered the security questions: birthday (found on Wikipedia), postcode (public knowledge) and where she met her husband (at high school; also known due to her public profile). With these three answers the student was able to authenticate himself as Palin and pretend that he was her.[lxxix]

Access control

If you have a database containing customer data, then you will want to give certain users certain rights of access to this database. This is done through *access control*, i.e. limiting who can access what sort of data in what ways. The question of who should be able to access certain data is often rather straightforward. What is often less obvious is that there are various access modes, including read, write, modify, erase, copy and export a given dataset.

For example, in the case of Your Model Car we want to give our customers (users) the ability to read all of their personal data (name, address, credit card etc.). We also want to give them the ability to modify some of their data, say, if they have changed their address. Likewise, we might want to give the customers to access some of our employee data. We might want to provide them with the contact details of their customer service manager. However, the information a customer has about the service manager should be restricted to only, say, their work email address. We would not want them to have access to their private details or to data about employees other than their service manager. And we certainly don't want to give customer the ability to modify our employee data.

Encryption (cryptography)

The third basic security tool is encryption. *Encryption* refers to the process of concealing data to protect it against unauthorized access by encoding it so that it cannot be deciphered.

By encrypting data, we can protect it from being read, manipulated or fabricated. Encryption is like a magic box that takes data as an input and twists it around so that it is ciphered and puts out the data in a different, encrypted form. Such a magic box is referred to as a key. In order to bring the data back to its original form so that it can be read again, it has to be decrypted again with a key.

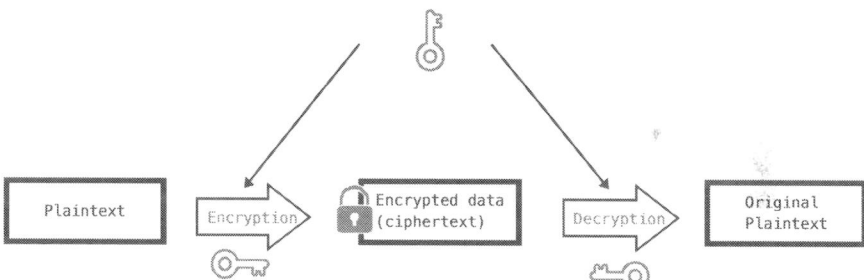

Figure 72.1 Overview of the encryption process

Encryption is especially important if *data is in motion* and therefore it plays a significant role in cloud architectures where data physically changes locations between computer systems. To take data from a local computer system and put it into the cloud requires data to physically move. This exposes the data and makes it especially vulnerable to threats.

However, data encryption is increasingly being applied to data at rest as well (i.e. data that does not physically change location but remains on a certain system) to add another level of security. Before data is stored on a system it is encrypted and then it needs to be decrypted upon access.

Data encryption therefore offers another layer of security in cases where other measures, such as authentication or access control, fail. All cloud providers offer ample customizable encryption both for data at rest and data in motion along with other security measures to make sure that their customers' data is safe.

Personal data as the link between data security and data protection

It is in the interests of every company to keep its data assets secure. No company wants its data leaked or modified in an unauthorized way. This in itself is a serious problem, and it damages the company's reputation and its customers' trust.

So data security is a goal that everyone wants to achieve – to a certain degree. In some cases, data security is only a desirable goal, because the company can decide how seriously it wants to take the issue. But in other cases, for certain types of data the data security is a *compulsory requirement*. This is especially the case with the collection, storage and processing of *personal data*.

> **Case study 31**
>
> **One of the largest data-security breaches in history**
>
> In 2013 and 2014, the email accounts of some three billion Yahoo! accounts were compromised. The data hacked included users' names, email addresses, telephone numbers, security questions and answers, dates of birth and passwords. Even though Yahoo! claimed that the majority of accounts were encrypted, the damage to Yahoo's reputation was disastrous. The data breach also had hard monetary consequences: Yahoo! continues to face lawsuits filed against it and the scandal led to a decrease of US$350 million in the final price that Verizon Communications Inc. paid to acquire Yahoo! In 2017.[lxxx]

73 | What is personal data?

When talking about the legal and security aspects of collecting, storing and processing data, one type of data always requires special attention: personal data. The reason is that any handling of personal data is subject to special laws and regulations.

The European Commission defines *personal data* as any information that relates to an identified or identifiable living individual.[lxxxi] To put it less technically: if you have data that is clearly about a specific person who can be identified, it is personal data. A person is identifiable if they can directly or indirectly be identified through a reference, such as name or some sort of ID.

Table 73.1 What is personal data and why does it matter?

> **What is personal data?**
>
> Personal data refers to any piece of information that can be related to a specific individual. That means that if there is some sort of (combination of) data that is about an identifiable individual, this constitutes personal data.

> **Why does it matter?**
>
> The distinction between personal and non-personal data is extremely important because the collection, storage and processing of personal data is subject to various rules and regulations.

Personal data

Examples of personal data include:[lxxxii]

- Name and surname
- Home address
- An email address like name.surname@company.com
- ID card number
- Internet protocol (IP) address
- Cookie ID

Personal data that has been de-identified, e.g. through pseudonymization, is still personal data if this de-identification is reversible. An example of a pseudonymization is if you, say, have a table with customer data and you replace the obviously identifiable data fields (customer ID, name, address etc.) with a new cryptic, artificial ID. Then you store a new linking table that contains the link to the new cryptic ID and the old customer ID. Then data would still be personal, because the pseudonymization is reversible by means of the link table.

If personal data has been rendered de-identifiable so that the individual is no longer identifiable then it is no longer considered personal data. But for that, the de-identification has to be irreversible. In the case of the customer table, this would mean deleting the new link table so that there is no longer any way of linking the data to a given individual.

Non-personal data

Here are some examples of data that is not personal:

- Irreversibly anonymized data
- An email address like info@company.com
- Any type of information that cannot be linked back to a specific individual

Differentiating between personal and non-personal data

In many cases the boundary between personal and non-personal data is somewhat difficult to discern. For example, say your company has a dataset about employees with only one column for their highest education degree ("no school degree", "high school degree", "bachelor's degree", "master's degree", "postgraduate degree"). If it is a company with a small number of employees, this information might already enable the identification of some individuals. In contrast, if the company is a multinational with thousands of employees then this data is probably not personal. If you add in the gender, this increases the amount of information and therefore also the likelihood that a person can be identified by means of these two variables. Add a third variable, such as their height, and the chances increase again, and so forth. Hence, while the definitions of personal and non-personal data are rather straightforward, there is some leeway in what constitutes identifiability and therefore also personal data.

Also note that no matter how big and extensive a dataset might be, it is not personal data unless it enables the identification of a living individual. You might have an Internet of Things (IoT) use case that uses billions of data points from machines in your production hall and none of it is personal data. However, if the use case also makes use of, say, data from wearables that are being worn by people and by means of which they can be identified, then the use case does involve personal data.

74 | What is data protection (privacy) and why is the distinction between non-personal and personal data so important?

In a lot of countries around the world, the collection, storage and use of personal data is subject to a number of restrictions and regulations that do not apply to non-personal data. For example, Your Model Car does not have to comply with any regulations in order to store data from sensors in the production hall, but it has to adhere to an entire legal framework in order to store customer data. So if a company (or individual) wants to store and use personal data, it has to pay a lot of attention to these special restrictions and laws. These regulations are called *data protection*, and they protect the privacy rights of individuals with respect to the collection, storage and use of personal data.

Table 74.1 What is data protection (privacy) and why does it matter?

What is data protection (privacy)?
Data protection and data privacy essentially mean the same thing. They refer to the regulations for and practice of protecting the privacy rights of individuals with respect to the collection, storage and processing of personal data.

Why does it matter?
In a number of countries an individual's right to privacy is enshrined in the law, sometimes even as a basic human right. As a result, when dealing with personal data you must adhere to the comprehensive set of rules and regulations of data protection.

Different approaches to data protection around the world

Data protection laws and their restrictiveness vary across the globe. The EU and the US, for example, have rather restrictive regulations concerning the collection, storage and use of personal data. A lot of Asian countries, e.g. India and Indonesia, have much laxer laws in place. In fact, there seems to be a correlation between the restrictiveness of a country's data protection laws and its political system. Liberal Western democracies – i.e. the US, European countries, Australia and New Zealand – have much stricter regulations than other countries.

One reason for this difference in laws is the way countries view a person's right to privacy. "The privacy of individuals" refers to people's ability to seclude themselves and thereby express (i.e. share information about) themselves only selectively. Privacy has several dimensions to it, including privacy of:[lxxxiii]

- Person – the right to keep bodily characteristics to yourself (e.g. biometrics and DNA)
- Thoughts and feelings
- Behaviour and action
- Communication

In the age of data, where the collection of mass data has become technically and economically viable, it has become extremely easy to gather personal data that intrudes on these spheres of privacy. In many cases we voluntarily give up our privacy; for example, if we use a dating app and reveal our name, gender and sexual identity. But there are a number of ways in which the privacy of individuals can easily be infringed upon without them fully realizing – just think of all the data that your smartphone collects and reveals about you as a person (📋 15).

Depending on your political views and inner core values, you might regard the right to privacy as something inherently valid that needs to be safeguarded at all times. With the technological possibilities extending, you might be dreading what the traditionally privacy-concerned Germans are calling the *gläserner Bürger* (the transparent citizen), about whom everything is known by the government and companies so that their privacy is fully eroded. It is certainly scary to imagine that private and public institutions know a great deal about us, an idea that has been extensively explored in many dystopian books and movies.

At the same time, if the right to privacy was fully adhered to at all times, public life would be difficult to run. It would be impossible to give out passports and ID cards, maintain a citizen register, plan schooling, etc. Humans are intrinsically social animals and our cooperation requires a degree of organization that is bound to curtail some of the privacy of individuals. So inherently the right to privacy stands in conflict with other goals and a trade-off has to be struck between these conflicting ends.

This trade-off is handled in different ways across the world. Some countries and societies place greater emphasis on the right to privacy (and other human rights) than others. For example, the EU places a lot of weight on the right to privacy, so much so that it explicitly stipulates it in Article 8 of the Charter of Fundamental Human Rights of the European Union: "Everyone has the right to the protection of personal data concerning him or her."[lxxxiv]

This charter has been legally binding for all EU members states since the adoption of the Treaty of Lisbon in 2009. Almost diametrically opposed to this philosophy, the Chinese government has been following an approach that many refer to as "mass surveillance" for several years now. It has introduced a social credit system by which Chinese citizens are assessed, and this is meant to improve public behaviour. Individuals who fail to pay fines, for instance, are downgraded in this system and face negative consequences. For example, in 2018 some 17.5 million would-be plane passengers were blocked from buying plane tickets as a punishment for offences they had committed.[lxxxv] Thus, China trades off its citizens' right to privacy with the other ends it pursues.

Overlap between data protection and data security

Data protection is related to data security. Personal data is extremely valuable and sensitive information, so there should be an intrinsic motivation to make sure that this data is secure at all times.

Furthermore, data protection laws often stipulate how personal data is to be secured by a company or organization. Thus, there is an overlap between data protection and data security, where the former dictates requirements for the latter in the field of personal data.

For example, the General Data Protection Regulation (GDPR) – which is arguably the most extensive legal framework for data protection worldwide at this time – stipulates a number of regulations concerning how personal data is to be secured, e.g. through encryption methods.

> **Case study 32**
>
> **Survey of a language instruction provider**
>
> A private language institute wants to conduct a survey of its alumni in order to find out how many of the students who took a language class have landed a job in the language in which they were instructed.
>
> The language institute decides to ensure the data collected is not classified as personal data, so that it is not subject to the GDPR. It takes a few precautions so that the respondents cannot be identified. Firstly, the online survey does not ask for any personal details such as name, address or contact details. Secondly, the IP address is not recorded. Thirdly, since class sizes are small and therefore students could be identified by knowing what class they took in what month, respondents are grouped by the year rather than the month they took a class.
>
> These measures blur and anonymize the data to such a degree that respondents cannot be identified and the data collected does not count as personal data.

75 | General Data Protection Regulation (GDPR) – who, what, where and why?

Just hearing the words "General Data Protection Regulation 2016/679" or simply "GDPR" can make a lot of people, especially those in business, relive traumas that occurred in 2018. Especially in the run-up to the GDPR taking effect on May 25th 2018, you could walk into almost any data-related department of any company and see sheer horror, panic, confusion and frustration on people's faces. For many, the GDPR is synonymous with an unmanageable mountain of confusing regulations that impede business activities.

We focus on the GDPR here as an example of data protection laws for a number of reasons. Firstly, the GDPR is the most comprehensive and toughest set of regulations for the use of personal data that has ever been passed.[lxxxvi] Secondly, due to the economic weight of the EU and its integration in a globalized world, the GDPR essentially applies to every business across the world, even if it is headquartered outside the EU. Thirdly, as a result of the latter, the GDPR has developed into a global standard that has been imitated by other organizations and governments.

How did the GDPR come about and why was it considered necessary?

There are a number of reasons why the European Commission initiated the drafting of a new set of regulations concerning the processing of data in 2012:

- There was a piece of legislation in place already that dealt with the use of personal data in the EU, the so-called Data Protection Directive.[lxxxvii] The problem was that this directive dated back to 1995 and therefore was from the digital Stone Age. Back then the internet had been around for just a few years and was not really a thing yet, and Nokia was working on a mobile phone what would develop into a classic, the Nokia 3110.[25] Fast-forward two decades and it should not come as a surprise that the laws passed in 1995 were not really adequate to regulate the new, data-driven world of smartphones, the internet and tech giants like Google. In a world where data is the new oil and currency, a new set of regulations was needed to govern the use of this asset.
- Despite the Data Protection Directive, the laws governing the use of personal data were mostly in the hands of the respective member states of the EU. The patchwork of different regulations was simply unviable and detrimental from an economic and administrative point of view. Today, data crosses national boundaries easier than humans, goods or money so there was a to integrate the patchwork of EU member states. The GDPR was meant to harmonize the national laws and is therefore a prime example of EU integration.

---

25. It would be released two years later, in 1997.

- The EU wanted to strengthen the rights of its citizens in the digital age, especially in the face of tech giants like Google and Facebook collecting massive amounts of data, often without the knowledge, let alone consent, of EU citizens.

For these reasons, the European Commission announced that it would initiate the drafting of a comprehensive framework to regulate and harmonize the use of personal data across the EU in 2012. After four years of tough negotiations between member states, interest groups and other political actors, in 2016 the GDPR was adopted by the EU institutions.[lxxxviii] The idea was to give companies sufficient time to prepare before all of the laws would be applicable, so the GDPR did not come into effect until May 25th 2018 – a day that for many companies was tantamount to doomsday.

What is the goal of the GDPR?

The GDPR regulates the use of personal data. Its primary aim is to strengthen the privacy rights of citizens by granting them more control over their personal data and also to create a level playing field for companies.[lxxxix] The GDPR consists of 11 chapters containing 99 articles.[xc]

When does the GDPR apply?

The GDPR applies if either

- *Data controllers* (companies or organizations that collect data) or *data processors* (organizations that process data on behalf of data controllers) process personal data and are based in the EU – regardless of where the actual data processing takes place.
- A company established outside the EU processes personal data in relation to offering goods or services to so called *data subjects* (individuals about whom data is collected) in the EU.[91]

Note that the GDPR still applies to a non EU-company – based, for example, in the US or China – If it collects data about individuals in the EU. In a globalized world where a lot of trade and commerce are conducted online, this essentially means that any company that does business in the EU Or with individuals in the EU must adhere to the GDPR.

Obviously, the EU cannot enforce its laws beyond its borders. So if, say, a Chinese company failed to adhere to the GDPR, it could be sued in a European court. If it was fined, the company could cease to do business in the EU and withdraw from EU territory entirely so that the fine could not be enforced (given that there are no extradition treaties between the EU and China). But given the economic weight of the EU and the fact that it is one of the largest consumer markets, internationally operating companies naturally have a strong interest in conducting business on EU territory and/or with EU residents. In an interconnected world, you cannot afford to ignore this economic giant.

Managing Data in a Company

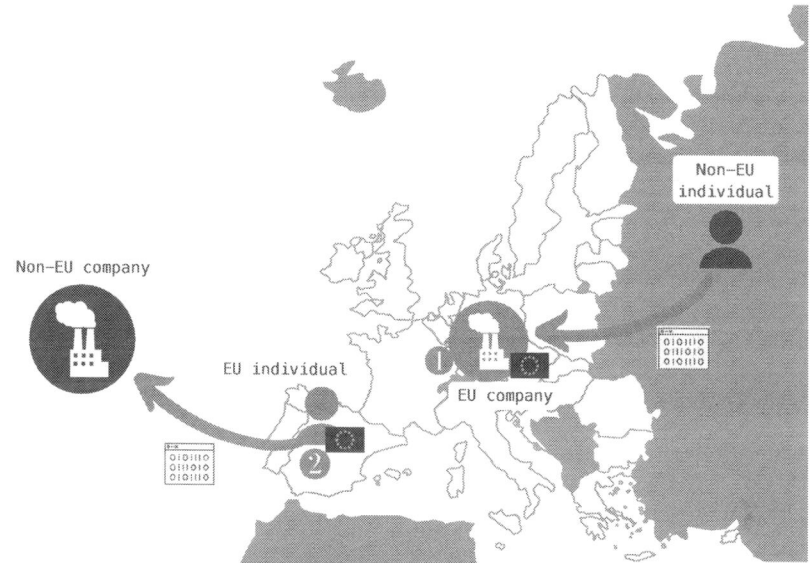

Figure 75.1 When does the GDPR apply?

Due to its global importance and economic dominance in the world, the EU can dictate the terms by which business is to be conducted. This is known as the *Brussels effect*, where standards that are implemented in the EU become global standards, since companies who want to sell to the European market adopt them.[xcii] And the Brussels effect can clearly be seen in the impact the GDPR has had globally. For example, Microsoft announced that it would implement GDPR compliance for its customers globally.[xciii]

Is the GDPR legally binding?

In short, yes. The EU essentially has two ways to pass laws: directives, which are guidelines that have to be transposed into national laws by the member state governments, and regulations, which immediately become directly applicable in all member states and for every EU citizen. The GDPR is a regulation and it came into effect on 25th May 2018. It can be enforced in the national courts of the EU member states directly.

What happens if there are conflicts between the GDPR and national laws?

All EU member states had some sort of data protection laws in place before the GDPR came about. For example, in Germany the Bundesdatenschutzgesetz (BDSG) has been regulating the use of personal data for decades. These national laws essentially became superfluous when the GDPR came into force.

Due to the EU law supremacy doctrine, the GDPR stands above national law. Even though some national courts have kept some space to manoeuvre and uphold national laws, especially at the constitutional level, courts in virtually all EU member states recognize EU supremacy. So there might be some cases where the GDPR and national law are in conflict that have to be resolved in the courts, but most of the time the courts interpret cases in the light of the GDPR and apply the regulation.

What are the most relevant stipulations of the GDPR?

The GDPR greatly enhances the right to privacy of individuals (who are referred to as *data subjects* in the GDPR). It also greatly affects the rights of companies (or other *data collectors*) to collect, store and use data.

There are 99 articles in the GDPR. In the following sections we summarize the most important stipulations.[xciv]

Data subjects

The data subject is imbued with a number of important rights, including:

- **Right to be informed:** If personal data is collected about a data subject, they have to be given explicit notice and the consent of the subject has to be explicitly given. This is why you have to explicitly consent to all cookies being collected about you when you visit a website today (yes, there were times when this was not the case).
- **Right of access:** Data subjects can request at any time that a company give them the personal data about them that it has stored. For example, if you have a Google account, you can visit https://takeout.google.com to get an export of the data about you that Google has stored.
- **Right of erasure:** A data subject can request that a company erase their personal data from its systems.

Data collectors

The core intention of the GDPR is to emphasize and protect the right to privacy of individuals. At the same time, it poses challenges to data collectors and puts them under pressure to maintain a solid and comprehensive data governance in order to meet the GDPR requirements.

The following stipulations affect data collectors:

- **Principles of lawful, fair and transparent processing:** Companies that use personal data have to do so in a way that is lawful, fair and transparent for the data subject.
- **Limitation of purpose, data and storage:** Companies are expected to collect only the data that is necessary for the specific purpose that they are collecting it for, and to store personal data only for as long as is necessary for the specified purpose.
- **Data breaches:** In the case of a personal data breach, the data collector has to:
    - ❏ Document the data breach.
    - ❏ Report that a data breach has occurred to the supervisory authority.
    - ❏ Inform the data subject about the data breach if it poses a high risk to the rights and freedoms of natural persons.

- **Data security:** The GDPR is mostly about privacy, but unlike its predecessor, it also touches on the topic of *how* personal data is to be secured. It suggests measures such as:
  - Pseudonymization (i.e. reversible anonymization) and encryption of personal data
  - Ability to restore the availability of and access to personal data in a timely manner in the case of a physical or technical incident
  - A process for testing, assessing and evaluating the effectiveness of data security measures

What happens if a company fails to adhere to the GDPR?

Companies that fail to adhere to the GDPR can expect hefty fines. The severity depends on a number of factors of the infringement, including:

- Nature of infringement
- Intention
- Cooperation with supervisory authorities
- Types of data

Fines can be up to €20 million or 4% of the company's worldwide annual revenue for the prior financial year, whichever is higher.

What are the consequences of the GDPR?

It is no exaggeration to say that the consequences of the GDPR were felt across the globe immediately after it took effect. Some companies dealt with the new regulation better than others. For example, a number of US newspapers, including the *L.A. Times*, simply blocked access to their website from EU territory on the 25th of May 2018, since they had not figured out how to adhere to the GDPR.[xcv] Even weeks after the GDPR taking effect, various US websites and newspapers were still not offering their online services to European IPs.

With our own customers, we saw entire departments coming to a complete standstill in the run-up to the GDPR taking effect, because managers were confused as to what the GDPR entailed and were scared they would infringe the laws. The 4% of revenue fine was an effective measure to draw the attention of top managers and scare them.

A lot of companies had to invest (and are still investing) remarkable amounts of money in order to ramp up their data standards to adhere to the GDPR. It is estimated that the costs to do so stand at some €37.3 billion for US companies and €214 billion for EU companies.[xcvi]

Even though a lot of companies have invested heavily in (human) resources and have set up entire GDPR compliance departments, the GDPR remains a challenge. In 2019, Cisco released its Data Privacy Benchmark, a survey of 3,200 data security professionals in 18 countries across a variety of industries. Some of the highlights of the survey are:[xcvii]

The Ultimate Data and AI Guide

- Though 97% respondents said the GDPR applies to their company, only 59% said they were meeting all GDPR regulations.
- The major challenges for companies are meeting data requirements (42%), internal training (39%) and staying on top of the ever-evolving interpretations and developments as the regulation matures (35%).

On the flip side of the coin, companies also reported some benefits of the GDPR. It is like the GDPR forced companies to put their house (or rather data governance) in order. For example, 42% of the respondents said the GDPR enabled agility and innovation through having appropriate data controls.

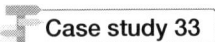

Case study 33

Would Your Model Car have to adhere to the GDPR if it were incorporated in the US?

While the GDPR is a territorial regulation, its scope transcends EU boundaries. That is, it is also applicable to companies that are not based in the EU if they are processing personal data of individuals in the EU. That means that all internationally operating companies have to adhere to the GDPR if they have customers within the EU.

Imagine that Your Model Car is incorporated in the US and is thus an American company. Does it need to adhere to the rules and regulations set out by the GDPR? Well, it depends. If Your Model Car exclusively does business outside the EU and has no EU customers, then of course it does not have to abide by EU law. So if we want to store, say, data about our customers and none of them are related to the EU, then we can do so while ignoring the GDPR. Things look very different, however, if our company addresses EU citizens or the EU market. In that case, the full set of GDPR regulations apply – even though Your Model Car is a US company incorporated outside of EU borders.

Since Your Model Car is an online shop conducting its business online and virtually, there are no physical assets within the EU. So how do we determine whether such a globally operating tech company is addressing the European market? We look at our core business. For example, if we are offering a version of our website in a European language other than English, then this indicates our intention to address that market. The same holds true if we offer shipping to European countries, or if we accept payments in euros or another European currency on our website. Our domain name might also point towards addressing a specific market; for example, www.yourmodelcar.com/nl indicates that we are targeting the Dutch market.

Thus, if such signs of addressing the EU market exist, we have to adhere to the GDPR regulations, even though we are a non-EU company that is incorporated and conducts its main business outside of EU borders.

Part III

The Engine: Artificial Intelligence and Machine Learning

"Just as electricity transformed almost everything 100 years ago, today I actually have a hard time thinking of an industry that I don't think AI will transform in the next several years."[xcviii]

Andrew Ng, one of the world's most famous and influential specialists in ML and AI

6 Understanding Machine Learning as the Key Driver Behind Artificial Intelligence

6_1 Understanding AI and ML

76 | What is AI?

Some years ago, if you went to a conference on innovation and the latest digital technologies and listened to a speaker, you would hear sentences like, "We are Company X and we are using *data mining* to power our business." Fast-forward a couple of years and you would hear the same sentence from another speaker, only "data mining" would be replaced with "big data". A few years later it would be "predictive analytics", and then at some point "data science".

Fast-forward to a conference in the year 2020, and the buzzword is *artificial intelligence* (AI). Nowadays, self-driving cars are fuelled by AI, logistic chains are optimized through AI, medical diagnoses are enhanced with AI and so forth. AI has truly arrived and is peaking in the hype cycle.

While the spotlight is helping the discipline of AI in many ways, e.g. in attracting funding, the hype around it has blurred the concept even more than it already was. The term AI is used in such an inflationary way that it is hard to know what people actually mean by it. This has exacerbated the confusion around AI that already existed for two reasons:

- AI is a lot of things to different people. It is an academic discipline, it is a goal that is sought after, it refers to software or technologies that exhibit a certain characteristic, and many more things. As an extremely wide field of research it has been rather dispersed, and the different strands that have been trying to research the topic have not been in collaboration.
- AI touches on a lot of other fields and topics. It is related to data, robotics, philosophy, ethics, neuroscience, knowledge reasoning, deep learning, natural language processing, machine learning (ML) etc. With the tremendous progress made in AI, it also increasingly has consequences on a political and societal level.

We want to avoid going into the discussion of what AI is at this point. Suffice it to say that in this book when we speak of AI we mean computer systems (or machines) that display intelligent, human-like behaviour and capabilities such as natural language processing, computer vision and reasoning.

Understanding Machine Learning as the Key Driver Behind Artificial Intelligence

Table 76.1 What is AI and why does it matter?

What is AI?

AI is computer systems or machines that display intelligent, human-like behaviour and capabilities that allow them to perform tasks that would usually require human intelligence.

Since the notion of intelligence is complex, it helps to distinguish weak from strong on a continuous scale. *Weak* (or narrow) AI refers to systems that are able to perform a narrow and specific task, e.g. classifying an email as spam. *Strong* (or general) AI refers to systems that are able to perform an entire spectrum of tasks that require human intelligence, including visual perception, verbal communication, emotional interpretations and empathy. We are still far from creating strong AI.

The academic discipline of AI has been trying to create intelligent agents and machine for decades and there have been various approaches to achieve that goal. Today, the vast majority of attempts to create AI are based on ML methods, and these are the most successful attempts.

Why does it matter?

With AI systems becoming increasingly sophisticated, they will be able to perform and thereby automate more and more human tasks. This has profound consequences on economic, political and societal levels.

It is often said that the previous industrial revolutions driven by the steam engine and electricity have equipped us with *muscle power*. AI is quipping us with *mind power*, i.e. systems that are able to perform tasks that require profoundly human traits such as creativity and perception.

Determining intelligence

One of the problems with considering AI as intelligent systems or the study thereof is that "intelligent" is a relative term. This has given rise to the so-called *AI effect*, which describes the fact that advancements in creating AI are discounted and dismissed as not really being intelligent. As AI researcher Rodney Brooks famously put it: "Every time we figure out a piece of it, it stops being magical; we say, 'Oh, that's just a computation.' […] We used to joke that AI means 'Almost Implemented'".[xcix]

Just consider the following AI systems, each of which exhibits some degree of intelligence. Is a calculator that can perform simple algebraic tasks intelligent? If not, is AlexNet, an algorithm able to recognize objects in images, intelligent? If not, is a self-driving car intelligent? If not, is Google's personal assistant, Google Duplex, which is able to have phone call conversations without humans noticing they are talking to a machine, intelligent? If not, is AlphaGo, which taught itself to play the board game Go and beat every human on planet earth in that game, intelligent?

Weak versus strong AI

To help with the discussion of what constitutes intelligent behaviour, we can situate intelligent computer systems on a "strength" scale according to how powerful they are, from weak to strong.

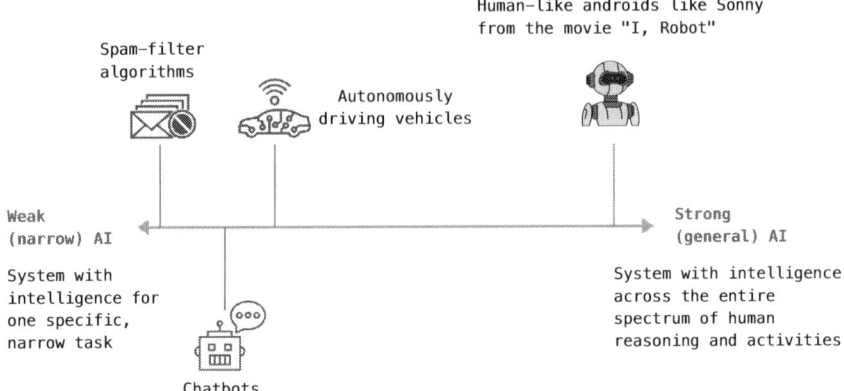

Figure 76.1 Weak versus strong AI

Weak AI refers to systems that are able to do only one or a few tasks at a (super) human level. As it turns out, there are a lot of systems and algorithms that can be considered weak AI already. Today, there are algorithms that sort out emails containing spam or hazardous content, assist in creating medical diagnoses, detect objects in images or videos, hold conversations with humans etc. All of these systems fall at the lower end of AI, but some of the models are arguably more intelligent than others.

At the other end of the scale, *general* or *strong AI* is defined as a computer system that is able to perform the entire spectrum of tasks that require human intelligence, including visual perception, verbal communication, emotional interpretations and empathy. Paired with the right robotics, strong AI would be something like Sonny from the 2004 movie *I, Robot* – or, arguably somewhat below the Sonny level of AI, the Terminator.[26]

The impact of AI

While the current hype around AI might be something of an exaggeration, AI is and will be a real game-changer for everyone. Our capability to create intelligent systems has been dramatically progressing in recent years, so that on the weak-versus-strong AI scale we are en route to the strong side at a considerable pace. In fact, what is already possible with AI can be quite daunting (📑 78).

It is often said that AI systems are equipping us with *mind power*. During the previous industrial revolutions, machines powered by fossil fuels and electricity equipped us with *muscle power*. Through the conversion of fossil fuels into kinetic energy, machines increasingly took the burden of physical labour off our

---

26. The Terminator can do a lot of things that appear human, such as perceiving information and reacting to it in the best possible way in order to achieve his goal, and learning to use the "thumbs-up" gesture to signal that everything is good. Yet in contrast to Sonny, the Terminator still lacks human traits such as feelings and acts accordingly, which makes his actions and reactions not very human.

shoulders. Just think of agriculture, industrial production, real estate construction and all the other areas where heavy machinery saves us elbow grease. This has had profound effects on economic, political and societal levels.

With AI systems advancing and getting ever more sophisticated, we will increasingly be equipped with *mind power*. That is, machines will increasingly be able to perform tasks that require human intelligence: analyse text documents, make medical diagnoses, communicate and scan visual input, etc.

This will lead to a new wave of automation of tasks and entire jobs previously performed by humans – in every sector. The potential and the consequences of AI are thus enormous.

> **Case study 34**
>
> **How Google Duplex is taking virtual assistants to the next level**
>
> In 2018, Google CEO Sundar Pichai announced a new service that Google would soon provide: Google Duplex. This service, which complements the Google Assistant, consists of an AI robot that will make phone calls for users to make reservations at restaurants or appointments at hair salons, just as a human personal assistant would.[c] The presentation of this service, which included a real-life demonstration of it, drew a lot of attention for a number of reasons.
>
> In the demonstration, the AI system appeared so human that the hair salon owner at the other end of the phone line did not even recognize she was talking to a robot. Some of the characteristics that make the system appear so human are that it uses stop words, it stutters a little bit and it even uses dialects.[ci]
>
> The sheer idea and quality of such an AI powered virtual assistant has given rise to a number of considerations. These include ethical questions, such as whether is it morally okay to have a human engage in a conversation with a robot without her knowing it. There are regulatory considerations surrounding privacy if such calls are recorded. Apart from this, there is also an entire economic and societal dimension to such rapid progress of AI if we imagine that all the work that is currently being performed by personal assistants could soon be automated. Moreover, which job role will we automate next?

77 | Where can AI be applied and how have approaches to create AI developed over time?

The ability to create machines that are able to think, reason and act like humans will find its way into every business area and aspect of our lives. Naturally, AI touches on many exciting fields where it is going to lead to mind-blowing innovations. Given that AI has the potential to automate tasks that require human intelligence and cognitive abilities, it can be applied in every sector where such skills are required – in short: everywhere. As Andrew Ng, one of the most influential figures in the field of ML and AI reckons: "Just as electricity transformed almost everything 100 years ago, today I actually have a hard time thinking of an industry that I don't think AI will transform in the next several years."[cii] Because AI can be applied in so many areas, it is often referred to as a *general purpose technology* – a technology whose impact is so large that it affects entire economies and societies, e.g. the steam engine, the computer and the internet.

Arguably, the most exciting field is the junction of mind power (AI) and muscle power (robotics). The notion of intelligent robots performing human tasks is very familiar to us through a lot of science fiction movies. While we are still far from scenarios envisioned in films like *I, Robot*, *Star Wars* and *Terminator*, we have already achieved several milestones and our progress continues to be steady. For example, in 2019 a restaurant in India introduced robots to replace human waiters.[ciii] The Hong Kong-based company Hanson Robotics has been developing several humanoid-like robots, one of which has even obtained citizenship from Saudi Arabia.[civ] The field of robotics and AI is thus likely to have several awesome – and sometimes also scary – innovations in store.

Other important aspects of AI that relate to robotics are *computer vision* and *natural language processing*. The ability to see and to communicate with words comes so easily to us, but these are immensely complex tasks that are extremely difficult to emulate. After all, they are the result of millions of years of evolution. In recent years, advancements in these fields have been tremendous and in fact we see the results in our everyday lives already. For example, no doubt you have been in contact with a chatbot on a website already. Another famous use case that falls under the area of computer vision is autonomous driving.

AI touches on plenty of other fields where it is going to lead a new wave of innovation. Unfortunately, going into the depths of all these fields is beyond the scope of this book. We refer back to some of these fields occasionally when talking about examples of where and how AI can be used. However, rather than looking at where AI can be applied, we chose to focus on how the ML approach to AI has developed (78).

How have approaches to create AI developed over time?

The vision to create a system or machine that mimics human behaviour and intelligence is by no means new and dates back at least to the ancient Greeks. However, 1956 is often considered as the birth year of the academic discipline of AI. That year an elite group of ten researchers and practitioners convened for a workshop to "find how to make machines use language, form abstractions and concepts, solve kinds of problems now reserved for humans, and improve themselves".[cv] Even though the workshop did not yield any noteworthy results, it did bring together and create a network of some of the smartest people in the field of AI and computer science at the time. These visionaries and university professors, along with their colleagues and students, would dominate the field and bring about major advancements in the following decades.

What ensued was waves of enthusiasm for the idea of AI and its research. Over the past six decades, there have been a number of approaches to creating AI that sparked interest in and enthusiasm for the discipline. More often than not, however, it turned out that these approaches were not viable, at least not with the technology and computational power at the time. The result was that the waves of enthusiasm were often followed by periods of disinterest and disappointment, during which attention and funding into the field became extremely limited. These periods are often referred to as *AI winters*.

A famous example of an approach that soon had to be discarded is an early attempt at machine translation. At the end of the 1950s and beginning of the 1960s, the US National Research Council funded the development of a program to speed up the translation of Russian scientific papers in the wake of the launch of *Sputnik 1* in 1957. This attempt was based largely on looking up words in a dictionary and trying to rearrange words in accordance with some grammatical rules. The problem was that language is way more complex than that. The results were disappointing. One famous example is that the program translated "The spirit is willing but the flesh is weak" into "The vodka is good but the meat is rotten".[cvi] This is what is called a rule-and-logic-based approach to creating intelligent machines. The idea behind such approaches is to ingrain certain logical rules into a computer program in order to solve a certain problem.

This is just one of several approaches to AI that have been used. AI has attracted researchers from a wide range of fields, including mathematics, computer science, philosophy and neuroscience, who have tested a range of other methods. For example, another field that AI has drawn on a lot is *genetic algorithms*. The idea behind this approach is that by making small mutations to a machine code program that is able to solve a given problem, you can generate a program that performs well in any particular task.[cvii]

While all of these approaches are extremely exciting, we do not have the space to delve into each of them. Instead, in this book we focus on the current approach to creating AI: *machine learning*.

Today, the vast majority of breakthroughs in the field of AI are based on ML methods. Maybe even more importantly, the vast majority of applied AI systems are based on ML methods. In fact, the breakthroughs in the field of ML a decade ago, notably in the field of deep learning, were so profound that they reinvigorated the field of AI after it had lain dormant. Now ML is even considered to be a subfield of AI, having previously been a sub-discipline of computer science.

78 | What is currently possible with AI and what are some top breakthroughs?

One of the questions we get asked quite frequently is: When will AI arrive? The answer is: It is already here. AI systems are used in a lot of products and services of companies that we make use of today (📑6). It is true that these systems still have to be considered as rather weak AI, since they are only able to perform the specific task they were designed and trained for. But with more and more data available and ML algorithms advancing, we are definitely moving to the right on the scale of weak versus strong AI.

It is difficult to give a simple answer to the question of what is currently possible with AI, since it varies across the fields of application and even from use case to use case. But Andrew Ng, one of the leading experts in the field of AI, has come up with a simple rule of thumb. He reckons that "pretty much anything that [requires human intelligence and that] a normal person can do in <1 sec, we can now automate with AI".[cviii] An example is recognizing a face or a voice.

To clarify and demarcate the borders of what is possible at present, in Table 78-1 we provide a list of use cases and research results that are pushing the envelope in a number of areas. All of these breakthroughs are based on (mostly supervised) ML methods. Creating such AI systems with ML methods requires data, so we have provided the datasets used.

Table 78.1 Top breakthroughs in the field of AI

	Field	Use case	Data
1	Medical/ psychological research	Use images from people's Instagram account to detect whether they are (inclined to be) depressed. Relevant features for the ML model were, among others, colours in photos (grey, blue and darker images were more likely to be posted by depressed people) and number of people in a picture (healthy people tended to have more people in their pictures). The trained model was able to identify patients who had depression 70% of the time. A review of studies has shown that the respective number of doctors identifying depressed people is 42%.[cix]	43,950 Instagram pictures of 166 individuals.
2	Creativity/art/ music	The Luxembourg-based start-up AIVA has created a neural networks able to compose entire rock songs or symphonies by itself. AIVA trained the model using the works of Bach, Beethoven and other composers (in the machine-readable MIDI format) to find common patterns and predict the next tone or chord in a song. The symphonies and songs created by the algorithm are of super-human quality and you would not be able to tell that they were composed by a machine.[cx]	Works and songs from a number of composers and artists such as Mozart, Bach and Beethoven stored in MIDI format.
3	Science and image recognition	Scientists from the University of Oxford have created a deep neural network that is able to recognize and track the faces of chimpanzees in the wild. This can significantly decrease the time wildlife researchers spend analysing video footage.[cxi]	Ten million images of wild chimpanzees.

	Field	Use case	Data
4	Medical research	Some breast biopsy results are extremely complex to interpret in order to check for possible cancer (sometimes doctors even disagree with their previous diagnosis when shown the same image again). Researchers from the University of California, Los Angeles have developed an algorithm to analyse and detect breast cancer from biopsies that promises to be more accurate than doctors' diagnoses.[cxii]	240 breast biopsy images.
5	Agriculture	The app Tumaini is able to use a picture of a banana to detect banana diseases and pests. The app was designed to be used by farmers to detect potential threats to their banana plantations.[cxiii]	20,000 images of bananas with visible signs of disease or pests.
6	Medical/ psychological research	Researchers from the NYU School of Medicine have created an algorithm that is able to detect whether a person is suffering from post-traumatic stress disorder (PTSD) based on voice recordings of them speaking. It is 89% accurate in distinguishing between those with PTSD and those without.[cxiv]	Hour-long interviews with 131 Iraq and Afghanistan War veterans (53 suffered from PTSD, 78 did not).
7	Medical/ psychological research	A research group has created an algorithm that is able to diagnose Alzheimer's disease earlier than was previously possible. The algorithm detects changes in the metabolism of a patient which are subtle and can be difficult to recognize for humans. The symptoms are early signs of Alzheimer's disease.[cxv]	2,100 tomography brain images from 1,002 patients.
8	Art	A group of researchers has created an algorithm that is able to create images of *The Flintstones* based on scripts and descriptions. So, for example, it is able to paint a *Flintstones* scene from the description "Fred, wearing a red hat, is walking in the living room".[cxvi]	25,000 videos of *The Flintstones* with descriptions.
9	Medical/ psychological research	Researchers from the University of Stanford have created an algorithm that is more accurate than humans at detecting a person's sexual orientation from images of their face. Based on one facial picture, it was able to tell whether a person was gay or heterosexual in 81% of the cases for men and 74% for women. This compares to a human judgement with much lower accuracy of 61% for men and 54% for women.[cxvii]	35,326 facial images from online dating websites.
10	Video footage	Deep fake algorithms are already commonly used today. They are able to superimpose images or videos onto source images or videos. For example, deep fake algorithms can swap the faces of people in videos.[cxviii]	Various implementations exist already.
11	Natural language processing	Facebook shut down two chatbots after they created their own languages to communicate and exchange information with each other. This language was not understandable to humans.[cxix]	
12	Natural language processing and computer vision	Google's translation app is able to translate text from pictures taken of book pages or other written, analogue text. It is thus a mix of a character recognition and machine translation algorithm.	

	Field	Use case	Data
13	Natural language processing and computer vision	The accessibility team at Facebook created a feature called "automatic alternative text". This feature enabled an algorithm to describe an image (e.g. "image contains a pizza and a smiling person") to help blind users use Facebook.[cxx]	
14	Natural language processing	Deep learning specialists from OpenAI have created an algorithm that is able to detect the sentiment of a word, phrase or even sentence.[cxxi] So, for example, it would classify the sentence "This development is amazing" as having a positive sentiment.	82 million Amazon reviews.
15	Games	The algorithm Angelina, developed by a researcher at Goldsmith University, is able to create computer games by itself.[cxxii]	
16	Medical/ psychological research	Researchers from Columbia University have created an algorithm that is able to "read thoughts". By examining brain signals measured with electrodes placed directly onto patients' brains, they were able to create an algorithm that translates these signals into words. However, this experiment is still in its infancy and only one-digit numbers could be deciphered.[cxxiii]	Five patients undergoing open brain surgery.
17	Games	ML algorithms have been trained to play various games and have been beating humans in more and more complex games. Today, algorithms play at a super-human level in the following board/video games: Go (board game)[cxxiv] Quake III Arena [cxxv] Star Craft II[cxxvi] Dota[cxxvii] It is likely that we will see many more AI-powered bots perform at super-human level in other games in the very near future.	
18	Robotics	Researchers from NVIDIA have developed a deep-learning-based system that enables a robot to complete a task simply by observing a human doing it. This could ultimately be used to teach robots to perform a task alongside humans, e.g. in a production hall.[cxxviii]	Synthetically generated data.

79 | Why is AI almost tantamount to ML (AI = ML + X) today?

Today, breakthroughs in the field of AI, as outlined in 📄 78, are commonplace. If you have subscribed to a newsletter in the field, you will regularly read headlines like "AI-powered system is now better at task XYZ than human". What all of these breakthroughs have in common is that they were built with the same methodology: ML methods.

ML is the discipline concerned with the study and creation of algorithms that are used to perform a specific task without having been explicitly programmed to do so.

Understanding Machine Learning as the Key Driver Behind Artificial Intelligence

Upon its conception as an academic discipline in the late 1950s, ML was extremely closely linked to the field of AI and regarded as one of the main approaches to attaining the goal of creating AI. However, with other approaches evolving and being en vogue in the quest for AI, a growing rift between AI and ML developed. As a result, by 2000 ML had reorganized as its own academic discipline,[cxxix] often considered a subfield of computer science (and typically also taught within computer science departments).

But since the turn of the century, ML has flourished and brought about incredible results. A lot of these successes pushed the envelope in the creation of intelligent computer systems and thus reinvigorated interest in the field of AI – so much so that today ML is considered a sub-discipline of AI again. More than that, it is considered the primary and most feasible approach to creating AI, so that today:

$$AI = ML + X$$

Today AI systems are almost exclusively created with ML methods. Furthermore, in the vast majority the ML methods used are based on deep learning, which refers to using an ML model class called neural networks. Many other ML model classes exist, but in recent years neural networks have outperformed these other model classes in many fields. Why this is so is the topic of Chapter 117.

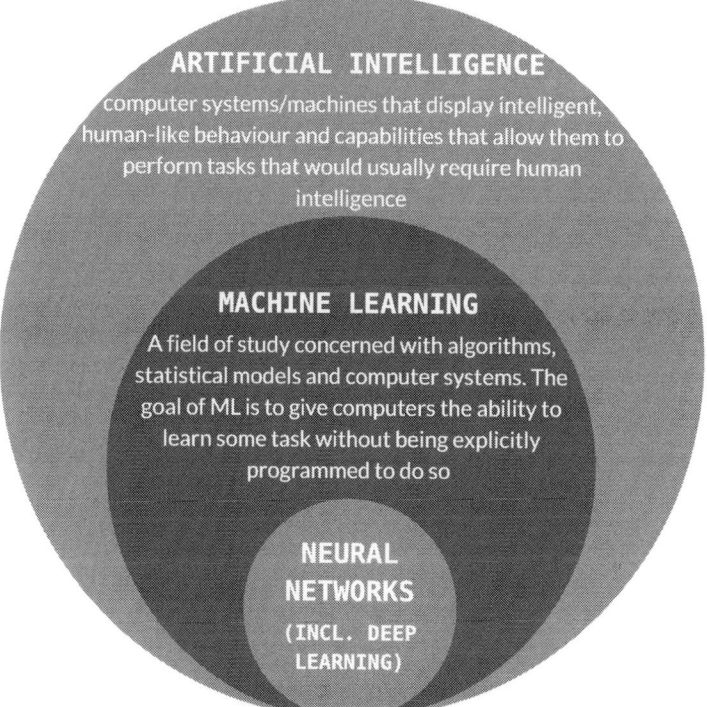

Figure 79.1 AI, ML and deep learning

The previous AI breakthroughs are, for the most part, attributable to ML methods. But what led ML to becoming the primary tool in the quest for AI creation, and why has it happened now? There are several reasons:

- For ML algorithms to work, a lot of data is needed – the more, the better. Therefore, with the surge of data availability in almost every sector, the performance of ML algorithms improved significantly.
- The masses of data that suddenly became available also had to be processed and analysed. This was possible because the growth in data was met with a growth in computational power at the same time. In fact, ML draws on a lot of ideas that had already been conceived in the second half of the last century. But while the idea existed already, the implementation thereof often failed due to a lack of computational power.
- The ML discipline itself evolved and witnessed considerable success in terms of its methodologies and algorithms. Above all, the advancement of one type of model family called "artificial neural networks", to which the field of deep learning pertains, had some breakthrough moments.

Case study 35

Automated post-hurricane damage estimation

An insurance company wants to create an AI system that can estimate the cost of roof damage a house incurred during a hurricane from aerial drone pictures. Since natural disasters entail large financial compensations for its clients, this is necessary in order to plan and optimize the cash flow of the company. Before, these estimates were done manually by specialists, which took a significant amount of time and therefore also money. The goal of the company is to make the process more time- and cost-efficient by automating this process with an AI system creating the estimates.

The company uses data relating to previous roof damage and employs a deep learning algorithm that is able to learn from this historical data. The result of this deep learning approach is an algorithm that automatically creates a dollar estimate within seconds when it is provided with an aerial image of a house with roof damage.

80 | What is ML and how can it create AI?

Machine learning is the discipline concerned with the study and creation of algorithms, statistical models and computer systems used to perform a certain task without being provided explicit instructions on how to do so. With ML we are able to create computer programs that act autonomously in an intelligent manner, predict the future and even automate certain tasks for us. The crux, however, is that we do not have to put in the manual labour of programming the model with explicit instructions (📄 81). Instead, an ML model learns on its own from historical data.

Understanding Machine Learning as the Key Driver Behind Artificial Intelligence

ML is the main driver behind the latest progress in the quest to create AI. While the engine behind muscle power (e.g. heavy machinery) is a mechanical motor and the fuel to power it is oil, the engine behind mind power and AI is ML and its fuel is data.

Considered a subfield of AI, ML draws on methods from various disciplines, notably computer science, mathematics and statistics. In fact, because it uses so many statistical methods, it is also referred to as statistical learning.

ML is applied in a broad range of fields. This reflects the fact that the range of tasks that ML models can perform is extremely wide too, including rather simple tasks such as classifying email content as spam or hazardous but also extremely complex tasks such as autonomous driving. In a lot of cases, the task to be performed is concerned with making predictions, often about the future. For example, in Your Model Car an ML use case would be to predict how many model cars we are going to sell on a given day, or we could predict the probability that a given customer will click on a certain product when browsing through our website.

Table 80.1 What is ML and why does it matter?

What is ML?

ML is a field of study concerned with algorithms, statistical models and computer systems. The goal of ML is to give computers the ability to learn some task without being explicitly programmed to do so.

Since ML uses so many statistical methods, it is also often called statistical learning or applied statistics. In contrast to statistics, it uses more computer science (programming) and typically has a slightly different goal. Nevertheless, statistics and ML have many methods in common.

Why does it matter?

ML and the increased availability of data are the main drivers behind the creation of AI systems. Almost all major breakthroughs in the field of AI and the top AI systems today have been created with ML methods. This trend is going to continue, given that data, the fuel to power the ML engine, will become even more abundant.

So how do ML and its models work? When talking about how ML is used to create AI systems, we need to differentiate between creating such a system and using it.

How is an AI system created with ML?

The creation of an AI system with ML methods is the topic of Chapter 7. But in a nutshell, you need:

- A certain task that is to be performed by the model and that requires some level of intelligence
- An ML model (or algorithm)
- Historical data from which the model can learn how to perform the task

For example, in Your Model Car we could create an AI system that predicts the probability that a customer visiting our website will click on a certain product link. Then we can tailor the links shown to a customer to their profile in order to maximize the likelihood of their clicking on a link. To create the AI system, we take an ML model and provide it with historical data. In this case the historical data refers to how customers have behaved in the past and what products they have shown an interest in. It might be that women, or a certain age group, or customers from a given country have shown an interest in specific products. The ML model is then able to identify such patterns and correlations.

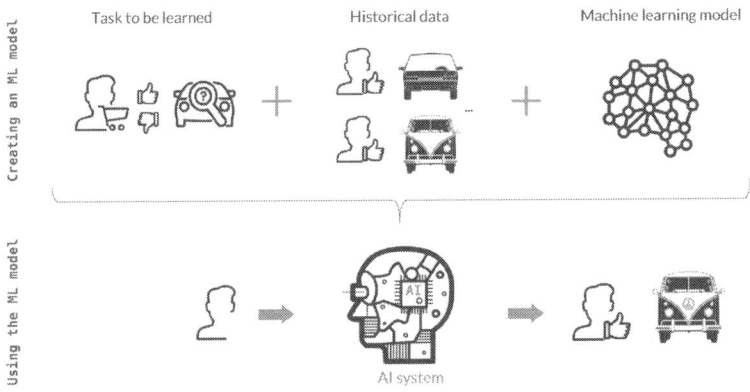

Figure 80.1 How an ML model is created and used

Once created, how is an intelligent system used?

After the model has learned to perform its task, it can then do so. It applies all the things it has "learned" from historical data. Having identified patterns and correlations in the data, it uses these to aid it in its task.

In the Your Model Car example, while learning from historical data the model might have identified that customers from Germany are twice as likely to be interested in antique Mercedes models than American customers. When a customer visits our website, we provide our model with the relevant data it needs to do its job. In this case, we provide it with the location from which the customer is accessing the website. Having learned how similar customers have behaved in the past, the model can perform its task and calculate the probability that this specific customer is interested in product XYZ. Ultimately, this knowledge can then be used to recommend the right products to the right customer.

81 | How is a machine able to learn and why is ML often considered "Software 2.0"?

How do machines learn?

Machines can learn to perform a certain task in a number of ways. These are usually grouped into three categories: supervised ML, unsupervised learning and reinforcement learning. To understand these ways of learning, it is helpful to consider how we humans pick up new skills and knowledge.

It turns out machines and humans aren't that different when it comes to the way they learn. Parents know how many iterations are necessary to teach a baby the concept of certain objects, e.g. a car. They point out a four-wheeled vehicle and label it as "car" dozens or hundreds of times before the baby is eventually able to identify and label cars on their own.

And in fact, we should not be frustrated by the fact that learning what a car is takes a while. There are plenty of other metal things moving around in our streets and worlds – bicycles, motorcycles, trucks, tractors, buses, etc. So there is plenty of room to confuse all of these vehicles and it is not an easy task to differentiate a car from, say, a truck. Both have wheels, both are made of metal, both have an engine that makes a sound, both drive, both have a driver, both have a windshield. Yet eventually, just by pointing out to a baby often enough that Vehicle A is a car and Vehicle B is a truck, they will get the hang of it and be able to correctly classify all the vehicles driving around. This is called *concept learning*.

There is another way that we humans learn: by trying things out and thereby collecting life experiences. For some people this way of learning is much more effective. "He that will not hear must feel": sometimes kids won't listen, and parents have to just let go and let their kids pay dearly for their experience. Sometimes kids need to touch fire to know it's too hot, go too fast on a bike and fall to see that it is dangerous, or touch a knife to know that it will leave a painful scar.

Machines can also learn in different ways in order to acquire the capability to perform a certain task or know a certain thing. Like in concept learning, we can teach a machine to classify or predict a certain thing if we just tell it often enough what it looks like. This is what happens in supervised ML (📑 84). We can also leave a computer to find patterns for itself *(unsupervised learning,* 📑 86) or even have it experiment to make its own experiences *(reinforcement learning,* 📑 88).

The only difference is that humans learn from fellow human beings, from the environment and from life, while machines learn from *data*. The more life experience we have, the wiser we get. The more (and the better) data an ML model ingests, the better it becomes at doing its job.

ML as "Software 2.0"

We as humans have always told computers to do something for us. After all, computers were invented to perform tasks for us, e.g. calculate something. ML – especially the latest advancements in deep learning – is often considered a game-changer in that respect. Andrej Karpathy, the director of AI at Tesla, has called deep learning models that have been created through ML "Software 2.0".[cxxx]

Traditional software development consists of manually written lines of code. Each line of code is explicitly written by the programmer and fulfils a certain function of the entire software. In contrast, when models are created with ML techniques, there is a higher degree of automation, since models *are training and learning on their own* and therefore in a way they write themselves without the need for further human input.

The Ultimate Data and AI Guide

The difference is best clarified by means of an example. Let's suppose we want to create software that takes pictures of vehicles as an input and classifies them into cars and not-cars. We could write a program that would conceptually look something like this:

If number_of_wheels = 4 AND
If height_of_vehicle < 2,5m AND
...
Then vehicle = car,
Otherwise vehicle ≠ car

We could now give this software images that it will classify according to our set of rules. Obviously, discerning and writing down all of these rules by which a car can be classified as a car is tedious and requires quite a lot of manual work and brainpower.

We could also choose to use the ML approach. Here things work the other way around. We simply have to choose a certain ML model, tell it what kind of things it has to pay attention to and then provide it with data from which it learns to classify a vehicle as a car – completely by itself, without further human input.

So instead of having to explicitly tell the program "vehicles with four wheels are probably cars", we just need to tell it "pay attention to the number of wheels and other factors XYZ, as they are important attributes by means of which vehicles can be differentiated". We then only have to feed the model with enough pictures of objects, some of which contain a car. With enough data, it will learn by itself how to correctly classify a car. For some models, we do not even have to tell the model explicitly what attributes to pay attention to; the model will determine these factors by itself. Conceptually, the code for such an ML model would look something like this:

Choose model ABC
Pay attention to attributes [number of wheels, height, length, size of wheels...]
Use data XYZ
Train yourself and learn

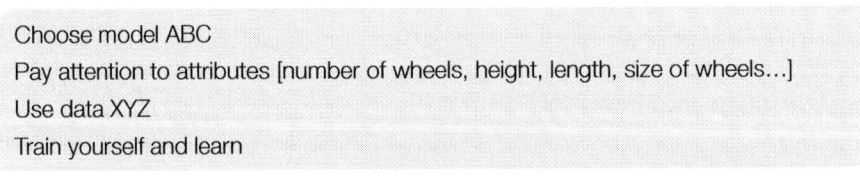
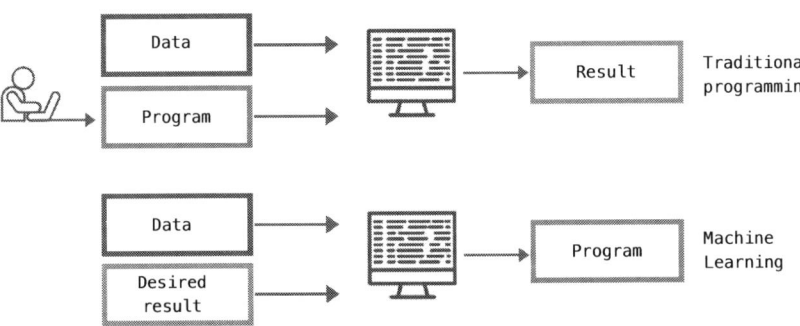

Figure 81.1 Traditional software programming versus ML

Understanding Machine Learning as the Key Driver Behind Artificial Intelligence

The big advantage of the ML approach is that you need way less human input and expertise to create an intelligent system (and it typically performs way better). The big "disadvantage" is that you need data instead, preferably a lot of it. The more complex the task, the more data you need. So with the increasing availability of data, we will definitely see more and more cases where ML is used.

But that does not mean that traditional software development will fade away. Rather than replacing traditional software development, ML will augment it as a new methodology.

Case study 36

The paradigm shift in programming machine translation algorithms

One of the constituting fields of AI has always been the area of natural language processing (NLP), which is concerned with enabling computers to process, understand and analyse human language. Within NLP, one of the main disciplines is machine translation.

The history of machine translation is symbolic of the entire field of AI. Academia first began studying NLP in the 1950s. Back then the primary approach to teaching a machine how to translate text was the method of rule-based logic. The idea was to create computer programs with certain rules that they would use to translate a piece of text; for example, explicit grammatical rules of the specific language to be translated. This required extensive manual labour for programmers as well as domain knowledge of both languages, and the results of the approach were extremely limited. So much so that in 1966 all US government funding for academic translation projects was cancelled.[cxxxi]

Over the course of history, various other approaches have been tried. Today, presumably all major machine translation providers have switched to creating translation machines with ML methods; to be precise, with deep learning methods. For example, Google Translate switched to using deep learning methods to create and improve its translation software in 2016 (that year, Google Translate already translated over 140 billion words per day).[cxxxii]

Rather than programming rules explicitly, an ML model learns from historical data. In the case of translation, one source of data from which it can learn is the texts of the UN and EU, which of course are available in various languages.

Not only has the switch to ML-based approaches for machine translation led to a reduction in manual programming labour and required domain expertise, but it has also led to a significant improvement in the translation results – as everyone who has used machine translation 20 years ago and today will agree with.

82 | What is a machine able to learn – can it predict the future?

When we tell people we are data and AI consultants, one of the first things they say is, "Wait, so you can predict the future?" The answer is: "Yes, you'll have a good marriage with 3.5 kids and live happily ever after" – or in other words, "It depends."

With ML we are able to create models that can take a decision autonomously or predict something by learning from historical data. Often such predictions concern future outcomes, such as how much are we going to sell or whether a customer will be interested in a given product.

To answer the question of what a machine is able to learn, it is necessary to introduce the concepts of noise and signal. Processes or outcomes can be divided into noise and signal.

Signal refers to an underlying pattern in a process, and pattern here refers to something repeatable or predictable. For example, there is a pattern in the occurrence of lung cancer and how many cigarettes a person smokes on average per day. The higher the average daily cigarette consumption, the higher the risk of developing lung cancer. In Figure 82-1 we provide a graph of a process with a clear signal, but which is subject to noise. It depicts the number of views a product in Your Model Car has received in the first quarter of 2020 and how often it was sold.

Noise refers to random influences that dilute an underlying pattern. For example, while we know that smoking cigarettes increases the chances of developing lung cancer, we cannot make exact predictions of how many consumed cigarettes lead to what likelihood of getting cancer. The reason is that there is a lot of *noise*, i.e. other factors we cannot predict, involved in this process that also play a role and thus dilute the pattern. An example of noise here is the genetic predisposition. In Figure 82-2 we provide a graph of a process with a clear signal and which is subject to almost no noise. It depicts the pressure of gas in a container for various container volumes (Boyle's law).

Table 82.1 What are noise and signal and why do they matter?

> **What are noise and signal?**
>
> In ML we split up a process or outcome into *signal* and *noise*.
>
> Signal refers to the underlying pattern in the process: a repeatable and predictable part that we hope to capture and distil with a model in order to explain and predict the process.
>
> Noise refers to the parts in the process that we cannot explain and that dilute the signal. Essentially, it is all the things that get in the way of us identifying and distilling the signal of a process.
>
> Some processes are noisier than others. The stronger the signal and the weaker the noise in a process, the better it can be predicted and the better an ML model will be at performing a task related to it.
>
> The goal of ML is to distil the signal from the noise in processes in order to predict or explain (future) outcomes.

> **Why do they matter?**
>
> Breaking up a process or outcome into signal and noise helps us to understand a lot of questions in statistics and ML.

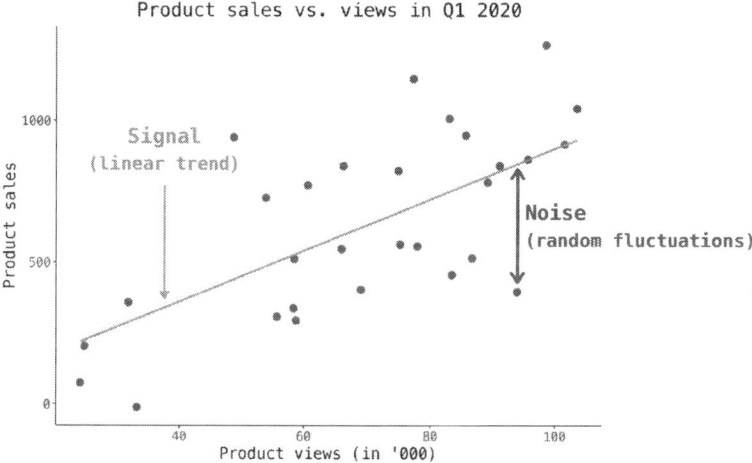

Figure 82.1 A process with a signal but also noise (product views and sales in Your Model Car)

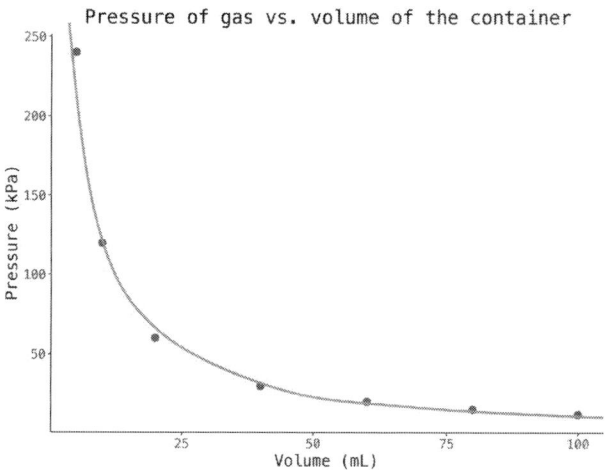

Figure 82.2 An almost noise-free process[27]

The basic answer to the question of what a machine is able to learn is:

A machine is able to learn *patterns*.

---

27. Artificially created data

The job of an ML algorithm is to try to find and identify and pick up such patterns. To do so, the ML algorithm needs an underlying pattern, it needs the pattern to be as free from noise as possible and it needs the data that contains this pattern, as outlined in the following sections. An important point to note is that any ML-model will only be able to make predictions with a certain probability. There is no 100% certainty when it comes to the predictions and accuracy of ML models.

The process or outcome needs to have a signal

The process or outcome that we are trying to predict needs to have a pattern in it. We can have as much data as we want and use the most sophisticated algorithm there is, but if a process simply does not have any patterns then we will not be able to predict it. In other words, there needs to be a *signal*.

There are some processes in the real world that have very strong and discernible patterns. For example, think of boiling water in a pan. If you turn the hotplate up to setting 1, then heating one litre of lukewarm water until it boils will take X minutes. If you double the strength of the hotplate (setting 2), the time will be cut in half. There is a very clear pattern: the more energy you transfer with the hotplate, the faster the water boils. In fact, this signal is so obvious that we as humans would be pretty good at predicting the boiling time and we would not deem ML methods necessary here.

In contrast, there are processes that lack an underlying pattern. For example, take whether and when an earthquake will occur in a given area. While there might be some extremely complex underlying patterns, to us it is essentially a random process. That means there is no theory or underlying pattern with which we could predict that "San Francisco will experience an earthquake on the 23rd of May 2035 at 14:35". There are no factors – such as, say, ground temperature, air pressure or current distance from Earth to the sun – that act as a pattern. The occurrence of an earthquake is a pure noise process.

The signal needs to be as free from noise as possible

For a process to be predictable, the signal needs to exist *and* it needs to be discernible. That means that it should be as free from noise that dilutes the signal as possible. The noisier a process or the weaker the signal in it, the less likely it is that we can predict or explain it.

Note that a signal in a process might not be visible to the human eye, but that does not mean that it is absent. In fact, that is exactly the point of ML. If we are trying to predict a variable by means of hundreds or thousands of input variables, we as humans are simply not able to decipher or make sense of such complex processes. In contrast, ML models can do this, given that we have data on all the variables. So while it does not need to be visible to the human eye, the signal does need to be discernible from the noise.

Let's return to our example of lung cancer and smoking. It is obvious that there is a pattern between the two. However, there are so many other influencing factors that dilute this signal that is difficult to discern it and create a forecast of when a person will get lung cancer based on how many cigarettes they smoke per day. The signal will be influenced by the person's genes, nutrition, lifestyle, medication they might take, how much sport they do and a whole lot of other random factors beyond our control that in everyday vernacular we often refer to as "good/bad luck". The greater the number of factors that influence an object of interest or process, the more difficult it is to identify underlying patterns in such clutter.

We are only talking about probabilities

When we talk about predictions, we are always talking in terms of *probabilities*, never in terms of certainties. In ML there is no such thing as 100% certainty. The accuracy of predictions of classifications therefore largely depends on how strong the signal and noise are in a process.

Consequently, there is no clear-cut way we can say, "If a process has that weak a signal or that much noise, it is unpredictable or explainable." Rather than a "predictable versus unpredictable" dichotomy, it is a spectrum. So with decreasing signal and increasing noise strength, our ability to accurately predict a certain process decreases.

For example, we know that smoking significantly decreases people's life expectancy. But we cannot make an accurate prediction of when somebody will die based on how much they smoke. We can only say it increases the probability of their death by X per cent. And somebody may still beat all the odds. For example, at 122 years of age Jeanne Calment was one of the oldest people ever documented in human history, and she was a heavy smoker. So even though her odds of living that long were slim, she still beat them.[cxxxiii]

The ML model needs sufficient data that captures the underlying signal

We need data that contains the pattern that we are using to make future predictions. Remember that the purpose of data is to model the real world and depict it in digital form. Thus, if we want to predict or explain certain aspect of that real world with data, we obviously need the data that reflects that aspect of the real world.

It is important to understand that an ML model makes predictions by extrapolating patterns it has identified during its training with historical data. Therefore, it can only predict outcomes in the future if they follow the same pattern that exists in the training data. Or to put it simply: an ML model is only able to predict what it has already seen in the past. If you have a sample of only white swans, then the algorithm will not be able to predict that there is a black swan. That also means that unique, unprecedented events fall off the list of things that can be predicted with data (or to put it more accurately, events that are the result of patterns that have not existed before or are not present in the data).

Table 82-2 provides examples of outcomes and processes that would be predictable or unpredictable.

Table 82.2 Predictable and unpredictable processes

Processes that cannot be predicted (or at least are extremely difficult to predict)	▶ Who will win the US election in 2028:
	  ❏ Lack of data (we would need data on all factors that influence an individual's decision to vote for a certain candidate)
	  ❏ Too complex a process that includes too many variables and that is too far in the future (so that many random events might happen until then)
	▶ Lottery or other games of chance:
	  ❏ This is a prime example of a random process with no underlying patterns (there is no signal).
	▶ Who will win the FIFA World Cup 2022:
	  ❏ Too complex and noisy of a process with a lot of random factors. (That is the beauty of football: anything can happen at any time and even an underdog can beat the favourite.)
	▶ Gender of your child at the moment of conception:
	  ❏ There is no underlying pattern (or at least it has not yet been discovered) to determine or influence gender upon conception.
	▶ Volcanic eruption/earthquake:
	  ❏ While there are long-term predictions for volcanic eruptions and earthquakes, such as "There is a 62% chance of a major earthquake in the San Francisco Bay area in the next 30 years", accurately predicting the day or week of such disasters is not possible because the underlying processes are not sufficiently understood.
	▶ The weather next year at a given time and place:
	  ❏ While we are able to make predictions about the (change of) the climate, it is not possible to make specific predictions about the weather on a certain day that go beyond, say, 14 days, because the weather is too complex a system with too many variables having an influence.
	▶ When, how or with whom you will fall in love:
	  ❏ Not only do we lack data about this phenomenon, but we do not understand its workings – that's the beauty of it.

Processes that can be predicted (to a certain degree of accuracy and given that we have the necessary data)	▶ How many products we are going to sell ▶ Which products on our website interest a customer ▶ What query you are looking for on Google (based on the first characters you type) ▶ Whether or not you will click on a link when browsing a website ▶ For more examples, see 📄 6 and 📄 78.

6_2 Types of ML

83 | What types of ML are there and how do they differ?

The range of tasks that a machine can learn is extremely wide. In general, we distinguish between three different ways that a machine is able to learn these tasks:

Understanding Machine Learning as the Key Driver Behind Artificial Intelligence

supervised ML, unsupervised learning and reinforcement learning. In 📑 84 to 📑 88 we look at the three ML types in detail. Here, we provide an overview.

Essentially, the three learning types differ in terms of two aspects:

- The type and existence of the so-called *target variable*
- The way the models are trained

Table 83.1 What are the types of ML and why do they matter?

What are the different types of ML?

A machine can learn to perform a certain task in three distinct ways:

- Supervised learning
- Unsupervised learning
- Reinforcement learning

These types of ML differ in terms of how the machine learns as well as the shape of the target variable of the ML case. While there are other minor types of ML, these three are the major ones.

By far the most significant and important type is supervised ML. In the majority of cases that are implemented today and that lead to an AI system, supervised ML methods are applied.

Why does it matter?

When approaching an ML problem, one central task is to understand the underlying problem and know what type of ML is appropriate to tackle it.

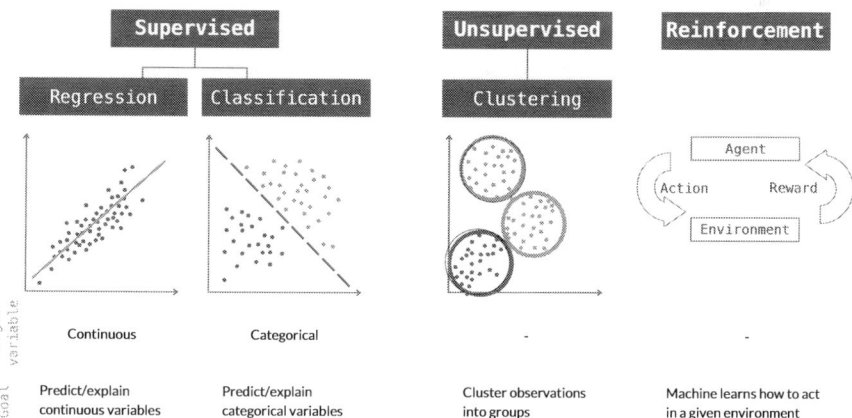

Figure 83.1 Types of ML

Target variables

Supervised and unsupervised learning can be distinguished by means of the existence of a target variable for a given task. *Target variable* refers to the variable that represents our object of interest (the thing we want to predict, make a decision about or automate) and therefore also the task we want the machine to learn. For example, let's say that with Your Model Car we are interested in creating an AI system that predicts if or when a machine in our production hall will break down. In this case our object of interest is "machine is operating versus machine breaks down". The task we want our AI to learn is to predict whether a certain machine in the production hall will be operational or broken at a certain point in time.

Table 83.2 What are target variables and input variables and why do they matter?

What are a target variable and an input variable?

In an ML model we distinguish between two different variables.

The *target variable* (also referred to as the label variable, response variable, predicted variable, explained variable, dependent variable and outcome variable) represents the object of interest for us. It is the variable that we are trying to predict or determine with the model.

The *input variables* are the variables that we use in a model to predict or determine the target variable. Input variables are also referred to as predictor variables, input variables, input variables, explanatory variables and simply features of a model.

Why does it matter?

The distinction between target variables and input variables is crucial in order to understand the workings of ML – and the remaining chapters of this book.

Labelled and unlabelled data

In a lot of cases, we have a certain object of interest but lack the data about it. In the Your Model Car example, we might have equipped our production machines with sensors that record the temperature and pressure of a given machine, but not whether or not the machine was operational at some point. In cases where we have a theoretical object of interest but lack the data on it, we talk about *unlabelled data*. An area where unlabelled datasets are common is computer vision. For example, in autonomous driving a central task of the computer system is to detect objects in an image. While we have plenty of videos and photos, very few are *labelled*, which in this case means having a verbal description of what objects a picture contains.

In cases where we have the data on our object of interest, we have a *labelled dataset*. So in the Your Model Car example, that would mean we have a variable in our dataset that tells us whether a given machine was operational or broken at a given point in time. In figure 83-2 we provide a labelled dataset for a predictive maintenance use case: we have the necessary data on our target variable representing our object of interest (the status of a production machine). If this variable was absent, it would be an unlabelled dataset.

TIME	TEMPERATURE	PRESSURE	STATUS
10:40	67.3	109.1	Operational
10:41	70.4	114.5	Operational
10:42	74.5	111.8	Operational
10:43	67.3	109.1	Operational
10:44	71.8	101.3	Operational
10:45	80.5	120.5	Broken
10:46	83.9	128.3	Broken
10:47	88.0	135.9	Broken
10:48	95.5	145.5	Broken
10:49	105.4	157.2	Broken
10:50	70.9	130.2	Broken
10:51	50.8	125.0	Broken
10:52	48.2	105.5	Operational
10:53	54.5	112.7	Operational
10:54	52.7	107.3	Operational

(Target variable; Labels — annotations pointing to STATUS column)

Figure 83.2 Labelled versus unlabelled data

Based on whether a dataset is labelled or unlabelled for a use case, we determine whether supervised or unsupervised ML is applicable to a given dataset.

Supervised learning

To apply supervised ML, we need labelled data. The goal of supervised ML algorithms is to create a model that determines or predicts a target variable as accurately as possible.

Within supervised ML we distinguish between regression and classification problems, which differ in terms of the shape of the target variable:

- *Regression problems:* The target variable is *numerical*. Examples of numerical target variables are number of products sold and the likelihood of a website visitor clicking on a link.
- *Classification problems:* The target variable is *categorical*. Examples of categorical target variables are "Does an email contain spam, yes or no?" and "What colour is the traffic light currently, red, yellow or green?".

Unsupervised learning

If we are dealing with unlabelled data, it is not possible to apply supervised ML methods. The reason is simple: if there is no target variable that we can determine or predict, then we cannot apply supervised ML to create a model that is supposed to do exactly that.

Just because we lack the labels for our desired target variable, however, does not mean that we cannot do anything with the data. By applying *unsupervised learning*, we can still identify patterns in the dataset that might be of interest. The goal of unsupervised learning is not to determine or predict a target variable, but to find other patterns that might exist in a dataset. The most widely used unsupervised learning methods are *clustering methods*, where we try to organize our data into groups of similar observations.

For example, we might be interested in understanding our customers more profoundly and so we want to assign them to a certain group, e.g. "male, regular customer" or "young, one-time purchase only". In this case our target variable would be the "type" of a customer. Unless we conduct a survey and ask every customer to tell us what type of customer they are, we lack the data for this target variable. Therefore, our data is unlabelled. However, with clustering algorithms we might still group similar customers together by means of, say, their sociodemographic characteristics such as their age and gender. This algorithm can then be used to assign a new customer to a certain group automatically.

Compared to supervised ML, the things you can do with an unlabelled dataset are rather limited. In the vast majority of cases we are interested in creating a system that is able to determine or predict a certain target variable in order to automate a certain task. Labelled datasets are therefore considered to be of much higher value. Accordingly, practitioners have a saying: "Data is cheap, but labels are expensive." In fact, there are entire companies, such as Scale AI, that specialize in providing data labelling services, and this will turn into an even bigger market in the future.

Reinforcement learning

Reinforcement learning differs substantially from both supervised and unsupervised learning methods. In both supervised and unsupervised learning, we provide the algorithm with historical data from which it can learn in order to "become intelligent" and perform a certain task.

In reinforcement learning, the algorithm is not provided with historical data. Instead, it is put into an environment in which it is supposed to find the optimal action in order to maximize some sort of reward – think a computer program being left to learn how to behave through trial and error.

84 | What is supervised ML?

Of all the ML types, supervised ML is the most important one. Not only is it the most widely used, but it is also the basis of most of the recent AI system breakthroughs. This is in contrast to, say, reinforcement learning, which is still in a scientific and research phase. So while you might see unsupervised or reinforcement learning being used every now and then, in the majority of cases when we implemented an ML project in an organization we employ supervised ML to create AI.

Supervised learning is applicable when our dataset is labelled; that is, we have data for our target variable. The idea of supervised ML is to create a system that performs a certain task by determining or predicting a certain target variable. For example, to optimize our stock levels in Your Model Car, we would have to know how many items of product X we are going to sell on a given day. Our target variable is thus "sales of product X".

The necessary underlying assumption of supervised ML is that there are some factors that have an influence on this target variable or are somehow related to it. There has to be a signal. When we think about the sales of our product, such factors include the product's price, how much we have advertised it, what day of the week it is and whether it is on offer. These variables are called input variables.

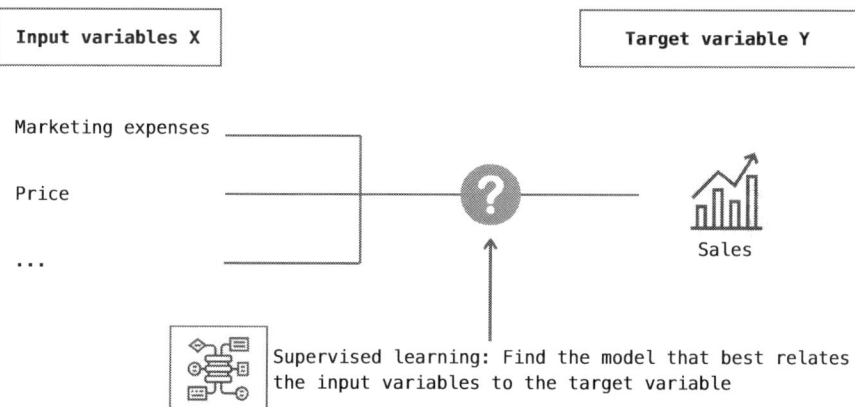

Figure 84.1 Overview of supervised ML

The goal of supervised ML is to create a model that finds and uncovers the patterns by which these factors are related to the target variable. In ML parlance we speak of finding a mathematical function (= model) that maps the input variables as well as possible to the target variable, so that we can determine and predict the latter.

This mathematical function is found by having a look at historical data to see how the input variables and the target variable have been behaving and interplaying before. This process is called *model training*. During model training, the model uncovers and detects the patterns that (ideally) exist between the input variables and the target variable, and learns to emulate these patterns as well as possible in order to use them to predict future data points.

Table 84.1 What is supervised ML and why does it matter?

What is supervised machine learning?
Supervised ML is one way in which a machine is able to learn a task from historical data. Its goal is to find a model (i.e. a set of rules) by means of which a set of input variables can be used to predict a target variable as well as possible. This is possible if there are underlying patterns (correlations) between the input variables and the target variable.
Because the goal is to determine or predict a target variable, supervised ML requires labelled data.

> **Why does it matter?**
>
> Supervised ML is by far the most important type of learning. In the vast majority of recent breakthroughs in the quest to create AI, supervised ML methods were used. In contrast to other learning methods, supervised ML is extremely widely used in the majority of ML projects.

It is called *supervised ML* because during this training phase the model receives feedback on how well it is doing in terms of determining or predicting the target variable. That way, the model is able to find its optimal form in order to emulate the relationships between independent and target variables with the highest possible level of accuracy. This feedback can be likened to a teacher supervising the learning process of the model.

Once a model has been created with supervised ML, it can then be used to perform the task it was designed for. Because it has picked up the patterns that exist between input variables and the target variable, it can apply these patterns to determine or predict the outcome of unknown data. For example, we could use such a model to predict how many of product X we will sell next month if we put the product on sale and reduce the price by 20%.

85 | What is the difference between regression and classification?

In supervised ML we distinguish between regression and classification problems. They differ in the form of their target variable.

In *regression* problems the target variable is numerical, i.e. it takes on numerical values, such as –15.6 or 822.1212. Therefore, the goal of regression is to determine or predict a target variable that takes on numerical values. Examples of numerical values are temperature measurements and probabilities.

In contrast to that, in *classification* problems the target variable is categorical, i.e. it takes on categories as value. The values could be binary values such as 0 or 1, male or female, yes or no. It could also be a multinomial variable that can take on one of several mutually exclusive categorical values, such as the type of a product (e.g. antique model car, sports model car etc.).

In some cases, a task to be learned and later performed by an ML model can be approached as both a regression and a classification problem. For example, if we were to create an AI system that determines what type of model car is in an image, this is a classification problem. Our target variable is "model car type" and can only take on categorical values. However, we can reframe the problem. Instead of taking "model car type" as the target variable, we could train a model that computes the probabilities of a model car being type X, Y or Z. By choosing the car type with the highest probability, we could then categorize vehicles with a regression approach. In such situations, there is no right or wrong way to model the target variable. Which approach to use will depend on a number of factors, such as the ultimate underlying goal and the nature of the problem.

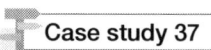

Case study 37

Optimization of mini loan applications

Customers can apply for a mini bank loan (less than €2,000) online. The bank employs supervised ML to automate the task of background checking to assess whether an applicant is creditworthy or not. Therefore, ultimately it is dealing with a classification problem, where the algorithm has to decide for each applicant "grant loan" or "deny loan".

However, the task to be learned by the ML-model is framed as a regression problem. Instead of "grant loan" vs. "deny loan", it is trained to predict the probability that a given applicant will pay back the loan. Being provided with historical data, the algorithm identifies factors (input variables) that influence this probability. These factors include, for example, their gender and monthly income.

By predicting the probability of payback rather than categories, the bank can decide how much risk it is willing to take with its applicants which gives it more transparency and control.

86 | What is unsupervised ML?

In unsupervised ML settings, we are dealing with unlabelled data, i.e. we do not have data on the target variable we are interested in. That means that, unlike in supervised ML, we cannot create a model to determine or predict a certain target variable we are interested in – simply because there is no target variable.

But just because a dataset is unlabelled and we lack the data on our target variable, that does not mean we cannot do anything with the unlabelled dataset. We can still discern patterns that might exist in the data and draw conclusions from it in several different ways. This is exactly what unsupervised learning methods do.

Arguably, the most frequently used unsupervised learning method is clustering. In clustering, we try to group together data points that exhibit some sort of similarity in order to discern what distinct groups there might be.

For example, suppose we have a dataset of images that all contain some sort of model car. If for each image we had the data on the target variable "model car type", we could use this dataset to create a system that is able to classify the type of model car in an image.

But what if we lack the target variable? Then we are left with only images and no information about what kind of model car they display. But one thing we could still do with this data is group similar model cars together. For example, we could put all vehicles that are a certain colour in one group. Or we could separate vehicles with two wheels from vehicles with four wheels or more wheels. In other words, based on some characteristics we could identify and create certain clusters of similar observations in the data. Even if we didn't know that two-wheeled vehicles are called "motorcycles" and we lacked the label that would provide us with this information, we could still group them together.

Table 86.1 What is unsupervised learning and why does it matter?

What is unsupervised learning?

Unsupervised learning is the second major way in which a machine is able to learn. It is applicable in situations where we lack data on our target variable, i.e. when we are dealing with an unlabelled dataset.

The goal of unsupervised learning is to find patterns or structures among the input variables, e.g. clusters of similar observations.

Unlike in supervised ML, there are no right or wrong answers because we lack a target variable that we are trying to determine or predict. Given this, we cannot give a model feedback on how well it is doing in predicting a target variable. Instead, we have to let it find patterns on its own, without supervision – hence the name *unsupervised* learning.

Why does it matter?

Unsupervised learning is the go-to solution when we have a dataset but we lack labels on the target variable. supervised ML cannot be applied in these cases, but that does not mean that use cases yielding added value cannot be implemented. Through unsupervised learning, above all clustering methods, interesting insights can still be generated.

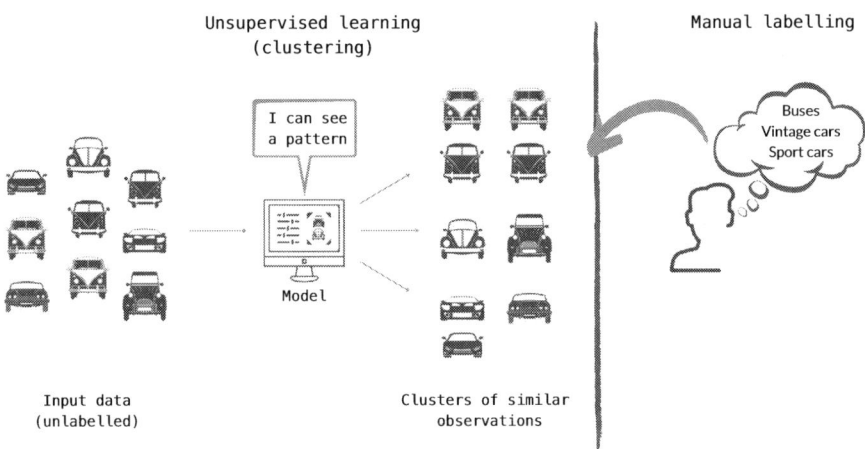

Figure 86.1 Schematic overview of clustering

In many cases, unsupervised learning methods are also used to alleviate the problem of unlabelled datasets. Let's continue with the example of images containing model cars. Suppose we have applied a clustering algorithm to 300,000 images in order to identify 25 different clusters of model types. We could manually look at some instances of each cluster and have a model car specialist label them. For example, it might be that Cluster 1 contains sports cars, Cluster 2 contains vintage cars and so forth. This additional information is effectively labels, so we finally have data on a target variable. With these labels, we can then apply supervised ML methods; for example, to create a system that is able to classify the type of model car in an image.

> **Case study 38**
>
> **Clustering similar car-part failures to increase repair efficiency**
>
> An in-house repair shop of a car producer repairs several dozen cars per day. Before a car can be repaired, it needs to be diagnosed. Finding out what is broken is complex given that there are many parts that may potentially be broken. Starting every diagnosis from scratch takes time because it requires the mechanic to think their way into the problem.
>
> To increase efficiency, the repair shop employs a clustering algorithm that groups cars with similar symptoms together by means of the cars' sensor data. Then mechanics can dedicate themselves to cars with similar problems, which makes diagnosing easier because a general direction is already suggested.

87 | What are the most commonly used methods in unsupervised learning?

Unsupervised learning spans a number of methods that differ in terms of what a machine learns. We do not have room in this book to present all the ML methods that fall under the category of unsupervised learning, so here we focus on the most important ones.

Clustering

Clustering is, arguably, the most frequently used method in unsupervised learning. The goal of clustering observations of a dataset is to create groups of observations that are similar *within* a certain group but different *between* groups. To implement such a clustering, we use several algorithms (models). Let's look at how one of them works: k-means clustering.

Suppose that with Your Model Car we want to implement a customer segmentation. Since our customers don't tell us upfront what kind of customers they are, we lack the target variable "customer type". The data that we do have, however, includes details about our customers such as their age and the value of their orders on our website. The graph in Figure 87-1 plots some customers by relating the value of their last order on our website to their age. Each dot represents one customer and the value of their last order.

Just by looking at the graph we can see that there seems to be a pattern. There are some areas in the graph where the points are denser than in other areas. These are ideal conditions for applying a clustering algorithm.

The k-means clustering algorithm is a very simple iterative algorithm that works as follows. Firstly, we have to tell the algorithm into how many clusters we would like to split our dataset. In our case, simply by looking at the data it seems that three distinct groups are a good start. The k-means clustering algorithm will carry out the following steps:

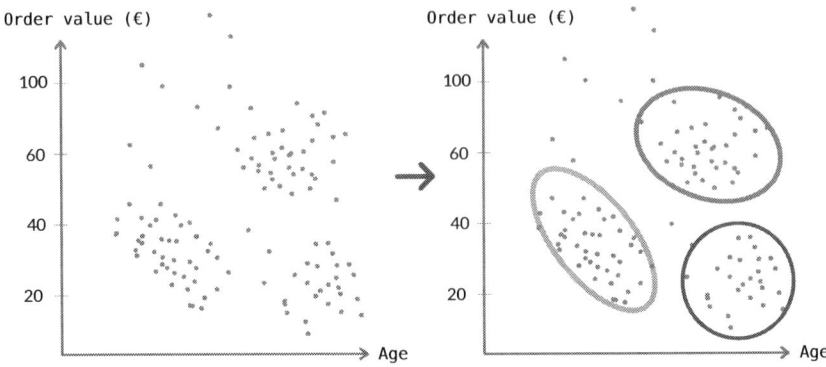

Figure 87.1 Example of clustering on customer data

1. Randomly choose three data points, each of which will be a cluster-centre
2. Repeat the following steps:
   a. Look for each observation in the dataset which cluster-centre is closest.
   b. Assign the observation to that cluster.
   c. When all observations are grouped into a cluster, calculate the new cluster-centre for each cluster. (You can think of this as finding the middle of the cluster. In the first round the centre is the randomly chosen initial observation; in later rounds it will be the mean value of all the observations in one cluster.)
   d. Start over at step 2.a.

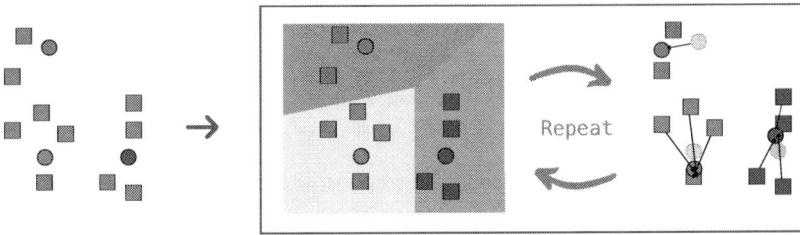

Figure 87.2 Overview of k-means clustering algorithm

By repeating these steps, we end up with the desired number of clusters. It is a bit like every observation is grouped into the solar system and it gravitates towards the centre. The result is that observations that are close to each other (and therefore similar to each other) belong to one group. In the Your Model Car example, "similar" means that two customers have a similar age or that their last orders were similar in value.

Once the algorithm has identified and demarcated clusters of similar observations, we can examine, characterize and manually label these clusters and the observations therein. In our customer segmentation case in Figure 87-1, some sensible labels for our clusters would be:

Understanding Machine Learning as the Key Driver Behind Artificial Intelligence

- Cluster 1 (light blue): Young smart shoppers
- Cluster 2 (dark blue): Senior smart shoppers
- Cluster 3 (orange): Senior premium customers

Anomaly detection

Another commonly used method in unsupervised learning is anomaly detection. The goal of anomaly detection algorithms is to detect outliers and anomalies in a dataset. Anomalies are observations that are rare and/or significantly differ from the other observations. Such anomaly detection is useful in a wide range of use cases; for example, to detect fraudulent transactions and behaviour in credit card usage.

Outliers and anomalies can be detected in various ways, a lot of which fall under unsupervised learning. One example is the local outlier factor algorithm (LOF). It is similar to the k-means clustering algorithm in that it characterizes points by means of their neighbouring points, or rather the distance between them. Specifically, the LOF algorithm computes for every observation of a dataset the distance to its X nearest neighbours. Figure 87-3 shows such a calculation where X = 3. Next, for every observation we calculate how big a circle around the point is if we include all three of its nearest neighbours in that circle. For all of the points pertaining to the point cloud on the right side of Figure 87-3, this circle is rather small. For Point A on the left side, the circle is extremely big and this gives an analytical confirmation of what is visible: Point A is an outlier and thus an anomaly in the dataset.

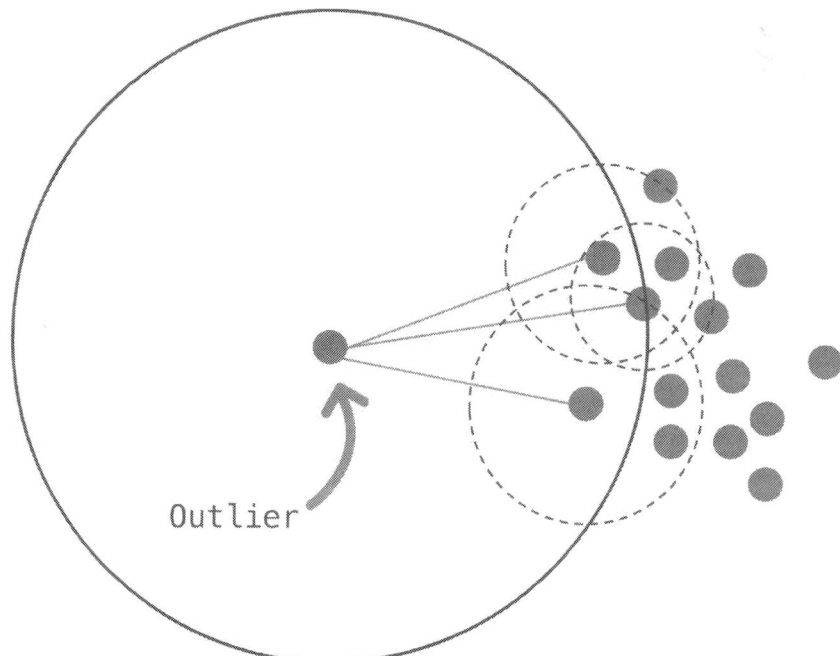

Figure 87.3 Example of the local outlier factor algorithm

The Ultimate Data and AI Guide

Other popular unsupervised learning methods

There are a number of other methods used in unsupervised learning to solve a range of problems.

Autoencoders are algorithms that are trained to learn an efficient representation of a given dataset by encoding the main aspects of it whilst ignoring the redundant information. Such autoencoders can be thought of as packaging algorithms that put the relevant information of a dataset in a more compact form.

Another method in unsupervised learning is *association rule learning*, which can be used to find frequently occurring patterns in data. Such algorithms are used, for instance, in affinity analysis, where shops want to find out what products are often bought together. With this information at hand, product recommendations of such complementary goods can increase the rate of cross-selling (selling an additional product to a customer even though they might have initially been looking for only one). The idea is simple: such algorithms look at the data and identify patterns that occur frequently. For example, in preparation for their holidays customers will buy bathing suits, sunglasses and sunscreen together. Somebody who is looking for sunglasses will therefore likely react to being offered sunscreen.

We could go on with this list of unsupervised learning methods, but that would go beyond the scope of this book. The takeaway point is that even if you are dealing with unlabelled data so that supervised ML cannot be applied, there is usually some sort of method you can use to extract something useful from a dataset.

Moreover, it is not like supervised and unsupervised learning are mutually exclusive. On the contrary, in a lot of use cases we use both of them to achieve our final goal. For example, a customer segmentation with an unsupervised clustering algorithm can create different groups of customers. These can then be manually labelled so that afterwards we can use a supervised ML algorithm to classify new customers into one of the respective clusters.

Case study 39

Predictive maintenance for motors of heavy machinery

A service provider for the maintenance of heavy machinery wants to create a system that is able to predict if the spark plug engine of a motor for heavy machinery will break down. The breakdown of a spark plug influences the capacity of the engine, but it often goes unnoticed because a certain degree of fluctuation in the capacity of the engine is normal.

To implement the use case, a labelled dataset would be necessary (target variable: spark plug is broken or not). However, neither humans nor sensors currently record this data. The dataset is unlabelled.

To create the necessary labels an anomaly detection algorithm is employed. It is known that if a spark plug breaks down, there are sudden impacts on variables for which data is available (e.g. voltage and temperature). The algorithm detects such unusual events, which are then

> examined by specialists to confirm whether they are indeed signs of a spark plug having broken. In this way the service provider obtains data on the target variables that can be used for supervised ML.

88 | What is reinforcement learning?

Compared to supervised and unsupervised learning, the third pillar of ML, reinforcement learning, is an entirely different breed. The concept of labelled/unlabelled data does not apply here. In fact, data does not need to exist in advance at all in a reinforcement learning setting. Instead, with reinforcement learning the computer learns by trial and error – simulations, if you will.

Remember that humans can learn in different ways: by being told about it (supervised learning), by figuring out patterns themselves by looking at something (unsupervised learning), and – probably the most effective way – by just trying things out and seeing how they go. Reinforcement learning works pretty much in the latter way. Instead of giving a computer data from which it is supposed to learn, we put it into an environment where it is supposed to simply try things out and learn how to behave optimally in that environment.

One main area of application for reinforcement learning is games, and the board game Go is a famous example of how powerful this kind of learning can be. Go is a popular board game that is extremely complex, a lot more so than chess. It is estimated that there are some 2×10^{170}[28] board positions in the game. Google Deepmind, a research department at Google, has developed and improved several AI systems that is able to play Go.

Earlier versions of the algorithm were taught the game with supervised ML methods by looking at previous games, and they were already beating human world champions in the game. However, in 2017 a different version of the algorithm, called AlphaGo Zero, was presented. Instead of learning to play the game by looking at historical data, it learned to play it from scratch, without any historical data, through reinforcement learning methods. That is, it created its own training data through simulations. After 40 days of playing games against itself, it was able to beat all previous versions of AlphaGo (which were already beating human champions).[cxxxiv] Its successor, AlphaGo Zero, is now considered the best Go player in the world.

This was truly a milestone in the field of reinforcement learning and AI: without the input of historical data, a computer learned a game all by itself and now outperforms every human on this planet. Not only that, but with its style of playing completely "untainted" by human ways of interpreting the game, it even serves as an inspiration to the Go player community. The Go world has already started picking up the playing styles of the various versions of AlphaGo. Instead of humans teaching an algorithm what to do and how to behave, AlphaGo Zero has turned the tables. The computer learned by itself and is *now teaching us humans*. Professional GO player Mok Jin-seok said this of playing AlphaGo Zero:

---

28. That's a 2 followed by 170 zeros

At first, it was hard to understand and I almost felt like I was playing against an alien. However, having had a great amount of experience, I've become used to it (...). We are now past the point where we debate the gap between the capability of AlphaGo and humans. It's now between computers.[cxxxv]

Table 88.1 What is reinforcement learning and why does it matter?

What is reinforcement learning?

Reinforcement learning is the third major way in which a machine is able to learn.

The goal of reinforcement learning is to have a model take optimal decisions in a certain environment. For example, a reinforcement learning algorithm for autonomous driving would aim to take decisions that ensure all traffic is safe and flows smoothly.

Unlike in supervised and unsupervised learning, where we use historical data, in reinforcement learning the model is put into an environment and is left to explore, and thereby create data, by itself. This can be likened to a simulation.

Why does it matter?

Reinforcement learning is increasingly drawing attention in the ML community. Unlike other types of learning, it does not rely on the availability of historical data, since it generates its own data on the fly through simulations, and so it can be used in a variety of different situations. While reinforcement learning is still at a research stage, we can expect to see it used with ground-breaking developments in the creation of AI.

How does reinforcement learning work?

To understand how reinforcement learning works, it is necessary to put the concept of supervised/unsupervised learning aside and introduce some new concepts. The main idea of reinforcement learning is to put a (software) *agent* into an *environment* where it can take *actions* to maximize a *reward* for itself. Figure 88-1 breaks this down in an illustration.

The agent is some sort of ML model, often a deep neural network. Just like in supervised ML settings, this model is able to create an output from some sort of input. Or in other words, it is able to observe its environment (input) and take *decisions on how to behave* (output). We put the agent into an environment where it is confronted with a situation (i.e. some input) and have it take actions within the environment. This (virtual) environment could be anything: a game of Go, chess, Super Mario, a flight simulator, a road simulator for learning how to drive autonomously etc.

We then "watch" the action that the agent takes in that environment and give it feedback: we give it rewards for taking desirable and good actions (e.g. certain moves in Go or stopping at traffic lights in a road simulator) and punishments for bad actions (e.g. driving over children or crashing into walls).

We tell the model: "Try out all kinds of actions and try to maximize your reward." The reward needs to be defined by humans and is not always easy to

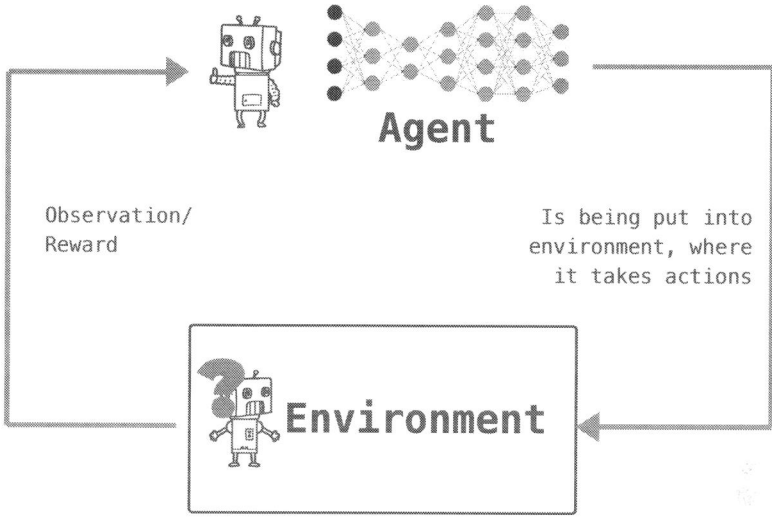

Figure 88.1 Visualization of reinforcement learning

quantify. Super Mario provides an illustrative example of what such a reward could look like. In the Super Mario game, the reward would be equal to the player's score, which increases when the player moves to the right on the screen and collects the coins, and decreases with every second elapsed. The agent will then enter an exploration phase where it will try out different actions and collect data on what action led to what kind of reward. If set up correctly, in the case of Super Mario it will try to get to the right as quickly as possible and collect as many coins as possible without dying (which is the ultimate punishment).

The appeal of reinforcement learning

The notion that a machine is able to learn a task or even behave without the input of historical data is pretty amazing. However, while the idea of reinforcement learning seems very appealing at first, it is not an easy concept to implement. There are a large number of challenges and problems to be solved in this discipline, which is still in its infancy.

Accordingly, at present reinforcement learning is barely used in any sector and very few companies have publicly stated that they are embracing this type of learning in their business. Car manufacturer Audi claims to have used reinforcement learning in the context of autonomous driving. Presumably, other companies active in the field of autonomous driving are also using or at least experimenting with it, given that autonomous driving is a prime use case for applying reinforcement learning. But apart from that, there has been very little information about its use in the business world, which means that either companies are keeping it classified or they are just not using it. It is probably a mix of both.[cxxxvi]

Even though reinforcement learning is not mature, however, that does not decrease its appeal. The notion of creating an intelligent software agent from scratch without needing historical data is extremely powerful and will probably be an important cornerstone for the future progress of AI. We will likely see reinforcement learning increasingly be applied in a number of fields, e.g. robotics and autonomous driving of any kind of vehicle.

So far the application of reinforcement learning has mostly been limited to games. Today, intelligent bots play ego shooters such as Quake III and complex strategy games such as Dota and StarCraft at super-human levels. A notable exploration into other fields is the research of OpenAI, which has created an entire AI gym where different reinforcement learning agents can be tried out and tested in various environments. For example, there are plenty of environments where human-like 3D stickmen are learning locomotion behaviour: to run, jump over obstacles, go upstairs, fight each other etc.[cxxxvii] These are all extremely complex actions and behaviours that we humans learned through thousands of years of evolution.

The next logical step after having a 3D stickman learn to walk and move around is to implement that in robots. There is still a long way to go with reinforcement learning and many challenges and problems to be solved, but research suggests that at least the software side of such robotic implementations will be ready in the not-too-distant future.

6_3 Popular ML tools

89 | What types of ML tools are there?

When you implement an ML project, you quickly encounter a plethora of tools, e.g. Hadoop, R, Python, SQL, Tensorflow, Keras, Splunk and Zeppelin. It can be really confusing to distinguish these tools by means of their type, let alone their capabilities.

Types of ML tools

In general, we can distinguish between three different types of tools that are used to create an ML model:

- Dedicated ML software
- Programming languages
- Libraries used in programming languages

Let's put these into context.

When you want to create an ML model (or really do anything) with a computer, the main goal is to give the computer a set of instructions so that it implements whatever you want it to do. In order to do that, you need an *interface*, which is something that makes two systems able to communicate. If you are in a restaurant, the interface for you as a customer to communicate with

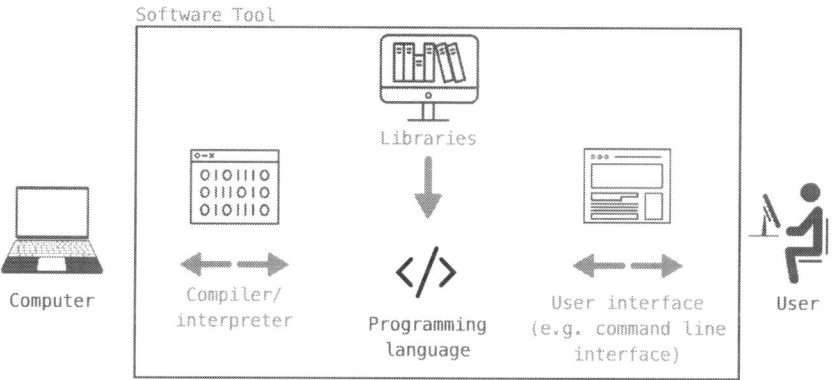

Figure 89.1 Types of ML tools

the kitchen is the waiter. With regard to a computer, the interface between the system "human" and the system "computer" contains a lot of components, both hardware (e.g. screen, keyboard and mouse) and software (e.g. operating system and software that runs on that operating system).

Computer programming languages and software tools differ in how comprehensive they are as an interface for a human to communicate with a computer. Programming languages are pretty basic. If you download a programming language such as Java or Python, then you essentially download a *language compiler*. You can think of a compiler as one big dictionary for your computer. Once you have downloaded such a compiler, you can talk to your computer in the respective language. So if you "install" Python on your computer, then your computer will be equipped with that dictionary, so you can give it instructions in Python language.

Programming languages come with so-called *packages* or *libraries*. You can think of these as add-ons that you can download, much like Google Sheet and Excel have add-ons that you can install to get certain extra features. These packages are pre-written code that you can download and use. Programming languages that are used in ML, for example, have a lot of packages that implement ML or statistical methods. So instead of going through the tedious process of writing the necessary steps to calculate an ML model, you can simply download a library and use it.

Obviously, if you want to communicate with a computer (or computer cluster) by means of a programming language, you need to speak that language. Like with any other language, it takes time to learn it. In contrast, software tools are often easier to pick up. Such software tools add another layer on top of a programming language in order to provide a more user-friendly interface between humans and computers so as to facilitate communication between the two. This additional layer could be a graphical user interface with a drag-and-drop menu for the user. In the background, the input the user provides is translated into bits and bytes using a certain programming language.

The Ultimate Data and AI Guide

Commonly used ML tools

Figure 89-2 shows the results of a survey of which tools data scientists and ML practitioners use. Today, most practitioners use the programming language Python to create ML models. This is a change to some years ago, when the programming language R, designed for statistical analysis, was more popular. As we see in Chapter 📖 32, SQL is an indispensable language that is used to retrieve and manipulate data in a database. But proprietary software tools such as RapidMiner are also popular.

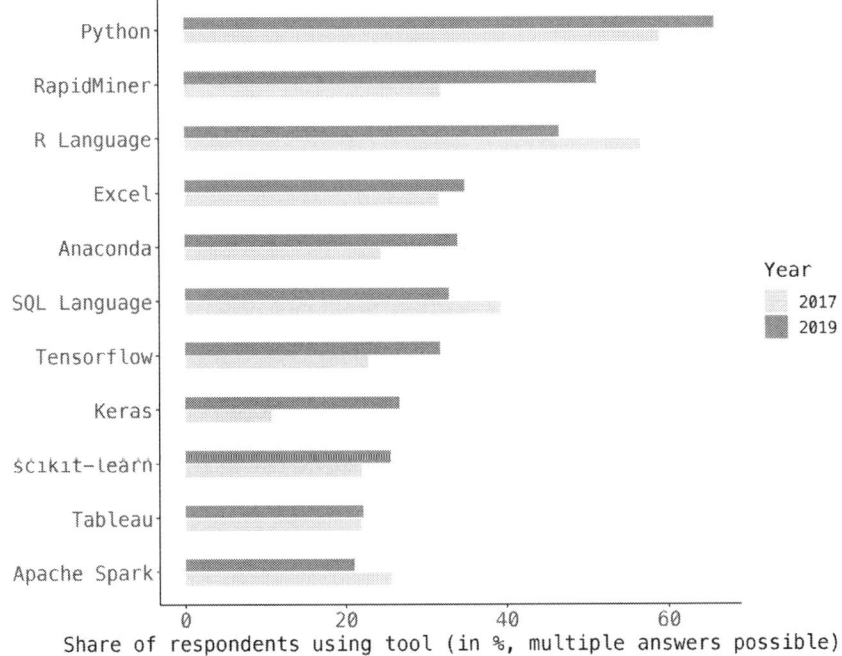

Figure 89.2 Poll of the most popular ML tools
From "Python leads the 11 top Data Science, Machine Learning platforms: Trends and Analysis" by Gregory Piatetsky, 2019 (https://www.kdnuggets.com/2019/05/poll-top-data-science-machine-learning-platforms.html). Copyright 2019 by KDnuggets. Reprinted and modified with permission.[cxxxviii]

These are just a few of the most commonly used tools in ML. The programming languages and the respective tools all work in a fairly similar manner. What matters most is developing data-driven thinking, knowing what you want to do and having the necessary knowledge of ML methods. The tool with which you implement the ML is secondary. This is much like with photography. A good photographer knows where to go and from what angle to take a shot in order to get a good picture. Whether they use a high-end camera or a simple SLR standard model does not matter so much – the camera is "just" a tool. Having said that, there are obviously differences in the tools that make them especially suitable or unsuitable for certain use cases.

90 | What is Python?

Table 90.1 Overview of Python

What is Python?

Python is a general purpose programming language. It is open source.

Why does it matter?

Today, Python is the most widely used tool for data science and ML. On top of that, Python is widely used in other fields, notably software development.

It has a large, active community that develops packages and helps to solve problems. It is really hard to think of a question or problem in Python that has not been asked by someone else already.

Python is regarded as an elegant and neat language. It is extremely readable and easier to pick up than other programming languages. It offers a wide range of packages, especially in the area of deep learning and neural networks. It is also a rather reliable and efficient language.

Where is it used?

Python is used in most ML projects and beyond, especially in projects where neural networks and deep learning are applied. Python can be used for data processing, modelling and visualization, since it offers a wide range of packages.

91 | What is R and RStudio?

Table 91.1 Overview of R and RStudio

What is R?

R is a programming language designed for statistical analysis. It is open source and often used in conjunction with RStudio, a user-friendly interface that facilitates writing R code.

Why does it matter?

R is the go-to programming language for conducting statistical analyses. R is popular mainly for its richness in libraries, above all for statistical analyses. That means in R a lot of statistical methods and models are already pre-implemented and can be used off the shelf.

Accordingly, R is widely used in a number of academic disciplines that use statistical methods, and it is used in business. It also has a large and active community that develops libraries.

Over the past few years, R has increasingly lost its edge to Python, especially in the business environment, because Python is a more elegant and efficient language that can be used in a wider range of fields and the Python community has been catching up in terms of creating libraries.

> Because of its many libraries, R is great for projects that include mostly statistical analyses and visualizing data. However, R is regarded as a pretty ugly language, especially by computer scientists. Furthermore, R is not a very efficient language. It is mostly used in projects with small or medium-sized datasets.

92 | What is scikit-learn?

Table 92.1 Overview of scikit-learn

What is scikit-learn?

> Scikit-learn is an ML library for Python. It contains all sorts of algorithms used to implement both supervised and unsupervised ML methods.

Why does it matter?

> Python has developed into the most popular tool for creating ML models. However, Python is just a programming language. The library scikit-learn provides a rich set of pre-written code with which you can easily create ML models without having to write the code for all of these models from scratch by yourself.

Where is it used?

> Whenever we want to train, validate and test ML models in Python.

93 | What are Tensorflow and Keras?

Table 93.1 Overview of Tensorflow and Keras

What are Tensorflow and Keras?

> Tensorflow is a library used to implement and calculate neural network models and implement deep learning. In the wake of the hype around deep learning, the popularity of Tensorflow has been surging.
>
> Tensorflow is used above all in Python programming language, but it is available in other ones. There are also other libraries that are based on and therefore use Tensorflow.
>
> Tensorflow in itself is a rather complex package. While it saves the user from writing a lot of complex code, there is still quite a lot of programming to do. This is where Keras comes into play.
>
> Keras is another library, also mostly used in Python programming language. Keras builds on Tensorflow (or other packages) and acts as an interface between the user and Tensorflow. Keras makes working with Tensorflow much easier and more user friendly.

Why do they matter?

Tensorflow and Keras have developed into the standard packages for calculating neural networks. They therefore lie at the heart of all deep learning.

Where are they used?

Whenever we want to train neural networks and apply deep learning.

94 | What are MLLib, PySpark and SparkR?

Table 94.1 Overview MLlib, PySpark and SparkR

What are MLLib, PySpark and SparkR?

Spark is a big-data framework that is used to process data on computer clusters and distributed systems (📄 41). MLLib is a library that enables you to implement ML methods on such clusters within Spark.

PySpark and SparkR are application programming interfaces (APIs). These APIs enable the integration of Spark with Python and Spark with R respectively. That means that they enable you to use Spark as a big-data framework by means of using Python or R programming language.

Why do they matter?

ML becomes much more complicated when we are dealing with datasets that are so large that they cannot be processed on a single-node computer. In that case we have to use computer clusters and big-data frameworks like Spark.

The conventional ML tools, such as Python or R, do not work in these environments. That is why we have to use the functionalities of big-data frameworks such as Spark and its native MLLib directly, or we have to be able to use Spark through other programming languages. This is enabled through PySpark and SparkR as APIs.

Where are they used?

In cases where we want to apply ML methods to datasets that are too large to be processed on a single-node computer.

95 | What are some popular cloud-based ML tools?

Table 95.1 Cloud-based ML tools

What are the cloud-based ML tools?

The major cloud service providers offer services that enable you to create and directly deploy (📄 126) ML models. These often come with user-friendly graphical user interfaces. The services offered by the major cloud providers are:

- Microsoft Azure Machine Learning Studio
- AWS Machine Learning and SageMaker
- Google Cloud Machine Learning Engine
- IBM Watson Machine Learning

Why do they matter?

You can build your own ML model from scratch in, say, Python. However, this comes with a lot of manual work. Many ML projects fail when models are deployed and put into operation. This step is much easier to do with the ML services of cloud providers, because they provide the entire necessary infrastructure and environment along with numerous other services that enable easy deployment of models.

Where are they used?

Given that cloud-based ML tools are proprietary software for which users need to pay (there is also a free option with limited functionality), they are mostly used in the business environment.

7 Creating and Testing a ML Model with Supervised Machine Learning

7_1 Creating a machine learning model with supervised ML methods

96 | What ingredients do you need and what is the recipe for creating an ML model?

Machine learning (ML) can be applied in any sector as long as sufficient representative, high-quality data is available. Yet the approach to creating an ML model and the ingredients needed for it are always the same. Step by step over the course of this chapter, we develop a model with supervised ML in the context of Your Model Car and cover the necessary theoretical concepts along the way.

These are the ingredients for creating an artificial intelligence (AI) system with ML:

- *An object of interest that we are trying to determine or predict:* In our example this object of interest is the sales of a given product in Your Model Car. Furthermore, we need some factors that influence this object of interest. In our example, some such factors are the product's price and how it is advertised. This influence needs to be in a systematic way or according to some pattern.
- *Historical data that represents this real-world process:* In the data world, the object of interest is the *target variable*, the factors that influence it are the *input variables*, and the systematic patterns by which the input variables influence the target variable are the *correlation* or *signal*. The historical data should encompass all of these things.
- *An ML model:* This model is provided with the historical data so that it can identify and learn the underlying patterns. This is called model training. Before we provide the model with data, we have to decide to which input variable we want it to pay attention. This process is what we do during feature engineering (📄 99) and feature selection (📄 100). After a model has been trained, it goes through a validation and testing phase to check how well it does its job. A number of factors can influence the ability of a model to determine or predict the target variable. The most notorious bugbear, which is one of the central challenges in ML, is called overfitting (📄 105). Fortunately, there are various remedies (📄 106–📄 108).

The Ultimate Data and AI Guide

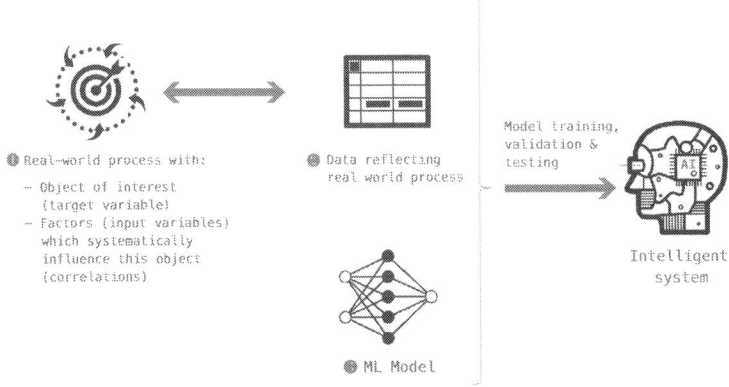

Figure 96.1 Ingredients to create a ML model

At the end of this entire process you will have an ML model that is able to perform the task it was trained for. This could be to take an autonomous decision, predict or determine a variable, or automate a certain task.

> **Case study 40**
>
> **Creating an AI system to predict the daily sales of a product in Your Model Car**
>
> To optimize our stock and logistics system, we want to create a system that is able to predict how many of a product we are going to sell on a given day in the future. For that we will use supervised ML to train a model with historical sales data.
>
> Our real-world process is therefore sales, and our object of interest is daily sales of a given product. We have historical data of the daily sales of the product "1992 Ferrari 360 Spider red (scale 1:18)" with the product ID "SC12_5355". Our data dates back to 2016, when we included the product in our portfolio. As Figure 96-1 and Table 96-1 show, sales of the product have been growing over time.
>
>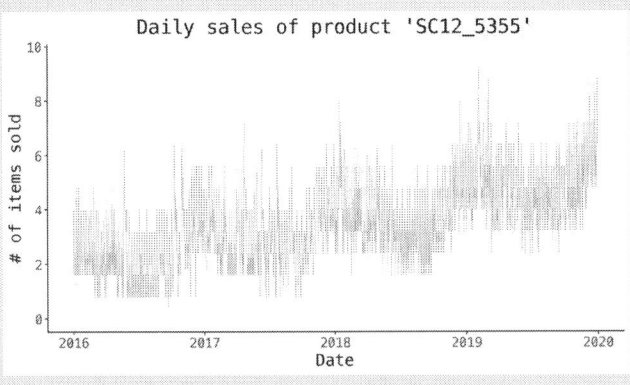
>
> Figure 96.2 Line chart of daily sales

Table 96-1 Dataset of daily sales

Daily sales table "SC12_5355" (1,461 observations, 3 variables)

PRODUCT_ID	DATE	SALES
SC12_5355	2016-01-01	5
SC12_5355	2016-01-02	6
...		
SC12_5355	2019-12-30	9
SC12_5355	2019-12-31	6

97 | What is an ML model?

A *model* in its broadest sense is a simplified representation of reality. We use models to explain, communicate or predict a process, object or idea. This also holds true for ML models, where we are focusing on a specific aspect of the real world. Models exist across all academic disciplines and beyond.

There are many ways to communicate and express a model. For example, say we want to model the weight of a person and how it relates to their height. We could represent this model with words (verbal representation), with a graph (graphical) or in mathematical language (mathematical), as in Figure 97-1, where we depict a model to predict a person's weight based on their height. While verbal and graphical expressions of models might be more accessible to a wide audience, expressing complex processes that involve a lot of variables becomes unviable. That is why in most scientific disciplines we use mathematical representations, which are much more effective and enable us to express more complicated processes. Furthermore, they enable us to communicate the model to a computer.

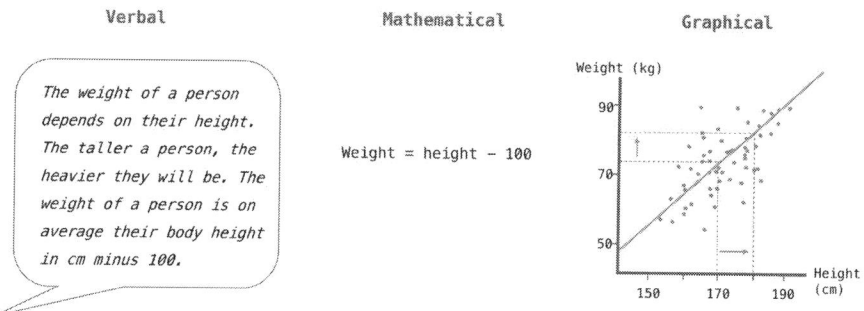

Figure 97.1 Verbal, graphical and mathematical expressions of a model[29]

---

29. Fictional data

A model should be parsimonious. That means it should only model the aspect of the world that is relevant for its purpose and leave out all the rest. This is because reality is way too complex to be captured in its entirety and unnecessary components of a model are just clutter.

Maps are a good example. The goal of a map is to help us orientate ourselves and be able to navigate. There are different types of maps, but the ones we typically use model the aspects of the real world that are relevant for the specific purpose of navigating: streets, street names, a proportional depiction of distances between places, maybe the kind of geographical landscape (town, forest, city) etc. These components are enough for the map to serve its purpose, and everything beyond that is unnecessary clutter that would only dilute the effectiveness of the model. We don't need to see all the details of the real world, e.g. the colour of streets, the height of buildings, the form of leaves on a tree, the shape of roof tiles, etc.

This also applies to ML models. In fact, things are even more rigorous. In supervised ML, we typically have one specific object of interest that is represented by our target variable, e.g. the weight of a person. Usually, we want to create a model that is able to determine or predict this variable as well as possible. We do that by having the model relate a set of input variables to the target variable.

Table 97.1 What is an ML model and why does it matter?

What is an ML model?
A model is a representation of some aspect of the real world. Good models are parsimonious, i.e. they focus on the parts that are relevant to them. In ML, models also represent an aspect of the real world. More specifically, they usually attempt to determine or predict a certain target variable by using input variables.
An ML model consists of mathematical functions (i.e. sets of rules) that are supposed to reflect underlying patterns between the target variable and the input variables.
ML models are created through what is called model training.
There are a number of model classes in ML and they differ in the way they attempt to depict the real world. Depending on the underlying problem, some model classes are more appropriate to reflect a given process than others.

Why does it matter?
ML models lie at the heart of the vast majority of today's AI systems.

Thus, in supervised ML a model is supposed to determine or predict a target variable as accurately as possible by relating relevant input variables to it. In ML parlance we speak of finding a *mapping function* that relates the input (the input variables) to an output as well as possible. *Function* in this case refers to a set of rules. The more this set of rules represents underlying patterns that exist in real life, the more accurately the model will be able to do its job. In the height–weight example, the input is the height of a person, the output is a prediction of their weight and the model is a set of rules (expressed mathematically) that we can use to calculate the person's weight. In this case the set of rules is easy: "Take a person's height in cm, deduct 100 and that will be their weight." We could extend this model by including other factors that are likely to influence a person's weight, such as gender and age.

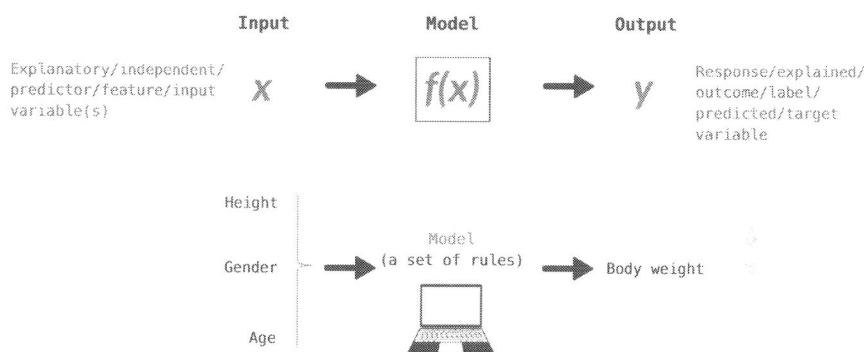

Figure 97.2 Overview of supervised ML

ML models are created through a process called model training. During model training, we provide an ML model with historical data from which it can identify and unveil the relevant patterns between independent and output variables. In our height–weight example, the model is the result of training a model on a dataset of a few dozen people.

When we train a model, we have to choose a model class. There are different types of model classes in ML; for example, linear models, tree-based models and neural networks. These model classes differ in the way they depict real life. Consequently, some model classes are especially apt for certain problems. For example, neural networks try to emulate the structure of the human brain to reflect real-world processes and are extremely good at computer vision and natural language problems.

> **Case study 41**
>
> **Using a decision tree from the model class "tree-based models"**
>
> To predict the daily sales of a product in Your Model Car, we are going to use a simple decision tree from the model class "tree-based model", because it is very intuitive to understand. The idea behind a decision tree is that it arrives at a prediction or outcome after applying a set of simple if-then rules. The order and specification of the if-then rules are from the historical data the model is trained on. Each of these if-then rules can be depicted graphically as a decision node in a hierarchical tree structure.

Here is a simple schematic overview of what a decision tree to predict daily sales could look like. This tree has only two decision nodes.

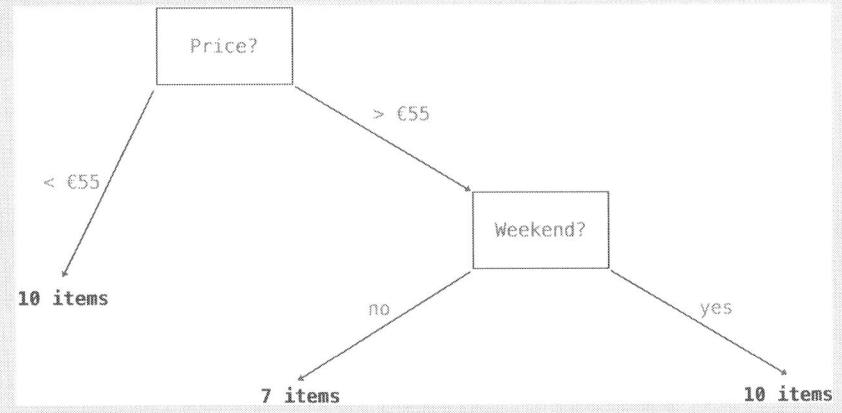

Figure 97.3 An example of a simple decision tree model to predict daily sales

98 | What is a correlation and why is it necessary for ML models?

In order for ML models to produce results there *must* be an underlying pattern in the real world by which the independent and target variable(s) of the model are related. In statistics and ML, we call this a correlation.

Correlation refers to the degree to which two variables fluctuate together or are associated with each other. Our world is full of such correlations. For example, there is a very strong correlation between a person's height and their weight, or the number sales of a product and its price, or the season and the type of clothes bought (summer versus winter).

The job of ML models is to uncover and memorize correlations that exist between the input variables and the target variable. And this only works if such underlying patterns actually exist in real life.

For example, say with Your Model Car we want to create a model to predict the likelihood that a website visitor will click on a product link. Lots of factors are correlated with this likelihood, e.g. the time of day, the price of the product, whether the customer has looked at similar products before, their taste, their current income and savings, the time of year (e.g. before Christmas) and many more. If we had data on all of these factors, then we could train an extremely accurate and therefore powerful ML model that would uncover and internalize all of these correlations.

However, if either of the following two conditions is present, then even the best ML model will create useless results:

Creating and Testing a ML Model with Supervised Machine Learning

- *In the real world such correlations between factors exist, but we do not have the necessary data that captures these patterns.* This happens frequently. In the example, it will be practically impossible to know the taste, earnings or savings of a customer who is visiting our website.
- *In the real world such correlations and patterns are absent.* There is an infinite number of correlations between a certain pair of variables. However, there is also an infinite number of variable pairs that have nothing to do with each other. For example, the current weather in the Pacific Ocean will not affect the sales of our model cars.

Therefore, the existence of correlations in the process or situation that an ML model is examining is the central building block for it to work.

Table 98.1 What is a correlation and why does it matter?

What is a correlation?

A correlation is a measure of the relationship between two variables. There are various types of correlations and they are measured with various correlation coefficients.

The most commonly used is the Pearson correlation coefficient, which measures the *linear* correlation between two numerical variables. It can take on values between –1 and 1.

If two variables are positively correlated, then their correlation coefficient will be between 0 and 1. This means that as one variable increases in value, the other one also tends to increase. If two variables are negatively correlated, then their correlation coefficient will be between 0 and –1, so as one variable increases in value, the other one tends to decrease. The closer the value of a correlation coefficient is to 1 or –1, the stronger the relationship between the two variables.

Presented graphically, the correlation coefficient between two variables indicates how closely aligned data points are to a straight line in a scatterplot.

Why does it matter?

Correlations represent patterns in a dataset and ML models work by identifying and picking up such patterns. Therefore, correlations between variables are the central building blocks that make ML models work.

The Pearson correlation coefficient

In statistics and ML there are a number of ways in which the correlation between two variables can be measured and quantified. The most famous one is the Pearson correlation coefficient. It measures the strength of the *linear* relationship between two numerical variables. It can take values from –1 (perfect negative linear relationship) and +1 (perfect positive linear relationship). In Figure 98-1 we provide three datasets, that differ both in the direction of their correlation and also in its strength, as measured by the Pearson correlation coefficient r.

The Ultimate Data and AI Guide

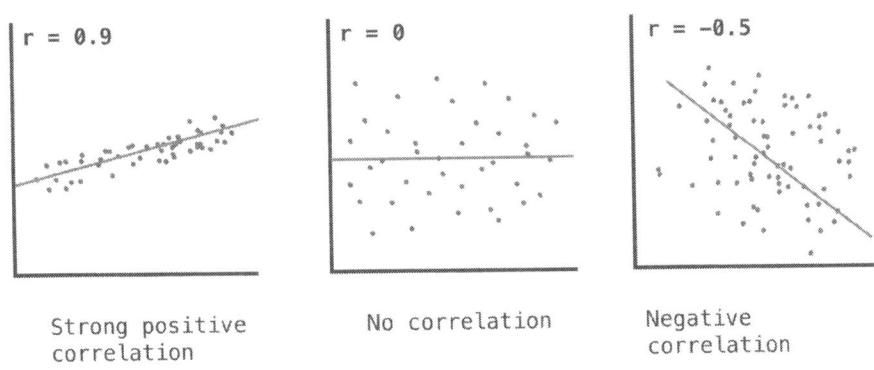

Figure 98.1 Various datasets that differ in the strength and direction of correlation between the x- and y-variable. This is reflected in the correlation coefficient values.

A *positive correlation* between two variables indicates that as the value of one variable increases, the value of the other variable also tends to increase. For example, let's look at the relationship between the number of times a product on Your Model Car has been viewed and how often it has been sold (Figure 98-2). There is a clear pattern between the two. The more often a product has been viewed, the more often it tends to have been sold. The two variables have a positive correlation, which indicates that they fluctuate together in the same direction.

The stronger a positive correlation between two variables is, the closer the coefficient will be to 1. In our case the correlation coefficient between a product's views and its sales is at 0.56. This is a moderately strong positive correlation, meaning that the more a product has been viewed, the higher its sales number tends to be. Graphically, the Pearson correlation coefficient indicates how closely the observations are aligned to a straight line in a scatter plot (regardless of how steep this line is).

A negative value of the correlation coefficient would indicate that two variables fluctuate in the opposite direction. That is, as the value of one variable increases, the value of the other one tends to decrease. An example of a variable pair that usually has a negative correlation is the price of a product and the sales of it. The more expensive a product, the less it tends to sell.

Separating correlation and causation

One extremely important aspect of correlation that is emphasized by statisticians and machine learners in an almost mantra-like fashion is that *correlation does not imply causation*.

Causation refers to situations where one process, thing or state contributes to the production of another process, thing or state. To put it differently, a cause is (partly) responsible for a given outcome, and likewise a given outcome is (partly) dependent on a given cause. For example, the outcome of you arriving late at work might be caused by there being an unusual amount of traffic.

Creating and Testing a ML Model with Supervised Machine Learning

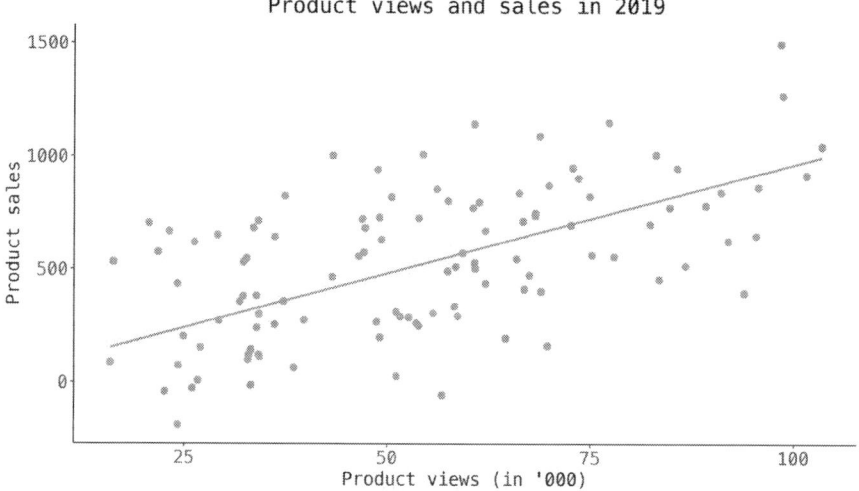

Figure 98.2 Example of a positive correlation

Typically, outcomes are multi-causal, which means they have many causes. You might be late for work because of traffic *and* because you forgot to set your alarm.

Correlation, on the other hand, merely refers to how or if two variables move in the same (positive) direction or opposite (negative) directions. For example, sales of sunglasses and ice cream are positively correlated. Sales of ice cream and winter gloves are negatively correlated. But one does not cause the other.

So there is a crucial difference between these two concepts, and correlation does *not* imply causation. Two variables, A and B, might have a strong correlation, but that does not necessarily mean that A causes B. People who are not aware of this might jump to conclusions prematurely. There are a number of ways in which two variables can be correlated without having the expected causation behind it. Here are some examples.

a) Reverse causation: B causes A

In a number of cases, the causational direction that exists between two correlated variables is the opposite of what is assumed:

The rotation of a windmill (A) is strongly correlated with the wind speed (B). Therefore, the windmill causes the wind.

Obviously, it is the other way around.

In some situations, the causation between two correlated variables might also be bidirectional. For example:

The level of happiness of a person will have a strong correlation with the number of times they smile. Therefore, happiness causes smiles.

While this might be true, it has also been shown that body language affects our mood. Thus "forcing" yourself to smile will lift your mood and make you happier[cxxxix].

b) Common cause (lurking/confounding variable): A and B are both caused by a third variable

Two variables might display a strong correlation with no *direct* causal link between them. Instead, there might be a third variable that influences both variables simultaneously and thereby creates the correlation.

The number of ice cream sales at the beach is strongly correlated with the number of shark attacks on humans. Therefore, ice cream sales cause sharks to attack.

Obviously, there is no reason to assume that there is a direct causation between these two variables in either direction. Instead, they have a common cause: the weather. The warmer and sunnier it is, the more people will be in the water and the more shark attacks on humans there will be. At the same time, the warmer and sunnier it is, the more people will buy ice cream.

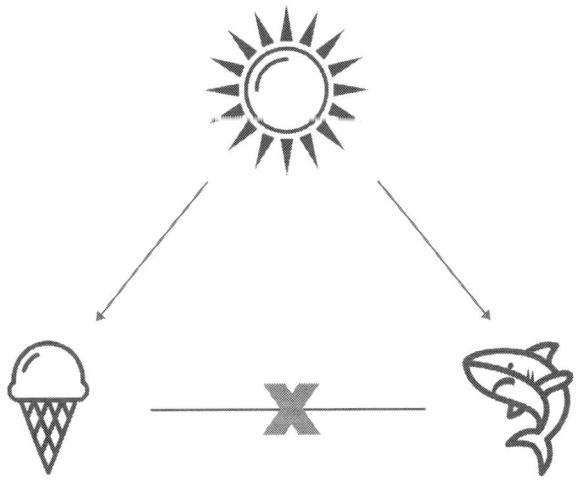

Figure 98.3 An example of a confounding variable

c) Coincidental correlation (spurious relationship)

Sometimes correlations can just be the result of pure coincidence. These are called "spurious" relationships between variables and they exist by mere coincidence. For example, it has been found that between 1999 and 2009 the US spending on science, space and technology correlated almost perfectly with the number of suicides by hanging, strangulation and suffocation in the US.[cxl]

99 | What is feature engineering and why is it considered "applied ML"?

Correlations between input variables and a target variable are the central building blocks for creating an ML model with supervised ML methods. Apart from choosing a type of model, we have to decide what kind of data we will feed it with. Ideally, we should provide the model with those input variables that in real life have a correlation with the target variable. The process of identifying such variables is called feature engineering.

The goal of feature engineering is to find the best combination of input variables to determine or predict the target variable. It is called feature engineering because we are trying to engineer the set of explanatory variables that will do the best job of explaining or predicting our target variable.

Table 99.1 What is feature engineering and why does it matter?

What is feature engineering?

Feature engineering is the process of creating relevant features (input variables) that are then used for training a model. The goal of feature engineering is to identify those factors that have an influence on the target variable. The quality of the input variables has a major impact on the performance and quality of the ML model.

There are various ways to create new input variables, such as:

- Simply creating/adding completely new variables
- Modifying existing variables
- Drawing and extracting information from existing variables
- Aggregating existing variables

During an ML project a lot of steps and phases can be automated or be performed by a computer. This does not hold true for feature engineering, which is a creative process at heart. It requires knowledge of and acumen in the subject at hand. Therefore, it is the phase during an ML project that requires the most domain expertise and knowledge.

Why does it matter?

Feature engineering plays a key role in ML and has a major impact on the quality of the model and its predictions.

The quality of the features used typically has a larger impact on the results of a model than the choice of model type. *Features trump complexity of the model.* That is, generally speaking with excellent features you can employ a mediocre model and still obtain good results, while the opposite is less true.

In fact, the phase of feature engineering is considered so important that applied ML is often said to be essentially feature engineering, since the rest of a project, such as data preparation and computing the models, is often diligent but routine work.

Feature engineering is extremely important and has a big influence on the results of the trained model – typically more so than the model type used. Better features beat fancier models. In ML the concept of "garbage in, garbage out" has been borrowed from computer science. Flawed or meaningless data produces a garbage output, regardless of what model class is used. Even a Ferrari will not drive if it is fuelled with water. So the importance of this phase cannot be stressed enough. For example, if we provided our model to predict sales with employee data that had nothing to do with the sales of a product, we could use the most sophisticated algorithm and we would still end up with entirely meaningless results.

Feature engineering is also the phase during an ML project that requires the most domain knowledge and creativity. The goal is to come up with input variables that have a high correlation with the target variable and can thus be used to determine or predict it. This requires both creativity and a profound knowledge of the underlying domain. Large parts of the supervised ML process can be automated, but coming up with relevant variables for the model requires the human brain and creativity. Andrew Ng, one of the leading figures in the field of AI, even goes so far as to say that "applied ML is basically feature engineering".[cxli]

There are various methods that are used in feature engineering.

Table 99.2 Types of feature engineering

Method	Description
Add external features	In many cases data from an external dataset can serve as great features. For example, we might be interested in predicting the traffic on our website. Apart from the date and time, which are likely to be important features, we might consider including weather data from an external provider.
Create new variables	Sometimes new variables can simply be created from scratch. For example, a supermarket chain has an interest in predicting how many products they will sell when and in which supermarket. Such sales might be affected by religious holidays. Before Christmas, Hanukkah and Ramadan the sales numbers of some products are likely going to change. So a new variable can be created that indicates the occurrence of these holidays.
Draw information from existing variables	A lot of information might be hiding in variables that you already have at your disposal. A prime example of this is email addresses. Imagine you want to launch a marketing campaign and reach out to your customers via email. Apart from their email address, you do not know much about the customer. But there is information in the email address already. In many cases you might be able to deduce the gender of the person just from their name, and you might get an idea of their location (.de, .fr, .co.uk, etc.). Also, you might get a sense of the consumer behaviour of the person. Most email providers are free (e.g. Gmail), but some email providers charge fees for their services. People who are using paid services might have a higher propensity to spend more money on products and could be addressed accordingly in a marketing email.
Modify existing variables	Some variables may contain good information for a model but still need modification to be consumable. For example, a variable called "age" created from the date of birth will typically be much more consumable for a model. In other cases it might be helpful to mathematically transform variables (e.g. take the logarithm or square them) so they have a nicer distribution.

Creating and Testing a ML Model with Supervised Machine Learning

| Aggregate variables | Variables might be too granular, in which case aggregating them can make a more useful feature. For example, a temperature sensor in a car engine might record data on a second-to-second basis. For the model it might be enough to aggregate this data into the average temperature on a minute-by-minute basis. |

These examples and techniques hopefully give a sense of how wide feature engineering is in its scope. Creativity and domain expertise in the underlying use case are key.

Case study 42

Your Model Car "feature engineering"

Feature engineering is all about identifying and collecting the variables that have an influence on our target variables. What are the relevant variables that are correlated with our sales?

Some variables should be apparent right away. For example, one obvious variable is the price of the product. We would expect there to be an inverse relationship (i.e. negative correlation) between the price and sales: the lower the price, the higher the sales figure. Usually, the price for a product is fixed, but because we have an online shop we put some products on offer every now and then. There is also the rating of the product, where we would expect a positive correlation (better rating, more sales).

Both of these variables are *product-specific*. External factors that are not product-specific include the day of the week (customers might tend to order on the weekends) and the season (e.g. the run-up to Christmas Eve is usually a busy time).

Furthermore, there is a factor that we directly influence, namely the marketing and advertisement of the product. For instance, we might put the product on the landing page of the website and thereby promote it very prominently. This will likely increase the sales of the product on a given day as well.

So, here is a reasonable set of features that we can engineer and use in our model:

- Day of the week
- Month
- Sales price (i.e. if a discount is offered)
- Advertisement (e.g. is the product advertised on the landing page?)
- Product rating

Can you think of more features that could be engineered and that influence this real-world process?

100 | What is feature selection and why is it necessary?

Once we have created a set of potential features to be used, the next step is to select the *right* ones among them. You might think that the more data, i.e. features, you use in your model, the better. After all, more features means more information with which the model can train, and what is the harm of including variables that might not be related to the target variable? So the easiest thing to do is to just give the model all available features with which to train and achieve its best performance, right?

Unfortunately, the opposite is the case. More features does not necessarily mean the better performance of a model. Features can be irrelevant, redundant and sometimes even detrimental when included in a model. Remember the function of a map: to help you navigate through a given territory. More information does not necessarily mean a better map. On the contrary, if you overload a map with unnecessary clutter, it will actually be more difficult for you to use the map. For instance, if you were to display every single tree on a map, this would not help you to navigate through the streets; it would just distract you and dilute the important information. The same holds true for the number of features that you include in your model.

The following sections outline reasons why you want to select features that are important for your model and therefore limit the number of features you use.

Increased chance of overfitting

We look into overfitting in detail in 📑 105, but here is a brief overview.

Overfitting refers to situations where a model that you train does not generalize well to unseen data because it picks up not only the signal but also the *noise* of the data it was trained on. Imagine you speak no English and would like to learn the language. So you take all the works of Shakespeare, lock yourself in a room and learn English from his 39 plays and 154 sonnets. Then you take a flight to London (or even better, New York) and start approaching people with "Thou lookest bewildering, methinks". You would probably not have much success, because the English you have learned does not generalize well to the situation. You have picked up the idiosyncrasies of Shakespeare's "data", which are unusable in today's world – you have overfitted your language skills to his works.

Increasing the number of features used in a model increases the likelihood of overfitting it to a given dataset as well. The reason is that the more features you have, the more likely you are to pick up idiosyncrasies of the given dataset you have. Just imagine you want to train a model to classify whether a picture contains a human or some other animal. Some basic features might be, for example, "number of legs" and "existence of a tail". A limited model would use only these two variables and would probably do quite a good job of differentiating between humans and animals in pictures. Now suppose you include "type of clothes worn" as an additional variable, and the pictures of humans in your dataset are taken from Wall Street, where the vast majority of people wear suits. Now the model will think that humans always wear suits. If you want to apply the model to pictures of humans who do not happen to be wearing suits, the model will perform poorly. This would not have happened if you had left out the variable "type of clothes".

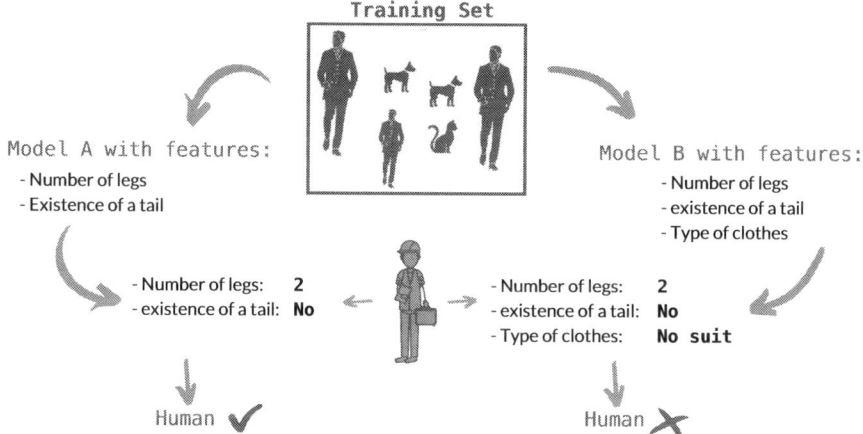

Figure 100.1 Overfitting due to too many variables

Collinearity

Collinearity (also called multicollinearity) refers to situations where input variables have a high degree of linear correlation with each other. Or in other words, they contain the same information and are therefore redundant. An obvious example is a car dataset that contains "weight in pounds" and "weight in kilograms". But even variables such as body height and weight usually have a very strong correlation.

Certain models in supervised ML can deal quite well with collinearity, but for others it can create problems in the sense that it makes them unstable. So if two variables contain the same information, the model does not know which of the two to use for its prediction. Usually, collinearity does not effect a model's predictive performance, but its robustness. That is, two models trained on the same dataset with only one observation exchanged might turn out very differently, even though the data is still essentially identical. So if there are collinear features, it is a good idea to remove them from your model.

Curse of dimensionality

The curse of dimensionality refers to a number of problems that arise when analysing data in very high-dimensional spaces (dimension is just a synonym for feature or input variable). What "very high-dimensional" means depends on the exact underlying problem, but typically we are talking dozens, hundreds or maybe even thousands of features, especially in use cases with sensor data. One such problem is the fact that the number of data points needed to fill a space increases exponentially with the number of features. Just consider the example in Figure 100-2.

Interpretability of the model

If features are redundant but still included in the model, they will make its interpretation more cumbersome. Irrelevant features are just clutter that draw your attention away from what actually matters.

The Ultimate Data and AI Guide

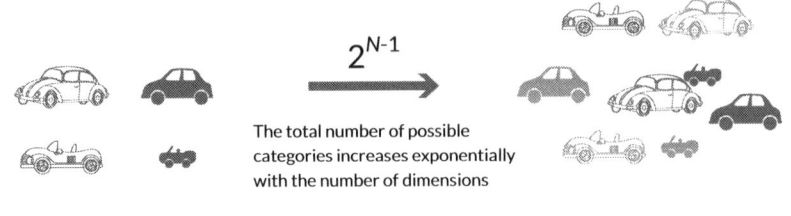

Figure 100.2 Example of the curse of dimensionality

Feature selection is important

So including more input variables might lead to a poorer performance by the ML model. That is why before training an ML model we try to sift out unnecessary input variables that add no value to the performance of the model. This process is called feature selection.

Feature selection is an important step in creating an ML model, especially in situations where we have a lot of input variables at our disposal. This is often the case when we are dealing with sensor data. For example, it is not unusual for a car today to be equipped with more than 100 sensors. If we are trying to determine or predict the breakdown of a part in that car, it is a good idea to trim down the number of input variables through feature selection.

Table 100.1 What is feature selection and why does it matter?

What is feature selection?

Feature selection is the process of selecting those features that are relevant for use in a certain model. As opposed to feature engineering, where features are created, feature selection is about identifying which of the available features are (most) relevant and should therefore be included in the model.

The goal of feature selection is to exclude irrelevant features from the model. This can be done both manually and with the help of algorithms that automatically select the most relevant variables.

Why does it matter?

Just because you have a lot of variables, that does not mean you have to use all of them. In fact, adding more variables often has a detrimental rather than beneficial effect on the performance of a model. Limiting yourself to using the most relevant variables decreases the likelihood of overfitting the model, of collinearity and of running into problems with the curse of dimensionality, and it increases the interpretability of the model.

But how do we know which features an ML needs in order to predict a target variable? There are a number of feature selection methods that we can use:

- *Manually remove features with domain knowledge:* Often you can remove features just with domain knowledge, either because they are redundant or because you know with certainty they will not affect the target variable. Say you have a dataset for predictive maintenance of car engines that contains hundreds of features in the form of sensor data. A domain expert such as a mechanical car engineer will know if some sensors certainly are not associated with the engine of a car breaking down. Manually removing features with domain knowledge is the most elegant way to reduce the number of features, but it requires expertise and brainpower.
- *Models with integrated feature selection algorithms:* Some models in supervised ML naturally and automatically select the features that are most relevant to them. For example, some ML models incorporate a so-called regularization, which puts a cost on including a feature in a model. Models with an automated feature selection functionality can relieve the burden of determining which features are important manually.
- *Dimensionality reduction algorithms:* These algorithms in ML are specifically dedicated to reducing the number of features of a dataset. One prominent algorithm is principal components analysis (PCA), which essentially enables you to extract the most relevant variables (principal components) of a dataset.

The result of feature engineering and selection should be a dataset that contains the target variable along with features that are relevant to (correlated with) that target variable – and *only* those ones.

101 | Why do we need to split a dataset into training, validation and test sets?

We have chosen what type of ML model we want to train. We have determined the target variable to be learned. We have chosen features that are correlated with the target variable and with which we therefore want to feed our model. We have a dataset of historical data from which this model can learn. Before finally training our model, there is one more step to do: splitting up our dataset.

If you are a patient in a hospital and the doctors take a blood sample from you, this sample is a precious resource. The doctors will split this sample up for various uses, e.g. for clinical trials, tests and as a sample backup. We do the same sort of thing in ML. We want to use the historical data – our precious resource – to train a model. But we also need to use the data for other purposes: to *validate* and *test* the model after we have trained it.

This is why before doing anything with the data, we split it up into three distinct parts that are named according to what they are later used for: the training set, validation set and test set. There is no clear-cut rule as to how big each of these should be, but in practice we usually size the training set at 60%

of the entire dataset, the validation set at 20% and the test set at 20%. So if we have a dataset of 1,000 customers, our training, validation and test sets comprise 600, 200 and 200 customers respectively.

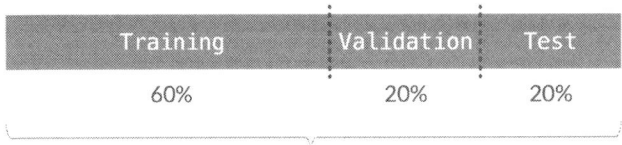

Total available data

Figure 101.1 A split into training, validation and test sets

Table 101.1 How do we split up a dataset and why does it matter?

What are training, validation and test sets?

In ML, the dataset containing historical data points has to fulfil several purposes: to train, validate and test a model. That is why we split our dataset into three distinct subsets:

- **Training set:** The part of the data on which the model is trained.
- **Validation set:** The part of the data on which a trained model is validated; that is, after the model has been trained on the training set, we use this dataset to validate how good it is.
- **Test set:** The part of the data on which validated models are tested to see how they would perform in real life.

The rule of thumb for the size of these subsets is usually 60–20–20% of the initial dataset. There are a number of ways to split up a dataset into these three distinct parts. Most commonly, the method of random sampling is used.

Why do they matter?

Splitting up the data into these three subsets is a vital part of training, validating and testing a model. Imagine we just used all of the data to train the model. That would mean we had no data left with which we could assess how well the model performs on data that it has not seen yet, i.e. which was not used during the training.

Withholding a validation set and test set enables us to evaluate and compare the performance of the model after it has been trained on the training set.

How should we split up the dataset?

The way we split up the dataset has a big impact on the performance of the model. The reason is that a *model can only identify and predict patterns in the future that it has already seen during its training*. If a model has only seen white swans in its training set, it will not be able to recognize a black one when it sees it.[30]

---

30. Actually, you probably could create an algorithm that would recognize a black swan as a swan as well, but we hope you get the point.

Creating and Testing a ML Model with Supervised Machine Learning

Let's return to the example of learning English from scratch. Say your goal is to be able to speak English in daily conversations with friends. The sources from which you learn English (your training set) will have a big impact on how impeccable your English turns out to be. For example, learning English from Shakespeare's works will result in your English being completely different than if you learned it from American sitcoms. If your goal is to have good conversational English then the latter "training set" is probably a wiser choice, given that the English spoken in American sitcoms is much closer to the English used in daily conversations. The English that we learn should be as close possible to the English used in the situations where we want to apply our skills.

The same holds true for an ML model. In ML we want the training set to display the same patterns that exist in a situation where we will apply the model to perform its task. When choosing a training set for a model, the goal is to make the training set as similar as possible to the data that it will be used on later in real life. In ML parlance, we say that we want the training set to be as *representative* as possible.

How can this be achieved? There are several ways to make sure that not only the training set but also the validation and test sets are representative. The most widely used method for splitting datasets while keeping all subsets representative is *random sampling*. In random sampling, the required number of observations from the entire dataset are *randomly chosen* to make up a subset. Choosing observations randomly means that each observation in the dataset has an equal probability of being picked. The best example of a randomly chosen subset is drawing the winning numbers in a lottery. Each number is equally likely to be drawn.

However, while random sampling does a good job of creating representative subsets of a dataset, it cannot be applied in every situation, such as in Case Study 43. In some instances, other sampling methods perform better. Choosing which sampling method to use depends on the underlying problem and is a science in itself.

Case study 43

Splitting the dataset in Your Model Car – why can't we use random sampling?

Random sampling is frequently used to split a dataset into representative training, validation and test sets. It is simple and effective in creating representative subsets. However, in our case we cannot use random sampling.

The reason is because we are dealing with so-called *time-series data*. This means we observe the same target variable over time and see how it develops. So instead of looking at one data point of an object or process, we have an entire sequence of data points. Stock prices are a prime example of a time series. In our case, the time series is the daily sales of our Ferrari model car over the course of four years. An example of a non-time-series dataset would be sales of all products on a given day.

Why can't we use random sampling? Because we are looking at time-series data, there is an inherent temporal dimension to our data that we have to respect. Let's assume we applied random sampling to our dataset to create a subset for training. We might end up with a training set that contains data points from 2019, whereas our validation set might contain data points from 2018. Consequently, we would be training our model to predict a future that it has already seen during its training. This obviously overestimates and distorts the performance of the model.

Therefore, we have use a simpler method that is often applied with time-series data. We just split up our dataset according to the temporal dimensions. So we take the earliest 60% of the observations for the training set, the next 20% for the validation set, and the next 20% for the test set.

Given that our dataset contains 1,461 observations in total with data from 01-01-2016 until 31-12-2019, we will end up with:

- **Training set**: Observation number 1 (date: 01-01-2016) – 877 (date: 26-05-2018)
- **Validation set**: Observation number 878 (date: 27-05-2018) – 1,169 (date: 14-03-2019)
- **Test set**: Observation number 1,170 (date: 15-03-2019) – 1,461 (date: 31-12-2019)

	ROW_ID	PROD_ID	DATE	SALES	YEAR	MONTH	DAY	PRICE	LAND_PAGE	RATING
Training Set	1	S18_5355	2016-01-01	5	2016	January	Friday	€55.00	0	4.3
	...									
	877	S18_5355	2018-05-26	7	2018	May	Saturday	€59.95	0	4.3
Validation Set	878	S18_5355	2018-05-27	6	2018	May	Sunday	€59.95	0	4.3
	...									
	1169	S18_5355	2019-03-17	4	2019	March	Thursday	€59.95	0	4.3
Test Set	1170	S18_5355	2019-03-15	6	2019	March	Friday	€59.95	0	4.3
	...									
	1461	S18_5355	2019-12-31	6	2019	December	Tuesday	€59.95	0	4.3

Figure 101.2 Splitting up our dataset

102 | What does it mean to "train an ML model" and how do you do it?

Once the dataset is split up, we can use the training set to train our model. To understand what model training entails, it helps to clarify that in ML we have to differentiate between a model class and an actual model:

Creating and Testing a ML Model with Supervised Machine Learning

- The *model class* (or model type) can be thought of as an off-the-shelf blueprint that we can use. We look at some model classes and how they differ in Chapter 8. To use a real-life analogy, vehicle classes would be "cars" or "motorcycles".
- An *actual model* refers to one realization or instantiation of a model class. There are countless shapes that a model from just one model class can take, just like there are countless cars that differ in shape, size, colour etc. – even though they are all of the same vehicle class, "cars".

Model training refers to the process of taking a blueprint of a model, i.e. a model class, and bringing it into a certain shape. This shape should be such that the model fits the underlying patterns in the real world as well as possible. We do this by providing the model with historical data from which it can learn these patterns. What we end up with after model training is an actual model, i.e. an instantiation of the model class that is specific to the underlying data.

Table 102.1 What is model training and why does it matter?

What is model training and what are model parameters?

Model training refers to the process of providing a model with training data from which it can learn. Through model training, the *parameters* of the model are estimated. Parameters are configuration elements of a model that determine its shape.

These parameters are obtained by having the model fit the data as closely as possible. This is why model training is also called model fitting.

The result of model training is an actual model (an instance) of the model class that we have used.

Why does it matter?

Model training is the step where a model is actually created or "born". By training a model and fitting it as well as possible, an undefined model with no parameters turns into an actual realization. This is much like a recipe is turned into a delicious dish through cooking.

The shape of a model is determined by its parameters, which are configuration variables of the model. For example, suppose we want to train the model of the model class "linear model" to predict a person's weight using their height. The blueprint of this model class is just a straight line as shown in Figure 102-1. Training a model means that we obtain the parameters that define the shape of the model in such a way that it fits the historical data as closely as possible. In the case of a linear model, the parameters that define its shape are the slope and the intercept of the line. In the case of cars, the parameters that determine the shape of a car are its height, width, weight, etc.

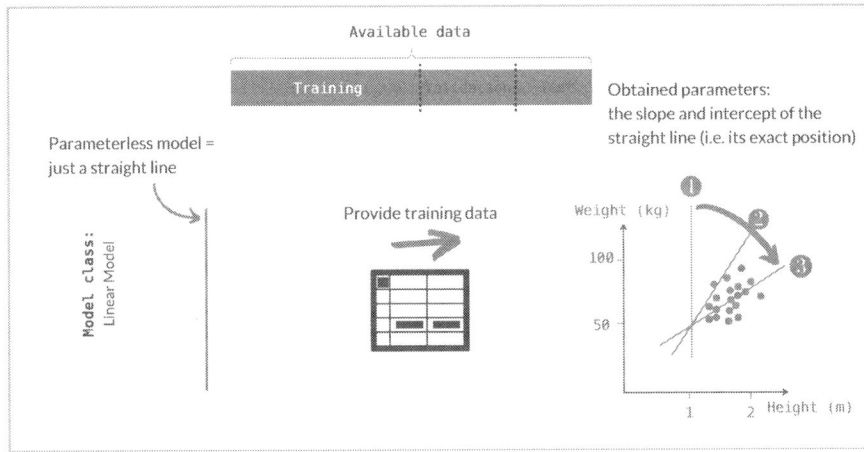

Figure 102.1 Model training example[31]

How exactly does model training happen?

Another way to put this is: how do we find the shape of a model class that best fits the data? This is quite a complex process that involves a lot of mathematical computation. We will spare you the minutiae of it at this point and provide some basic information.

Let's assume we want to train a linear model to predict a person's weight based on their height. As you can see in Figure 102-1, there are an infinite number of ways in which we could place the parameterless model (i.e. just a straight line) in the diagram. We could just leave it as a vertical line. But this vertical line would do a pretty poor job of enabling us to predict a person's weight. In fact, this model would tell us that the weight of a one-metre-tall person is infinity (1). That clearly doesn't correspond to reality, which is reflected by the data points. So we have to fit the straight line through the scatter plot of data. By tilting the line towards the scatter plot, we get a model which fits the data somewhat and seems more reasonable. However, it still overestimates the weight of a person based on their height (2). The straight line numbered 3 goes right through the scatter plot and therefore seems to fit the data best.

But what does "fitting" really mean? Intuitively, we would say that the line should be as close as possible to as many points as possible. This in turn means that what the model predicts (i.e. the straight line) is as close as possible to reality (the single data points). In other words, we want the prediction to be as accurate as possible. In ML, the discrepancy between a model (its predictions) and reality is called the model's *error*. So when we speak of training a model in ML, we refer to the minimization of the model's errors so that it fits the data as well as possible.

---

31. Fictional data

Creating and Testing a ML Model with Supervised Machine Learning

In the Figure 102-1 example, because things are pretty simple, we could just take a wild guess and try pushing around the line until in fits the data optimally and minimizes the model's errors. And in fact, that is what a lot of so-called approximation algorithms do in ML. Other algorithms have specific formulas for finding the best fit of a model to the data. Since finding this best fit is a little like finding a needle in an infinitely big haystack, you can imagine that this requires quite some computational power. That is why for complex ML model classes that use a lot of data, the training process can take some time (up to several weeks).

In the majority of cases, however, model training takes a couple of seconds or minutes. And the best part is that for us humans it is nothing more than one line of code or one click. All the complex mathematical computations that are necessary to fit a model optimally to a (training) set of data are packaged and automated in libraries (📘 89).

At the end of the model training phase we have a specific model derived from a certain model class. Remember that a model in this case is a mathematical function, i.e. a set of rules, by which our target variable can be calculated from a set of input variables. We can simply provide this trained model with input data and it will compute predictions on our target variable.

> **Case study 44**
>
> **Your Model Car "data split and model training"**
>
> We have split our dataset, identified the relevant features and chosen our model class. Now we can provide our model with the training data in order to obtain its parameters. In the case of a decision tree, these parameters are:
>
> - Which variable to use to split the data at a given decision node
> - What values to split by for a given variable
>
> This is the result of the trained decision tree are displayed in Figure 102-3. As you can see, the day of the week, the month and the sales price have been found during the model training to be the most important variables by which the daily sales can be predicted. What the tree would predict by means of looking at the bottom row of nodes. "y" indicates the predicted sales, "n" indicates the number of observations in the training set that fell within that category (e.g. in the bottom left node n = 16 indicates that there were 16 observations in the training set that
>
> - had a sales price of less than €55.00
> - were in January, February, April, November or December
> - were a Saturday or Sunday

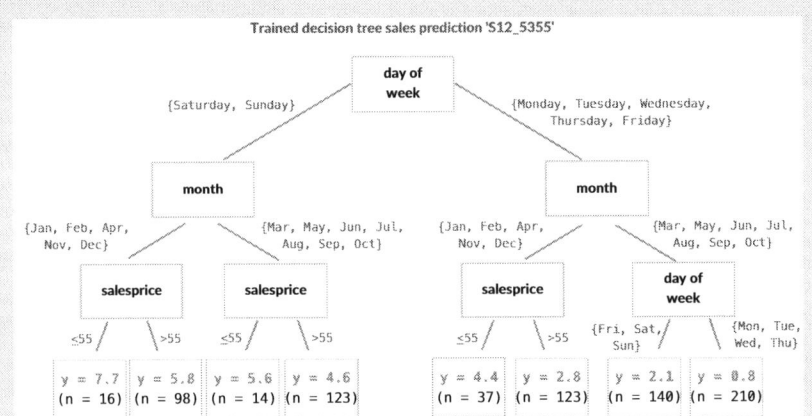

Figure 102.2 Result of training a decision tree to predict daily sales of product S12_5355

Thus, we finally have an actual model, i.e. a set of rules, that we can provide with input data to obtain the prediction for the output. During the training the model has learned that in order to predict how many pieces of "SC12_5355" we will see, it will implement the following set of rules:

- Look at the day of the week and distinguish between the weekend and weekdays.
- If we are talking about Saturday or Sunday, the next variable to consider is the month. If we are in…
- And so forth

Let's look at what the model would have predicted for our sales on 01-01-2019, a Tuesday on which Your Model Car gave a new year's discount and set the price below €55. Following the split nodes of the tree, we would arrive at a prediction of 4.4 sales of product "SC12_5355" for that specific day:

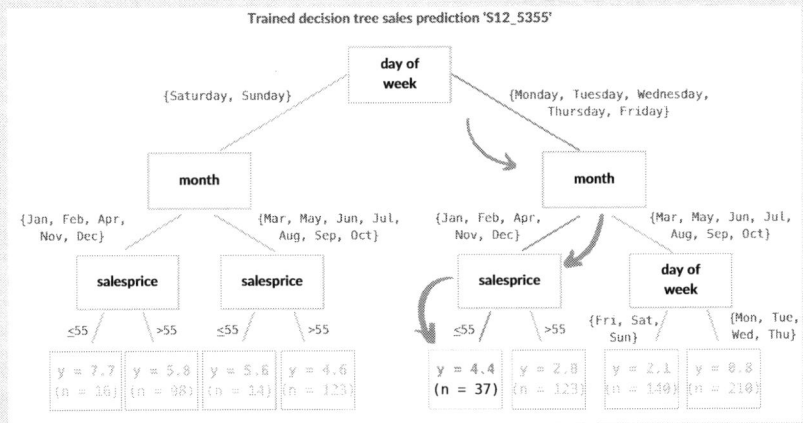

Figure 102.3 Example of a trained decision tree

7_2 Validating, testing and using a machine learning model

103 | What does it mean to "validate a model", and why is it necessary?

Let's say we have created an ML model to recommend products to website visitors of Your Model Car. After having trained a model, would you use it straightaway in real life? You could, but it's not a smart way to go about things. We don't know if the model that we have created makes sense at all, if it is good at the task it is supposed to perform. Also, maybe there are better models that we could use.

During the model training, we have created *one* model from a model class that fits the training data as well as it can. While this is good, there are two remaining questions:

- Our model fits the training data as well as it can, but does it also fit real life?
- Are there other models that would be even more accurate?

The first problem is the reason why after model training we enter a phase of model validation. To tackle the second problem, we train and validate not just one model but several models in the quest to find the best one.

Model validation refers to assessing (validating) how good a model is at determining or predicting the target variable after it has been trained. To understand the rationale of model validation you can think of cooking. Say you want to get really good at cooking ratatouille, and so you cook and subsequently eat a dish of ratatouille every day. And every day you make some changes to your recipe and thus refine it, until you have found the ultimate mix of ingredients that *you* think tastes best. But how can you claim that you cook the best ratatouille if no one else has tasted it and assessed its quality? By having some friends try your ratatouille, you get feedback on how good it actually is. This is exactly what we do during model validation. Your taste is the training set and your friends' taste is the validation set, by means of which you assess just how good your taste (the training set) really is.

Table 103.1 What is model validation and why does it matter?

What is model validation?
Model validation is the process of assessing (validating) how good a trained model performs.
The model is given unseen validation data (i.e. data that has not been used to train it) in order to make predictions. Since the validation set contains historical data, the predictions on the model can be compared to what *actually* happened. Thus, the validity of a model can be assessed and models can be compared in terms of their predictive performance.

The Ultimate Data and AI Guide

Why does it matter?

After a model has been trained, it is ready to make predictions, but we have no way of telling whether or not it is actually a good model. By means of the validation set, we can put the model to the test and gauge how good it is. This is much like having no idea whether a dish we have cooked tastes good or not – which is why we ask other people to try it and give feedback.

How does model validation work?

This is where the validation set kicks in. Remember that before training a model we had to split our dataset (which contains historical data) into three subsets. We used the training set to train our model. Now we would like to know how well the model that we have created performs on data that it has not seen during its training, i.e. data from the validation set. We can have the model make predictions on the validation set and then we can compare:

▶ The outcomes that the model predicts for the validation set
▶ The outcomes that are true

The smaller the difference between the two, the better our model is at its task of determining or predicting the target variable. So, in our example we have created a model to predict sales. To validate this model, we simply feed it with the input variables of the validation set. The model then computes its predictions on the target variable for these input variables. We can then compare these predictions to the actual values. The mismatch between prediction and reality gives us a sense of how good our model really is.

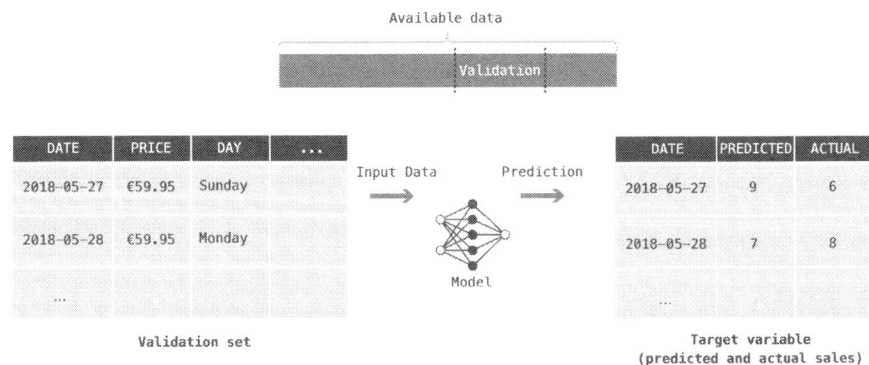

Figure 103.1 Example of model validation

We can quantify the performance of a model. However, doing so is not straightforward, because there are a number of metrics that we can use to assess the model's performance. After all, what does it mean if a model is "good"? The general agreement is that the model's predictions should be as close as possible to the actual values, but there are different ways to quantify and define "close".

For instance, in our example let's assume we have used two models to create predictions of the coming ten days. Which of the following models would you prefer?

- Model A: Over-/ underestimates the actual value by five items each of the ten days
- Model B: Over-/ underestimates the actual value
  - ❏ By two items on five days
  - ❏ By eight items on five days

On average, both models are equally accurate (because on average they both have a prediction error of 5) – but still extremely different. So the answer is not straightforward and depends on the underlying problem. What are the consequences if predictions are slightly off? What if some are very far off? How can we quantify these implications best in an indicator to reflect their value in real life? These are all considerations that have to be taken into account when choosing an appropriate metric to assess an ML model. There are many such evaluation metrics, and exploring them would go beyond the scope of this book. Choosing the most appropriate one for the underlying problem is a science in itself.

Train a model, validate – repeat

Choosing a metric to assess the performance of a model enables us to validate its strength. More importantly, however, it also enables us to compare its performance to other models.

In ML we do not limit ourselves to training and validating only one model – we train and validate several models. While we might have an idea of what model class and what input variables best reflect reality, we can never know for sure. That is why we have to try a few different setups of models and then see which one yields the best results.

We might refine our initial model and try to recalculate it with a different set of input variables. Or we might use a different model class altogether. Or we might do a combination of these things. We might also realize that there are some strong and unrealistic outliers in the training set that we can exclude. These are all ways in which we can tune and alter the model that we create with the training set. Each of these models will be different and create different prediction results. Because we do not know in advance which model class, which specific shape or which set of input variables is best, all we can do is try out some of these different setups. After all, the proof of the pudding is in the eating. In a way, the quest to find the best ML model is therefore a hit-and-miss endeavour.

So after we have trained and validated *one* model, we note down the validity of the model (as measured by the evaluation metric that we have chosen) and then we go through the entire process again, training and validating another model – and so on and so on. For every variation of our model we note down its performance on the validation set.

What we end up with is a list of trained models along with a score of how well they performed in creating predictions on the validation set. By means of

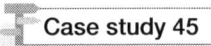

Case study 45

Your Model Car "model validation"

One metric that is often applied in time-series forecasts of sales is the *mean absolute error* (MAE). The MAE tells us how far off a model's predictions are on average from the actual values. For example, if our model had an MAE of 3.4, it would mean that on average in its predictions the model misses the actual values on average by 3.4 items. Thus, the lower the MAE of a model, the closer its predictions are to the actual values, and the better (i.e. more performant and accurate) it is.

In Your Model Car we can train a few models to calculate their MAE on the validation set and then we can compare their performance:

Table 103.2 Comparison of model scores on the validation set for three different models trained to predict sales in Your Model Car (measured in mean absolute error on validation set, MAE)

Model	Model Specifications	MAE on the validation set
Model X	▶ Model class: decision tree with three splitting levels ▶ Input variables: ❑ Price ❑ Day of the week ❑ Month ❑ Product rating ❑ Was the product advertised on the landing page?	5.3
Model Y	▶ Model class: neural network with more than 1000 parameters ▶ Input variables: ❑ Price ❑ Day of the week ❑ Month ❑ Product rating ❑ Was the product advertised on the landing page?	3.1
Model Z	▶ Model class: decision tree with three splitting levels ▶ Input variables: ❑ Price ❑ Day of the week ❑ Was the product advertised on the landing page?	4.5
...		

the evaluation metric we can then easily compare the different models in terms of their accuracy and choose the best one among them.

104 | What is the difference between validating and testing a model and why is the latter necessary?

So we have trained a few models that differ in a number of ways, e.g. in terms of their model class or in terms of what set of input variables they were provided with during their training. We have also reiterated and tuned these models so as to improve and optimize their predictive performance on the validation set.

Among these models there will be the best models that have the most accurate prediction results. Because these models have been validated with the validation set, it is safe to assume that:

- These are indeed the best models to determine or predict our target variable.
- The performance they exhibited on the validation set is also how they will perform if we put them to use in real life.

Right? Unfortunately, both of these points are untrue. To understand why, let's return to our cooking example. After several iterations and tuning your recipe, you have finally arrived at a version that all three of your best friends have agreed is the most delicious one. You want to take things a step further and open a ratatouille restaurant and claim that you make the best ratatouille in the world – a claim that is validated by you and your three best friends.

But there is a big problem with that. What if your friends all happen to have a very specific taste that is not shared by the majority of other ratatouille lovers? Because you have only had your ratatouille assessed by these three friends, it might be that you have honed it to cater to their specific taste. This could go right if their taste is shared by the majority of people, i.e. if it is representative. It will go wrong, however, if they happen to have some weird taste, because then your ratatouille will be specialized to cater to this weird taste.

The exact same thing holds true in ML. With the validation set we have found the models with the best performance – *on the validation set*. In fact, we have had several iterations and tried out different models in order to optimize performance on this specific set of data. This kind of optimization will go well if the validation set happens to be a perfect representation of the real world and the environment in which the model is to be used. But it will go wrong if the validation set is not sufficiently representative. In that case, our models might only fit the validation set. The problem is, we cannot know right now whether it will go well or go wrong.

This is where we turn to the test set. The test set is an untainted dataset that the model was neither trained nor validated on. It was not involved in creating the model at all. So the test provides real-life conditions that we can use to gauge how a model will perform in real life. We give the best models the data of the test set. Then, just like in the validation phase, we have them create predictions and we compare these predictions with the actual values.

The Ultimate Data and AI Guide

Table 104.1 What model testing and why does it matter?

What is model testing?
We use model testing to assess the final performance of a model and obtain an estimate of how it will perform in real life.
In model testing we give the model(s) that has been performing best on the validation set the (historic) test data, which the model has not seen during its training and validation. Just like in model validation, we then compare the predictions to what actually happened. This gives a realistic estimate of how the model will perform in real life.
Afterwards, the model must not be tuned again.
Why does it matter?
Model testing is necessary in order to obtain an unbiased assessment of how well the final model is going to perform in real life.

So what is the difference between validation and testing? The difference is that we do the model testing once – and that is it. It is the one and only time we use the test set. Under no circumstances do we refine any of the models again in order to increase their performance on the test set. Why? Because then we would deprive our test set of its purity and the fact that it has been completely excluded from the entire model-creation process. If we did refine a model to tweak its performance after having tested it on the test set, we would simply turn the test set into another validation set, and then the results would not be representative of how a model would perform in real life. The test set is like a group of new people tasting your ratatouille, so you can gauge how well it is received by someone who did not give you any feedback when you created the recipe.

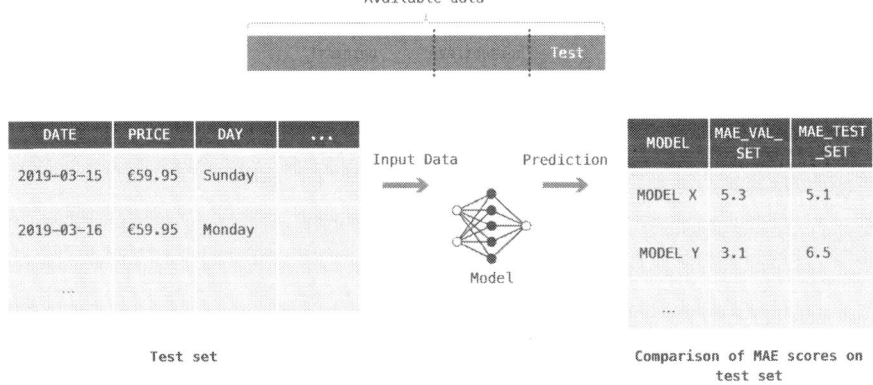

Figure 104.1 Example of model testing

So we can simply take the models with the best performance on the validation set and *test* their predictive performance on the test set. Again, we end up with a list of performance scores. Because we are not tuning any of the models afterwards, the performance results of the models can now be regarded as realistic and representative estimates of how the models would perform in real life. So all that is left to do is pick the model with the best performance and employ it in real life.

> **Case study 46**
>
> **Your Model Car "model testing"**
>
> Once we have trained and validated a number of models, we can shortlist the best ones and put them to the final test. Thus, we can compare their performance on the test set, which gives us a realistic estimate of how well they would perform in real life. Then we can choose the best model and put it to use in Your Model Car to have it predict future sales.
>
> Table 104.2 Comparison of model scores on both validation and test set for three different models trained to predict sales in Your Model Car (measured in mean absolute error, MAE)
>
> | Model | MAE on the validation set | MAE on the test set |
> |---|---|---|
> | Model X | 5.3 | 5.1 |
> | Model Y | 3.1 | 6.5 |
> | Model Z | 4.5 | 4.6 |
> | ... | | |

105 | What are overfitting and generalization?

In supervised ML, the overall goal is to create a model that is able to determine or predict a target variable as well as possible in order to automate a certain task. The ability to do so comes from looking at historical data to identify patterns that can then be used to make future predictions on the target variable.

If a model does a good job of identifying and picking up such patterns that exist in the training set (and assuming that this training set is representative of real life), it will do a good job of predicting the future (given that these patterns will continue to exist in the future). In ML we say that the model *generalizes* well to unseen data. Creating models that generalize well to unseen data is the ultimate goal in supervised ML.

But it is not an easy task, and there are a number of reasons why a model may fail to generalize well. The most important one is *overfitting*, which refers to situations in which a model fits the data it has been trained (or validated) on so well that it picks up the underlying patterns *plus* idiosyncratic characteristics of the training (validation) set.

Let's apply overfitting to the ratatouille example. Assume that the perfect ratatouille contains a balanced mix of tomato, onion, garlic and just a hint of thyme. This balanced mix is what the vast majority of people prefer. However, as tastes vary, there are some people who like their ratatouille extremely thyme-heavy. If the three friends who validate and tune your ratatouille recipe all happen to be thyme-fanatics, then your recipe will fail to pick up the underlying taste that exists in the general population. Instead, the recipe will be specific to your three friends, who happen to have an idiosyncratic and exceptional taste that is specific to them. So you will overfit to their taste and create an extremely thyme-heavy recipe.

In ML every dataset has data points that are in some way exceptional and have idiosyncrasies that make them diverge from the overall pattern, i.e. they are not representative. Such idiosyncrasies are called *noise* (📑82) because they dilute and hide the *pattern* (signal) that generally exists in the population. If a model overfits a dataset, it fits the dataset so well that it picks up the noise that exists in this specific dataset but is absent in the general population. Consequently, it does not generalize well. The opposite of overfitting is underfitting, where a model is so "bad" that it does not pick up noise but it also fails to pick up the patterns in the data.

Table 105.1 What are overfitting, underfitting and generalization and why do they matter?

What are overfitting, underfitting and generalization?

The goal of ML models is to make predictions on unseen data as accurate as possible. This is called *generalization*, i.e. we want a model to make predictions on a certain dataset (or real life) even though it has been trained on a different one.

That means when training an ML model the goal is to have the model pick up the underlying patterns (signal) of a dataset without picking up the idiosyncrasies (noise).

Overfitting refers to situations in which a model fits the data it has been trained on *so well* that it picks up the underlying signal plus the noise of the training set. There are a couple of factors that increase the likelihood of a model overfitting, e.g. the complexity of the model.

Underfitting refers to situations in which a model fails to pick up the underlying patterns of a dataset. As opposed to overfitting, where a model is so good that it captures the noise, with underfitting the model is so simple that it is not even capable of picking up the underlying pattern in the data.

Why does it matter?

Both overfitting and underfitting lead to poor predictive power in models. The central challenge in machine learning is to strike the balance between the two and find the optimal fit of a model so that it generalizes well to unseen data.

Overfitting can occur at two stages during the ML phase. It might be that a model overfits the training set. And it might also be that we overfit the validation set while trying out and tuning different models to find the one with the best performance on the validation set.

A graphical illustration

Overfitting and underfitting can be illustrated graphically. Consider Figure 105-1, which shows a training set of voters. Let's assume we want to create a model to predict the political affiliation of a person of a given age and yearly income.

Creating and Testing a ML Model with Supervised Machine Learning

Graphically, we want to find a line that best separates the dots from the crosses. Just looking at the point cloud it is clearly visible that there is a strong relationship between the input variables "age" and "income" and the dependent variable "political affiliation". The older a person and the higher their income, the more likely they are to vote centre-right.

Figure 105-1 shows three different models: one linear model to separate the voters, one that is parabolic and one that has a complex shape.

As you can see, a straight line already somewhat captures the underlying pattern of older, wealthier people voting centre-right. However, it would wrongly classify a good number of observations. While the model is going in the right direction, it does not seem to fully and perfectly capture the underlying pattern of real life. Since it does not seem to perfectly fit the data and therefore fails to pick up the underlying patterns and correlation, we say that it *underfits* the dataset.

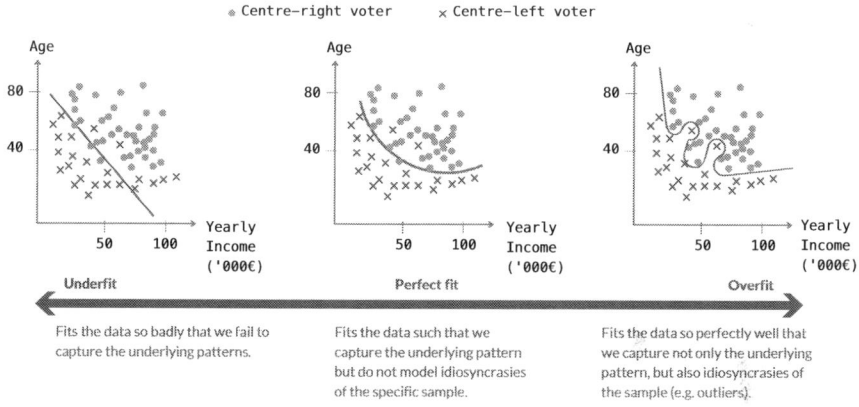

Figure 105.1 Overview of overfitting and underfitting[32]

In contrast, the model on the right is so good that it perfectly classifies all observations in the dataset! At first this might seem like a great thing. But if we look at the shape of the model, we see it seems like it really had to wriggle and meander through the point cloud in order to achieve that. The reason is that there are two data points that fall outside of the overall pattern of the dataset – two blue outliers in the ocean of orange points. These outliers are noise to the overall patterns that exist in the data. The problem with our model is that it is so good that it captures not only the underlying pattern but also the specific idiosyncrasies and noise of the sample it was trained on. It *overfits* the training set. The model does not generalize well and will probably have a poor predictive performance. The two wriggles of the overfitted model will likely lead to misclassifications on unseen data.

There is a golden midpoint between overfitting and underfitting. The perfect model captures the underlying patterns that exist in real life but ignores the noise of the sample it was trained on. In the figure this means it has some

---

32. Fictional data

parabolic shape and therefore is a better fit than the linear model on the left. But it spares itself the extra wiggles caused by the outliers and as a result will generalize better and perform better on unseen data.

Identifying overfitting and underfitting

How can we know whether or not we have committed either of the two? Unfortunately, there is no easy formula for knowing that. Trying to spot underfitting and overfitting is much like playing Sherlock or Dr House in search of a disease. But there are a couple of symptoms of the two "illnesses":

Table 105.2 Overview of symptoms of over- and underfitting of models

	...the training set	...the validation set
Overfitting...	▸ Small errors on the training set ▸ Very large errors on the validation and test set compared to the ones in the training set	▸ Small errors on the validation set ▸ Very large errors on the test set compared to the ones in the training set
	▸ Complex model with a lot of parameters (the more complex a model is, the more it tends to overfit; see Figure 105-2)	
Underfitting...	▸ Large errors on the training set ▸ Large errors on the validation and test set that have a similar magnitude to the ones on the training set ▸ Very simple model with only a few parameters	

> **Case study 47**

Checking whether one of our models overfitted

Looking back at the MAE scores of our models on the validation and test sets, we can see that Model Y exhibits clear symptoms of having overfitted the validation set. It is a complex model with a lot of parameters and the errors (measured in terms of MAE) on the test set are more than double as big as the ones on the validation set – this is an unusually high difference.

Table 105.3 Comparison of model scores on validation and test sets

Model	MAE on validation set	MAE on test set
Model X	5.3	5.1
Model Y	3.1	6.5
Model Z	4.5	4.6

106 | Preventing overfitting: how does cross-validation work?

Cross-validation is a model validation technique used to obtain a more accurate estimate of how a model would perform on unseen data. Cross-validation is very commonly used in practice.

Table 106.1 What is cross-validation and why does it matter?

What is cross-validation?

Cross-validation is a model validation technique used to get a more accurate estimate of the generalizability of a model.

Compared to a normal training/validation/test setting, it gives a more accurate estimate of how well a model will perform in real life on unseen data.

In cross-validation the process of training and validating a model is not done only once, but instead is repeated several times. Each time a different, randomly drawn training and validation set is used to train and validate the model. Repeating the process several times mitigates the risk of training and validating a model on an unrepresentative sample with quirky idiosyncrasies.

Why does it matter?

Cross-validation is heavily used in practice. It is easy to implement and yields much more accurate estimates of the performance of a model than only using one round of training-validation-testing.

The idea of cross-validation is simple. Instead of training and validating a model only once, we repeat the process several times on different subsets of the data. So instead of splitting our initial dataset into training, validation and test sets, we split it into a cross-validation set (typically 80%) and test set (typically 20%). We put the test set away and use it only at the end, as usual. We then start a loop using the cross-validation set where we repeat the following steps:

- Take a random subset, typically about 70% of the cross-validation set.
- Train the model on it.
- Validate it with the remaining data of the cross-validation set (30%) and calculate the error on the validation set with an appropriate evaluation metric.

Having repeated this process, typically five to ten times, we can then calculate the cross-validation performance of the model. For that we simply compute the average of the model performances on the number of runs we have executed.

As usual, this process can be repeated with a few different models. We end up with a number of models that we have trained and validated. We can then simply compare the performance of the models and assess their final performance with the test set. The difference is that this time we validate and compare the models based not on their performance on *one validation set* but on their cross-validation performance.

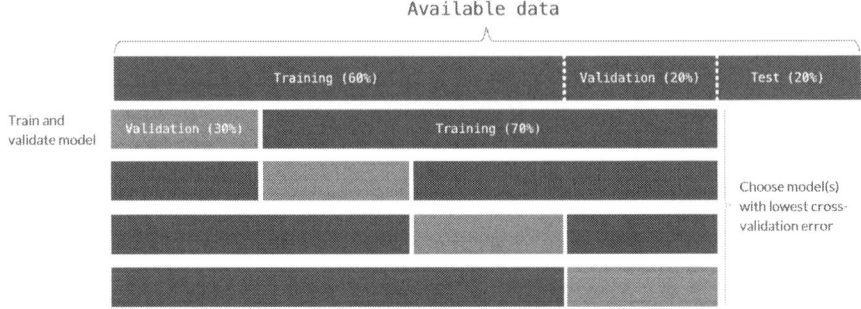

Figure 106.1 Overview of cross-validation

This gives us a much more accurate estimate of how well the models will perform on the test set and in real life. Why? Because we avoid overfitting the models to a given validation set. Cross-validation alleviates this problem, because we take several validation sets and so by definition we cannot run into the problem of overfitting to one specific validation set.

Cross-validation is heavily used in supervised ML. It is easy to implement, yet helps a lot in finding a strong model.

107 | Preventing overfitting: how does ensemble learning work?

The idea of ensemble learning is a bit like using the "wisdom of the crowd". The crowd in this case does not consist of humans, but different ML models.

Table 107.1 What is ensemble learning and why does it matter?

What is ensemble learning?

Ensemble learning is a method in which several models rather than just one are used to make predictions. For example, the most prominent ensemble learning method is the random forest, which consists of several decision trees (hence forest) that are being trained. If a prediction is to be made about a new dataset, then all predictions on the individual decision trees are aggregated to yield the overall prediction.

Drawing on and aggregating the predictive power of several models rather than just one increases the predictive performance. The principle behind this magic is akin to "the wisdom of the crowd" – but here the crowd consists of different models rather than humans. The idea is that individually the models might be underfitting and overfitting and performing poorly. But by forming a group, these "weak" models and inaccuracies in predictions cancel each other out and together they form a powerful ensemble.

Why does it matter?

Ensemble learning algorithms are heavily used in practice. Compared to just using one single model, ensembles typically have a higher predictive power, since they are less likely to overfit and underfit.

In ensemble learning we split up our dataset to obtain a training set, as usual. However, this time we do not use the entire training set to train one model. Instead, we create several subsets of the training set. We then use each of these subsets to train a different model. These different models could all be of the same model class. For example, we might train a decision tree on all of them to obtain a random forest. We could, however, also use different model types for each subset. What we end up with is a number of models that have all been trained on different subsets of the training set.

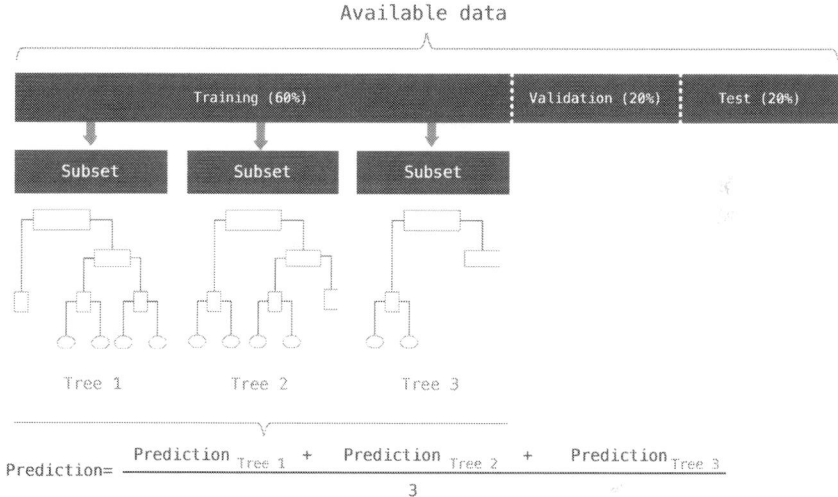

Figure 107.1 Example of ensemble learning

In order to make predictions on unseen data, we do not use just one of the models but *all of them* and aggregate their results. If our target variable is numerical, then we just take the average predicted value of all models. If we are dealing with a classification problem, then we can simply have all the models make their classification of the new observation and then decide by majority vote.

For example, say we have some customer data and want to predict whether or not a customer visiting our website will buy a product. We create a training set from historical data, take, say, 101 subsets of that training set and train a decision tree on each of these subsets. If we want to classify a new customer, we have all of the 101 trees make a prediction as to whether the new customer will buy or not. If the majority decide that they will, then the ensemble of decision trees as a whole makes the prediction "yes, the customer will buy something".

Ensemble learning is extremely powerful and works very well in practice. In fact, the random forest is arguably the most applied ML model by practitioners in supervised ML. The reason why ensemble learning works so well and is a good remedy against overfitting is because we are beating overfitting with its own weapons. If we train a given model on a subset of the training set, then we will very likely end up with a model that heavily overfits its subset. So it will pick up the idiosyncratic noise of it. But the point is that we use a number of models to make predictions, all of which overfit their respective training subset. So if we aggregate all of the overfitted models that picked up some strange idiosyncrasies of their respective subset, then eventually these individual overfitting tendencies cancel each other out. Everyone overfits individually, but together this effect is levelled again – the powerful wisdom of the crowd.

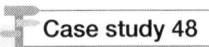

Case study 48

Ensemble-learning-based hedge fund

A company that has been taking ensemble learning to the edge is NumerAI. NumerAI is an "AI-based crowd-sourced" hedge fund that is using an ensemble to steer its investments. But in this case, the ensemble does not only consist of a couple of ML algorithms, but also a couple of thousand anonymous ML practitioners from around the world! Put in simple terms, a data scientist can submit to NumerAI an ML model that predicts stocks. NumerAI then aggregates the predictions on all the models it has received in order to analyse the market and steer its own investments. It can therefore prevent the overfitting or bias of using a single model (or group of models) from its own staff. The data scientists who have submitted the most accurate models are compensated in bitcoin.[cxlii]

108 | How else can overfitting be prevented?

Even in the world of data and ML there are approaches that still rely on brainpower. This is especially true when it comes to preventing models from overfitting their training set.

A very effective method is to simply reduce the complexity of models manually, with domain knowledge and/or a deep understanding of the applied models. In many cases models can be greatly simplified by just knowing what features will be relevant to predict the target variable. The number of features and parameters used can easily be reduced, and this will also help in determining what kind of model class is most appropriate for the underlying problem.

There are other methods and techniques to counter overfitting at all levels of the supervised ML process, but the aforementioned ones are definitely the most relevant and widely used. In practice we often use a combination of these methods depending on what type of model we are using, what the underlying problem is and what the data looks like.

109 | How much data is needed to train an ML model?

How much data you need for the ML model largely depends on two factors:

- *The complexity of the underlying process related to the target variable:* The more complex the process, the greater the number of variables that come into play and the more data you need in order to make sensible

Creating and Testing a ML Model with Supervised Machine Learning

predictions or explanations of that process. Take, for example, boiling one litre of water in a pan on a hotplate. This is a very simple process because there are few factors in play beyond the heat of the hotplate, the type of pan and maybe the air pressure. So even us humans would not need more than a few goes of boiling water to give a pretty accurate prediction of how long it takes to reach 100°C. A model to predict the time it takes for the water to boil will have a handful of data points. In contrast, consider the effect of smoking on the life expectancy of a person. While it is clear that there is a correlation between these two variables, the life expectancy is also subject to thousands of other factors, such as genes, nutrition, environment and lifestyle. Distilling the signal between the variables "smoking" and "life expectancy" in such a convoluted and intricate mix of factors will require lots of data points.

- *The complexity of the model:* Generally speaking, the more complex a given process, the more complex the model has to be in order to depict this real-world process. As such, the complexity of the model is a direct reflection of the complexity of the underlying real-world process. And the more complex the ML model, the more data you need to train it. For example, a simple linear model with a handful of parameters can already be calculated in a sensible way with a few dozen instances. A deep neural network with millions of parameters needs millions of instances in order to be trained.

Given these two factors, it is difficult to give a precise answer or rule of thumb as to how much data is needed to create an ML model.

Even so, there is one firm rule: you always need more instances in your dataset than there are parameters to be estimated in your model. There are a number of rules of thumb among practitioners for just how much longer than wider your dataset needs to be, such as the ten-times rule, i.e. you need ten times as many instances as features. But these are just rules of thumb that again depend on the complexity of the process, the model and the strength of the features.

So it is difficult to know exactly how much data you need in order to train an ML model. It could range from just a few observations for very simple processes and models to millions of data points to create a very complex ML model with a lot of parameters, such as a deep neural network. One thing that generally holds true, though, is: the *more (unbiased and high quality) data you have, the better*.

Case study 49

Creating AI that composes music

The Luxembourg-based start-up Aiva Technologies has created an ML model called Aiva that is able to write entire classical symphonies on its own. It is a deep neural network that was trained on a dataset of 3,000 scores by the greatest composers of all time such as Beethoven, Bach and Mozart.[cxliii]

Specifically, it has acquired the capability to predict the next note that is (or should be played) in a symphony and it applies this pattern to write new music. Given the hundreds of thousands of notes that are played by the various instruments in an orchestra during a symphony, this makes hundreds of thousands of data points from which Aiva was able to learn. Because it is a deep neural network with thousands of parameters, such a large dataset was necessary for its training.

8 Popular Machine Learning Model Classes for Supervised Machine Learning

8_1 Some classic ML models

110 | What model classes are there in ML?

In supervised machine learning (ML) we differentiate between various model classes. While all model classes have in common that they aim to model the real world, there are substantial differences between them in the following areas:

- *Their underlying philosophy or approach to depicting the real world:* For example, linear models assume that a target variable is the result of a linear combination of input variables, and neural networks are loosely inspired by the structure of the human brain and assume that a target variable is the result of a network of neurons. And so forth. So while all model classes might have the same goal, they approach the problem from different angles.
- *Their fit for a situation:* Certain models are especially appropriate for certain situations. There is no perfect model that does the best job of modelling all real-life situations there are (there is no free lunch). If the underlying problem is based on a linear process, then a linear model will do a much better job of modelling it accurately than, say, a tree-based model. While each model class has its strengths and weaknesses, some are more flexible than others. For instance, some model classes can only be used where the target variable is numerical, while other model classes can be used for both numerical and categorical variables. Other model classes, such as neural networks, are even so flexible that they can be used for supervised, unsupervised and reinforcement learning.
- *Their degree of complexity and flexibility:* In this context, we often speak of white box and black box model classes:
  - ❏ *White box models* are simple and easy to understand. After a model has been trained and is used to create predictions, we can look into the inner workings of the model and understand why and how the model works and makes its predictions. The results it produces are interpretable and we understand how a certain input variable affects our target variable. An example of a white box model is a simple linear regression.
  - ❏ *Black box models* are those that are complex and difficult to comprehend. We do not know how or why a model came to a given

prediction. Black box models do not allow us to understand the underlying patterns, i.e. how a certain input variable influences our target variable. Deep neural networks are an example of black box algorithms. Complex models tend to perform better, especially in complex processes and situations. That is why we often have to trade a model's complexity (and thus also interpretability) off against its performance.

We do not have the space to go into all model classes in depth. That is why in this chapter we limit ourselves to the model classes that are most widely used in practice. We devote an entire section to one model class: neural networks. Because the majority of breakthroughs in the field of artificial intelligence (AI) have been based on the application of neural networks, we have decided to do a deep dive into this and related fields.

111 | How do generalized linear models work?

Table 111.1 Overview of GLMs

What is a GLM and how does it work?	The generalized linear model (GLM) is arguably the most well-known and most commonly used model class in statistics and ML. It models the target variable as a *linear combination* of the input variables. A linear combination is the sum of all input variables multiplied by some parameters (see the example). GLMs are actually an entire model family that consists of a number of linear models, each of which has specific use cases. The two most commonly used GLMs are: • **Linear regression model:** Used to model a continuous dependent variable (e.g. temperature or body weight). • **Logistic regression model:** Used to model dichotomous variables (which can, for example, be used to classify vehicles into "car" or "not a car"). There are a lot of other types of GLMs. The simpler models are the workhorses for a lot of statistical and ML problems. They are well understood, intuitive and simple. In practice, we give these models a first shot at a problem, using them as a benchmark to assess the performance of other models. Some GLMs can be used for regression and some for classification problems.
Example	Let's suppose we want to model the average fuel consumption of cars. Our target variable is "average fuel consumption of car per 100 kilometres distance driven". Our target variable is thus continuous. What are the factors that influence the average fuel consumption of cars? Good candidates to begin with are probably the car's weight and its horsepower. So in a multiple linear regression model, you would assume the fuel consumption of a car is a linear combination of its weight and horsepower. We express this in mathematical symbols like this: $$\text{Fuel consumption} = \beta_1 * \text{weight} + \beta_2 * \text{horsepower}$$ where β_1, β_2 are Parameters and weight, horsepower are Independent Variables. Figure 111.1 Example of a linear model

Popular Machine Learning Model Classes for Supervised Machine Learning

Let's assume that you have data on a couple hundred cars, and you train a model and obtain the following trained model and its parameters:

```
Fuel Consumption (l per 100km) = 0.0031 x weight (kg) +
                                 0.017 x horsepower (hp)
```

Figure 111.2 Example of a specified simple linear model

According to this estimated model, the fuel consumption of a car (litres per 100 kilometres) can be predicted by multiplying its weight in kg by a factor of 0.0031 and adding its horsepower in hp multiplied by a factor of 0.017. So, for example, for a car that weighs 1,500 kg and has a horsepower of 110, we would predict the following fuel consumption:

```
Fuel Consumption = 0.0031 x 1500 + 0.017 x 110
                 = 6.52 (l per 100km)
```

Figure 111.3 Example calculation of a prediction with a simple linear model

Strengths and weaknesses	Strengths: • GLM are very intuitive, interpretable and understandable even for non-experts. • For a lot of processes in real life, they do a pretty good job of modelling. • They are computationally inexpensive: they do not need a lot of computational power to be trained or to make predictions. Weakness: • They perform poorly when modelling very complex processes with non-linear relationships; for example, if there are a lot of interactions between input variables.

112 | How do decision trees work?

Table 112.1 Overview of tree-based models

What is a decision tree and how does it work?	A decision tree is a set of hierarchically ordered if-then rules by means of which a target variable is predicted. It consists of a number of splitting points (nodes) with which a given observation is classified. Decision trees can be used for both regression (regression trees) and classification (classification trees). The decision tree is a rather weak model, especially due to its strong tendency to overfit, and so it is barely used in practice. However, it is used in ensemble learning to alleviate the problem of its tendency to overfit. In fact, while decision trees are barely used in practise, the so called random forest, which is an ensemble of decision trees, is an extremely strong and widely used model. It is a true all-rounder that can be used for almost any problem and produces splendid results.
Example	See Chapter 7.
Strengths and weaknesses	Strengths: • Decision trees are good at modelling non-linear relationships. • They are very intuitive to understand and to depict graphically. Weakness: • They have a strong tendency to overfit.

113 | How do ensemble methods such as the random forest algorithm work?

Table 113.1 Overview of ensemble learning

What is ensemble learning and how does it work?	Ensemble learning is not a model class as such. It refers to using several ML models (which may or may not be from the same model class), rather than just one model, to make predictions on a target variable. Ensemble learning can thus be thought of as harnessing the combined intelligence of an ensemble of models.

There are various ways to create such an ensemble, but the underlying idea is the same. Instead of using the entire training set to train a model, we draw, say, ten subsets of the training set and train a model on each of these subsets. We thus end up with an ensemble of ten models. When we want to predict our target variable with this ensemble, we provide each one of those ten models with the input data and have it make its prediction. We then aggregate the individual predictions. For example, in the case of a regression problem where we want to predict a numerical variable, we might take the average value of them, and in the case of classification problems we simply make the prediction by a majority vote.

The most commonly used ensemble learning algorithm is the random forest. It trains a number of decisions trees, say 500, and aggregates their single predictions.

Drawing on and aggregating the predictive power of several models rather than just one increases predictive performance. The idea is that individually the models might underfit and overfit and thus perform poorly. But in a group, these inaccuracies in predictions cancel each other out and together the individually "weak" models form a powerful ensemble.

Ensemble methods are heavily used in practice. They are real all-rounders that tend to perform well in almost any situation, with both regression and classification problems. Given that they alleviate the tendency of single algorithms to overfit, they usually have extremely strong predictive power. |
| Example | Let's assume we are training an ensemble of decision trees (random forest) to predict whether a website visitor will click on a product link on our website. Our input variables are the time of day, the location of the visitor (country) and whether they have visited the website. Usually, we would train dozens or hundreds of trees, but for simplicity we will just train three of them.

We draw three different subsets from our training set. On each of these subsets we train a decision tree.

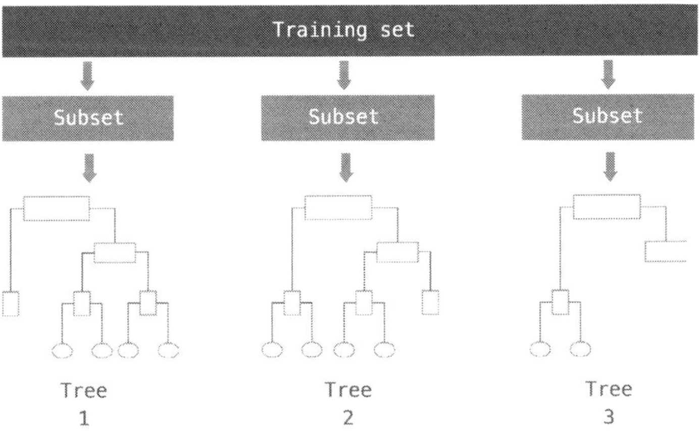

Figure 113.1 Example of a tree-based ensemble |

Once the various models are trained, we can use them to make predictions on unseen data. For that we provide each of the models with the input variables and have them make their individual predictions. Because we are dealing with a categorical target variable, we can aggregate their predictions by simply applying a majority vote rule. If the majority of models predict that a visitor will click on a link, then this will be the overall prediction.

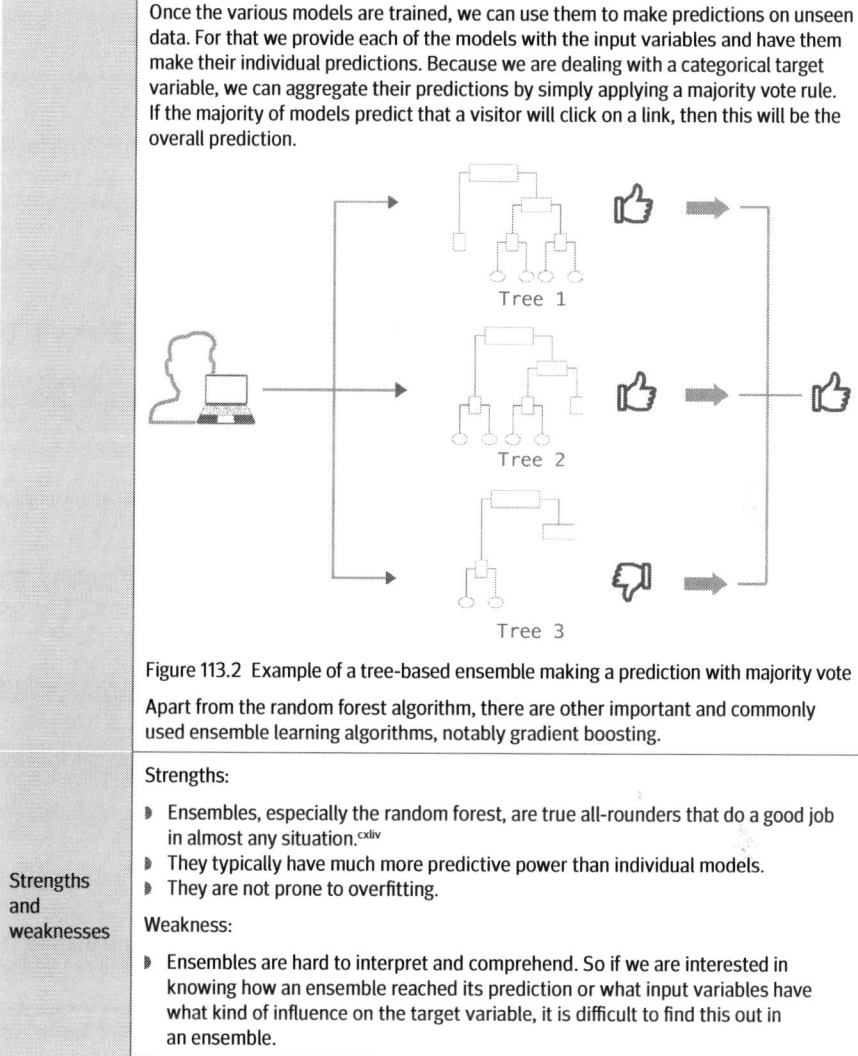

Figure 113.2 Example of a tree-based ensemble making a prediction with majority vote

Apart from the random forest algorithm, there are other important and commonly used ensemble learning algorithms, notably gradient boosting.

Strengths and weaknesses

Strengths:

- Ensembles, especially the random forest, are true all-rounders that do a good job in almost any situation.[cxliv]
- They typically have much more predictive power than individual models.
- They are not prone to overfitting.

Weakness:

- Ensembles are hard to interpret and comprehend. So if we are interested in knowing how an ensemble reached its prediction or what input variables have what kind of influence on the target variable, it is difficult to find this out in an ensemble.

114 | How do we choose the right ML model?

Unfortunately, there is no straightforward answer for how to choose the right model class for a given supervised ML problem. Every problem is different and there are a lot of factors to consider. Here are some questions that we as practitioners consider when implementing an ML model.

What does the target variable look like?

We consider the underlying process to be modelled and the target variable to be explained. Whether we are dealing with a continuous or categorical variable points us towards certain models. Or maybe we don't have labelled data and a target variable, so we need to use unsupervised learning methods.

What potential variables influence the target variable and how are they related to each other?

Do we already have an idea of the input variables that might influence the target variable? In what ways may they influence the target variable? Are the input variables related? How many input variables are there?

If, for example, a target variable is likely to be a linear combination of its input variables (and a lot of problems can be modelled like this), a GLM is a good candidate. But if we suspect there are a lot of interactions and non-linear relationships within the input variables, then a linear model will let us down and we will fare better with other model classes. For example, if there are hundreds of input variables (which is often the case with use cases dealing with sensor data) and the process is too complex for us comprehend, then neural networks might be a good start, since they are able to model such complex interactions and automatically select relevant features.

Is the interpretability of the model important?

Another factor to consider is the other end of the line: who will consume this information and how important is it that the results are comprehensible? Some models are more complicated to comprehend than others (black box), e.g. deep neural networks. They might be good at modelling an underlying business problem, but the way they do that and the predictions they create are opaque.

Using such a model in situations where we are interested in explaining a process and comprehending how factors influence a given target variable would be complete nonsense. We might be subject to legal or business constraints that force us to use a transparent model. For example, if we implement an algorithm that decides whether a loan applicant is granted a loan, we want to identify the factors that led to that decision so that we can communicate them to the applicant.

How much data do we have?

The amount of data also matters. We should consider three things:

- *How many input variables do we have?* (In the final dataset this translates to the number of columns.) If we have a lot of them and we suspect that a lot of them are relevant, then we likely have a very complex problem at hand and we probably want to consider models that are able to deal with such complex relationships.
- *How many observations do we have?* (This translates to the number of rows in the dataset.) If we have very few observations, then complex models will not pass the test. To train complex models with a lot of parameters, we need the necessary amount of observations.
- *What is the overall size of the dataset to be analysed?* If we are dealing with so much data that we have to make use of a computer cluster, then

by default some models are not available to us. Distributing tasks across computers is extremely challenging and not all algorithms and models can be distributed among many nodes.

We don't limit ourselves to only training one model

In practice, we do not limit ourselves to training only one model. That means that we can try out models from different model classes and see how they perform. For experienced practitioners, this is not a hit-and-miss process, however. Typically, we will take into consideration factors such as "Would a linear decision boundary work here?" in order to choose a few models that are likely to do a good job. Moreover, there are algorithms that automate the process of training and validating a number of models. This takes tedious manual work off our shoulders during the ML process.

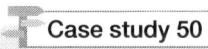

Choosing a model for political reasons

Another factor to consider when choosing which model class to use for a given use case can be a company's internal politics. For example, we have been in a situation where we were forced to use deep learning algorithms just for the sake of using deep learning. From an analytics perspective, it made little sense because we knew that given that dataset we were dealing with, deep learning would not have produced better results than other model classes. However, because the project was financed under the newly set up "AI and Deep Learning Department", we had to use deep learning models in order to gain the support of management and secure the funding for the project.

8_2 Neural networks and deep learning

115 | What are neural networks and deep learning and why do they matter?

One ML model class that has received increased attention in recent years is *neural networks*, along with a specific use of them called *deep learning*.

Even though neural networks are just one model class among many in ML, they have developed into something like a *primus inter pares*, given that virtually all of the major AI breakthroughs can be attributed to their use. In fact, some would argue that deep learning has reawakened the entire field of AI in recent years.

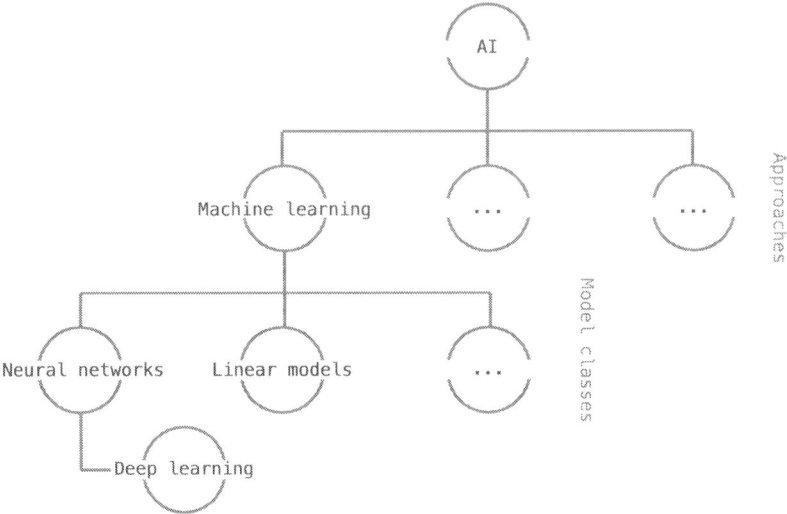

Figure 115.1 Relationship between AI and deep learning

Table 115.1 What are neural networks and deep learning and why do they matter?

What are (artificial) neural networks and deep learning?
Neural networks, also called artificial neural networks (ANNs), are one class of ML model. They are loosely inspired by the way biological brain networks function.
Neural networks consist of a number of interconnected units called nodes or artificial neurons (or neurons for short). Like synapses in the human brain, these units are connected and transmit signals among each other. Each of these units performs a mathematical operation when it receives a certain input: it transforms it and passes on an output to other neurons. Like this, an input signal moves through the network until it is finally transformed into an output, usually a prediction of a target variable.
The neurons are arranged in so-called layers of the network. Neural networks that consist of many such layers are called deep. The training and use of deep neural networks is called deep learning.

Why does it matter?
Neural networks have a number of characteristics that render them extremely powerful. An important one is their ability to model real-world situations where other ML model classes perform poorly fail because they are too complex, e.g. image recognition.
The use of deep learning has led to some ground-breaking successes in the creation of AI – so much so that some people consider the advancements brought about by neural networks to be the main reason that AI is enjoying so much attention at the moment.
Neural networks are especially appropriate and have led to impressive results in the fields of computer vision, natural language processing and other areas where traditional ML problems have so far yielded only limited results.

Popular Machine Learning Model Classes for Supervised Machine Learning

The idea of neural networks is to model the real world and analyse data by loosely imitating the structure of the human brain and biological neural networks. A neural network is a collection of interconnected units called *artificial neurons* (or simply neurons). Like the synapses in the human brain, each connection between the neurons can transmit a signal from one neuron to another. The neuron then processes the signal and possibly passes it on again.

The neurons in a network are arranged and ordered into *layers*. Every neural network consists of at least three layers: the first layer, where the data is fed into the network (input layer); the last layer, where the result/prediction of the network is brought out (output layer); and at least one hidden layer in which the input signals are transformed and processed (hidden layer). A neural network with more than one hidden layer is called *deep*. Training such deep neural networks is called deep learning.

Today, the most complex deep neural networks consist of hundreds of layers, millions of neurons and billions of connections between these neurons. In 2018, researchers presented a deep neural network with some 16 million neurons – about the size of the brain of a frog.[cxlv] This number is still dwarfed, though, by the c. 100 billion neurons in the human brain.[cxlvi] Of course, the brain has many substructures and is not structurally comparable to a neural network.

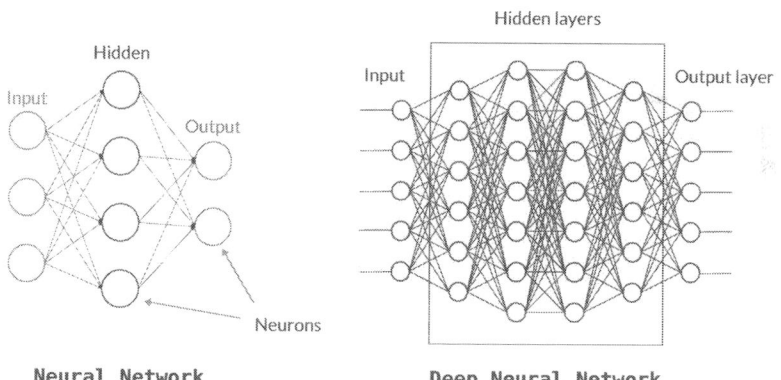

Figure 115.2 Overview of a neural network and a deep neural network

Neural networks are extremely versatile. They can be used for both regression and classification problems in supervised ML. They can also be used for a lot of unsupervised learning problems and in reinforcement learning. There is incredible hype around neural networks at present, especially deep neural networks. While we think it is good to keep your cool when confronted with hype, in this case the hype is justified to a certain extent. Neural networks have proven to be very powerful and have outperformed other ML model types in a wide array of fields.

One of the most important breakthroughs was in 2012, when a deep neural network won the ImageNet competition in a spectacular fashion (see Case Study 51). This reignited interest in neural networks and their use. More importantly, it reinvigorated the entire academic field of AI, because it was a major breakthrough in the field of image recognition and computer vision, where progress had previously been slow. The success in this field later spilled over into other areas of AI such as natural language processing.

Case study 51

How a deep neural network beat all other ML models and thus reinvigorated AI

In the late 2000s, Fei-Fei Li, a computer science professor now teaching at Stanford University, wanted to create better ML models. However, instead of focusing on improving the models, she and her team focused on improving the *data*. So they gathered some 3.2 million images from the internet and labelled these images with the objects they displayed, e.g. sailboats, furniture, dogs and vehicles. Thus was born the so-called ImageNet dataset, which now contains over 13 million labelled images drawn from the internet.[cxlvii]

Additionally, the team organized an annual competition where researchers and practitioners could submit models that would classify objects in these images. The ImageNet database has since developed into something like the gold standard for benchmarking and testing computer vision models, i.e. seeing how well a model is performing its task of correctly classifying objects in images.

The first competition took place in 2010 with okay results. In 2011 there was a very slight performance increase in the models submitted. That year, the winner was a team from the Xerox Research Centre Europe. They applied a variant of a support vector machine algorithm, a classic ML model class, and were able to classify some 75% of the images correctly.[cxlviii] The other major competitors had error rates of around 30% and were therefore well behind the winners.

The next year, however, was a watershed moment for the competition and beyond. In 2012, a team from the University of Toronto – including Geoffrey Hinton, who today is seen as one of the heroes in the advancement of neural networks – submitted a deep neural network called AlexNet that turned out to be a real game-changer. It outperformed previous models and other competitors by a huge margin. While other teams' models achieved errors rates of around 25%, AlexNet's error rate was well below 25%: it had pushed the previous champion by some 10% in performance!

The following year, 2013, almost all of the major competitors were below the 25% error rate. This is because everyone was following the approach of AlexNet and using a deep neural network for the competition. As a result, after 2012 every single competition was won by a deep neural network. With the major competitors using deep learning approaches, the performance as a whole and at the top had increased to stunning levels by 2017, where the best model was close to perfect and the vast majority of models submitted had an error rate of less than 5%.[cxlix] This result is all the more impressive when you consider that human performance on the dataset stands at around a 5% error rate as well (i.e. humans are not able to classify all objects perfectly and also make errors).[cl]

But the legacy of AlexNet was not only bound to the ImageNet competition itself. If a computer can classify images with such a high degree of accuracy, then this is a big step in the field of computer vision, which could above all be applied in autonomous driving. The impressive performance of the deep neural networks competing at ImageNet showed that such computer vision was indeed possible and feasible with neural networks. This was arguably one of the main contributing factors in the increased interest and hype around deep learning, which had been in hibernation for decades at that time.

And it did not stop there. If deep learning could enable computer vision, what else could be done with it? Deep learning models were now applied in other fields, such as voice recognition. All of these applications and advancements drove the current hype around AI.

116 | How do neural networks work?

Neural networks loosely emulate the structure of the human brain and create predictions on a target variable by transmitting a signal through a network of neurons.

Setting up a simple neural network

Let's look at how a neural network creates predictions by means of an example.

Imagine we have created a neural network to predict whether a person going into a cafe will order a doughnut. The neural network we have trained consists of only one hidden layer with only one neuron. We have two variables of the person going into the cafe: their level of hungriness (scale of 0 = "not hungry" to 10 = "could eat a bear") and their appetite for something sweet (scale of 0 = "I feel like something savoury" to 10 = "I want pure sugar right now"). Since we have two input variables, our input layer consists of two neurons. We want to know whether the person will buy a doughnut, so the output layer of our network will consist of one neuron that outputs either yes or no (or rather 1 or 0).

The Ultimate Data and AI Guide

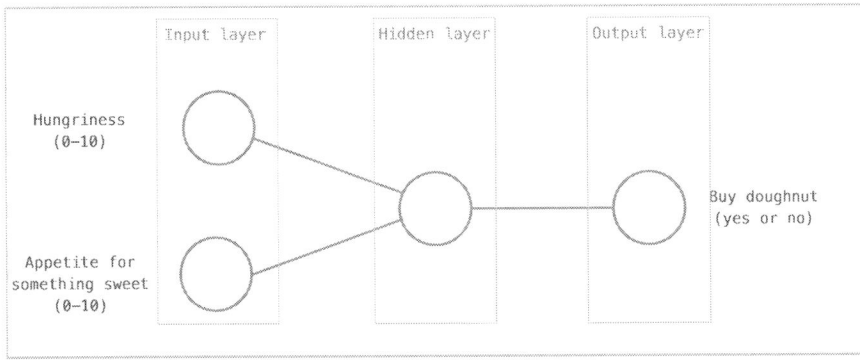

Figure 116.1 Example of a simple neural network

In basic terms, a neural network functions like this: each neuron takes the input it receives, performs a mathematical function with this input and passes on the output.

In our example, things are easy. The neuron in the hidden layer gets as an input the level of hungriness of a person along with their appetite for something sweet. It seems sensible to assume that the level of hungriness and the appetite for sweetness are equally important in the buyer's decision. Both have to be given for the result to be a doughnut purchase. No hunger would mean no purchase; hunger but appetite for something savoury would mean the purchase of a salty snack.

So this is a sensible mathematical function to apply to these two variables: sum the values and divide them by two to obtain a theoretical variable like "sweetness-hunger". If the "sweetness-hunger" score is above a certain threshold, say 5, then the person will buy a doughnut. So if someone has a score of 6, then the network will output: "Yes, this person is going to buy a doughnut." A dataset with a couple of people with varying hunger levels would yield the following predictions:

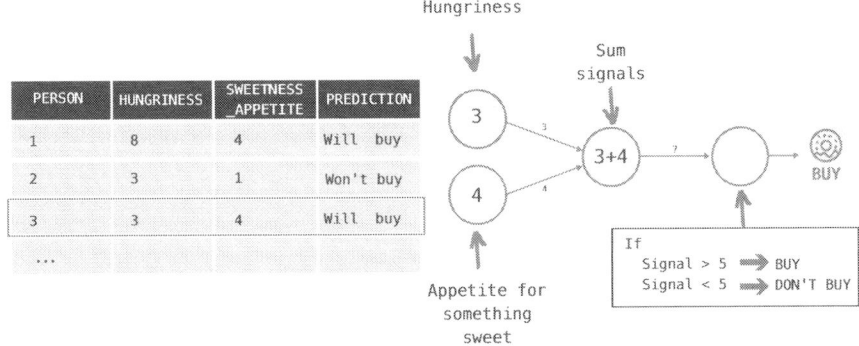

Figure 116.2 Example of the workings of a neural network

Popular Machine Learning Model Classes for Supervised Machine Learning

It might be that in reality the hunger is far more important. In that case we might adjust the mathematical function so that we put more weight on the input "level of hunger", say in a ratio of 3:1, as compared to the "appetite for sweetness". Such adjustments to increase or decrease the strength of a given input variable for a neuron are called *weights* and are crucial for the functioning of a neural network.

The weights that determine how strongly a neuron pays attention to an input signal are one parameter in a neural network. The other one is whether and how strongly a neuron passes on a signal, which is called the *bias*. When a model is trained, the weights and biases in the network are adjusted so that they fit the underlying data as well as possible. In our example, if in reality the level of hunger turns out to be ten times more important than the appetite for sweetness and this is reflected in the training data, the neural network will assign the weight parameters accordingly.

Setting up a deep neural network

Neural networks are extremely powerful for a number of reasons that aren't really apparent when looking at such a simple example. Whether or not a person buys a doughnut depends on other factors as well. For example, there are personality-related factors such as the ability to resist temptation, the current mood and the level of health-consciousness, and there might be external factors such as the weather, temperature and time of the day. There are strong interactions between these influencing factors; for instance, mood is strongly influenced by the weather. In short, there are actually *many* factors that influence a person's decision to buy a doughnut or not. While the outcome is a simple yes or no, the process behind it is extremely complex.

Imagine we have data on all of these variables. If we continue to try to model this extremely complex process with such a simple neural network, we won't be able to capture the complex underlying processes. So let's make our model more complex. Instead of one hidden layer, we set up our model with, say, ten hidden layers that contain thousands of neurons (this is a more typical size of a neural network). Now we have a deep neural network.

There are two advantages to using such deep neural networks and these get more pronounced the "deeper" a neural network gets:

- Deep neural networks are extremely flexible. Just imagine that you have a network of thousands or even millions of interconnected neurons that transmit signals between them. This enables them to capture even highly intricate processes with a lot of input variables that are subject to complex interactions. In general, the deeper a network gets, i.e. the more neurons and hidden layers it contains, the more complex the situations it can model.
- During their training, neural networks automatically implement their own feature engineering and selection mechanisms. Remember that one of the central parameters is the weight that a neuron assigns to a given input. If a network is fed with irrelevant input variables, the weight assigned to

them by the various neurons will automatically be low – an automated feature selection. Likewise, the interplay of several neurons often results in situations where a certain neuron transmits a signal that reflects a factor that actually exists in real life.

Training the neural network

Given the sheer size of most neural networks, they can take a long time to train. For instance, AlexNet had a stunning 60 million parameters that needed to be computed during its training.[cli] While classic ML models barely take more than a couple of seconds on normal computers, the training of neural networks can take days or even weeks.

This is largely due to the fact that there is no simple formula to calculate the optimal parameters of a neural network during its training. Instead, they have to be determined with approximation methods, which essentially means repeatedly trying a set of values for the parameters and seeing how well they fit. The algorithm that is implemented in all ML tools to train a neural network is a form of the gradient descent algorithm.

Model types

Within the neural networks ML model class there are several model types. These differ in their architecture, i.e. the way in which neurons are connected and transmit signals among each other.

The model type that we looked at in the doughnut example is a (deep) feedforward neural network, which is the simplest type of neural network. In a feedforward network, the signal is only passed on from left to right once. In other architectures, neurons can transmit a signal back to themselves, which is especially useful for handling problems that have a temporal or sequential dimension. Some examples of other popular and widely used neural networks are long short-term memory (LSTM) networks, convolutional neural networks and recurrent neural networks.

Because neural networks are a black box algorithm, little is known about what kind of architecture works well for what kind of problem. So it is a work in progress to experiment with and improve the various neural network types.

117 | What is so special about deep neural networks compared to classic ML model classes?

Compared to other ML model classes, neural networks have some features that come in extremely handy and make them very powerful, especially if they are deep neural networks.

Partly automated feature engineering and selection

Arguably, the biggest convenience when working with neural networks is that, due to the way they function, they inherently engineer and select features from the data put into them.

Popular Machine Learning Model Classes for Supervised Machine Learning

Remember that during model training the neural network determines the optimal weights and biases for each neuron. In doing so, the network excludes redundant variables that carry no information. If a variable is unimportant, no neuron will assign a great weight to it, so it will play no role in computing the prediction in the output layer.

Neural networks also create certain abstract features *by themselves*. This comes in handy for processes that deal with a lot of features and are so complex that there is no way for us humans to discern any intricate relationships in the data. Certain neurons capture and depict abstract variables that exist in the data and have meaning in real life.

This can best be clarified with neural networks that are trained to detect objects in an image. During the training, certain neurons or layers assume different responsibilities. The first layer might be responsible for detecting the edges in a picture. The second layer can build upon these edges and discern certain traits or higher-level abstract features. These can then be used by the following layer to classify these traits into objects, and so forth.

Note that the neural network creates these abstract features by itself. We as model trainers do not have to provide the input that a certain image contains edges and colours, let alone where in an image these edges and colours are. Neural networks have the ability to do all of this by themselves. This is one of the main reasons why deep learning algorithms are so popular.

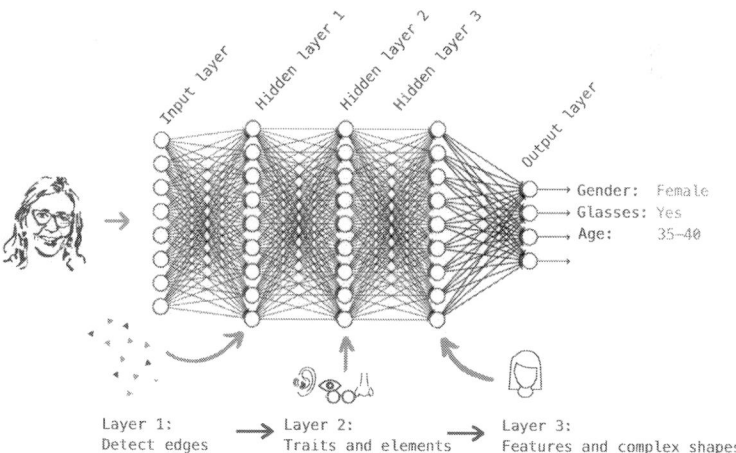

Figure 117.1 Automated feature engineering of a deep neural network

Therefore, the ability of neural networks to create and select features by itself automates the ML process right at the point that requires the most domain knowledge and manual input: feature engineering and selection. So the beauty of neural networks is that in a way they democratize the application of ML, because they enable the creation of models in areas where we do not have profound domain knowledge.

There is a big "but", however. To be clear: that does *not* mean that feature engineering is unnecessary when employing neural networks. A neural network can identify features and select them in a dataset without being explicitly told about them, but only if this information is already contained in the input variables that we give the neural network. One of the main jobs in feature engineering is to develop new features that provide additional and novel information. So if we hold back information from a neural network that it cannot get from anywhere else, it won't be able to "engineer" that by itself. For example, let's assume we train a neural network to predict our daily sales of a model car and we provide it only with the day of the week as input variable. An important variable influencing our sales that we withhold from the model in this case will be the price we set for the product on a given day. Let's assume that, the price we set is not correlated to the day of the week, i.e. we don't give offers only on certain days. Then the neural network will not be able to model the influence the effect the price has on sales and it cannot recreate it from the other input variable "day of the week".

So, feature engineering is still essential, and deep neural networks are not in fact a one-size-fits-all solution. A lot of practitioners just throw deep neural networks at every problem they see without thinking clearly about the underlying business problem and processes. This may work sometimes, but in our experience for use cases in the business world, domain knowledge and smart feature engineering trump even the most sophisticated neural networks.

Flexibility and therefore capacity to model even complex processes

The second big selling point of neural networks is their high degree of flexibility, which enables them to model almost any kind of relationship. In fact, the *universal approximation theorem* states that neural networks can approximate any continuous mathematical function.[clii] That also means that they can model extremely complex and weird relationships that happen to exist in the real world.

Thanks to the millions of neurons and billions of connections between them, a neural network is able to pick up and discern the complexity inherent in some real-world processes. A lot of processes actually follow rather simple patterns, and classic ML model classes do quite a good job of explaining and predicting them. There are, however, some extremely complex processes in nature (e.g. image classification) that cause classic ML models to hit their boundaries. These are exactly the areas where neural networks have recently excelled, leading to impressive advancements.

Case study 52

One neuron in a multi-million neuron network can classify the sentiment of words and phrases

Deep neural networks combine the input of several neurons to create an output that has some meaning in real life. This is what happened with a neural network trained by OpenAI, a research institute solely dedicated to the field of AI.

> In 2017, OpenAI trained a large neural network in order to predict the next character and word in a sentence (the training took about one month on high-end computers).[cliii] They used 82 million Amazon product reviews to train their model. Essentially by chance, they found that the output of a small number of neurons could be used to gauge the sentiment of a word and sentence (positive versus negative sentiment). Using the power of this neuron, they were able to classify the sentiment that prevailed in a piece of text. For example, the sentence "The package received was blank and has no barcode – a waste of time and money" would have been correctly classified as exhibiting a negative sentiment.

118 | Why are neural networks so good at natural language processing and computer vision?

ML can be applied in a wide variety of cases to solve a variety of problems and thereby automate a variety of tasks. Some of these problems are rather easy to solve. But then there is the "Champions League" of ML problems: processes and problems that are so complex to solve that for a long time even the most complex among the classic ML models and other approaches would do an unsatisfactory job.

Enter the neural network, and suddenly, from 2010 onwards, these problems seemed to be within the realm of the solvable again. In fact, neural networks had been conceived of in the 1960's already. But what changed some ten years ago is that we have started to have the necessary amounts of data and computing power to train deep, complex neural networks. With more data and computing power, the application of neural networks turned out to be a real game-changer by bringing about breakthroughs in several fields of AI, notably in two of the most complex ones: computer vision and natural language processing.

Computer vision

Visual perception is one of the most complex processes. What comes so easily and naturally to us without our even thinking about it requires the constant processing of incredible amounts of data. We use our eyes in everything we do in life and vision is arguably the most important sense – and an extremely sophisticated one that took a long time to develop.

Around 540 million years ago a major event happened on our little planet known as the Cambrian explosion.[cliv] During this event, which lasted some 20–25 million years, an explosion of new life forms appeared on Earth. One of the theories for why this explosion of species occurred is that at that time the first animals developed visual perception.[clv] Life before that seemed to happen at random and was based on other senses, such as smell and touch. But animals opening their eyes was a real game-changer. Suddenly, there were predators who were able to target their prey, which created a lot of pressure on every other animal to be able to see in order to dodge and escape. Suddenly, it mattered how you looked in order to attract the opposite sex and mate. Suddenly, it mattered how you behaved, because fellow animals were able to observe and interpret your behaviour. Our eyes and visual sense are the result of the ensuing evolution. It took nature some 500 million years to develop and hone our visual perception to the level it is at today.

Teaching a computer to see like humans do has long been on the minds of researchers. Even though there had been advancements and successes in that field, things changed when neural networks entered the scene. Thanks to their ability to model the complex relationships they led to a leap of performance in the fields of object recognition and computer vision (see Case Study 51). So suddenly the creation of AI system to automate extremely complex tasks that seemed impossible some 20 years ago such as autonomous driving, were put within the realm of possibilities sooner rather than later.

To understand why vision is so complex and interspersed with intricate relationships, consider the picture in Figure 118-1. For us, the situation is clear from just a split-second glance: a pretty bad traffic jam in a big city at night. Not only can we immediately discern the objects in the picture, but we also automatically get the context and understand what is going on (it is noisy, the air is polluted, drivers stuck will be frustrated, etc.).

Figure 118.1 A photo of a traffic jam in Jakarta by night

Things look different for a computer. What a computer "sees" is an array of pixels. Each pixel has a colour code, usually expressed as a mix of the strength of red, green and blue (RGB colour model). This strength is typically quantified on a scale of 0 to 256. So for each pixel a computer has the three RGB values that yield the colour that the pixel is displaying. Through the interplay of the various pixels arranged and coloured in a certain way, we get the image as a whole.

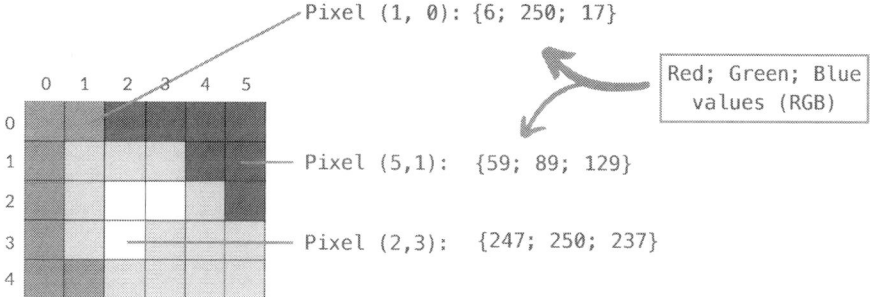

Figure 118.2 How a picture is broken down into pixels

For us, an image is the interplay of millions of visual inputs and objects whose interrelationships make up the whole, which eventually gives us meaning. For a computer, an image is just another array of 0s and 1s put together in a strange way. A computer does not just know that a certain arrangement of pixels and colours is the entity "car" in an image whereas a different arrangement is the entity "building". But we can get a machine to *learn* to name the entities in an image.

To understand just how complex it is to teach a machine vision, consider the following. If you take a picture with an iPhone X, you create an image with a size of 12 megapixels, i.e. 12,000,000 pixels. Taking the RGB 256 code, each of these pixels could be coloured in 16,777,216 ways.[33] So this is how many ways there are to arrange the pixels and their colours in an iPhone picture:

$$16{,}777{,}216 \wedge 12{,}000{,}000 = \text{an incalculable figure}^{34}$$

Whatever the figure is, it is more than the number of atoms in the entire universe, which is estimated to be 10^80 atoms.[clvi] These staggering numbers show just how intricate vision is. The brain is a high-performance, supercomputing engine that processes tons of information every millisecond from the eyes alone.

It should not come as a surprise, then, that if we were to train, say, a GLM to detect an object in an image, we would not get very far. There are far too many relationships and they work in ways that are too difficult to be discerned by a linear model. But deep neural networks, with their millions of neurons and billions of connections between them, are able to make sense of such a mess. Through their ability to create and discern abstract features in a dataset, they can discern edges, traits and ultimately objects in an image. This has enabled significant advancements in computer vision. Today, neural networks have been trained to perform incredible tasks, e.g. recognize all sorts of images in a picture (Case Study 51) or detect the sexual orientation of a person based on facial traits (📑 78).

---

33. 16,777,216 is the number of colors in the RGB code-system. A pixel's colour is determined by the value of its red, green and blue intensity, each of which can take on a value between 0 and 255. That makes for 256 * 256 * 256 = 256 ^3 = 16,777,216 colour combinations.
34. No calculator can calculate that number – we *have* tried.

Most of these advancements are in object detection and classification. While these are impressive, there is still a long way to go before algorithms can compete with human vision, and this will probably not happen anytime soon. You could download a deep neural network that would correctly detect a building and cars in Figure 118-1. But right now you could not teach the computer the context and the meaning behind these objects – what it means to be stuck in a traffic jam, how frustrating it is, what it means to miss an appointment or arrive home late, etc.

Natural language processing

Another major area where neural networks have excelled recently is natural language processing, which is the field of study concerned with enabling computers to learn human (natural) languages. This involves a wide array of fields, including:

- Speech recognition (e.g. in personal assistants)
- Language and text understanding
- Natural language creation (e.g. summarizing and creating text)
- Machine translation

Like vision, human language has been a key factor in the survival and development of our species. And like vision, it is an extremely complex task on which previous approaches and models have performed poorly. This is because in human language context matters a lot and the semantics of words depend on this context.

For example, "set" is the word with the most distinct meanings in English: 430.[clvii] We automatically know which of the hundreds of different meanings is meant when somebody uses the word "set". But we can only infer the semantics of a word if we are given the context it is used in (and even then we sometimes get confused). This context is extremely complex and subtle and you need a lot of experience to decipher and interpret it. Furthermore, even small changes in punctuation or intonation can change the meaning of something that is written or spoken. Just consider the sentence, "Let's eat, Grandpa!" Omitting the comma completely changes the meaning (to cannibalism): "Let's eat Grandpa!"

There are other major challenges when trying to teach a computer to understand our human language. For example, modelling things like sarcasm and irony is extremely difficult and usually requires human interaction beyond words. Furthermore, we tend to create new words and abbreviations of words daily.

Despite these challenges, the use of deep neural networks has led to impressive improvements in a wide range of natural language processing fields. This is thanks to their ability to capture and make sense of the intricate interplay of meanings and context that make up our human language and communication.[clviii]

Over the past couple of years, we have seen personal assistants entering the market. Siri (Apple) and Alexa (Amazon) might have been flawed in their alpha versions. However, with the adoption of a deep neural network as their core engine,[clix] these personal assistants have experienced an impressive improvement in performance and keep getting better at understanding and communicating with a human much more accurately.

Machine translation is another field where neural networks have led to significant performance improvements. For decades the progress of traditional machine translation approaches was extremely sluggish. When companies began using neural networks at the beginning of the 2010s, major improvements happened. Today, all machine translation providers, including Google Translate, have a deep learning model as their engine.[clx]

Text creation and understanding is another area. A number of email providers and social networks today offer suggestions for how to answer a message based on its content.

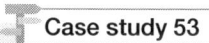

Case study 53

Autonomous driving

In contrast to classic ML models, neural networks require powerful graphics processing units (GPUs). For years, the company Nvidia has been at the forefront of producing and developing such GPUs.

As a result of this expertise, Nvidia has developed into one of the leading players in the field of deep learning today. One of its moves was to enter the market of autonomous driving with the goal of becoming a supplier of "self-driving unit kits" for automobile producers providing both the hard- and software for computer vision for cars. The models that are used for computer vision tasks such as obstacle, path, and wait condition perception are based on deep neural networks.[clxi] Today, Nvidia has partnered up with several major car producers including Volkswagen, Mercedes-Benz and Toyota to advance autonomous driving.[clxii]

119 | Are neural networks a universal cure for all ML problems or do they also have some drawbacks?

Deep neural networks have been outperforming other ML model classes in a number of fields, not only with highly complex problems such as visual recognition and natural language processing, but also in more down-to-earth business use cases, such as predicting sales. While a lot of these "standard" use cases can still be implemented with classic ML methods, the use of neural networks is becoming more and more widespread. You may be inclined to think that neural networks are a universal cure that can solve every ML problem. Fortunately[35], they are no universal cure. They also have some drawbacks.

---

35. Otherwise the field of ML would be too boring and we would no longer have our jobs.

Deep neural networks are black (or at least very dark) box

For a lot of use cases we want to be able to retrace how a model came to its prediction or decision. Sometimes we may even be required by law to do so. For example, if we deny a bank customer a loan, we certainly want to provide the grounds on which we came to that conclusion. Just saying "Our model told us that you are not a trustworthy customer and we do not want to conduct business with you" is not only detrimental to the image of the company, but it may also be unlawful in some countries.

That means we want to easily interpret and understand how models came to their decisions, i.e. we want white box models. While black box models, such as deep neural networks, might excel at creating predictions, it may be close to impossible to retrace how and why they reached certain decisions or predictions.

While drawing a dichotomy between white and black box models is too stark, there certainly is a difference concerning the interpretability and traceability of various ML models. The deeper a neural network gets, the more it is drawn to the dark side of interpretability.

To understand why, let's assume that we create two algorithms that decide whether to grant a bank customer a loan based on their socioeconomic data (age, income etc.): one simple linear model and one deep neural network with several hidden layers and several thousand parameters. Remember that when training an ML model, what we do conceptually is try to find a function (i.e. a set of rules) that best maps the input (here the socioeconomic data of a person) to the output (give a loan or do not give a loan).

With a linear model, this function is linear and therefore extremely easy to interpret. With such a model it is perfectly possible to say that the model classified Customer X as not creditworthy because, say, their income was too low.

We would not be able to do that with a deep neural network. In theory, it might be possible to unwind the functional form that is approximated and created by the millions of neurons and connections. But in practical terms when a deep neural network classifies a customer as not creditworthy, there is no way to say, "It is because their annual income is too low." It is simply too difficult to make sense of a model with millions of parameters where the result is a non-linear function of some neurons that in turn are a nonlinear function of some other neurons.

To be clear: in this case the deep neural network might do a much better job of classifying customers into creditworthy or not than the simple linear model. It might just be that the underlying relationships are indeed so complex and non-linear that the neural network is better at modelling the underlying patterns and functions, and so creating much more accurate predictions. The underlying business process may be so complex that it is difficult to know what input variables have what kind of influence. Then it is not really the "fault" of the neural network that is uninterpretable; it is simply the case that real life is uninterpretable and extremely complex. A linear model might not capture reality in its complexity and may oversimplify it, but at least the model enables us to make sense of the world.

It should also be noted that shallow neural networks can in fact be interpreted because their functional form is not as intricate. Furthermore, researchers are trying to make even deep neural networks interpretable so that we can say what variables play what kind of role in predicting the outcome. A notably example is local interpretable model-agnostics (LIME), a technique aimed at explaining the predictions of any ML model to make it both interpretable and trustworthy.[clxiii] Given the active research in the field of neural networks, we will likely see some fruits of these efforts in the future.

Deep neural networks usually require large amounts of data for their training

Remember that the number-one requirement for the amount of data needed to train a neural network is that there are more observations in the dataset than parameters in the model. One of the main assets of deep neural networks is that they are able to model extremely complex problems and processes because they have millions of neurons and billions of connections in between. That means that they need datasets with millions of observations for their training. There are several ways to work around and alleviate this problem, such as transfer learning (adapting pre-trained models), one-shot learning (learning from only one or a few training data points) and data augmentation (increasing the diversity of the dataset). However, in general training a deep neural network from scratch with a small dataset is difficult.

Deep neural networks do not necessarily outperform other ML model classes with small datasets

Even if a dataset is large enough to train a deep neural network, that does not mean it is large enough to ensure that the performance will be good. The predictive performance of a deep neural network increases with the amount of data. For extremely large amounts of data (millions of observations) the deep neural network's performance will typically be so good that other ML models cannot keep up.

If we are dealing with small datasets, however, things look very different. The predictive performance of deep neural networks is akin to that of other ML models if we are dealing with datasets that do not have observations in the range of hundreds of thousands or millions.

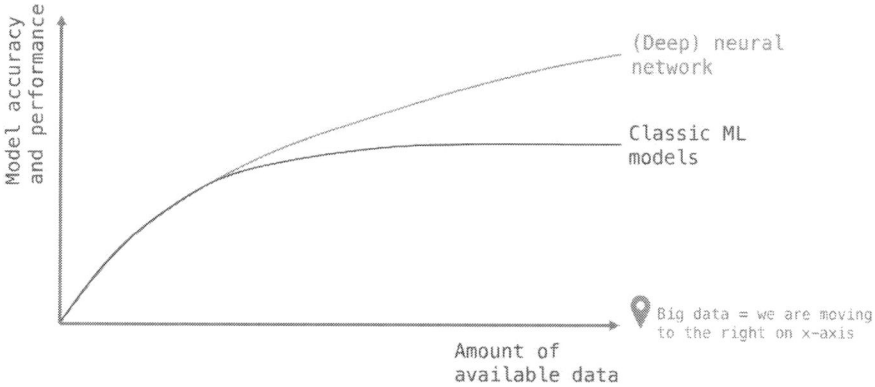

Figure 119.1 Schematic overview of the performance of deep neural networks vs. classic ML models

This means that just throwing a deep neural network at every ML problem will not necessarily lead to the best performance. If we are dealing with smaller datasets, then the expertise and domain knowledge of the ML engineer will be the deciding factors in the performance of a model, because the engineer will know which model will best tackle the underlying business problem. Such use cases with smaller amounts of data are a challenge that require brainpower.

Deep neural networks – nobody knows what they are doing

Another peculiarity about (deep) neural networks is that there are no guidelines or rules, let alone scientifically proven ways to architect and design them. Remember that there are different types of neural networks and each one can be architected in an infinite number of ways. This means that people training a deep neural network on a given problem do not know how many hidden layers there should be, how many neurons there should be, how these neurons should be connected etc. There are some ideas, hands-on experiences and examples of best practice out there, but so far there is no definitive proof that for a problem with *these* and *these* characteristics, neural networks with *this* kind of structure work best. So a lot of the neural network training is simply based on trial and error.

This also applies to other ML algorithms, albeit to a lesser extent. After all, we try out different model types and models to find the best one for a given problem, which is a hit-and-miss process. But since we comprehend better the functional form that other model classes approximate, deep neural networks have us in the dark even more than other models.

> **Case study 54**
>
> **Where are neural networks of no use?**
>
> Medical trials, for example to test the efficacy of new drugs, typically work with very small samples of patients. This is because recruiting patients who want to participate in experiments and have the right medical predisposition is extremely cumbersome and costly.
>
> Given that samples of a few dozen patients are not uncommon, neural networks will likely not be used anytime soon in these areas of medical research. In addition, not only is the available dataset too small, but in medicine we are mostly interested in understanding the underlying patterns, which requires the use of simple, white box models, e.g. linear regression models.

120 | What is transfer learning?

One of the drawbacks of (deep) neural networks is that they require large amounts of data for their training. Researchers have been attempting to alleviate this shortcoming. Arguably, the most important work in this area is the concept of *transfer learning*, in which knowledge acquired during model training is used to solve other ML problems and tasks.

Popular Machine Learning Model Classes for Supervised Machine Learning

For example, if a deep neural network has been trained to detect cars in an image, then it will likely have picked up some patterns that also enable it to detect other vehicles or objects. Therefore, if we want to create a model that detects other vehicles in an image, we do not need to train a new model from scratch. Instead, we can use the previously trained model as a base and simply have it acquire some minor adaptions during the next model training. The idea is to "recycle" the knowledge and skills that a certain model has already acquired in previous training in order to solve new problems.

Table 120.1 What is transfer learning and why does it matter?

What is transfer learning?
Transfer learning refers to the idea of using the knowledge that an ML model acquired during training to solve other tasks.
So instead of training an ML model from scratch, the idea of transfer learning is to *adapt* a pre-trained model for a certain task, thereby leveraging and recycling the knowledge that the model acquired previously.

Why does it matter?
Transfer learning is especially relevant for deep neural networks. Training deep neural networks from scratch requires large amounts of (typically labelled) data. When such data assets are not easily available (which is often the case), transfer learning is a viable option for creating performant ML models.

The cool thing about this approach is that adapting a pre-trained model requires less data than training a new one from scratch. Transfer learning is thus a viable option in situations where data to create an ML model from scratch is too scarce or where labelling a dataset is too expensive.

Transfer learning has enormous potential. In fact, Andrew Ng, one of the leading figures in the field of ML and AI, has gone so far as to say, "After supervised ML, transfer learning will be the next driver of ML commercial success."[clxiv]

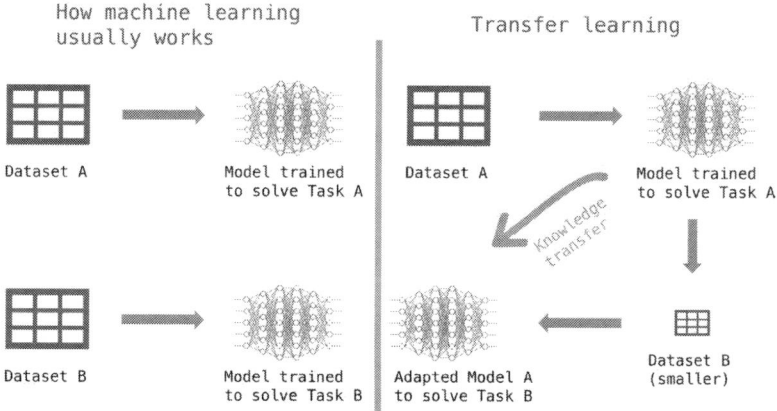

Figure 120.1 Normal ML versus transfer learning

Today, there are many deep neural networks available online that can simply be downloaded and used in transfer learning. The tasks they have been trained for range from object detection in images to facial recognition to natural language processing problems. While they may have been trained to solve a specific task, their inherent knowledge can be used to solve other ones.

121 | Deep neural networks – why now and what will their future look like?

For a long time, researchers who were trying to imitate how the human brain works by experimenting with neural networks seemed to be heading down the wrong path. The idea of neural networks dates back to the mid-20th century. Back then, the idea of creating a model that would imitate the structure of the human brain with its interconnected neurons and could be implemented on a computer seemed exciting and promising. Yet over time interest in the topic decreased. The outcomes of that research were too few, and it seemed there were too many challenges and hurdles to overcome in order for such networks to be used in practice.

Fast-forward half a century and the advancements in deep learning have created an immense hype, achieved things that we could previously only dream of, created widespread adoption of the method in a number of fields, reinvigorated the field of AI and affected the lives of everyone. How did this happen? And why has it happened now? There are essentially four reasons, outlined in the following sections.

Increased availability of data (big data)

Deep neural networks need large amounts of data to be trained, and the more data they have, the better they perform. Until the 1990s, data growth was sluggish and the total available amount of (labelled) data was simply too low for neural networks to outperform other ML model classes.

However, this changed with the advent of big data. Looking at Figure 119-1, you can see that since the advent of big data we have been moving to the right on the x-axis: more and more data is available, and so training neural networks has become viable and they have been outperforming classic ML models. Remember that this data growth did not happen in a linear fashion but followed an exponential path. Suddenly, scarcity of data was no longer a problem and the amounts of data in a number of fields were large enough to train deep neural networks.

What is more, most of the data that is washed onto our shores through the big data wave is exactly the kind of data that compared to traditional ML models, deep neural networks are good at handling and analysing: images, videos, text, speech, audio – in short, unstructured data, which due to its complexity is difficult to analyse and process with other ML algorithms.

Popular Machine Learning Model Classes for Supervised Machine Learning

More computational power

Training neural networks also requires more computational power than had previously been unavailable.[36] The deeper they get, the more power they need to be trained. Just think of deep learning networks that have millions of parameters to be calculated during training and you end up with algorithms that need weeks to train. So the mere availability of data is not enough – it is also necessary to have the computational architecture and power to process and analyse the data. In fact, in 2013 Dileep George, cofounder of the San Francisco-based AI company Vicarious, even went as far as to say that at least 80% of recent advances in AI is thanks to the availability of more computing power.[clxv]

Advancements in neural network methods

Even with the tremendous advancements in computational power, the widespread use of deep neural networks would probably not have happened if it weren't for improvements to the algorithms themselves.

In recent years, thanks to all the attention researchers have given to neural networks, the algorithms have been advanced significantly. Today, there are a number of off-the-shelf open-source libraries that allow everyone to implement neural networks on normal computers such as Keras and Tensorflow (📑 93). Compared to earlier versions, these packages are not only easier to use but also far more efficient, due to several breakthroughs in how the algorithms can be designed. And with the hype around deep learning, this research is likely to continue and bear further fruit in the future.

Marketing

Last but not least, academia and the business world have been doing a good job of branding and promoting deep learning. The public perception of a technology driven by AI or deep learning is that it is highly sophisticated and futuristic and works well. This reputation is also thanks to a number of companies that have publicly adopted such technologies and branded them as breakthrough innovations. The fascination for deep learning has also created an increased interest around it. Today, deep learning is extremely hyped and widely talked about. In December 2019 the interest in deep learning as measured in Google search queries was more than 49-times as high as in December 2009 (i.e. it increased by 49,500%).[clxvi]

The future of deep neural networks

As you can see, the main contributing factors in the advancement of deep learning are here to stay and will develop even further. We will have more data

---

36. Note that they need a lot of data and computational power in order to be *trained*. However, once they have been trained, they can be used to create predictions with rather limited computational power. That is, making predictions with an existing neural network is not computationally expensive.

in the future, we will have even more powerful computers and we will see further progress in the implementation of deep learning algorithms. Even though there may be some drawbacks and challenges with deep learning, you don't need an ML model to predict that the application of (deep) neural networks is going to expand in the future.

This expansion will be helped by the fact that some of the work that is being done in the field of deep learning is made available as open source. Companies and institutions such as OpenAI that have the access and resources to train massive neural networks often make their results and methodologies available. That means you can download a deep neural network they have previously trained right now and use it.

Therefore, compared to the other ML model classes, neural networks will likely continue to gain an edge. The more data available, the better the performance of a model – but while other models hit a ceiling eventually, deep neural networks turn this increased data availability into even better performance.

9 Managing Machine Learning in a Company

9_1 Phases of an ML project

122 | How does the ML process work (an overview)?

Machine learning (ML) projects are implemented by some geeks sitting in the basement of a company who spend their time coding to train models. This is the assumption that a lot of people make, but it could not be further from the truth.

The overarching goal of ML is to create added value from data by teaching a machine to perform a certain task. The process to get there is extremely multifaceted and requires the involvement and collaboration of a number of different job roles and stakeholders. Even though data and ML can be applied in essentially any sector, the ML process always follows the same pattern. It does not matter whether we are talking about creating a fraud detection algorithm for a bank to assess whether a transaction is fraudulent or creating a model to predict when a car part will fail – the process to create such models and data products is identical.

From the idea of an ML model until the model is deployed in an operational environment, a project has to undergo several phases:

1. Understanding and defining the underlying problem to be solved
2. Exploring and preparing the data
3. Training and testing the model
4. Integrating and continuously deploying the model in the relevant business process

While these phases happen in a sequential manner, in many cases reiterations are natural. For example, there will often be a back and forth between data preparation and modelling to conceive and integrate new features in a model. The first three phases constitute an ML project, while the (continuous) model deployment phase is a software engineering project, which requires the respective skillset.

The following sections provide an overview of what happens in the phases. The approach we present resembles the cross-industry standard process for data mining (CRISP-DM).[clxvii] CRISP-DM is an open standard process model that was conceived as an approach for data mining projects.

Phase 1: Business understanding and framing of the goal

The first step in every ML project should be to gain a deep understanding of the underlying (business) process, in order to identify the goal of the project and find out how data can be used to help achieve this goal.

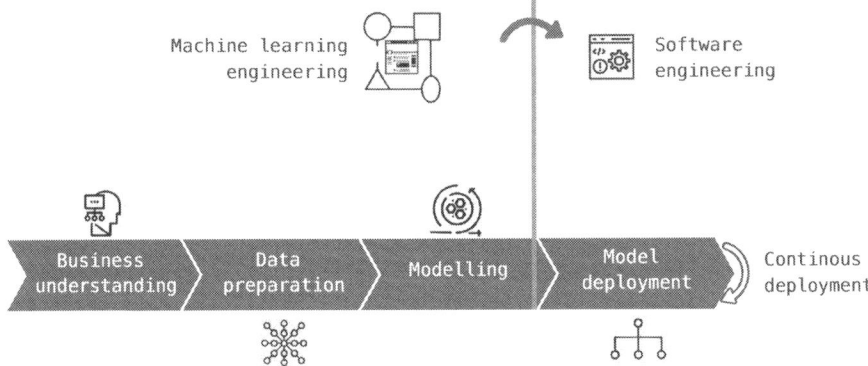

Figure 122.1 Overview of machine-learning project phases

Ideally, this phase should result in the underlying problem or process being translated into data. We need to identify:

- The target variable (if there is one) – what we are trying to predict/determine/automate
- Possible input variables that we can use to predict the target variable

We say this phase "should be" the first step in an ML project because in our experience this step is often omitted or done sloppily by companies. This is a big problem, because to truly understand the business problem and subsequently define the desired outcome is fundamental in every ML project. Everything follows from this. For instance, in this phase we determine what kind of data is needed, what granularity the data should have, how much data is needed, which algorithm should be used etc.

Phase 2: Data exploration and preparation

Once the problem is clearly defined, along with the target and input variables, the data exploration and preparation phase can begin.

In this phase, the relevant data is gathered and explored to check its overall fit with the given use case. Is the data quality good enough? Is there sufficient data or is more data needed?

It may well be that after an initial exploration the project stops, because the data is not appropriate to fulfil the goals of the project. Often the available data only partially captures the business process, or the quality of the data is not good enough to meet the requirements of a given use case. Unfortunately, you cannot implement fancy ML projects if the data basis is not right.

Once it has been established that the data does in fact meet the necessary requirements to implement a given use case, the data preparation phase can begin. In this phase, the relevant data is extracted from its sources, cleansed and brought into the necessary format for the modelling and analytics phase.

This process takes up most of the time in an ML project, typically some 60–70%.

Phase 3: Modelling

After the data has been cleansed and brought into the necessary shape, the modelling phase can begin. This is where the model training, validation and tuning, and testing happen (see Chapter 7).

Phase 4: Model deployment

The project does not end with the creation of the ML model. Remember that an ML model is nothing more than a set of mathematical functions. Putting these into use is what happens during the model deployment phase. Deploying a model means making it available to its end-users. These end-users could be humans or other machines.

Model deployment is a complex process and the vast majority of ML projects fail at this stage. The reason is that from here on an ML project essentially turns into a software engineering project. You have an ML model, but this now needs to be integrated into existing IT systems. This requires a very different skillset than during the rest of the project.

Once the model is successfully deployed and integrated into the existing IT infrastructure of a company, it has to be continuously monitored, maintained and updated. In the context of classic software engineering this is called continuous deployment (CD). Data pipelines to feed the model might have to be changed or updated, other components of the IT infrastructure that affect the model might need to be altered, and so on.

12.3 | Phase 1: How can ML use cases be identified?

A lot of companies underestimate the importance of the beginning of an ML project. This is where the underlying problem is analysed to find a use case where ML can help to contribute to the solution. Failing to do so properly can lead to severe problems during the later stages, which all build upon this phase.

The first phase of the ML project serves two purposes:

- Identify a problem in a business process to be solved, along with a solution that can be implemented with data and ML.
- Translate this solution from the business world into the data world so that it can be solved with ML methods.

Identifying problems and data-driven solutions

In our experience, ML projects either originate from data or a problem:

- *Data:* Someone in a company says, "Hey, we have all this data lying around. Why don't we try to do something with it?"
- *Problem:* The company wants to tackle an underlying problem in a certain process or outcome.

The first approach does not usually create much added value, simply because it is little goal-oriented and thus fails to solve a problem or improve a certain process. So what you end up with might well be a data-driven and ML-powered solution to a problem that does not exist.

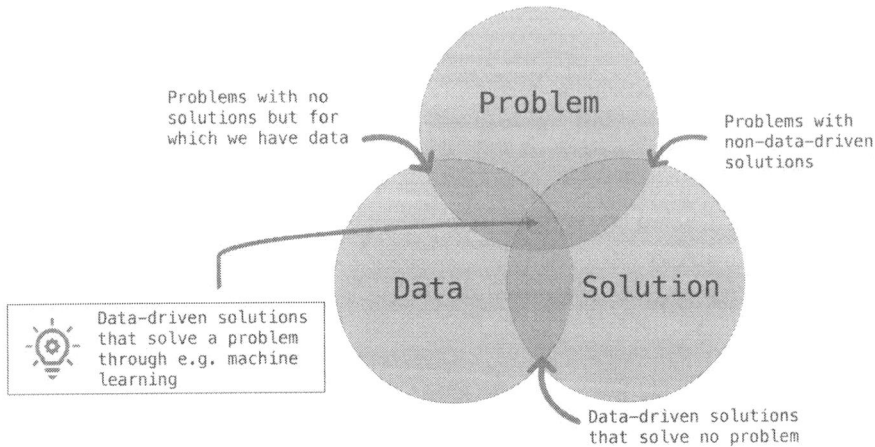

Figure 123.1 Venn diagram of problems, solutions and data

That is why we encourage the second approach, i.e. a goal-oriented and problem-focused approach to implementing ML projects. The central question is whether there is a problem or room for improvement in a given business process, application or situation. If the answer is yes, then the next step is to think about whether there are solutions that can alleviate this problem. Ideally, there will be various solutions. The next question to ask is whether some of these solutions are or can be data-driven. If all these conditions are fulfilled, then there is room to develop a data-driven solution to remedy the problem.

Ideally, such a data-driven solution features the use of an ML model. But it doesn't have to. In a lot of companies there is ample room to improve certain business processes or solve existing problems with a very simple use of data. Data visualization in dashboards can often yield real added value.

This phase is a fundamentally creative process. Identifying problems and finding and proposing solutions also requires domain knowledge of the underlying business process. That is why it is a good idea to have several job roles on board for this process, including data scientists, ML engineers, business analysts, domain experts and other stakeholders involved in the underlying process to be improved.

There are various methodologies that foster creativity in this regard. For example, design thinking has developed into a widely used method to help identify problems and solutions, including data-driven ones. Design thinking is a systematic, human-centred approach that offers a number of methodologies and tools in order to stimulate creative problem-solving and thinking.

Translating solutions from a business perspective into an ML perspective

Once data-driven solutions that can be implemented with ML methods have been identified, the next step is to translate them and reframe them in an ML context. Often, the problems and solutions are formulated in a somewhat blurry manner.

For example, say with Your Model Car we want to implement predictive maintenance for production machines. The underlying problem is that breakdowns of machines lead to downtime in the production hall, which causes heavy losses. The solution is to predict when a machine will break down and anticipate its maintenance.

This problem seems clear from a business perspective. However, when we translate it into an ML context, we find that a lot of areas lack clarity. What is the target variable here, the operational status of a machine or the probability it will break down? How far in advance do predictions have to be made? What granularity of data is needed and what is available (do we have sensor data on a millisecond, second, minute level)? What are possible input variables? Is the necessary data available? Is the data of sufficiently high quality? These are questions that are often overlooked in the business realm but must be answered once we get to the nitty-gritty of implementing an ML model.

Furthermore, it is crucial at this stage to define a key performance indicator (KPI) with which the success of the entire ML project can be measured. After all, we are trying to solve a certain problem or improve a business process, and if there is no metric to measure whether the problem has been remedied or the process improved, then there is no way to know whether the effort in creating an ML model was worth it. In our predictive maintenance example, a sensible KPI would be the total duration of unplanned downtime in the production hall per month. With the use of a predictive ML model integrated in the business process, this KPI should decrease.

Phase 1 checklist

By the end of this phase, the following checklist should be completed:

- A problem or room for improvement in a business process has been identified, along with a data-driven solution, ideally ML-based.
- The data to implement this solution is available and of sufficient quality.
- The solution has been reframed from a business to an ML perspective. The appropriate ML type has been identified, and the target and input variables are well defined.
- A KPI has been defined, by means of which the success of the ML project and model can be gauged.

Case study 55

What problem are we solving by predicting our sales in Your Model Car?

In Chapter 7 we create an ML algorithm to predict product sales. What might the underlying problem be that this data-driven solution solves? It might be that there is a problem with the logistics chain. For example, overstocking a product might have led to high storage costs. Likewise, a product being out of stock might have led to unsatisfied customers.

There are many solutions for this problem and a lot of them have nothing to do with data. For example, we could have changed the storage service provider to a cheaper solution, or we might have offered vouchers to customers who suffered from long delivery times due to a product being out of stock.

The solution that we have come up with is to "optimize" the logistics chain through a sales prediction. But what does that mean translated into an analytical ML framework? It means that we have a target variable called "sales of product X" that we are trying to predict by means of input variables that will influence the sales, e.g. "day of the week" and "marketing expenses for product".

What KPIs should we choose to measure whether the ML-based solution that we are implementing is actually successful? One KPI would certainly be the storage costs, which should ideally go down because we are able to avoid overstocking. Another one would be how many customers face out-of-stock situations, a figure that should also decline.

124 | Phase 2: What are data exploration and data preparation and why are they necessary?

After the goal of the project has been clearly defined and translated into an ML context, it is time to get the data ready for the modelling phase. For that, we go through three steps:

- Identify data sources and get hold of the necessary data.
- Get a first impression of the data through exploratory data analysis.
- Prepare the data for modelling.

Identify data sources and get hold of the required data

This first step, to identify relevant data sources and actually get hold of the data, may sound simple, but in practice it is often a real challenge for a number of reasons:

- *State of the data:* Most companies have sloppy data governance in place at best. This poor management of data typically results in a lack of information about where data is located in a company, how it can be technically accessed, who owns it and is the contact person, and what exactly the data depicts. Essentially, the state of the data is like a disorganized house move: all your things are in boxes that are wrongly labelled, that do not contain the things you expected and that are all over the place with no overview of where exactly they are.
- *Lack of documentation:* Data documentation is typically neglected. Accordingly, even if we identify relevant data sources and are able to

retrieve the necessary data, the corresponding metadata (i.e. data about the data) is often missing. Ideally, there would be data glossaries that describe what a certain data field contains and how this data was collected. For example, in our predictive maintenance case, if we are confronted with some cryptic sensor data, we want to know what the measurements depict and how are they collected.
- *Silos:* More often than not there are political obstacles to obtaining data. In many companies the data architecture is still highly siloed, so that an exchange between different data silos and owners is difficult, because data owners do not want to share their data.

Exploratory data analysis

Once the data has been identified and retrieved, the next step is to gain an initial understanding of it. We simply jump into the data and explore it. This process is called exploratory data analysis (EDA). Specifically, the goal is to examine the data and:
- ❏ Assess the overall quality of the data.
- ❏ Check whether there are some patterns in the data, e.g. correlations.
- ❏ Check whether/how various data tables and data sources are connected (identify the primary and foreign keys).
- ❏ Spot anomalies that suggest data quality issues.
- ❏ Check previous assumptions.
- ❏ Develop a first feeling for potential ways to model the target variable.

Table 124.1 What is EDA and why does it matter?

What is EDA?

Exploratory data analysis (EDA) is the initial analysis of a dataset. This is usually done with visual methods and descriptive statistics. Visual methods include visualizing data by means of boxplots, bar charts and displaying the distribution of a variable. Descriptive statistics draws on methods such as calculating the average value of a variable and calculating what percentage of a variable takes a certain value.

The goal of EDA is to get an overview of the data in order to answer the following questions:
- *Assess data quality and availability:* Does the data fulfil the necessary availability and quality requirements of the use case?
- *Spot anomalies:* Are there some things that seem fishy and require attention?
- *Discover patterns:* Are there some visible correlations between variables that could later be used during the analytics phase?
- *Check assumptions:* Does the data reflect what we have previously thought?

Why does it matter?

The EDA marks the first touchpoint with the data in a project and so it enables us to get a first impression of the data.

> Most importantly, the end of the EDA phase brings with it a pivotal decision. After we have an idea of the data, we have to decide whether or not the data meets the requirements so that we can make the investment and continue with the use case. In the best-case scenario, the answer is a clear "yes". More often than not, though, things aren't so clear: the data quality has significant shortcomings, so the outcome of the project is uncertain. The decision to proceed in these cases requires a degree of gambling and hoping that the data will yield what it is supposed to yield (yes, even in ML and AI there are still such things as gambling and hoping).

Various methods and techniques help us to acquire a basic understanding of the data and an overview of its structure, quality and availability. They generally fall under two categories. *Descriptive statistics* characterizes a dataset by means of a few of key indicators, such as the average value of a variable (e.g. the average number of orders per day). *Data visualization* uses graphical techniques to give an overview of the data, e.g. by displaying distributions or scatterplots of variables.

There are many EDA techniques and covering all of them would go beyond the scope of this book. Here is a list of some popular basic methods.

Summary statistics

Summary statistics describe the distribution of a numerical variable by means of some of its central characteristics, e.g. mean (average) value, the minimum/maximum value etc.

For example, on the right are the summary statistics of the variable "CUSTOMER_AGE". As you can see, the mean (average) age of our customers is 37.76 years. The youngest customer is 16 years old, while the oldest one is 67.

Table 124.2 Summary statistics of variable "CUSTOMER_AGE"

Number of observations	870,342
Missing values	0
Min. value	16
Max. value	67
Mean	37.76
Number of distinct values	51

Histogram

A histogram shows the number of observations of a variable (y-axis) that fall within a given value range (x-axis).

For example, Figure 124-1 shows the histogram of the variable "PRODUCT_PRICE". Each bar indicates how many products we have in the Your Model Car product portfolio for a given price range.

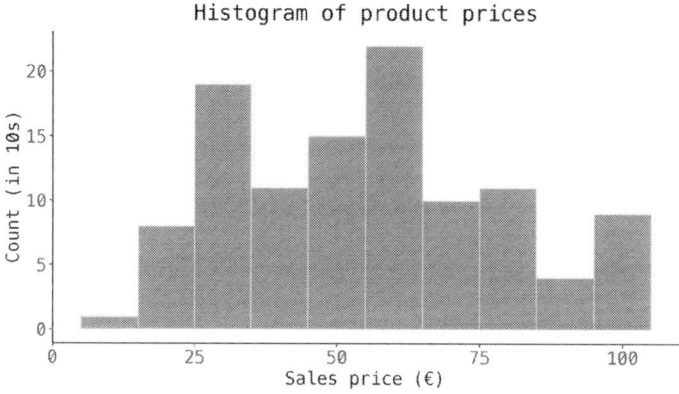

Figure 124.1 A histogram of product prices of Your Model Car product portfolio

Boxplot

Much like a histogram, a boxplot gives a visual representation of a variable. It does so by dividing a variable into its quartiles, i.e. blocks, each of which contains 25% of the total number of observations in the dataset. Two of these blocks are represented by the black lines, and two of the blocks are represented by the grey box, separated by the black separator line, which represents the median value.

Figure 124-2 displays boxplots of the product prices in different product categories. So the boxplot of "Ships" tells us that 25% of all products in that category have a product price between €15 and €30 (first black bar), 25% between €30 and close to €50 (lower half of light blue box), 25% between €50 and €60 (upper half of light blue box) and 25% between €60 and €85. The median value is indicated by the black line in the middle at around €50.

The distribution for "Model Cars" is much more dispersed, with 25% of the products having a price of between €10 and €50 alone (lower black line). There is also at least one product that costs close to €100.

Boxplots are a great way to identify outliers and compare the distributions of a variable between categories.

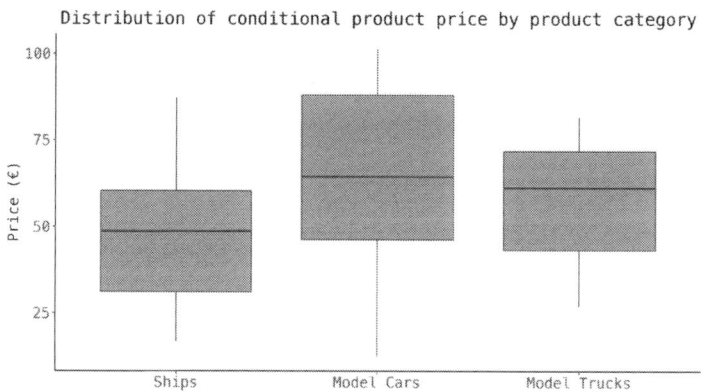

Figure 124.2 Boxplots of product prices per product category

Scatterplot

Scatterplots display the values of (usually) two numerical variables of a given observation.

Figure 124-3 displays the scatterplot of Your Model Cars product portfolio. It shows how often a product has been viewed and how often it has been bought in Q1 of 2020. Scatterplots are a fantastic way to discover potential correlations and relationships between variables visually. *Note*: Correlation does not imply causation (📑 98).

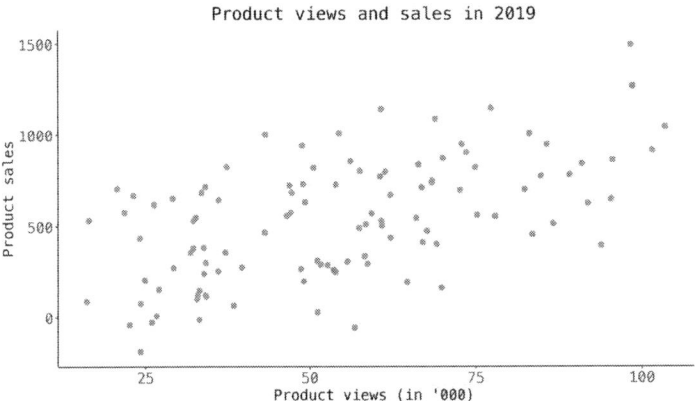

Figure 124.3 Scatterplot of product views and sales in 2019

Time-series chart

With time-series data we take measurements of the same entity at certain temporal intervals. The development of that specific entity over time can then be visualized through a line chart.

For example, Figure 124-4 displays the development of visitors per day on our website. We look at the same website (www.your-model-car.com) and track the development on a daily basis.

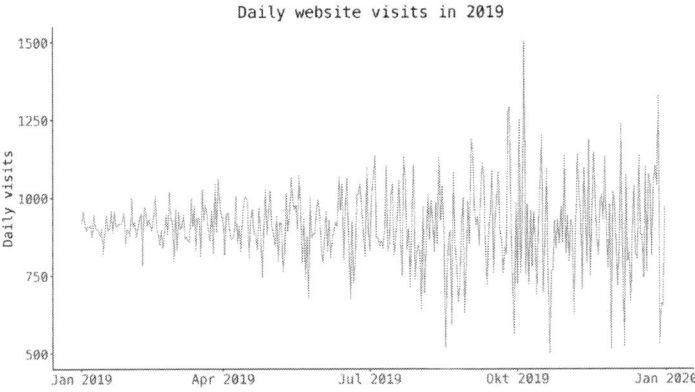

Figure 124.4 Line chart of website visits

Managing Machine Learning in a Company

By the end of the EDA phase, we should have acquired a basic idea of the data, its structure and its quality. The results of the EDA inform the decision as to whether to proceed with an ML project: will the data allow us to create an ML model to solve the underlying problem? If not, then this is the time to abort the entire project and acknowledge that, due to the shortcomings of the data, an ML model will not be able to fulfil its intended purpose. If the EDA shows us that the data looks good, then the project can proceed to the next step: integrating the data and preparing it for the modelling phase.

Data preparation

Data preparation is the least glamorous and most time-consuming part of the entire ML process. It is not uncommon for data preparation to take up 60% of the time and resources in an ML project. This is where we get our hands dirty and do the necessary plumbing work in preparation for the modelling phase.

By the end of this phase, the data should be consolidated, cleansed and brought into the necessary format to train an ML model. This typically requires a combination of the following measures:

Table 124.3 Overview of data preparation methods

Measure	Description	Example
Data cleansing	Data cleansing focuses on removing errors in the data to bring it into a true and consistent form.	▶ Missing values (i.e. "N/A" values) ▶ Inconsistencies (e.g. "04.08.89" versus "1989-08-04") ▶ Formatting errors (e.g. with umlauts and other special characters) ▶ Implausible values (e.g. age less than 0)
Data integration	Typically, the data required to implement a project resides in various sources and tables. These need to be collected and integrated.	▶ Join tables or data sources
Data transformation	Certain models require data to be in a specific form, so it needs to be transformed into that form.	▶ Encode the variable male/female into 0/1
Data aggregation	Often the granularity of data is too high and data is needed on an *aggregated* level. In these cases we might have to sum up, average or otherwise aggregate the data.	▶ Calculate the monthly sales of a product by summing all daily sales

Phase 2 checklist

By the end of this phase, the following checklist should be completed:

▶ The relevant data has been extracted from or accessed on the data sources.

- The data to be used has been explored (e.g. to identify possible patterns and correlations) and assessed with regard to its quality. This knowledge has informed whether or not the data meets the requirements to implement the ML project.
- The data has been transformed and prepared so that it is in analysis-ready shape for the modelling phase (at least for a first shot at the problem).

> **Case study 56**
>
> **Extracting and exploring data for the Your Model Car sales prediction**
>
> What variables influence sales of our 1992 Ferrari 360 Spider red (scale 1:18), on which systems are they stored and how can we get hold of them? Some obvious candidates are its price, product rating and whether it has been advertised or on offer. Luckily, most of the variables will be on internal systems, e.g. in some data mart in the data warehouse of Your Model Car. But we might also consider including weather data from external providers, because customers might order more on rainy days.
>
> Once the data is retrieved, the next step is to conduct the EDA. Then we will prepare and clean the data accordingly. We might, for example, encounter implausible values such as negative sales numbers (which might be indicative of product returns). Such data quality issues need to be fixed as far as possible to prepare the dataset for the modelling phase.

125 | Phase 3: What is model creation?

In this phase, we use the cleansed and prepared dataset to create, validate and test various ML models in order to solve the underlying problem. How this works is covered extensively in Chapter 7.

Hopefully, by the end of the modelling phase we have a model with good predictive accuracy. Often a first shot is only a prototype and we repeat the modelling phase several times; for example, we integrate more data and then repeat the feature engineering and selection for our model. However, after a few iterations we should arrive at a model that we actually want to put to use in our business.

Remember that a model is a set of mathematical functions. So really, what we have at the end of the modelling phase is nothing more than a few functions that we can provide with values of input variables to have our target variable computed. The next step is to integrate this set of functions sensibly into our business process and actually put the model to use.

126 | Phase 4: What is (continuous) model deployment?

Unfortunately, a lot of companies and practitioners think that an ML projects ends when the final model with a good predictive performance is created. In their minds, all that is left to do is to throw that model over the fence to the IT department and leave it up to them. This is not going to work.

In fact, model deployment is a crucial and rather complex task. Essentially, this is the point where the entire ML project turns into a software engineering project, which requires a very different skillset. Because this is often neglected and because the effort required to deploy a model is vastly underestimated, a lot of projects fail at this point, so that prototype models remain in their pilot phase and are never rolled out. One quote from the trenches is that "we have more pilots than any major airline".

Deploying the model

Model deployment refers to the process of making the model available to its end-users by integrating it into the business process it was intended to improve. The end-users of the model could be machines or humans. An example of humans as end-users is if we visualize Your Model Car sales predictions in a dashboard for the procurement department. An example where a machine is the user of the model is an automated product recommendation algorithm on our website. The product recommendations would be fed directly into the webserver.

Table 126.1 What is model deployment and why does it matter?

What is ML model deployment?
Deploying an ML model means making it available to its users. For that it needs to be integrated and embedded into the respective business process and IT infrastructure.
These users could be humans, e.g. if the finished data product is a visualization dashboard. The users could also be other computer systems. For example, a product recommendation algorithm could be embedded in a website, so its "user" is the website (which in turn is used by visitors to the website).
Because the deployment of a model requires software engineering skills rather than ML skills, at this point an ML project turns into a software engineering project.

Why does it matter?
Data product deployment is an extremely cumbersome and complex task that requires a very different skillset than during the other phases of an ML project. A lot of ML projects fail at this stage.

Integrating and embedding a model (a set of mathematical functions) into the respective business process is complex because it involves a number of questions and issues. What do the existing data and, more generally, the IT infrastructure look like? What hardware and software tools are available to deploy the model (what is the toolstack)? How big is the data – will computer clusters and distributed systems have to be used? Typically, ML models are developed in tools (e.g. R or Python) that are not part of the operational IT systems of a company, so they have to be translated or rebuilt to fit into the operational toolstack.

Furthermore, the integration of a model into the existing infrastructure also entails building and adjusting the data pipelines. How does the necessary data arrive at the model and where is it supposed to go after a model has done its job? For example, if we were to implement a recommendation system on our website, the model is likely going to run on a backend server and will have to communicate with databases or other microservices running in the background.

Putting the model into production: an analogy

Deploying an ML model is much like taking a new car model into mass production.

Training an ML model is like the development of a car. You design, tweak and fine-tune a prototype of a car, until you end up with the final version that you want to mass-produce and sell.

Thinking that the final model of an ML project can just be handed over to the IT to take care of the deployment is like taking the final prototype of the car, driving it up to the production plant and leaving the keys with the production supervisor, saying, "That's the final version of the brand-new XYZ-car series. We need a million made within the next three months." This will be challenging. The car that you have created in a garage in many iterations will probably contain a lot of features that are unviable for mass production, e.g. a super-smooth hand-polished surface or interior that can't be emulated by production machines. The production plant will also be producing other car series, so there is a capacity issue to be solved. Furthermore, where is all the material for the new car series supposed to be sourced from? The logistics also require careful planning and coordination.

Designing a nice prototype is one thing, but producing this prototype in an automated, cost-effective and economically viable way is an entirely different kettle of fish and is maybe even more challenging. Similar challenges and problems arise when putting an ML model into production.

Continuously deploying the model

Once the model is successfully deployed, this is not the end of the ML project. Because the model is part of the business process it was created for, it has to be monitored and updated to guarantee it is functioning properly. For example, a data pipeline in the IT infrastructure in which the model was deployed might change, thereby impacting the model. Or the performance of the model might decline over time because the underlying real-world process it is supposed to model is subject to changes. As a result, the model might have to be adapted, retrained, validated, tested and deployed. Just like in classic software engineering where components of a piece of software are constantly maintained and updated, these reiterations to maintain and update a deployed model are called *continuous deployment*.

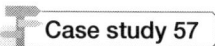

Case study 57

Deploying the sales prediction algorithm in Your Model Car

So we have an ML model (i.e. a set of rules) to predict how many Ferraris we are going to sell on a given day – what next?

First, we can use the model to help the procurement department in its operations, by integrating the model into the software that is used to monitor stock. Next, we might add a feature in that software that issues warnings as soon as a product is running out of stock. Ultimately, we might even be able to automate the procurement process completely.

All of these solutions sound easy, but integrating or augmenting a certain piece of software is an enormously complex software engineering project that requires ample time and resources.

9_2 Lessons learned from machine-learning projects

127 | How long does a machine-learning project take from the conception of the idea until the model is deployed?

We have to distinguish here between the theoretical case and how things actually go in real life.

In theory, if there were no human, political and technological obstacles and all the data and human resources were available immediately, then a possible project timeline for the Your Model Car sales prediction model could look something like this:

Table 127.1 Duration of an ML project[37]

Business understanding: identification of problem and solution	1 week
Data exploration	3–5 days
Data preparation (cleansing, integration etc.)	2 weeks
Data modelling	1 week
Deployment	3 weeks
Total:	**~8 weeks**

---

37. Here we assume that we have an interdisciplinary team with the necessary expertise and human resources, and that the underlying problem is of average difficulty.

Obviously, the speed at which a use case can be implemented depends on a number of factors. How difficult is the underlying business problem to be modelled and solved with the data? How much pre-processing and cleaning up of the data is necessary? How good and experienced is the team and do they get along well? How "big" is the data and what tools are available the toolstack of the IT infrastructure? And so forth. For a use case of average difficulty, though, we can say that somewhere between one and three months from the idea through to the deployment of the data product is theoretically possible.

But things look very different in practice. Based on our experience, it is not uncommon that in projects there are a number of factors that keep us from doing the job we were (initially) hired to do. For example, it might be that there is political rivalry within a company where Department A does not want to collaborate with Department B for a given use case. Or data Owner X is not willing to give out the data from their department. Or the legal department has reservations as to whether or not data can be used for a use case. The data steward, who happens to be the only person in the company who knows about the data that is relevant for a use case, is first off sick and then on sabbatical. External service providers need to go through a special accreditation procedure in order to gain access to the data. And so forth.

These are all challenges that can lead to significant delays in the implementation of a project in practise. The job roles in a team to implement an ML project therefore have to be able to navigate such politically difficult cultures that have nothing to do with the scientific work with data. It is about soft skills. Disregarding data quality issues, the vast majority of technical challenges, such as difficulty in modelling a business process and preparing the data, are minor and solvable. In contrast, political challenges halt and interrupt projects on a regular basis.

Such problems can slow down the implementation of ML projects, so that from the initial idea until the deployment of a data product months pass by – even for simple projects

128 | How many projects make it from the idea to the end and where do they fail?

Few projects succeed. When implementing an ML project, there are a number of challenges and hurdles that need to be overcome. These lurk at every phase of the project.

Table 128.1 The most common hurdles during an ML project

Business understanding: Ideas are utopian and unfeasible.	Some ideas are not even worth turning into projects. This is typically not because there are no good ideas where data-driven solutions could bring added value, but is rather because it is clear from the beginning that the idea would not be feasible. This might be due to various reasons: data might be missing or unobtainable, there might be political challenges within a company, there might be laws restricting the use of data etc.

Data exploration: The EDA reveals that the data availability and quality are too poor.	Insufficient data quality and availability is arguably the biggest challenge in ML projects. While suspicions might have been hovering around, a final and definitive diagnosis of both the data availability and quality is only possible after the EDA. A lot of projects are buried after this initial assessment.
Modelling: The target variable cannot be predicted sufficiently well.	Even if the data is good enough, there is still the hurdle of whether or not a business process or problem can be modelled, i.e. whether the target variable can be predicted with the available input variables. A given business process might simply be too noisy for the model to discern patterns for prediction or explanation – sales might be influenced by too many factors, the delivery time of a food order might be too erratic to predict, stock prices may behave randomly with no discernible pattern and so forth. Even with the best data at hand, such unpredictable or unexplainable events – which are influenced by too many factors that cannot be controlled – cannot be modelled with data.
Model deployment: The model cannot be integrated into the existing IT infrastructure.	Creating a proof of concept or prototype of a model is easy and typically done quite quickly. But as we explain in 📖 126, deploying such a model is a whole different story and requires a lot of effort. So model deployment is the hurdle that most companies struggle with. It might also be the case that a prototype has proven successful but the results are not valuable enough to justify the extra investment required to deploy the model.

So how many ML project *ideas* yield an actual *operational* ML model? Unfortunately, there is no data for that question, but based on our personal consulting experience, around 10% of all initial ML ideas make it into a fully operational and deployed model.

Keep in mind, however, that this number will vary greatly between different sectors and companies. For example, technology and data-driven companies will have much better data quality and in-house expertise, so their success rate will be higher. In contrast, companies in traditional industries that lack experience with data will likely have a lower success rate.

Furthermore, every company and every use case is different, and in many cases there are solutions or workarounds to the problems encountered in ML projects. For example, ideas can be adjusted or reframed to be viable, data quality issues can be remedied to some extent, target variables can be altered etc. Thus, a project is rarely dropped completely. Instead, the hurdles impede its success and the quality of its results.

129 | What are the most common reasons why projects fail?

There are a lot of reasons why an ML project might fail. The severity of these problems will vary from one company to another, but in particular traditional, non-data-native companies with steep and rigid hierarchies tend not to be fruitful environments for ML projects. Here are the main reasons we see ML projects fail.

The Ultimate Data and AI Guide

Data

This is the single most important success or failure factor. In an ML project, data is the fuel that keeps the entire engine running. If there is not enough fuel or if it is dirty, then even the most sophisticated ML model won't be able to do anything with it. Therefore, for a ML project to succeed the data must:

- Model the real-world process (target and input variables)
- Be sufficient in quantity
- Be available and accessible
- Be free of errors and be of high quality

These conditions are only met in companies that treat data as a highly valuable asset. In order to have abundant, high-quality data available, investment is necessary: investment in designing and implementing data-generating processes, in IT infrastructure, in skills and in the management of data with data governance. In most traditional companies, data has not been and is not regarded as a crucial asset, so data quality and availability are lacking. And the message to these companies is always the same: you need to fix your basics and collect high-quality data. Data is the basis for applying ML and thus creating artificial intelligence (AI) systems. So if the data is insufficient, then everything else built on top of it will be too.

Internal politics

The politics within a company are another big reason why projects fail. Unfortunately, in a lot of companies a culture of competition between departments prevails over a spirit of working together. For example, often responsibilities overlap between departments, which leads to competition and even hostility. The result is that neither data nor expertise is shared, which impedes the success of a project.

Lack of the right skills and people on board

Implementing a ML project from start to end is a complex endeavour that requires a lot of expertise in a number of fields. There is currently a shortage of such experts, and getting the right people with the right skills on board can be challenging, especially for companies that are struggling to attract new talent. Who would want to work for a small or medium-sized company somewhere in a rural area if they could work for a big tech start-up in a thriving city? Arguably, the most severe shortage at present is in experienced data engineers (📑 133).

Legal concerns

The fields of ML and AI are constantly expanding and developing. New breakthroughs and cutting-edge use cases are announced almost every week. This is all new for everyone involved. Consequently, there is a lot uncertainty as to what is legally allowed with data and what is not. This legal insecurity can impede ML projects and lead to failures.

The biggest and most fundamental game-changer in this regard has been the introduction of the General Data Protection Regulation (GDPR), which has created buzz, uncertainty and downright confusion for a lot of companies. The GDPR went into effect in May 2018, and many of our customers were unable to cope with its legal consequences. Approaching the "GDPR doomsday", one of our clients even put all data-related projects and work flows on hold in order to check whether it would be legal to continue these projects.

Even with statutory laws and regulations such as the GDPR that are supposed to govern what companies can and cannot do with data, uncertainty continues to exist. The new laws will have to be interpreted in judicial precedents, so final answers to questions may not be available for long time.

> **Case study 58**
>
> **Data sources that cannot be integrated**
>
> A global medical company lets its employees make purchases of minor operational equipment, e.g. petri dishes, pipettes, pencils, IT equipment etc. However, departments in different countries use product catalogues from different suppliers. The products are functionally equivalent, but some are more expensive and there are different pricing methods (e.g. volume discounts). There is no overview of the pricing across different suppliers.
>
> A lot of data-driven solutions could be implemented to improve this situation and save costs, including ML. Unfortunately, though, the data, which is stored in different systems, has too many issues. For example, products have different names and belong to different product groups in the various systems, so an integration of all the product catalogues is not possible. Some of the catalogues are outdated and don't reflect accurate prices. And so forth. The data quality is not sufficiently high for a data-driven solution.

130 | Why is model deployment the bottleneck for most companies implementing ML projects?

The hype around ML, deep learning and AI led to a major increase in both interest and investment in these areas within companies. In an enormous leap of faith, entire ML and AI departments were set up.

However, for a lot of companies these efforts did not bear fruit. While implementation begins in many ML projects, they get stuck at the model deployment phase. Companies end up with a plethora of ML model prototypes, but few are actually deployed and integrated into existing business processes.

The Ultimate Data and AI Guide

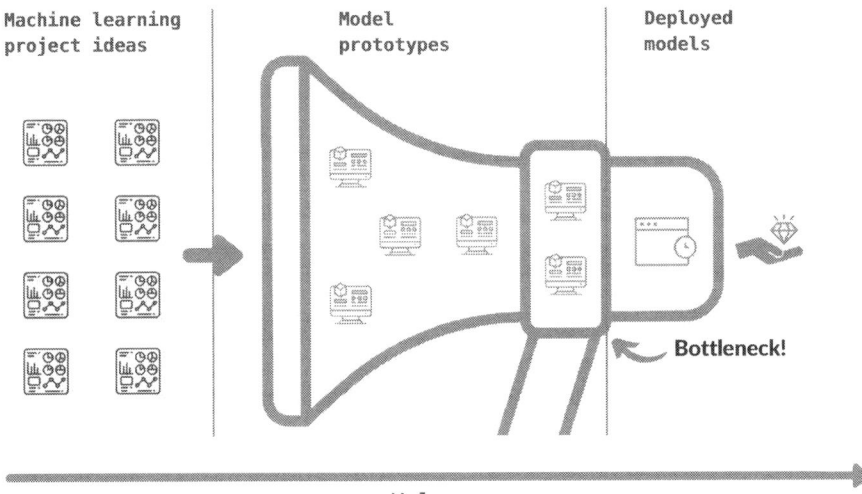

Figure 130.1 Model deployment as the bottleneck of ML projects

Why do so many projects fail at this stage? There are a number of reasons.

- *Developing an ML model and deploying it are two very different things:* Though companies often don't realise it, developing the model is an ML project but deploying it is a software engineering project. Solutions and workarounds that work in one do not necessarily work in the other. For example, during the development phase of an ML model it is common to retrieve data from the relevant sources and develop the model on local computers with local data. However, when deployed the model needs to run on the operational IT system, so it needs to be integrated and embedded into existing data pipelines in the architecture.
- *The necessary skills for development and deployment are lacking:* In the realm of ML and AI it is difficult to get hold of talent. In particular, data engineers with a background in software engineering and experience in working with data are scarce, and this is the job role required for deployment.
- *Deployment is a very challenging task from a technical perspective:* Companies have their own unique toolstack in their data and IT architecture that needs to be catered to when deploying an ML model. Furthermore, technologies for data processing and storage are quickly evolving, so it can be difficult to keep an overview of existing technologies and their compatibilities. Therefore, there is no standard procedure or technology for deploying models yet and different approaches are still being tested across companies. It will probably take a while before a technical cross-industry solution for deploying models evolves.
- *From an organizational perspective, the way ML projects are implemented is not appropriate:* In many companies, the structure still strictly separates the IT department from the business functions (and also data science

Managing Machine Learning in a Company

functions). The result is that the team implementing an ML project is often not in contact with the IT department, who own the operational IT infrastructure on which the model is supposed to be deployed. Instead, projects should be implemented by interdisciplinary teams that include at least one representative from the IT department who knows about the existing IT architecture and its capabilities.

> **Case study 59**
>
> **Chip tuning in cars**
>
> A car manufacturer grants warranties for engines that break down within the first five years of a car purchase. Some customers tune their engines, which increases their performance but also their risk of breaking down. Tuned engines are not eligible for a warranty. Customers who tune their engines typically cover their tracks, so it is impossible for mechanics to tell tuned from non-tuned engines when they come into the garage.
>
> To solve the problem, the car manufacturer turns to ML methods. It creates an algorithm that determines whether a car has been tuned based on the data recorded through the sensors in a car.
>
> The ML model has an impressive accuracy rate. However, integrating this algorithm into the business process is an entirely different project. How can the data from the sensors be extracted as soon as a broken engine under warranty enters the garage? Where and how is the data cleansed and prepared for analysis? How does the data get to the algorithm? Where is the algorithm hosted (in the cloud, on computers in the garage)? How are the results presented to the mechanic? These are all questions that need to be answered before the ML model can be deployed.

9_3 People and job roles in ML

131 | Which roles are required to implement an ML project?

Implementing an ML project is a complex process with several phases and steps, and it requires the collaboration of an entire team, rather than a single person.

In the following sections we outline a number of job roles that are needed in order to implement an ML project from start to end. Note we are referring to *roles* rather than *people*. In practice, teams can be rather small, so people may fulfil more than one role. These roles are not necessary at all times: certain roles are needed for certain phases of the project. What is more, there is often an overlap in roles that does not allow for a clear delineation. For example, a data scientist is regarded as something like a unicorn that combines the skills of a business analyst, data engineer and statistician.

Figure 131-1 gives an overview of the required roles and when they are needed during an ML project.

The Ultimate Data and AI Guide

	Business understanding	Data preparation	Modelling	Model deployment	Continuous deployment
Data scientist	Partly	Partly	x		
Data engineer		x		x	
ML engineer		Partly	x	Partly	
Software engineer				x	
Business analyst	x				
Domain expert	x	x			
Project manager	x	x	x	x	

Figure 131.1 Roles required during an ML project

Data-driven companies, such as Amazon, Spotify and Zalando, have been advocating the two-pizza-team principle to determine the healthy size of a team. According to this principle, the team implementing a project should be able to share two pizzas. Given that pizza sizes vary, this leaves some leeway, but usually it is said that teams should not be bigger than six or seven members and definitely not more than ten. The reason is that the cost of coordination and communication increases exponentially with the size of the team which decreases the team's agility and flexibility, both of which are crucial for implementing ML projects.

Ideally, team members have an understanding of what the other job roles do. That is, a good data scientist also understands how to prepare data and how to deploy an ML model. Collaboration between the job roles during the various phases of an ML project avoids hurdles at the transitions between phases, e.g. between modelling and deployment. This is necessary, because the phases of a project are not self-contained but rather intertwined. For example, feature engineering and selection might be reiterated after some first models have been trained in order to increase their performance.

> **Case study 60**
>
> **Setting up an ML and AI department**
>
> A clothes and sportswear company wants to set up and grow an ML and AI department. The goal is to create several independently operating teams that implement ML projects across departments within the company. The teams are to be interdisciplinary.
>
> The company sources software engineers from the IT department and gives them extra training in various data storage and processing technologies so that they can act as both data and software engineers.

Project managers and business analysts are drawn from the respective departments (e.g. online sales). ML experts and data scientists are recruited or sourced from external providers for specific projects.

132 | What does a data scientist do?

Table 132.1 Overview of the data scientist job role

What is the data scientist's role?	A data scientist is expected to be a jack of all trades. They have to be especially good during the modelling phase, but also able to prepare and visualize data, explore and assess its quality, and translate business problems into analytical ML solutions. The data scientist job role started to become increasingly popular from 2012 onwards, when it was named the "sexiest job of the 21st century" by the Harvard Business Review magazine.[clxviii] But while some companies still hire data scientists, many have realized that the job profile is too broad and few people can live up to it, and so they are splitting the responsibilities into more specific roles, e.g. ML engineer and data engineer.
What tools should they know?	● Python including relevant packages such as TensorFlow ● R ● SQL ● Qlik/Tableau/Power BI and other data visualization tools ● Spark ● Hive
What skills/ experience/ knowledge should they have?	Ability to translate a business problem into an analytical problem that can be solved with data and ML ● ML, including deep learning techniques ● Statistical analysis ● Basic knowledge of popular data storage technologies ● Data visualization ● Data preparation and basics of software development
A typical data scientist...	● Has a degree in a quantitative field such as ML, statistics or mathematics ● Enjoys geeking out by writing code while still keeping the business aspects of a project in mind
Average salary	US$95,998[clxix]

133 | What does a data engineer do?

Table 133.1 Overview of the data engineer job role

What is the data engineer's role?	Data engineers are needed mostly during two phases of an ML project: ● *Data extraction and preparation:* Their main role is to extract all the necessary data for the project from the relevant sources, cleanse it and prepare it. This requires profound knowledge of all sorts of data storage and processing technologies, such as NoSQL databases. ● *Technical deployment of the finished model:* Their main job is to turn the finished data product into an error-proof piece of software that can be deployed in operative systems. During the deployment, a data engineer is like a production-line engineer, who turns the prototype from the analytical phase into a reliable product that can be used in the day-to-day operations of a company.

What tools/ languages should they know?	- SQL - Spark - Scala (programming language) - Hadoop and related tools from the Hadoop Zoo, e.g. Hive, Pig - Python - Java - C++
What skills/ experience/ knowledge should they have?	- Profound knowledge of all sorts of data storage technologies - Knowledge of how computer clusters work - Software engineering skills and the ability to write and optimize reliable, error-proof code - Knowledge of cloud services and tools
A typical data engineer...	- Has a degree in computer science / software engineering - Has experience in dealing with (big) data - Is happiest when they get complex and puzzling problems to solve with data
Average salary	US$91,695[clxx]

134 | What does an ML engineer do?

Table 134.1 Overview of the ML engineer job role

What is the ML engineer's role?	An ML engineer combines the skillsets of a data engineer and a data scientist with a focus on ML. This means that they develop predictive models and apply ML methods in such a way that the transition of a prototyped ML model towards its deployment is as bump-free as possible. They combine coding or software development with predictive analytics skills.
What tools should they know?	- Python - Spark - Java - SQLs - Hadoop, including related tools
What skills/ experience/ knowledge should they have?	- Mastery of all sorts of ML methods – above all, supervised and unsupervised learning methods - Profound knowledge of the various ML model classes, including neural networks and deep learning - Ability to write proper code and develop software
A typical ML engineer...	- Has a background in software engineering with experience in predictive analytics, or the other way around - Understands as much about statistics as they do about programming
Average salary	US$111,657[clxxi]

135 | What does a statistician do?

Table 135.1 Overview of the statistician job role

What is the statistician's role?	Sometimes ML projects are statistics heavy and require the input of trained statisticians. For example, there might be a lot of missing values in a dataset which can be reconstructed with statistical methods (data imputation). In contrast to data scientists and ML engineers, the statistician's knowledge of statistical methods and models is typically more profound, but it comes at the cost of the ability to write code.

What tools should they know?	- R - SAS - SPSS - Matlab - Stata - Python
What skills/experience/knowledge should they have?	- Profound knowledge of statistical methods and models, including the design of experiments and data imputation methods.
A typical statistician...	- Has a degree in statistics
Average salary	US$72,189[clxxii]

136 | What does a software engineer do?

Table 136.1 Overview of the software engineer job role

What is the software engineer's role?	Software engineers are needed after a prototype of a data product has been developed and needs to be deployed. They are the ones who take the final ML model – which is nothing more than a set of mathematical equations – and integrate it into the existing data and IT infrastructure. Among other things, this requires setting up the necessary data pipelines for the model.
What tools should they know?	- Python - Java - C++ - Ruby - PHP and html - SQL
What skills/experience/knowledge should they have?	- Ability to write error-proof code - Ability to conduct software testing - Ability to turn a ML model prototype into a functioning component of an overarching IT architecture - Profound knowledge of the existing toolstack of the IT infrastructure of a company
A typical software engineer...	- Has a computer science degree - Can code well and make use of all sorts of methodologies that are popular in software engineering
Average salary	US$84,414[clxxiii]

137 | What does a business analyst do?

Table 137.1 Overview of the business analyst job role

What is the business analyst's role?	Business analysts are required mostly at the beginning of a ML project. Their role is to analyse business processes and identify problems where (data-driven) solutions can yield added value.
What tools should they know?	- Various methods used to analyse business processes - Creativity and problem-solving methods, e.g. design thinking

What skills/experience/ knowledge should they have?	▶ Analytical mindset and the ability to comprehend and analyse business processes ▶ Some domain knowledge in the respective field ▶ Experience in identifying data use cases and determining how much value they would create ▶ Superficial knowledge of data processing and storage technologies along with a basic knowledge of what ML is and what it is capable of, in order to gauge what is within the realm of possibilities
A typical business analyst...	▶ Has a degree in business administration or an analytical background ▶ Has an understanding of data-related topics ▶ Enjoys dissecting business processes to look for improvement potential
Average salary	US$68,364[clxxiv]

138 | What do other roles do?

An ML project typically requires the collaboration and help of many other job roles and stakeholders. Going into each of them would go beyond the scope of this book, but there are two more roles that are noteworthy:

- *Domain expert:* Essentially, ML can be applied in any sector. While the roles in the preceding sections are methodological experts in dealing with data, they cannot be experts in all the fields where ML is applied. This role is filled by domain experts. They could be mechanical engineers, for example, or sales experts, depending on the type of project. They are especially important at the beginning of a project, to make sure the underlying business process is well understood. Their input in finding possible solutions is also indispensable at that point. Furthermore, they play a big role during the feature engineering phase. Given their expertise in the field, their input in identifying factors that influence the target variable is extremely important.
- *Project manager:* Like any other project, ML projects require proper management. This is where the project manager comes in. Their responsibilities include the coordination of all stakeholders, resource management, the management of all activities within the team using methodologies such as Scrum or Kanban, and of course keeping an eye on the budget.

9_4 Agile organization and ways of working

139 | What is agile project management and why is it appropriate for ML projects?

Engineering and traditional IT projects are (or used to be) managed in a sequential and linear way – for example, by following the *waterfall model*, where a project is divided into a linear sequence of distinct phases and each phase must only begin after the previous one has been completed and yielded the required deliverables.

But using such sequential models has proven inappropriate for ML projects. The main reason is that ML projects are uncertain, in the sense that we do not know the outcome and challenges of a project beforehand. Even if there is a clear plan to use data XYZ and apply ML algorithm ABC to it, it is difficult to estimate just how successful the algorithm will be in achieving what it was intended to do. The data might have a different format or quality than was initially thought, the underlying process might be difficult to analyse and predict, the model might not behave as expected and so forth. Even if you are experienced and have a good idea of how these basic parameters will influence the outcome of the project, there is always a degree of uncertainty in the outcome. Therefore, following such a sequential model is unviable.

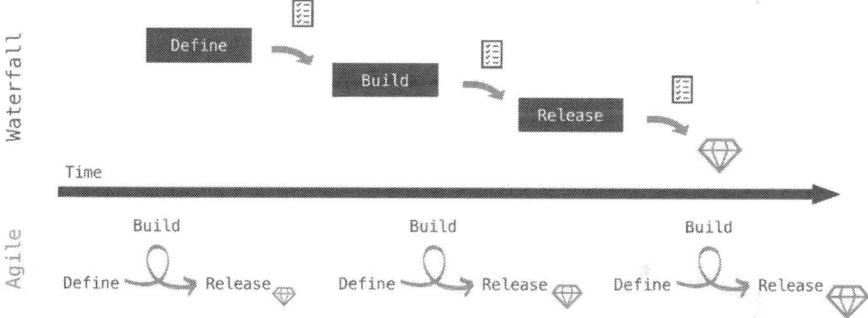

Figure 139.1 Waterfall versus agile project management

Instead, ML projects are proven to work best when implemented in an *agile project management* setting. Agile project management is an approach to managing projects that has been applied in the vast majority of software development projects for some time now. Instead of regarding the project as a linear sequence, it is implemented in an iterative cycle.

Table 139.1 What is agile project management and why does it matter?

What is agile project management?
Agile project management is an iterative approach to planning and managing a project.
With other project management approaches in software development, such as the waterfall model, you typically identify all the requirements upfront and plan a project meticulously from the beginning to the end. In contrast, in agile project management you do not set a project plan in stone. Instead, you break the project down into small parts and goals that are achieved in small sprints lasting anywhere from a day to a few weeks. That way a project is delivered incrementally and can be tested and adjusted frequently so that new requirements can be identified.

> **Why does it matter?**
>
> Agile project management has turned out to be an extremely useful approach in implementing ML projects. The main advantage of agile project management is that it is very flexible and so it can accommodate unforeseen changes, risks or issues that might come up during a project.
>
> This is the right setup for ML projects, in which – unlike projects in other areas – uncertainties are inherent. There are a lot of things you do not know beforehand. How good is the data quality? Can the process be predicted with data? Are models sophisticated enough to fulfil their goals? And so forth.
>
> With agile project management, answers to these unforeseen questions and other issues can be more easily accommodated.

Advantages of agile project management

Rather than dedicating specific roles or teams to phases like in the waterfall model, in agile project development the iterations of requirement definition, development and testing are implemented in a cross-functional team. Breaking the project up into small stages, each of which produces an outcome that contributes to the overall goal of the project, has two advantages:

- *Adaptability to change:* Changes to the requirements or other basic parameters of the project can be accommodated without jeopardizing the overall project plan. This ultimately leads to increased control over the project. This is crucial for ML projects, where the outcome and progress are so uncertain.
- *Early feedback can be incorporated*: The final goal of the project is chopped up into smaller chunks that can be presented to the end-user earlier than with a waterfall model. The end-user's feedback can be directly incorporated in order to increase the quality of the final outcome.

Agile project management frameworks

There are many methods and techniques for implementing agile project management. The two most notable frameworks employed in agile management are Scrum and Kanban, which we outline in the following sections.

Both Scrum and Kanban have found their way into the mainstream and are applied beyond the borders of software development and ML. Unfortunately, because they are often used in improper ways and in situations where they do not really create added value, they are often eyed critically. For ML projects, however, agile methods, be they Scrum, Kanban or something else, have proven to be extremely useful.

Scrum

In Scrum, the project is broken down into *sprints*, i.e. periods of fixed-length, usually of two weeks. By the end of a sprint, a specific deliverable should be produced. For example, one sprint in an ML project might be dedicated to data preparation, so the final deliverable should be the model-ready, prepared dataset.

The progress is tracked daily in *stand-ups* of the team. In these stand-ups (in which team members are supposed to stand to encourage succinctness of communication) each member reports their daily progress to the team and shares their plan for the coming day.

After a sprint, the team convenes to reflect on the progress of the sprint in a so-called *retrospective*. In these retrospectives not only is the project process evaluated, but team members also reflect on the overall state of the project and the team by engaging in exercises like identifying factors that are motivating or demotivating them.

Figure 139-2 shows how a Scrum sprint roadmap plan could look:

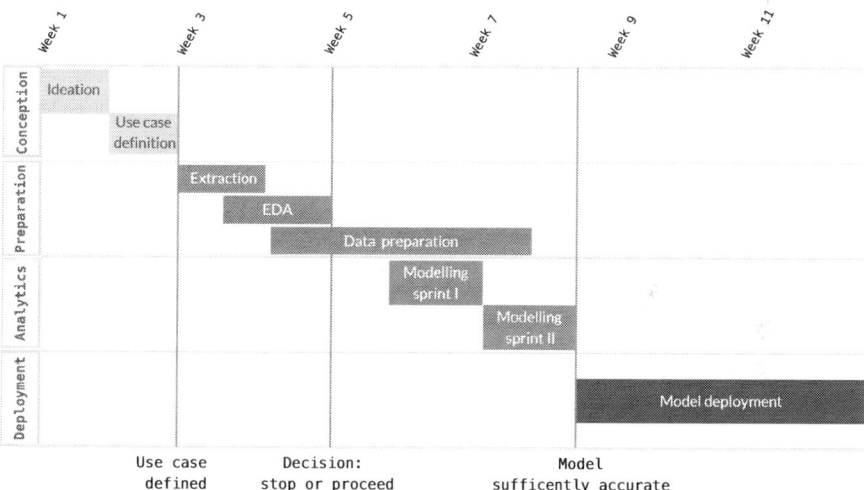

Figure 139.2 Project plan in a Scrum-like style

Kanban

Kanban is a method used to improve collaboration and manage the work of members in a team. The central tool is the Kanban board, where team members collect tasks that must be done in order to achieve the overall goal. The tasks are organized on the board depending on what state they are in (e.g. currently in progress, done, still to do).

By employing such a board, all members of the team can directly see what tasks are open, identify bottlenecks and coordinate their efforts to tackle the most pressing issues. If requirements change or other tasks come up, they are collected in the backlog, the central repository of open tasks.

Thus, a Kanban board is a great way to give team members an overview and to manage the workflow and resources within a team.

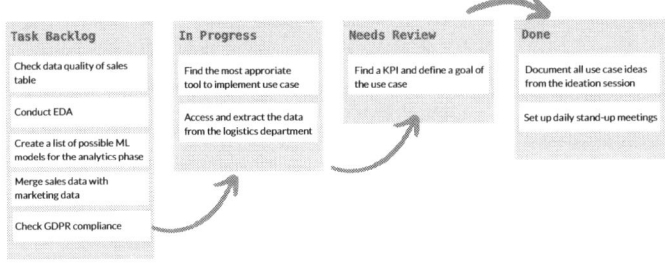

Figure 139.3 Example of a Kanban board

140 | What are DevOps and DataOps?

Most ML models that are deployed and go live need to be operated, maintained and supported. In traditional IT, software solutions are developed by one team and are then handed over to another team to do the operations and keep the lights on. This sounds logical at first, because every team can specialize in a narrow skillset in order to do their tasks better.

However, the traditional IT operations model has several major drawbacks. The most obvious one is that the development team and operations team have different KPIs:

- The development team needs to deliver a solution that pleases the users and matches specifications as quickly and with as little resources as possible.
- The IT operations team needs to minimize the costs to run and support the software solution; keep failures, bugs and downtimes to a minimum; and have fast error resolution times.

As a result, the development team does not have many incentives to deliver a solution that is easy to operate, maintain and support, because their sole focus is on the user and time to market. And consequently, the operations team sets ever higher criteria for deployment, to protect themselves from badly implemented and documented software that leads to a lot of additional work for the development team.

Often, this leads to unnecessary bureaucratic procedures and mistrust. Handoff meetings between both sides can turn into formal, frosty events with little knowledge sharing and a lot of paperwork. This, in turn, leads to less collaboration and discussion, which makes it hard for the development team to understand how software can be improved in the future in order to prevent problems in operations. A vicious cycle.

The main idea of DevOps is to put both sides into one team: hence the same team that develops also runs the code afterwards. The benefits of this approach can be quite impressive:

- There is no need for mistrust, as everyone is now responsible for the process of the software lifecycle.
- Solutions can be delivered faster and in smaller chunks, since more pragmatic approaches to deployment are used as and there is a more efficient way of organization.

- Because developers have to fix bugs and provide support for their own software, they have a big incentive to program clean and well-documented code and automated tests.
- Providing support and removing bugs from your own code is much less time consuming than doing so with code that somebody else programmed. Even if another person in the team did the coding, it is easy to ask the actual developer questions, at least in the first critical phase after going live.

DevOps

DevOps is usually combined with agile methodologies in software development. It is particularly suitable when there is a need for frequent deployments, in contrast to a fixed half-yearly or quarterly release plan. Therefore, many DevOps teams work under the continuous integration and continuous deployment (CI/CD) logic, with the ability to deploy code to production at any time. In such situations, cloud infrastructures are of huge benefit, as hardware and middleware resources can be switched on and off very easily. Moreover, dependencies between software applications during releases with other IT infrastructure teams can be limited.

There are four architectural prerequisites in order for software for DevOps to make sense and be effective. These are that the software can be:

- Deployed
- Modified (because it is likely to be changed)
- Tested against defined specifications
- Monitored to detect problems automatically and, if possible, before they even happen

Usually, with DevOps the team aims to automate the procedures to test software solutions as much as they can. To achieve a higher grade of automation, there are many new software solutions that support the DevOps way of working. For example, tools like Ansible and Terraform allow you to create, share and deploy infrastructure as code, which means that a new project does not need to rebuild the entire infrastructure manually but can reuse and adapt previously built infrastructures. This is mostly relevant for cloud infrastructure environments.

Table 140.1 What are DataOps and DevOps?

What is DevOps and DataOps?
DevOps is the approach of combining development, deployment and operations of IT solutions in one joined team that takes care of a software product from beginning to end. It includes new roles, processes and tools that can support the implementation of DevOps.
DataOps builds on DevOps and adds further aspects that are specific to ML products, with a focus on ensuring that data and model quality are well monitored and maintained.

> **Why do they matter?**
>
> DevOps and DataOps overcome a major drawback of traditional IT organization: that the development team and operations team have different KPIs, which kills good collaboration between them. They incentivize developers to implement higher-quality code and ML models and to document better, while making operations managers less inclined to build bureaucratic barriers to the deployment of software and AI products.

DataOps

So what is DataOps then? DataOps builds on DevOps, as ultimately all ML models we build are algorithms that are ultimately embedded into software code. While DevOps was developed with a clear focus on the software engineering world, DataOps adds further aspects that are specific to ML products, with a focus on ensuring that data and model quality are well monitored and maintained.

A key technique of DataOps is statistical process control, which is applied to constantly track the data analytics pipeline. In this way every step in the data flow can be automatically monitored to allow for the early detection of problems with the data quality and the model output quality. At certain points in the flow, people might need to check regularly whether the data input and model output look reasonable and match their experience.

A further core principle of DataOps is to automate manual data preparation done by data engineers and make these processes as robust as possible to anticipate and prevent errors coming from varying data input feeds and make them ready for higher data volumes.

Last but not least, DataOps includes the management of the data used following data governance management principles; for example, by establishing a well-maintained data dictionary which allows people to understand data faster when problems need to be resolved during operations.

Implementing DevOps and DataOps

DevOps and DataOps are a paradigm shift compared to traditional IT. It is therefore highly recommended that companies redefine roles, processes and technologies before starting to implement DevOps and DataOps. The implementation typically needs a lot of management attention and change management, as changes are quite substantial for those companies that have been around longer.

141 | What are the popular organizational structures and best practices?

When the board decides to put a higher focus on digital, data and AI transformation as part of the corporate strategy, the chief information officer (CIO) is often tasked with leading this transformation. This might seem intuitively the right thing to do, as the IT department probably has the best knowledge on information technologies.

But at a second glance, the situation looks different. How does IT react when it is asked to do something new? It typically starts gathering business requirements to buy a new software tools and hardware while expecting the *business departments* to have a clear view on what is innovated. For decades, IT was pressured to become more and more efficient in providing the enabling IT infrastructures. So the main focus of IT today is to provide the needed infrastructure in the most cost-efficient way. Additionally, CIOs are charged with so many responsibilities – managing IT assets, sourcing, staffing, security and development – that they may struggle to add running business transformation programmes to implement a digital strategy, big data analytics and data governance. What is missing is the ability of IT to drive business innovation.

Companies that are leaders in digital innovation have realized that the IT department led by the CIO are not the right people to solely own the digital innovation and transformation agenda. New executive roles have been created that focus specifically on data and digital, in particular the chief data and analytics officer (CDAO). Typically, this comes with a new central organization for data, analytics and AI led by the CDAO. Digital and data steering councils are formed to act as cross-departmental governance bodies that coordinate, distribute budgets and govern the transformation towards a data-driven organization. Moreover, IT is transformed too. The traditional IT department continues to operate and maintain the enabling IT infrastructure in the most efficient way, but in addition a new IT department is created that focuses on the agile piloting, development and operations of new digital innovation ideas using DevOps.

Organizing data roles

A key organizational design decision is where to place data professionals and how the coordination and steering works between them. There are three main ways that data roles can be organized.

Centralized data department

The first approach is to create a centralized data department where most of the data roles are located. This is usually the preferred option when the data analytics strategy and data analytics skills still need to be developed and the overall data maturity of the company is comparably low. It has the big disadvantage that the centralized department is often perceived as being innovation in the ivory tower that is not spreading and bringing value across other business departments.

Centralized data & AI department

Hybrid (hub & spokes model)

Decentralized data & AI specialists

Figure 141.1 Types of data and AI organizational setups in a company

Decentralized data roles

Another option is to keep data roles completely decentralized, so that they are scattered across many different business divisions and functions and make innovation happen where the money is made. This allows data scientists and data engineers to solely focus on activities that directly make an impact on a particular business department.

On the positive side, business departments are much more open to data innovations that are produced by people within their department. On the downside, it is difficult to develop skills, as everyone is scattered around the business, and data scientists and data engineers can feel like loners who are misunderstood by everyone around them. It also can lead to money being wasted through duplicate investments in infrastructure, and – even worse – to the situation where nobody pays for infrastructure modernization because nobody feels directly responsible.

Hub and spoke model

There is a hybrid option between centralization and decentralization that is known as the hub and spoke model. As organizations become more mature in their data analytics journey, they tend to turn to this.

In this model, strategy development and alignment and investments in the main data infrastructure are done centrally, to ensure that synergies between business divisions can be realized and necessary central investments are made. The CDAO is typically at least responsible for the data platform, data operations and data governance. In this model, a CDAO can own their own data teams that work side by side with decentralized data teams to realize value in each of the business departments.

The hub and spoke model usually finds a good balance between centralized and decentralized steering and investments and mitigates the downsides of the two former approaches. The biggest challenge with this model can be overcoming cross-departmental politics and aligning the activities of several business departments.

Organizing agile teams: the tribe model

Another important organizational aspect is how to organize agile teams wherever they sit in the organization. There is a multitude of different, well-proven approaches, and the optimal approach really depends on the particular setup and culture in your organization.

One innovative concept is to use the tribe model, which is based on leveraging groups within a company and cultivating those tribal structures to drive new behaviours or skills in the company.[clxxv] An early adopter of this organizational design was tech innovator Spotify,[clxxvi] along with other growth companies. Some traditional companies started to adopt the model too, including global bank ING (see Case Study 61).

An organizational setup of *tribes*, *squads* and *chapters* in the agile community can help companies to effectively utilize their data science digitization resources in order to innovate their business.

- *Squads:* The most granular group, a squad has a clear long-term mission and a responsibility for a business product (e.g. a mobile app or an analytics model). It consists of three to nine people, working together in a joint physical location and is able to deliver its mission from start to end. Each squad is led by a product owner, who has the final say in everything for the squad and represents the squad in the business. Squads are self-steering teams that consist of different skillsets and roles. Since they can focus on one particular mission for a long time, the members of a squad can become real experts in their area.
- *Chapters:* Coordination between the subject matter experts across the squads happens in chapters, e.g. all software testers get together in one chapter and all data scientists meet in another chapter. In a chapter, people meet other people with similar skills and competencies. This makes sure that economies of scale are realized through knowledge sharing and creating together tools and assets that are shared across tribes and squads. Each chapter has a chapter lead, who is the line lead for all the chapter members. The chapter lead is also responsible for the coordination within the chapter and with other chapters.
- *Tribes:* Several squads that have interconnected missions form a tribe. A tribe consists of fewer than 100 people. A tribe lead makes sure that knowledge and insights are shared within the tribe, establishes priorities, allocates available budgets and forms the interface with other tribes. The idea is that more and more employees want to follow the tribes or tribal leaders on the path to excellence. In that sense, tribal leadership is more of a talent magnet than a prescribed organizational model where you deploy talent based on old-school, controlling principles of headcount, funding and share of business growth. With the right talent and tribe leaders in place, companies can not only encourage internal talent but also lure external talent to move into that space. Tribal leaders should be the face of the company to demonstrate its ambitions and analytics capabilities at conferences, professional network events, in the media and universities.

Case study 61

The tribe model at ING bank[clxxvii]

The tribe model is used at ING bank. There are a number of squads, each of them with a clear scope of responsibility. A squad for mortgage applications, for example, is responsible for providing a user-friendly and efficient path from first mortgage request to final approval. A squad for search engines is responsible for developing the best and most effective search engine across all digital channels of ING bank. In one squad, we

> can find people from marketing, product management, formula management, data analysis, user experience and IT. The mix of people is determined by the mission of the squad. One tribe is responsible for mortgage services and another tribe is responsible for securities and private banking. There is also the role of the agile coach, who coaches individuals and squads on agile methods. Last but not least there is the guild, an organic and wide-reaching community across squads and tribes that shares knowledge, tools, code and practices.

9_5 Data ethics in ML

142 | What is data ethics?

Ethics, also referred to as moral philosophy, is a branch of philosophy that is concerned with the moral correctness of conduct. Ethics seeks to systematize, defend, recommend and establish the concepts of right or wrong behaviour and actions. Data ethics is ethics applied to the use of data.

Data ethics is actually something of a misnomer. Data itself cannot be ethical or not. It is the actions and activities around data – i.e. the collection, storage, use, deletion and so forth – that are, or should be, subject to ethical considerations.

Data ethics will increasingly play an indispensable role in the field of ML and AI. The reason is simple: more and more aspects of our lives are regulated by data-driven algorithms and AI rather than humans. Thus, the sphere that should be governed by ethical standards is constantly expanding and gaining importance.

Table 142.1 What is data ethics and why does it matter?

What is data ethics?
Data ethics is the field of study concerned with establishing, systematizing and recommending the moral correctness of behaviour and actions related to the use of data.

Why does it matter?
More and more aspects of our lives are regulated by data-driven algorithms. This forces us to think about what rules we want to put around them and their creation. While there may be comprehensive rules and regulations in place in some countries that govern these new spaces, the law cannot govern everything. Much like in other parts of society, there is also a need for good behaviour that goes beyond mere adherence to the law.

A lot of conduct in relation to the use of data is already regulated by laws. For example, collecting personal data about EU citizens is only legal if it is done with the person's explicit consent. However, not every action is and can be regulated by laws. Not only would this inflate laws to an unviable extent, but it is simply impossible to regulate every action around the use of data in detail, given the innovations that data-driven technologies bring about on an almost daily basis.

If something is lawful, that does not necessarily mean that it is deemed right by society. For example, finding loopholes in the tax system to avoid paying taxes may be legal, but most people would agree that it is not ethically right. That is why there is a need for a moral benchmark for the use of data that goes *beyond* the legal regulations that are already in place. Given the different sets of values that not only individuals but also entire societies and cultures hold, creating a global standard is not a straightforward task.

As we have seen throughout this book, creating an AI system with the help of ML methods is an extremely complex process that involves a number of phases, skills and people. The various stages of an ML project give rise to ethical issues, which we outline in the following sections. Rather than attempting to answer these ethical questions, we refrain from giving our personal opinions and focus on presenting the issues.

143 | What are the ethical considerations in data collection?

Even the most sophisticated AI systems have data at their heart. To harness this resource, the collection of data assets is necessary, e.g. through the digitization of a business process. This step alone raises a multitude of ethical questions.

Legal regulations already exist to mitigate ethical concerns. For example, the collection, storage and use of personal data of EU citizens is comprehensively regulated by the GDPR, which makes collecting personal data about people without their explicit consent illegal. The vast majority of people would agree that collecting personal information about somebody without their knowing let alone agreeing to it is morally wrong.

While the GDPR regulates a great deal of conduct relating to personal data, it is far from complete and a lot of ethical questions remain open. These affect a number of stakeholders, such as private companies, the producers and sellers of sensors, public organizations and so forth. Some of the ethical questions are as follows.

Who owns the data?

Given that data is essentially a valuable commodity, this question is one of the most fundamental ones to ask. If you are at the heart of a data generating process, do you own the data?

Let's say you purchase a car that is packed with sensors that constantly generate data which is stored on the servers of the car manufacturer. The data could include information about the location of the vehicle, how often and when it is used, how it is used, etc. Do you as the owner of the car own that data, or is the owner the car manufacturer, or maybe even the producer of the sensors?

If the data is of such a nature that it can be considered personal, then ownership leans towards you. You would have to give explicit consent for the data to be collected, and you could request that it be deleted from the servers of the car manufacturer ("right to be forgotten").

But what if the data is of a non-personal nature? Say the car manufacturer collects GPS data of the car in such a way that it is not considered personal data. Let's further assume that the car manufacturer then monetizes this data by selling a traffic jam prediction service to customers based on the GPS data of all its vehicles on the road. Is that ethically okay? Is the car manufacturer entitled to all the profits, or does the car owner co-own the data and is therefore entitled to a share of the profits that the company makes?

How long should data be stored?

This is a question that has largely been answered by the regulations of the GDPR already. An organization can only store personal data for as long as is necessary to fulfil the purpose for which it has been collected. But while this stipulation acts as a guideline, it leaves ample room for interpretation, since the purposes of data can be manifold.

Should data collection be prohibited in some cases?

There are areas in which the collection of data raises ethical questions that extend into philosophical debates. A pressing example is the entire insurance industry.

In a number of countries, the public health insurance system is based on the principle of *solidarity*: everyone pays the same percentage of their income regardless of their health status, i.e. irrespective of whether they are healthy or ill (and therefore incur medical treatment costs). Consequently, no matter how sick a person is, they will still be accepted into the public health system.

In contrast, private insurance companies do discriminate according to health status. While the information they are allowed to collect might be regulated, devices such as wearables greatly expand the ability of companies to assess an applicant's health. This information can be used to alter the risk premium and enables discrimination by means of the health status of a person, which erodes the principle of solidarity. The people who happen to have good genes and lead a healthy lifestyle can be favoured over the ones who were born with diseases or have acquired them during their lifetime.

This raises the question of how far the collection and use of such data should be allowed. Should a health insurance company be allowed to give out wearables to applicants and offer discounts to healthy people or apply surcharges to unhealthy applicants?

The same holds true in other insurance areas. For example, the car insurance provider Progressive Insurance grants up to 10–15% discounts to drivers who are willing to have their driving behaviour tracked with a connected device.[clxxviii] Should such collection of data, which forms the basis for discriminating against applicants, be allowed? Or should it be prohibited in order to uphold the principle of solidarity, which aims to tame the forces of the free market?

How far does and should the right to privacy go?

As we explain in 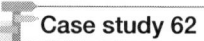74, privacy is so highly valued in the European Union that it has been enshrined as a fundamental human right: that is, everyone should have the right to lead a life without having to disclose it to the public. However, there are some situations where we want to subordinate the right to privacy of individuals to the greater good; for example, the common good of society. For example, the "Uniting and Strengthening America by Providing Appropriate Tools Required to Intercept and Obstruct Terrorism Act" (USA PATRIOT Act), which was enacted in the wake of 9/11, gave federal US agencies the right to infringe on the basic rights, including the right to privacy, of citizens for the sake of national security.[clxxix] While this is certainly a contentious topic, most people would agree that there are certain situations in which we subordinate the right to privacy for a greater good. But under which circumstances should this be the case?

> **Case study 62**
>
> **Should cancer patients be obliged to supply their data for research?**
>
> We can take curtailing the right to privacy a step further and ask the question: are there situations where we do not only want to limit the right to privacy but even reverse it and oblige people to make their data public?
>
> Cancer would be an appropriate area of application. By using ML it is possible to create AI systems that are able to detect cancer earlier and more accurately.[clxxx] That, however, requires the availability of health-related data, which is extremely precious and sensitive.
>
> Given that it would lead to significant improvements in medical care, should patients be obliged to supply their data for research and to train such models? What about a system where only people who provided their health data got access to better medical treatment that was enabled through the "public good" or health data? How far do we want to trade privacy concerns off against the greater public good of improved cancer treatment?

144 | What are the ethical considerations when creating ML models?

Another major area where the use of data is subject to a number of ethical considerations is during the training of ML models. If data is readily available, the next step is to select the data that will be used to train the algorithms in order to create the data product. This step raises ethical questions.

Has the data been collected in ethical ways?

In the future, we will have to treat data just like any other commodity or resource from which products are created. And just like with other commodities, say an ore or meat, there will be different providers that process it in different ways. Meat can be produced at a cheaper price when animal and environmental considerations are ignored. This is why in a number of countries certifications and labels inform customers of the positive ethical status of meat (e.g. fair trade and organic labels).

If we transfer this logic to data, we could conceive of something like a "clean data" label for data that has been collected and processed in ethically desirable ways; for instance, where the right to privacy has been respected. We might therefore impose an ethical due diligence obligation on anybody who uses data to force them to check that the data they are using was collected ethically.

Is the data selected for the model biased?

There have been headlines on a frequent basis about algorithms that are subject to racial bias. For example, Amazon's facial recognition technology to identify the gender of a person was found to work far more poorly on dark-skinned people.[clxxxi] The reason for this is that often algorithms are trained with biased data that is not representative of the population on which they are supposed to be employed.

Another example is the case of women being presented with worse-paid jobs when googling vacancies than men. This was likely due to the fact that the algorithm had been trained on a dataset in which men tended to have better-paid jobs than women.[clxxxii]

Because an ML model behaves and makes decisions according to the data it has seen during its training, the training data *must* be representative and not subject to any sort of discrimination or unconscious bias.

What variables are acceptable for use as features for a model?

There might be cases where the data that is available for training an ML model is dubious. In the United States the collection of data on somebody's "ethnicity" is still common practice. Is it okay to create an intelligent system that decides whether or not a loan applicant is granted a loan and provide it with ethnicity data on the grounds of which it can base its decisions? Or should such discrimination on racial grounds be prohibited?

We could also take the issue a step further and ask if algorithms that decide people's fate actually *should* discriminate on the grounds of race and sex in an attempt to implement "affirmative action". Let's reconsider the model that decides whether or not a bank customer will receive a loan. There is currently significant racial discrimination when it comes to giving out loans and determining the interest rates. For example, it has been found that historically black colleges and universities pay higher underwriting fees to issue tax-exempt bonds compared to similar non-historically black colleges and universities.[clxxxiii] If we take the decision to grant a loan out of the hands of humans and have an algorithm do this, we could decide not to include ethnicity as a variable and so try to make the algorithm "colour blind". However, we could go a step further and argue that we have a moral obligation to right the wrongs of our society and so include "race" as a variable in order to favour racial minorities in their odds of receiving a loan. Minorities that have faced discrimination in the past could thus be compensated by increasing their likelihood of getting a loan or lowering their interest rate. A similar logic could be applied to mitigate sexism.

Should algorithms replace human decisions in cases where human objectivity is not a given?

We could take the previous example even further.

Today, most of the decisions that govern our lives are still taken by humans. Judges decide whether or not somebody is guilty and what their sentence should be. Banks decide who gets a loan and with what conditions. Doctors decide what illness a patient has and what the treatment should be.

The problem is that humans, as we all know, are not perfect. It has been shown that the longer it has been since a judge's last break, the more severe their judgment.[clxxxiv] Happy is the culprit who is judged right after lunch! Likewise, employees of banks might base their decision on whether to give credit to a person or company on subjective feelings rather than hard facts. And everyone who has talked to a doctor who is doing their residency in a hospital knows that they are often very overworked and so it should come as no surprise that doctors sometimes make mistakes because they are exhausted.

Algorithms, on the other hand, will never be tired, subjective or moody. They might never be "perfect" and they do also make mistakes. However, if trained with the right data, they do not make decisions that are subject to racial or sexist discrimination. This raises the question of whether algorithms should replace humans where possible. Do we have a moral obligation to use algorithms in courts and hospitals if they provide better services than humans?

This question gives rise to a whole range of considerations. For example, think of technological unemployment. If we were to replace humans with machines wherever they are better, then what about these humans? Do they have a right to work even if they might be worse at their profession than a computer? Should they be compensated if they are being replaced?

On a more profound level, if we replace more and more humans and their jobs with machines, this means that we are slowly shifting more and more power and influence in our society into the hands of the coders and data scientists who create such technologies and algorithms. Unlike in medical studies, philosophy and ethics are not covered in any computer science or statistics degree. Is it okay to shift the power into the hands of these tech-savvy graduates without having given them ethical training that lives up to the power they will later have?

How white box do algorithms have to be?

Another aspect to consider if we are to give more decision power to machines is the question of how transparent they have to be.

We have seen that there are certain algorithms where the influence of a given variable on the outcome and prediction can be perfectly quantified, e.g. simple linear models (📑 111). For other models, though, the effects of the input variable on the dependent variable cannot be traced back, let alone comprehended.

Even if such algorithms are extremely good at their task, is it right to use them? Would it be morally okay to sentence somebody to life in prison without knowing exactly how the algorithm came to its decision? Should patients have a right to know how the decision about their diagnosis was reached, or is it okay to leave them in the dark so as long as the diagnosis and the predicted optimal medication are right? Should the state prohibit black box algorithms for certain use cases?

How should we choose the right metric to train and assess an ML model?

Another issue that arises in ML projects is how to choose the right metric for an algorithm and how to resolve conflicting goals. The prime example of such a conflict is autonomous driving. Say an algorithm has a choice between running over a group of people or steering the car with one passenger into a tree? How should the algorithm decide? How much is a human life worth, how much an injury? With AI there is no space for human error or spontaneity. Everything is computed and calculated, which is a curse and a blessing at the same time because it forces us to think about and decide on these issues beforehand.

Should ethical training exist for those involved in creating ML models?

These ethical obligations during the creation of a ML model are largely in the hands of the team implementing the ML project, i.e. data scientists, data engineers, ML engineers etc.

The fact is power and influence in our society are being shifted from humans and centralized in AI and algorithms. This increases the power of the people who are involved in creating such algorithms and puts an incredible ethical burden on them. In the light of that, it seems essential that these people receive adequate ethical training.

145 | What best practices and principles can ensure the ethical use of data?

The issues raised in 📑 143 and 📑 144 are just a few of those that arise when dealing with data and creating intelligent systems with ML methods. It should be clear from these examples that talking about right and wrong when it comes

Managing Machine Learning in a Company

to the use of data is not straightforward. The world is complex, and every AI system and ML project is different. Logically, there cannot be a one-size-fits-all solution or guideline for how to ensure the ethical collection, storage and processing of data.

Nonetheless, there are some principles that can serve as general guidelines:

- *Adhere to the law, but realize that the law is often the minimum bar for ethical behaviour.* A lot of what is ethically right and wrong with regard to the use of data has already been established in laws and regulations. So the most fundamental step for the ethical use of data is to not break the law. In the EU, the GDPR includes principles such as an individual's right to control what data is collected about themselves, consent when collecting personal data and transparency of data processing purposes. Furthermore, the Charter of the Fundamental Human Rights stipulates a wide range of ethically correct behaviour and forbids, for instance, discrimination on the grounds of race, sex, ethnicity and religion. So a great deal of ethical behaviour is covered already. Unfortunately, however, we do not have laws to cover every aspect of the ethically good use of data. Therefore, laws should act as moral minimum bar rather than a sufficiency.
- *Put people at the centre of development.* Companies mostly strive to make a profit. While this is not ethically wrong as such, during the development of data products it is essential that the interests of people and nature prevail over the pursuit of profit and other values.
- *Foster a culture of critical thinking, openness and discourse.* Teams or companies that are highly hierarchical and do not encourage people to share critical thoughts have a couple of disadvantages. Not only do they suppress discourse around the moral use of data, but they also hinder innovation and the development of ideas. So it is in the best interests of a team or company to encourage critical thinking and openness in discussion and participation.
- *Strive for and safeguard diversity in developer teams.* Teams should be diverse in terms of all conceivable features: gender, educational background, economical background, ethnicity, age etc. This ensures that the development of an AI system or ML model is scrutinized from different angles, which prevents blind spots and ultimately leads to higher-quality algorithms. If you have a diverse team developing an algorithm, the likelihood that it will fall prey to discriminatory biases is much lower, simply because you may well have somebody on board who would be a victim of such discrimination.
- *Make data ethics training compulsory for people who develop algorithms and AI.* With more and more power being given to sophisticated algorithms and AI, there is a need to provide the people creating such systems with ethical training during their education and beyond.
- *Delineate responsibilities and communicate them clearly.* A clear delineation of responsibilities within developer teams ensures that tasks

and therefore also liabilities are clearly separated and distributed. This is not only a question of morality; it can have severe legal consequences when it comes to determining the liability of a given model or algorithm. Accountability should be communicated clearly to the team. For example:
- ❏ Who is responsible for obtaining data?
- ❏ Who is responsible for making sure that the data is legally and ethically okay to use?
- ❏ Who is responsible for choosing the right assessment metric for the algorithm?
- ❏ Who can be held liable if an algorithm makes detrimental decisions?

- *Make algorithms white box and transparent where possible.* There will often be a trade-off between the transparency of an algorithm and its performance. In some cases, having a white box algorithm which can be fully comprehended comes at a high cost in terms of its performance. But whenever this cost is justifiable, we should opt for making algorithms as transparent as possible. If machines and algorithms increasingly dictate our lives, then at least we should have the right to know how.
- *Foster an open and informed public discourse about data ethics.* This is really important. Discussions about data ethics are likely to be extremely heated and they may trigger intense debates. But only if the public understand and care about data ethics will there be pressure on politicians to act and regulate the use of data further – in the interests of society.

Purpose of ML and AI: we have the power – what are we doing with it?

We have looked at ethical behaviour during the process of developing algorithms. Lastly and most importantly, ethical considerations arise with regard to *what we are using data and ML-based AI systems for.*

Given that AI and ML are general purpose technologies, they can be used in a multitude of ways. They are tools, and just like any tool, they can be used for good, evil and every conceivable shade in between: on the one hand, ML and AI can be used to improve medical treatment for patients, and on the other hand, they can be used to improve military equipment and weapons.

So the most important best practice for the ethical use of data, ML and AI is to align the cause of a project with your inner ethical compass and readjust that compass by engaging in discussions with other stakeholders. What is the right thing to do with the power of data, ML and AI? Ensuring the ethically correct use of data, ML and AI is a shared responsibility. Companies should foster a culture where people are encouraged to speak up about their concerns and listen to each other.

PART IV

Where will we go?

"It's going to be interesting to see how society deals with artificial intelligence, but it will definitely be cool."[clxxxv]

Colin Angle, CEO and Founder of iRobot

10 The Future of Data, Machine Learning and Artificial Intelligence

146 | How are AI and its drivers going to develop?

Earlier in the book (📄 78), we explain what is currently possible with artificial intelligence (AI) and how "intelligent" the systems that are created today really are. How will the quest for AI develop in the future?

Remember that AI is driven largely by machine learning (ML) and in particular deep learning. Assuming that this will continue to be true (which, unless there is a sudden breakthrough of another approach to creating AI, seems a sensible assumption to make), then the development of AI will depend on the factors that are driving advancements in ML. So to predict how AI is going to develop, we need to look at the factors behind ML.

Data

The single most important resource for ML and the quality of ML models is data. It is the fuel of ML and therefore also AI. If you want to launch bigger rockets and eventually send a rocket to the moon, then you need more (and better) fuel. Therefore, data is a crucial determinant in the progress of AI and ML.

Looking at the past trajectory of data growth and the future predicted growth, it is safe to say that data will continue to grow. Whether this growth will follow an exponential path or will eventually slow down remains to be seen. But it is beyond doubt that we will have more data collected, stored, processed and thus also available in every conceivable sector. Figure 146-1 shows the predicted trajectory of data growth. In 2020 the total amount of data in the world stands at around 50 zettabytes (that is 50 billion terabytes). This number is expected to more than triple by 2025 to some 175 zettabytes.[clxxxvi]

Data growth does not automatically mean the growth of high-quality, structured, labelled data. Remember that the vast majority of ML use cases that yield added value and achieve the creation of intelligent systems are implemented with supervised ML methods, and this type of learning requires structured, labelled and high-quality data. So data growth – as mind-blowing as it might be – is not automatically enough. The data will also have to be in good shape. Nevertheless, with more companies devising and implementing data strategies that contain both digitization and data governance measures, it seems reasonable to assume that more and more of the collected data will be of high quality.

The Future of Data, Machine Learning and Artificial Intelligence

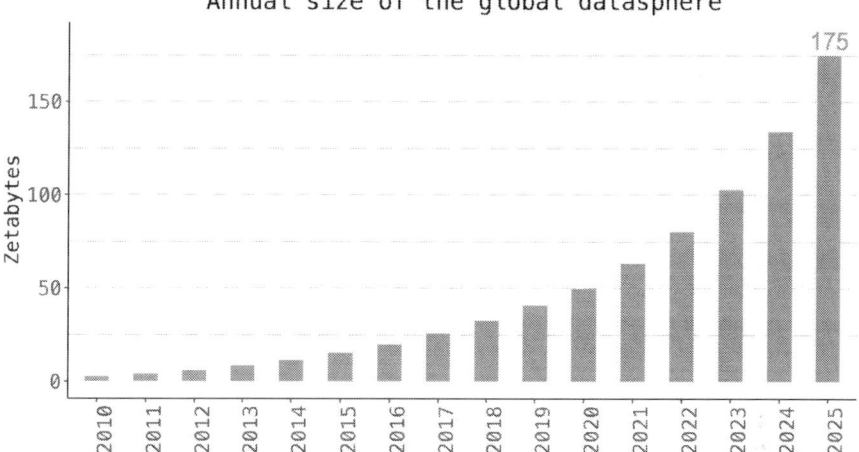

Figure 146.1 Projected growth of data
From IDC Data Age 2025 Study, sponsored by Seagate, Nov 2018. Copyright 2019 by IDC. Reproduced with permission.[clxxxvii]

Conclusion: As the primary enabler and driver of AI, data will continue to grow, but the speed and quality of the growth are difficult to predict. From a data perspective, the signs point to AI advancing rapidly in the future.

Computational power

Along with data, a major enabler for success in ML and AI was the incredible increase in computational power. If we apply Moore's Law for the future development of computers, we assume that machines will double in their computing capacity every two years, and so rapid advancements in AI are a given from the computing side. Even if we diverge from Moore's exponential trajectory and follow a slightly slower path of growth, what is sure is that computational power will continue to grow and thereby enable the development of more sophisticated AI systems.

What is more, there are countless research projects, some of which are still in their infancy, that might lead to leaps and breakthroughs in computing technology. DNA digital data storage and quantum computing are two such examples that might bring about a significant revolution in computer science.

Conclusion: As with data, the speed of growth of computational power is uncertain; it could continue to follow an exponential growth or slow down somewhat. However, the one thing that is certain is that we will continue to have ever-increasing computational capacities. Therefore, "computational power" will be a favouring rather than a restraining factor in the future progress of AI.

Advancements in algorithms and methodologies

Advancements in algorithms used in ML, notably in the field of deep learning, have led to success in the creation of AI. It is close to impossible to gauge how far we can expect further breakthroughs in the research and practice of the algorithms behind AI. What we can do, however, is look at how much interest and money is flowing into AI research and take that as a determinant of the progress of future research.

This interest in AI, ML and deep learning can be approximated with a number of indicators, such as:

- *Number of AI papers published annually:* The number annually published AI papers has been growing continuously in all regions of the world since the year between 1996 and 2017 – so fast that it has outpaced other areas of research. By 2017 the growth in papers relative to 1996 had increased more than 8-fold for AI papers. In contrast to that, the number of academic papers in all areas had not even increased 3-fold.[clxxxviii]
- *Job openings:* The growth of job openings requiring AI related job skills has also been surging as measured by the number of job openings on the job portal website https://www.monster.com/. Between 2015 and 2017 the growth in job openings requiring ML skills has increased around 5-fold, the job openings requiring deep learning skills has even increased 34-fold.[clxxxix]
- *Venture investment in AI:* The money that is being invested in AI in the start-up sector also confirms that interest in AI is on a growth path. Venture capital (VC) funding for U.S. AI startups increased 350% between 2013 and 2017. This is in contrast to the VC funding for all active startups which had increased only 100% in the same time period.[cxc]

We could explore a lot more indicators from a lot more fields, but it should be clear by now that essentially any indicator that allows us to gauge interest in and resources allocated to the fields of AI and ML has been following a growth path. While there may be challenges lurking along the path of research, we can surely say that these indicators point to our being able to overcome them and improve our capabilities to create AI. It is therefore sensible to assume that we will continue to see breath-taking breakthroughs.

Moreover, much of the knowledge created through research into ML and AI is made available to the public, and so knowledge and innovations are disseminated freely across the globe. A lot of the newest algorithms and frameworks are being made publicly available for everybody's use. For example, Google has released the deep learning frameworks TensorFlow and Keras (📘93), which you can download and use on your home computer right now.

Conclusion: Given the vast amounts of interest, money and (human) resources that AI and ML are attracting, it seems sensible to assume that we will see the algorithms and the fields in general continue to evolve faster than most other areas of research.

Legal regulations

The use of data is going to open up a lot of new possibilities. Like with other general purpose technologies, there will be use cases that clearly benefit society; for example, improvements in medical diagnoses through image recognition will earn universal approval and endorsement. But there will definitely also be cases where data is used in ways that are undesirable. ML and AI is a tool, and the way it is employed depends on the user. Unfortunately, not all people, companies and governments out there have purely good intentions.

With this increase in possibilities, we will also see an ever-increasing need to regulate all activities surrounding the use of data. A number of such regulations concerning the use, storage and processing of data are in place in most countries. The most comprehensive regulatory framework is the General Directive on Data Protection (GDPR) introduced by the European Union. The GDPR regulates and strongly curtails the rights of companies and institutions to store personal data of citizens of the European Union.

The run-up to the GDPR taking effect was a perfect example of how rules and regulations can determine the course of data-related projects. The confusion that prevailed in the industry during the months before the GDPR took effect in May 2018 was just unbelievable. We saw entire departments of major international companies putting every project that involved the use of data on halt for days and or even weeks until they had figured out whether they were complying with the GDPR.

On the one hand, such regulations establish barriers and therefore create clarity for companies and institutions as to what they can legally do with data. On the other hand, the restrictions that such regulations introduce slow down companies and research in pushing the boundaries in these fields.

Conclusion: We can expect to see more frameworks that regulate the use of data in the future, which will hinder the progress of ML and AI and other data-related use cases. How far they will slow the creation and progress of ML and AI is difficult to predict and will vary across countries.

147 | What are the implications of ML and AI for companies?

The fact that we have an ever-increasing amount of data available and are able to create more and more sophisticated, intelligent systems is changing the rules of the game. And to continue playing the game, companies have to adapt to this new environment. Some companies will adapt faster than others. Some might be too slow to survive.

ML and AI are essentially one aspect of digital transformation – arguably, the central one. It is not news that digital transformation is affecting every industry and that to remain competitive companies have to transform digitally, e.g. by becoming more data-driven and digitalizing their business processes. With regard to the adoption of ML methods and AI systems there are some specific factors that companies need to take into account.

The Ultimate Data and AI Guide

Create a data and AI strategy as roadmap

First of all, organizations need to craft a *data and AI strategy*. This business strategy looks at the current capabilities of the company and how they are applied in the chosen market to create a competitive advantage.

AI is likely to require changes to the core parts of the business strategy: which customer segments are actually addressed, which products and services are offered to customers, how these products and services are created, and how the company counters the strategies of existing and new competitors. At the very least, the way the company creates products and services will be substantially transformed by data and AI.

The data and AI strategy should address which key parts of the value chain will require major changes as a result of AI, how these changes should be approached, and how value is generated with data and AI in the organization, e.g. how could processed be made more efficient or products and services be augmented with AI.

Organizational design and culture change for data and AI

For many companies, especially traditional ones, building new capabilities and extending existing ones for data and AI will require changes in roles and responsibilities, organizational structures, business processes and corporate culture. Such roles include chief data officers, data scientists, data stewards, data engineers and data architects (Chapter 5_1).

The challenge of integrating and managing innovation in the company with data, ML and AI might require organizational restructuring of companies away from traditional hierarchical set ups to. One way forward can be the hub-and-spoke model, with a strong central Data and AI unit (📄 141). This should go in lock-step with the use of the new ways of working, such as the DevOps (📄 140).

Finally, the most difficult task of the data and AI transformation is cultural change, which needs to draw on best practices and lessons learned in change management. All these capabilities and organizational changes should be aligned with and focused on the implementation of the data and AI business strategy and the corporate values.

Get more data: make strategic data acquisitions

In an AI-driven economy, the strength and value of data assets is a crucial determinant of a company's ability to compete. Data is the most basic resource in the data-driven world. The more data a company owns, the more power it has.

As opposed to the ML methods that are used to create AI, data assets give a company a *defensible comparative* advantage. Knowledge of methodologies is disseminated across research institutions and companies eventually – because they are often made publicly available, but also because it is difficult to prevent knowledge and methodologies from spreading. In contrast to that, data assets are highly defensible and give a comparative advantage to companies that competitors struggle to close. As such, data is a tangible asset.

A number of companies have realized this and have devised their company and digital strategies accordingly. For example, a lot of companies are attempting to build a platform around their brand that acts like a bubble: the customer does not have to leave and within the bubble everything that the customer does can be tracked. This is why, for example, Tencent, the company behind the App WeChat, has such powerful and invaluable data. Tencent offers so many services with its app (chatting, social media, payment, ordering taxis, etc.) that it can paint a frighteningly accurate picture of users' lives. Such precious data enables so many ML and AI use cases.

Personal assistants are another great way of accumulating masses of data, and this data is extremely precious, given that the assistants pervade users' personal lives. It is an extremely smart move of Google (Google Assistant), Amazon (Alexa) and Apple (Siri) to offer products and services that "help" their customers in everyday life while collecting invaluable information about them: their preferences, interests and habits.

There are a lot of other examples of companies trying to enrich their data assets. In a lot of cases these services are "free", like the vast majority of services offered by Google. "Free" means we do not have to make a monetary transfer in order to use the service, but we do pay: with data about us. Given that data drives innovation, this is a key strategic move for major companies across all industries.

Manage the data correctly: establish data governance and a unified data architecture

Having a large amount of data is one thing; structuring and managing it correctly is another. In an AI- and data-driven world, companies have to make sure that they put their data assets to the best use. This requires them to put effective data governance in place. The data needs to be managed so that it is of high quality and accessible to the right people at the right time within an organization.

This directly feeds into the broader strategy and culture of a company. Companies with silos will face the problem that their data assets cannot move around easily to reach the employees that need them for a given use case. A unified and well-structured data architecture is key for creating AI or indeed any form of value from data. This will likely involve a shift from the current IT infrastructures towards more cloud-driven IT infrastructures.

Use the data: implement ML methods to create AI systems

In order to cope in an AI-driven world, companies have to embrace the (hopefully well-managed) data assets they own and put them to use effectively. This means they need to resort to data-driven solutions and embrace ML methods in all areas of their business. This includes for example the optimization of business processes through automation and the use of intelligent algorithms that aid employees in their daily operations. It also includes augmenting and improving existing services and products with smart algorithms, potentially even creating entirely novel fields of business such as in Case Study 63.

> **Case study 63**
>
> **Creating a data asset by augmenting the traditional product-based business model with a platform-based business model**
>
> John Deere, a company founded in 1837, is known by most people as one of the leading manufacturers of agricultural machinery. By 2016 it was the number one farm equipment manufacturer with worldwide revenues of US$26.2 billion. For most of its history, its main business model was to develop and sell tractors, harvesters, field sprayers and the like.
>
> However, in 2012 the company made a strategic move to augment its traditional business model with a data-based one. It launched the platform "My John Deere". By installing several sensors in its sold equipment, it was able to collect valuable data about the operations of farmers. This was a smart move to create a precious data asset, which it now uses to offer new services to its customers through its digital platform, e.g. remote diagnostics of machines or field and operations overview dashboards.[cxci]

148 | We benefit a lot from AI, but will it cost me my job?

The effects of the progression of AI for us as individuals and for our societies will be profound, just like in the previous industrial revolutions. Predicting all of the implications of the age of AI is way too difficult. It seems clear, however, that there will be both positive and negative impacts.

On the positive side, we will see products and services delivered that are of a higher quality and a lower price. The gains in economic efficiency achieved through automation in companies will probably be at least in part passed on to us consumers. We will also enjoy new kinds of services and features of products that are enabled through the use of AI.

If we liken the changes brought about by the rise of AI to the spread of electricity, the best way to develop a sense of what is lying ahead of us is probably to talk to our parents and grandparents. The previous generations suddenly saw fridges becoming available to the mass market, revolutionizing domestic life. Mixers, telephones, transport, televisions, radio – these are all technological innovations that were enabled by electricity in the first place. Prior to their invention, people could probably not imagine their existence, let alone the impact they would have on their life. The same will be true for our generation with AI and AI-powered products and services – who would have guessed 20 years ago that we have machines that act as virtual assistants and that we can talk to today? So on the one hand, we are definitely looking forward to very exciting times.

On the other hand, there will also be negative repercussions. Arguably, the biggest discussion will revolve around the technological unemployment that the rise of AI will create. Technological unemployment refers to the loss of jobs brought about by technological change and innovation. This debate is by no means a new one: it ensued in the wake of every industrial revolution and major innovation. Fuelled by the fear of job losses and being replaced by increasingly intelligent machines and algorithms, this debate has heated up again.

Are we really in the process of making people superfluous as a workforce and disrupting ourselves?

The answer is clear: we have no clue about the net effects of AI on the job market. Some say it will obviously lead to the loss of jobs, full stop; others reckon that job losses are going to be offset by job creation effects, so that the net results will be positive. There are prominent proponents on both sides of this debate. For example, Andrew McAfee (associate director of the Center for Digital Business at the MIT Sloan School of Management) and Erik Brynjolfsson (director of the MIT Initiative on the Digital Economy) have published the books *Race against the Machine* (2011)[cxcii] and *The Second Machine Age* (2014)[cxciii] in which they raise concerns about technological unemployment brought about by automation and AI. On the other side, the current US secretary of the treasury, Steve Mnuchin, reckons that automation is not going to have a big effect on the economy for at least the next 50 years.[cxciv]

From the latter position, we can argue that these concerns are raised each time automation spreads due to an industrial revolution, and yet in many "developed" countries that have adopted automation technologies, unemployment rates are at record lows.[cxcv] Obviously, there are a lot of factors to consider here, including the definition of unemployment, the way the data is gathered and aspects such as underemployment and precarious job situations. But it is safe to say that the current state of the world is far from the worst-case scenarios that anti-automation proponents painted decades and centuries ago. Just look at the rise of computers. Sure, they took over a lot of tasks and jobs. But also think about all the innovations and new business fields they opened up and the jobs they created (the World Wide Web, website development, online marketing, software engineering, etc.). History may not repeat itself, but there are certainly patterns. Therefore, by extrapolating historic developments of previous radical revolutions, we could reach the conclusion that the rise of AI is not that worrying at all.

On the other hand, as McAfee and Brynjolfsson argue, the rise of AI has a different quality than previous technical revolutions. While they were mechanical, this one is digital: previously, machines have replaced the need for our muscles, but the rise of AI is replacing the need for our *minds*. Historically, machines have saved us from doing strenuous physical labour such as construction, agriculture and manufacturing and have augmented our physical power. But the human intelligence to steer these extended muscles has always been necessary. This time, machines and algorithms are not only becoming intelligent but also creative. Of course, even if machines become better at cognitive tasks that require intelligence there are still a lot more unique qualities that make us human, e.g. empathy and feelings. Unfortunately, these qualities are less sought after in a lot of sectors and jobs. Therefore, so goes the argument, by giving machines cognitive abilities to imitate intelligence, we are eroding one of the main unique selling points of humans in the labour market. What is more, combine AI with advancements in robotics and we humans really start to look snookered.

Can we turn to data and get down to the facts to get answers? Yes, but the answers will not give us any more clarity. Countless studies by renowned universities, international organizations, governments and private companies have looked into this question and each has come up with a different answer. Table 148-1 shows the results of some selected studies on the subject.

Table 148-1 Predicted jobs that automation will create and destroy

Prediction for	Study released in	Where	Jobs Destroyed	Jobs Created	Net effect	Predictor
2020	2017	worldwide	1,800,000	2,300,000	+500,000	Gartner[cxcvi]
2020	2016	sample of 15 countries	7,100,000	2,000,000	-5,100,000	World Economic Forum (WEF)[cxcvii]
2027	2017	US jobs	24,700,000	14,900,000	-9,800,000	Forrester[cxcviii]
2030	2017	worldwide	400,000,000 -800,000,000	555,000,000- 890,000,000	-245,000,000 to +490,000,000	McKinsey[cxcix]

As you can see, the only conclusion that can be reached is that no one agrees. The predictions concerning the effects of AI on the job market range from highly optimistic to absolutely catastrophic with all shades in between. This is largely due to the fact that studies employ their own methodologies to assess the effects of automation and AI.

The study by the McKinsey Global Institute, for example, examined 2,000 work activities in 800 different occupations. The study concludes that about half of the tasks (not jobs or occupations) currently carried out by workers are automatable. This is true for tasks that are highly predictable and take place in structured environments (e.g. data collection and entry in accounting). It is less true for jobs that include the management of other people, providing expertise and interfacing with stakeholders. "Half of the tasks" may sound scary. However, the authors also state that only around 5% of jobs are automatable. For the vast majority of jobs, only certain *tasks* within them are automatable, as opposed to the entire job.

We could take a deep dive into other studies published on this topic, but the overall picture and message would not change. Whether or not the increasing application of AI in the working world will create or destroy jobs remains to be seen. What can be said with certainty is that AI will have profound consequences. While we may not know its net effect on the amount of jobs, we can say with certainty that it will *change occupational profiles a lot*. In the near future, rather than being replaced by algorithms, we will be working *with them*.

This is exactly what we are seeing with our clients as well. In many of the use cases that we help clients to implement, the immediate goal is to support employees becoming more productive and better at their tasks. Dashboards with sales forecasts help procurement make better buying decisions. End-of-line checks of car parts in manufacturing are done by an algorithm to help the controller.

Obviously, these might be the first steps towards full automation. In the far future, algorithms might create sales forecasts and automatically reorder products. End-of-line checks might rely entirely on AI. But for that to be the case, a good amount of deep neural networks will have to be trained. And by then, who knows what other kinds of jobs there will be for humans to do?

So what can we do to prepare ourselves for the wave of change that is about to hit us in as yet unknown ways? Apart from keeping updated on the latest developments in data-related fields, it seems that the only actionable lesson that we can take from the discussion is this: flexibility will matter rather than skills. The traditional approach to work of being skilled in a certain area and becoming an expert in it will gradually fade away. Instead, job profiles, requirements and task will be changing in yet unknown ways. Our only chance is to be able to react to these changes. We will all have to be lifelong learners and develop the flexibility to acquire new skills and knowledge quickly.

149 | Which nation will win the AI race?

Given the power that comes with AI, a hotly debated subject is which nation will win the AI race (many believe it will be China or the US). But casting the topic in this light is problematic.

Firstly, if there is a race, then where is the finish line? There is no clear or concrete goal towards which nations are striving when it comes to AI. Instead, the debate seems to aim at who will achieve a general dominance within AI-powered services and products. The problem is that "dominance in AI" is an extremely vague concept that is difficult to measure. This is leading to journalists, businesspeople and government officials publishing selective reports and articles that do not always give the full picture or a systematic break down and discussion of the question.

Secondly, it makes little sense to pit nations against each other in this debate. While public research institutions, universities and government bodies play a certain role, the truth is that the majority of innovation in the field of AI is happening in the private sector. Out of the top 30 AI patent applicants only four are universities or public research institutions. The other 26 are private, internationally operating companies including the top three which are IBM (more than 8,000 AI patent applications), Microsoft (almost 6,000) and Toshiba (more than 5,000).ᶜᶜ Virtually all approaches to AI creation are from an ML perspective, which requires data, and private companies have the largest and most valuable data assets. The bigger the company, the more data it tends to have. Such large companies operate globally and consequently cross national boundaries.

So "Which nation will win the race?" is the wrong question. Rather, the question to ask is where the companies, institutions and organizations that develop and adopt AI systems are located. Let's look at some data.

Where are the top digital companies located?

Classifying, comparing and assessing companies with regard to their adoption of AI and influence on AI development is difficult. Nonetheless, there are a number of rankings that try to do exactly this.

For example, in 2018 Forbes released The Forbes Digital 100, a ranking of the top 100 publicly traded IT, hardware, media, digital retail and telecommunications companies shaping the digital world. The list was led by Amazon, Netflix and Nvidia. Companies hailed from 17 countries. In total, the list included 49 US companies, which heavily dominated the top 20 places. Sixteen companies were Chinese. European companies were hardly to be found on the list: there were only two companies in the top thirty.[cci]

Looking at the question by means of this indicator, therefore, we could surmise that the US has a massive lead at the moment, China is the other great player, and the rest of the world does not play a significant role.

AI-related patents per country

Another indicator we can use to measure who is pushing the envelope in the development of AI is where most AI patents are filed. The World Intellectual Property Organization (WIPO) released a comprehensive study on this in 2019[ccii].

When we look at the AI patents filed in the national patent offices, we can see that the first patents were filed in the 1980s in Japan. Since then the number of patents filed has massively increased across the globe. The US had developed a big lead from the mid-1980s (when around 1,000 patent applications were filed annually in US patent offices) into the mid-2010s (when the number of patent applications filed annually in US patent offices had increased to over 6,000). This lead, however, has recently been closed by China: in 2014, with almost 14,000 patents there were more patents were filed here than in the US for the first time. It should be noted that the number of patents filed says nothing about their quality of impact. What is more, only 4% of the AI patents filed in China are subsequently filed in another jurisdiction.[cciii]

The US has an edge, but China is catching up

These indicators of the current state of adoption, research and dominance in the field of AI paint a rather coherent picture. The US still has an edge, but China is catching up rapidly. Other countries and regions, notably Europe, play only a minor role. Europe is already said to have a digital gap, because its adoption of digital technologies and its level of digitalization are comparatively low. It seems that Europe also has an AI gap.

How are things going to develop in the future?

The next question that arises is whether the status quo is going to change, and if so how. Are Chinese companies going to "take over" American ones? There a couple of arguments on both sides.

China and AI

A number of factors are likely to foster China's rapid advancements and adoption of AI technologies:

- *The Chinese political system:* The government of China is not subject to as many political players and adversaries as Western governments. Imagine the area of self-driving vehicles expanding to trucks and therefore the logistics sector. This would likely lead to upheaval from truck driver unions in the West to which governments would need to react. In China there are no such powerful worker unions, NGOs or other institutions that would impede companies' or the government's ability to collect and use data.
- *Chinese regulations and culture:* These are more conducive to the adoption and development of AI. Societies in the West have concerns about and are extremely careful with data privacy and security. This is already reflected in strict regulations concerning the collection, processing and use of data; for example, the GDPR in the EU. Regulations are much laxer in China, largely due to the fact that in China, much like other Asian countries, few eyebrows are raised if a company or government institution wants to collect data about you. The Chinese seem more willing to trade off convenience for privacy.[cciv] As a result, it is much easier there to collect data in sensitive areas and use it with AI. Healthcare is likely to be such an area. There are numerous potential use cases involving health data (e.g. self-diagnosis apps that would aid or replace doctors), and getting hold of such extremely sensitive data is possible in China, unlike in Western societies.
- *Attitude towards AI:* China seems to be embracing and emphasizing the importance of AI much more. In a global study of 1,378 CEOs, 72% of respondents from Asia-Pacific agreed or strongly agreed with the statement "AI will have a larger impact than the internet", compared to only 44% from North America.[ccv] The importance that the Chinese place on AI can also be seen in the fact that the government has a digital strategy. It even provides substantial subsidies for AI start-ups. In contrast to that, AI efforts, research and adoption are much more dispersed in Western societies. Most Western governments are doing little, if anything, to aid and promote the development of AI and are far from having comprehensive digital or AI strategies.
- *China's market:* This combines the best of the European and US markets: it is even bigger than the European market, but at the same time it is homogenous, like the US market. This makes it more lucrative to research and implement AI-powered products and services in China.

Therefore, China is likely to excel in the time to come.

The US and AI

There are also a number of factors that support the view that the US will maintain its lead.

Most of the leading digital companies are still headquartered in the US – and companies are the entities that own the most valuable data assets. The thing about data- and AI-driven products and services is that once they are launched, they enter a virtuous circle. First, in order to offer an AI-driven product or service, companies need to have data on which the algorithms can be trained so that the product can be developed. Once the product is developed, it is deployed and used in real life, and it creates and collects data. This data can then be used to refine and improve the product further, etc.

This virtuous circle propels an exponential growth path. Since US companies already have an edge in all the elements of this virtuous circle, it will be very difficult for others to catch up, close the gap and overcome the existing data monopoly structures. In a way, with US companies being the forerunners, it seems like the cards have been dealt already.

The US also has a competitive advantage in drawing top talent to its shores. A lot of the world's best universities are in the US, and so the brightest minds will continue to flock to them, especially at the graduate level. And due to the proximity of the top digital companies to the top universities, it is likely that they will not face a shortage of talent anytime soon. The US remains a desirable country to live in for a lot of people.

The big picture

To summarize, it seems like China is catching up and will continue to catch up even faster, given that it has a number of factors working in its favour, notably

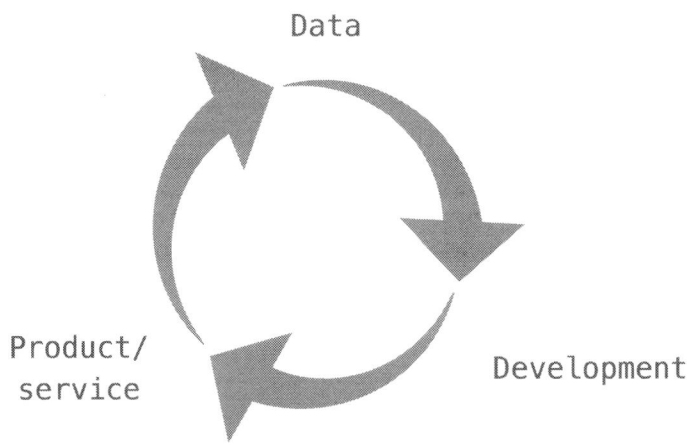

Figure 149.1 Virtuous circle of data creation, digital product/service and development

its political system, culture and attitude towards AI. The speed will be especially fast and outpace that of the Western world in areas that use sensitive data, which is cumbersome to collect in liberal democracies.

The US definitely has a lead that is difficult to close, given that US companies arguably possess the largest and most valuable data assets in the world. Recreating such valuable and large data assets to be on par with US companies would take other companies years. Regulations and restrictions might contribute to the US losing its lead, however.

How do things look for Europe and the rest of the world?

For Europe, things look bleak. Essentially, Europe shares all the downsides of the US (lack of AI vision and strategy, and strict rules and regulations for the collection and use of data) without sharing its comparative advantages. The situation for Europe is further exacerbated because it lacks the venture capital investment culture and spirit to innovate that make the US so powerful.

As a result, for the most part European companies simply lack the data assets that are needed to get the AI train running. There is no European Google/Baidu, social network or other digital service provider that competes with the US and Asian counterparts. And while European universities provide excellent educations at much lower costs for students, top talent will still mostly be drawn from the flagship universities in the US.

Given that rather restrictive rules surrounding the collection and use of data apply in most European countries, it also seems unlikely that European companies will be able to kick-start the virtuous circle of data creation, digital product/service and development (Figure 149-1). We might see European (and also US) companies embracing a form of "data colonialism", as Yuval Noah Harari[ccvi] has called it. That is, European companies might escape strict regulations by using their global network to collect data in countries with laxer regulations, typically developing countries, in order to train and feed their models in the headquarters in the West. An example where we will probably see such a development is in AI use cases involving medical data. European companies will have a hard time collecting the relevant patient data for this field of application, but they might try to collect it abroad and ship it back in order to circumvent domestic regulations. But it seems unlikely that embracing such a practice will give them the necessary momentum to catch up with US and Chinese companies, which will be able to develop and adopt AI systems much faster.

150 | When are we going to see the creation of general AI?

Looking at the main determinants of how AI is going to develop in the future, it seems that it will continue to advance rapidly. This opinion is shared by leading AI researchers across the globe. In 2016, researchers from Oxford and Yale universities conducted a survey of 352 leading AI researchers to collect their estimates of whether and when we will see the creation of general AI. The results suggest that the community is rather optimistic and sees a real chance of general AI evolving within the next 100 years or so. The results also show, however, opinions and estimates differ vastly.

The AI experts were asked to provide their estimate of the probability of human-level machine intelligence (HLMI) during the next 100 years. HLMI was defined in the survey as the point "when unaided machines can accomplish every task better and more cheaply than human workers", which is equivalent to how we have defined strong (general) AI in the book (76). Figure 150-1 summarizes their answers; each light grey line represents the estimate of one respondent. The thick red line is the aggregate forecast, the interval around it represents the 95% confidence interval of the aggregate forecast.[38] We can see that the respondents believe that there is a 50% chance of HLMI existing in 2066 and a 75% chance of it existing in 2116.

The survey also included a breakdown into narrow AI systems. That is, respondents were also asked to give their estimate of when AI systems will be able to perform certain milestone tasks at a human level. Figure 150-2 shows

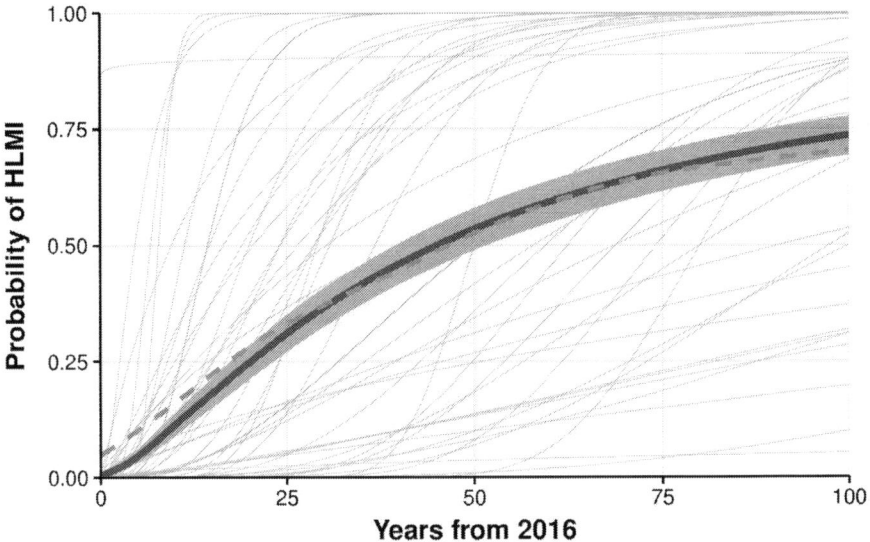

Figure 150.1 Results of a poll of AI experts of what year we will see human-level machine intelligence (HLMI) arise with what probability

From "Viewpoint: When Will AI Exceed Human Performance? Evidence from AI Experts" by Grace, Salvatier, Dafoe, Zhang, & Evans, 2018 (https://doi.org/10.1613/jair.1.11222). Copyright 2019 by AI Access Foundation Inc. Reprinted with permission.[ccvii]

---

38. The dashed grey line represents the locally estimated scatterplot smoothing (LOESS) curve. If you don't know what that is, just ignore it for now.

the results. Each dot represent the median estimate of all respondents, the black line shows the 50% probability intervals.[39]

What is interesting about these results is that certain tasks are already being performed by ML models at the time of writing – contrary to the expectations of the AI experts when they took the survey just three years ago, in 2016. Transcribing speech to text was estimated to be possible within ten years, but in 2019 most smartphones already come with built-in functions to do this.

What seems clear is that we will not see general AI arise anytime soon. However, the use of sophisticated ML algorithms that imitate parts of our intelligent behaviour will become increasingly widespread. Therefore, the current development of more and more tasks being automated and performed by machines will continue, probably at an even greater speed than most of us expect. AI will be able to make better diagnoses than doctors, interact with customers faster and more cheaply, and summarize, translate and create text more effectively than us humans.

Just like around a century ago electricity brought about innovation after innovation, the increasing availability of data will enable more and more areas of application for AI. Around a century ago, people suddenly had devices to create artificial light and cool their food, and companies suddenly had machines to run their operations and production. In the future, we will have applications that give us diagnoses at the click of a mouse and companies will have algorithms that supervise and manage their production.

---

39. For technically interested people: Specifically, intervals represent the date range from 25% to 75% probability of the event occurring, calculated from the mean of individual CDFs as in Figure 150-1. Note that these intervals represent the uncertainty of survey respondents, not estimation uncertainty. For further information on the methodology we refer you to the original paper (s. reference).

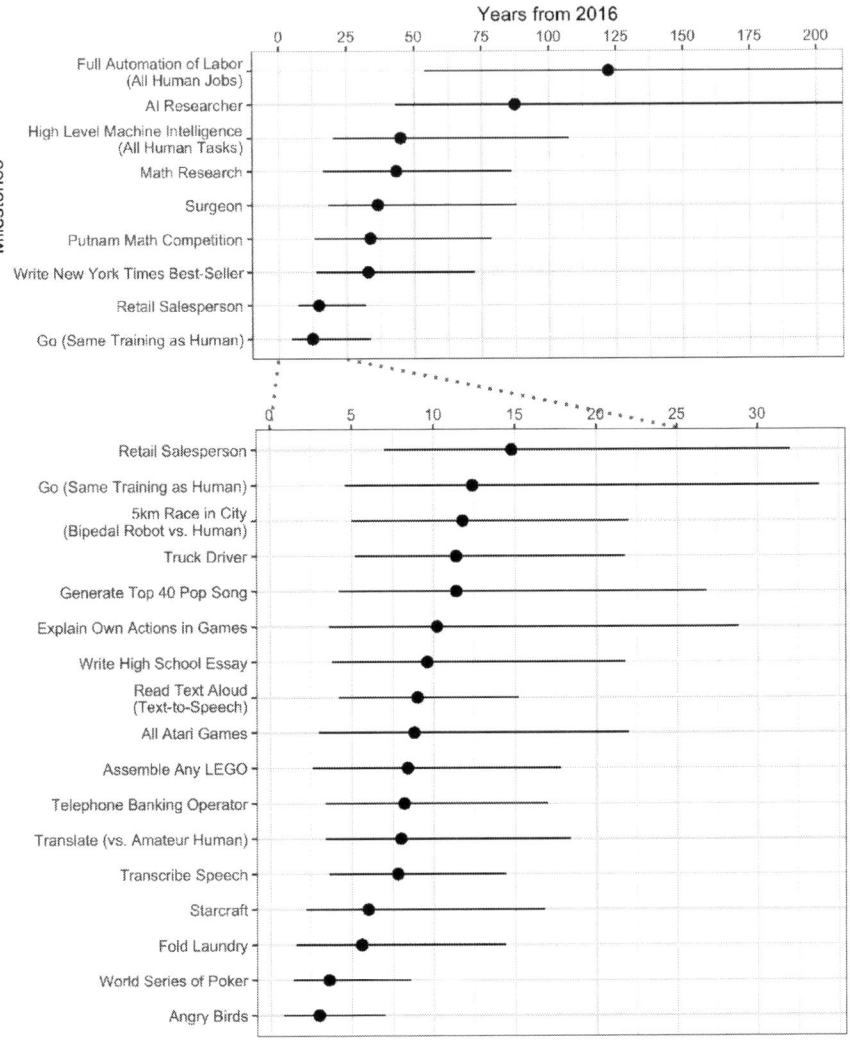

Figure 150.2 Results of a poll of AI experts of what year we will narrow AI system being able to perform a task at (super-)human level

From "Viewpoint: When Will AI Exceed Human Performance? Evidence from AI Experts" by Grace, et al., 2018 (https://doi.org/10.1613/jair.1.11222). Copyright 2019 by AI Access Foundation Inc. Reprinted with permission.[ccviii]

Appendix

List of Abbreviations

3 V's	Volume, Velocity, Variety (Big Data)
AI	Artificial Intelligence
ANN	Artificial Neural Network
API	Application Programming Interface
BI	Business Intelligence
CDAO	Chief Data and Analytics Officer
DB	Database
DBMS	Database Management System
DWH	Data Warehouse
EDA	Exploratory Data Analysis
ELT	Extract, Load, Transform
ETL	Extract, Transform, Load
FK	Foreign Key
GDPR	General Data Protection Regulation 2016/679
GLM	Generalized Linear Model
ML	Machine Learning
NLP	Natural Language Processing
RDBMS	Relational Database Management System
NoSQL	Non-relational / No-SQL / Not Only SQL Database
PK	Primary Key
SQL	Structured Query Language

List of Tables

Table P-1 Key facts about the content of this book

Table I-1 Summary statistics and overview of chapters

Table I-2 Route 1: Data and AI in a nutshell for busy people and managers

Table I-3 Route 2: Technical trip into data for (aspiring) practitioners

Table I-4 Route 3: Technical Trip into AI and ML for (aspiring) practitioners

Table I-5 Route 4"Why should I care route?" for the average person

Table I-6 Route 5: The impress-me route for people looking to be entertained

Table 1.1 What is digital transformation and why does it matter?

Table 1.2 Examples of digitization, digitalization and digital transformation

Table 2.1 Publicly traded companies with highest market value in 2010 and 2020

Table 4.1 Examples of digital transformation driven by digitization and digitalization versus driven by AI

Table 6.1 Examples of ML-based AI systems in manufacturing

Table 6.2 Examples of ML-based AI systems in banking and insurance

Table 6.3 Examples of ML-based AI systems in healthcare

Table 6.4 Examples of ML-based AI systems in telecoms

Table 6.5 Examples of ML-based AI systems in energy and utilities

Table 6.6 Examples of ML-based AI systems in travel

Table 6.7 Examples of ML-based AI systems in e-commerce

Table 15-1 How much data do you generate every day?

Table 15-2 Cryptic sensor data

Table 15-3 What is data and why does it matter?

Table 17-1 What is the data generating process and why does it matter?

Table 17-2 Human versus machine generated data

Table 18-1 The scales of data size

Table 19-1 What is data quality and why does it matter?

Table 19-2 Example of data quality issues

Table 19-3 Types of data quality issues

Table 21-1 Structured, semi-structured and unstructured data

Table 21-2 Example of structured data

Table 21-3 Unstructured structured data

Table 22-1 Master versus transactional data

Table 22-2 Example of master data

Table 22-3 Example of transactional data

Table 23-1 What is streaming data and why does it matter?

Table 24-1 What is big data and why does it matter?

Table 24-2 An alternative definition of big data

Table 26-1 What is a database and why does it matter?

Table 28-1 What is a database model and why does it matter?

Table 28-2 A flat-file data model of employees

Table 29-1 What is a relational database system and why does it matter?

Table 29-2 Ranking of database systems according to popularity

Table 31-1 What is a key attribute and why does it matter?

Table 32-1 What is SQL and why does it matter?

Table 35-1 What is a computer cluster and horizontal scaling and why do they matter?

Table 37-1 What is a NoSQL database and why does it matter?

Table 38-1 Comparison of relational and non-relational databases

Table 40-1 An overview of Apache Hadoop

Table 40-2 An overview of the Apache Hadoop Ecosystem

Table 41-1 An overview of Apache Spark

Table 42-1 An overview of relational database providers

Table 43-1 An overview of NoSQL database providers

Table 44-1 What is a data architecture and why does it matter?

Table 46-1 What is a DWH and why does it matter?

Table 48-1 What is a data pipeline and why does it matter?

Table 50-1 An overview of ETL tools

Table 51-1 What is a data lake and why does it matter?

Table 53-1 Comparison of a data lake and DWH

Table 54-1 What is the cloud and why does it matter?

Table 56-1 Types of cloud services

Table 58-1 What is a serverless architecture and why does it matter?

Table 59-1 Popular cloud providers and services

List of Tables

Table 60-1 Role of a chief data and analytics officer

Table 61-1 Role of a data architect

Table 62-1 Role of a database administrator

Table 63-1 Role of an ETL developer, data quality specialist and data artist

Table 64-1 What are data governance and data democratization and why do they matter?

Table 65-1 What are the key elements of data governance and data democratization?

Table 67-1 What are data dictionaries and data catalogues?

Table 70-1 Data governance zones

Table 72-1 What is data security and why does it matter?

Table 73-1 What is personal data and why does it matter?

Table 74-1 What is data protection (privacy) and why does it matter?

Table 76-1 What is AI and why does it matter?

Table 78-1 Top breakthroughs in the field of AI

Table 80-1 What is ML and why does it matter?

Table 82-1 What are noise and signal and why do they matter?

Table 82-2 Predictable and unpredictable processes

Table 83-1 What are the types of ML and why do they matter?

Table 83-2 What are target variables and input variables and why do they matter?

Table 84-1 What is supervised ML and why does it matter?

Table 86-1 What is unsupervised learning and why does it matter?

Table 88-1 What is reinforcement learning and why does it matter?

Table 90-1 Overview of Python

Table 91-1 Overview of R

Table 92-1 Overview of scikit-learn

Table 93-1 Overview Tensorflow and Keras

Table 94-1 Overview of MLlib, PySpark and SparkR

Table 95-1 Cloud-based ML tools

Table 96-1 Dataset of daily sales

Table 97-1 What is an ML model and why does it matter?

Table 98-1 What is a correlation and why does it matter?

Table 99-1 What is feature engineering and why does it matter?

Table 99-2 Types of feature engineering

Table 100-1 What is feature selection and why does it matter?

Table 101-1 How do we split up a dataset and why does it matter?

Table 102-1 What is model training and why does it matter?

Table 103-1 What is model validation and why does it matter?

Table 103-2 Comparison of model scores on the validation set for three different models trained to predict sales in Your Model Car

Table 104-1 What is model testing and why does it matter?

Table 104-2 Comparison of model scores on both validation and test set for three different models trained to predict sales in Your Model Car

Table 105-1 What are overfitting, underfitting and generalization and why do they matter?

Table 105-2 Overview of symptoms of over- and underfitting of models

Table 105-3 Comparison of model scores on validation and test sets

Table 106-1 What is cross-validation and why does it matter?

Table 107-1 What is ensemble learning and why does it matter?

Table 111-1 Overview of GLMs

Table 112-1 Overview of tree-based models

Table 113-1 Overview of ensemble learning

Table 115-1 What are neural networks and deep learning and why do they matter?

Table 120-1 What is transfer learning and why does it matter?

Table 124-1 What is EDA and why does it matter?

Table 124-2 Summary statistics of variable "CUSTOMER_AGE"

Table 124-3 Overview of data preparation methods

Table 126-1 What is model deployment and why does it matter?

Table 127-1 Duration of an ML project

Table 128-1 The most common hurdles during an ML project

Table 132-1 Overview of the data scientist job role

Table 133-1 Overview of the data engineer job role

Table 134-1 Overview of the ML engineer job role

Table 135-1 Overview of the statistician job role

Table 136-1 Overview of the software engineer job role

Table 137-1 Overview of the business analyst job role

Table 139-1 What is agile project management and why does it matter?

Table 140-1 What are DataOps and DevOps?

Table 142-1 What is data ethics and why does it matter?

Table 148-1 Predicted jobs that automation will create and destroy

List of Figures

Figure P-1 Wordcount of selected key words in the book

Figure I-1 Route 1: Data and AI in a nutshell for busy people and managers

Figure I-2 Route 2: Technical trip into data for (aspiring) practitioners

Figure I-3 Route 3: Technical Trip into AI and ML for (aspiring) practitioners

Figure I-4 Route 4: "Why should I care route?" for the average person

Figure I-5 Route 5: The impress-me route for people looking to be entertained

Figure I-6 Screenshot of fictional website of Your Model Car

Figure 3.1 Mutually reinforcing drivers of digital transformation "altered customer behaviour" and "technological innovation"

Figure 4.1 Muscle versus mind power

Figure 5.1 Virtuous cycle of data, AI and digital transformation

Figure 7.1 Overview of buzzwords in the data and AI sphere

Figure 12-1 Overview and relationship between data science, data mining, data analytics, predictive analytics, business intelligence and ML

Figure 15-1 Data as a representation of facts

Figure 15-2 DIKW pyramid

Figure 16-1 Different types of data analytics

Figure 21-1 Example of semi-structured data (employee data)

Figure 21-2 Example of unstructured data (product data)

Figure 24-1 What happens in 60 seconds on the internet?

Figure 25-1 Screenshot of a file system

Figure 26-1 Visualization of a database system

Figure 29-1 Visualization of a relational database system

Figure 30-1 Simple table in the relational model with terminology explained

Figure 30-2 Example of two interconnected tables

Figure 30-3 Example of relational data model of Your Model Car

Figure 31-1 An example of a join operation

Figure 32-1 Popularity of programming languages

Figure 32-2 Example of an SQL query

Figure 32-3 Another example of an SQL query

Figure 32-4 Visualisation of results of an SQL query

Figure 35-1 Horizontal versus vertical scaling

Figure 35-2 A computer cluster

Figure 36-1 Schematic view of how a file is stored on a distributed file system

Figure 36-2 Schematic overview of how data is processed on a computer cluster

Figure 37-1 Example of a key-value store

Figure 37-2 Visualization of the CAP theorem

Figure 37-3 The CAP theorem in practise

Figure 39-1 Overview of data storage technologies

Figure 40-1 Overview of a Hadoop-based computer cluster

Figure 44-1 Data architectures compared to cities

Figure 44-2 Data architecture versus database

Figure 47-1 Schematic overview of a DWH

Figure 47-2 Example of an ETL process

Figure 47-3 Example of a data flow in a DWH

Figure 52-1 Schematic view of a data lake

Figure 52-2 Example of a data flow in a data lake

Figure 53-1 A wardrobe as a metaphor for a data lake

Figure 55-1 Types of cloud architectures

Figure 56-1 Client–server model

Figure 56-2 IaaS, PaaS and SaaS

Figure 57-1 Flexibility of the cloud

Figure 58-1 Schematic overview of a serverless architecture

Figure 71-1 Overview of data security and privacy/protection

Figure 72-1 Overview of the encryption process

Figure 75-1 When does the GDPR apply?

Figure 76-1 Weak versus strong AI

Figure 79-1 AI, ML and deep learning

Figure 80-1 How an ML model is created and used

Figure 81-1 Traditional software programming versus ML

Figure 82-1 A process with a signal but also noise

Figure 82-2 An almost noise-free process

Figure 83-1 Types of ML

Figure 83-2 Labelled versus unlabelled data

Figure 84-1 Overview of supervised ML

Figure 86-1 Schematic overview of clustering

List of Figures

Figure 87-1 Example of clustering on customer data

Figure 87-2 Overview of k-means clustering algorithm

Figure 87-3 Example of the local outlier factor algorithm

Figure 88-1 Visualization of reinforcement learning

Figure 89-1 Types of ML tools

Figure 89-2 Poll of the most popular ML tools

Figure 96-1 Ingredients to create a ML model

Figure 96-2 Line chart of daily sales

Figure 97-1 Verbal, graphical and mathematical expressions of a model

Figure 97-2 Overview of supervised ML

Figure 97-3 An example of a simple decision tree model to predict daily sales

Figure 98-1 Various datasets that differ in the strength and direction of correlation between the x- and y-variable.

Figure 98-2 Example of a positive correlation

Figure 98-3 An example of a confounding variable

Figure 100-1 Overfitting due to too many variables

Figure 100-2 Example of the curse of dimensionality

Figure 101-1 A split into training, validation and test sets

Figure 101-2 Splitting up our dataset

Figure 102-1 Model training example

Figure 102-2 Untrained model versus trained model with obtained parameters

Figure 102-3 Example of a trained decision tree

Figure 103-1 Example of model validation

Figure 104-1 Example of model testing

Figure 105-1 Overview of overfitting and underfitting

Figure 106-1 Overview of cross-validation

Figure 107-1 Example of ensemble learning

Figure 111-1 Example of a linear model

Figure 111-2 Example of a specified linear model

Figure 111-3 Example calculation of a prediction with a simple linear model

Figure 113-1 Example of a tree-based ensemble

Figure 113-2 Example of a tree-based ensemble making a prediction

Figure 115-1 Relationship between AI and deep learning

Figure 115-2 Overview of a neural network and a deep neural network

Figure 116-1 Example of a simple neural network

Figure 116-2 Example of the workings of a neural network

Figure 117-1 Automated feature engineering of a deep neural network

The Ultimate Data and AI Guide

Figure 118-1 A photo of a traffic jam in Jakarta by night

Figure 118-2 How a picture is broken down into pixels

Figure 119-1 Schematic overview of the performance of deep neural networks vs. classic ML models

Figure 120-1 Normal ML versus transfer learning

Figure 122-1 Overview of ML project phases

Figure 123-1 Venn diagram of problems, solutions and data

Figure 124-1 A histogram of product prices of Your Model Car product portfolio

Figure 124-2 Boxplots of product prices per product category

Figure 124-3 Scatterplot of product price and sales in 2019

Figure 124-4 Line chart of website visits

Figure 130-1 Model deployment as the bottleneck of ML projects

Figure 131-1 Roles required during an ML project

Figure 139-1 Waterfall versus agile project management

Figure 139-2 Project plan in a SCRUM-like style

Figure 139-3 Example of a KANBAN board

Figure 141-1 Types of data and AI organizational setups in a company

Figure 146-1 Projected growth of data

Figure 149-1 Virtuous circle of data creation, digital product/service and development

Figure 150-1 Results of a poll of AI experts of what year we will see human-level machine intelligence arise with what probability

Figure 150-2 Results of a poll of AI experts of what year we will narrow AI system being able to perform a task at (super-)human level

List of Case Studies

Case Study 1: How the Blockbuster night was replaced by Netflix binge watching

Case Study 2: Next-best-action marketing by a software company

Case Study 3: Digitalizing business processes in a hospital

Case Study 4: How an airline can use data to employ different types of data analytics

Case Study 5: Human and machine generated data in the production process

Case Study 6: A flawed data generating process in the production line, Part I

Case Study 7: A flawed data generating process in the production line, Part II (Case Study 6 continued)

Case Study 8: Collecting structured and unstructured data from insurance claims

Case Study 9: How master data management can save costs

Case Study 10: Streaming data of bank customers withdrawing money

Case Study 11: Setting up a database to replace Excel

Case Study 12: Setting up a database to digitalize business processes

Case Study 13: Digitizing the certification process with a relational database, Part I

Case Study 14: The power of key attributes in creating a comprehensive picture

Case Study 15: Digitizing the certification process with a relational database, Part II (Case Study 13 continued)

Case Study 16: Digitizing the certification process with a relational database, Part III (Case Study 15 continued)

Case Study 17: Telemetric automotive data

Case Study 18: Spotify uses Apache Cassandra (NoSQL database) to store user-profile data

Case Study 19: Connected multi-cooker kitchen machine

Case Study 20: Centralized view of insurance claims

Case Study 21: How the Your Model Car DWH works

Case Study 22: Data pipeline in food retail

Case Study 23: Enhanced data storage requirements of a logistics provider

Case Study 24: Implementing a data lake at Your Model Car
Case Study 25: Netflix migration into the AWS cloud
Case Study 26: Hybrid cloud architecture to reduce storage costs
Case Study 27: Data visualization as SaaS
Case Study 28: The way into the cloud for a global insurance company
Case Study 29: Completely serverless backend
Case Study 30: Usama Fayyad – the first chief data officer
Case Study 31: One of the largest data-security breaches in history
Case Study 32: Survey of a language instruction provider
Case Study 33: Would Your Model Car have to adhere to the GDPR if it were incorporated in the US?
Case Study 34: How Google Duplex is taking virtual assistants to the next level
Case Study 35: Automated post-hurricane damage estimation of houses
Case Study 36: The paradigm shift of programming machine translation algorithms
Case Study 37: Optimization of mini loan grants
Case Study 38: Clustering of similar car-part failures to increase repair efficiency
Case Study 39: Predictive maintenance of block-type thermal power stations
Case Study 40: Creating an AI system to predict the daily sales of a product in Your Model Car
Case Study 41: Using a decision tree from the model class "tree-based models"
Case Study 42: Your Model Car "feature engineering"
Case Study 43: Splitting the dataset in Your Model Car – why can't we use random sampling?
Case Study 44: Your Model Car "data split and model training"
Case Study 45: Your Model Car "model validation"
Case Study 46: Your Model Car "model testing"
Case Study 47: Checking whether one of our models overfitted
Case Study 48: Ensemble-learning-based hedge fund
Case Study 49: Creating AI that composes music
Case Study 50: Choosing a model for political reasons
Case Study 51: How a deep neural network beat all other ML models and thus reinvigorated AI
Case Study 52: One neuron in a multi-million neuron network is able to classify the sentiment of words and phrases
Case Study 53: Autonomous driving
Case Study 54: Where are neural networks of no use?

List of Case Studies

Case Study 55: What problem are we solving by predicting our sales in Your Model Car?

Case Study 56: Extracting and exploring data for our Your Model Car sales prediction

Case Study 57: Deploying the sales prediction algorithm in Your Model Car

Case Study 58: Data sources that cannot be integrated

Case Study 59: Chip tuning in cars

Case Study 60: ML and AI departments

Case Study 61: The tribe model at ING bank

Case Study 62: Should cancer patients be obliged to donate their data for research?

Case Study 63: Creating a data asset by augmenting the traditional product-based business model with a platform-based business model

Reference List

1 Digital Transformation: The Role of Data and Artificial Intelligence

i. Brysbaert, M. (2019). How many words do we read per minute? A review and meta-analysis of reading rate. Retrieved 2020-01-02 from 10.31234/osf.io/xynwg

ii. Brysbaert, M. (2019). How many words do we read per minute? A review and meta-analysis of reading rate. Retrieved 2020-01-02 from 10.31234/osf.io/xynwg

iii. Brysbaert, M. (2019). How many words do we read per minute? A review and meta-analysis of reading rate. Retrieved 2020-01-02 from 10.31234/osf.io/xynwg

iv. Schmidt, E. and Cohen, J. (2013), *The New Digital Age: Reshaping the Future of People, Nations and Business*. London: John Murray.

v. N.a. (2010, December 31). FT Global 500 December 2010: Prices and market values at 31 December. *Financial Times.* Retrieved 2020-01-01 from http://media.ft.com/cms/253867ca-1a60-11e0-b003-00144feab49a.pdf

vi. YCharts Inc. (2020, January 2). Apple Inc. *YCharts.* Retrieved 2020-01-02 from https://ycharts.com/companies/AAPL/market_cap

vii. YCharts Inc. (2020, January 2). Microsoft Corp. *YCharts.* Retrieved 2020-01-02 from https://ycharts.com/companies/MSFT/market_cap

viii. YCharts Inc. (2020, January 2). Alphabet Inc. *YCharts.* Retrieved 2020-01-02 from https://ycharts.com/companies/GOOG/market_cap

ix. YCharts Inc. (2020, January 2). Amazon.com Inc. *YCharts.* Retrieved 2020-01-02 from https://ycharts.com/companies/AMZN/market_cap

x. YCharts Inc. (2020, January 2). Facebook Inc. *YCharts.* Retrieved 2020-01-02 from https://ycharts.com/companies/FB/market_cap

xi. YCharts Inc. (2020, January 2). Alibaba Group Holding Ltd. *YCharts.* Retrieved 2020-01-02 from https://ycharts.com/companies/BABA/market_cap

xii. YCharts Inc. (2020, January 2). Berkshire Hathaway Inc. *YCharts.* Retrieved 2020-01-02 from https://ycharts.com/companies/BRK.A/market_cap

Reference List

xiii. YCharts Inc. (2020, January 2). Tencent Holdings Market Cap. *YCharts.* Retrieved 2020-01-02 from https://ycharts.com/companies/TCTZF/market_cap

xiv. YCharts Inc. (2020, January 2). JPMorgan Chase & Co. *YCharts.* Retrieved 2020-01-02 from https://ycharts.com/companies/JPM/market_cap

xv. YCharts Inc. (2020, January 2). Visa Inc. *YCharts.* Retrieved 2020-01-02 from https://ycharts.com/companies/V/market_cap

xvi. Sheetz, M. (2017, August 24). Technology killing off corporate America: Average life span of companies under 20 years. CNBC. Retrieved 2020-01-01 from https://www.cnbc.com/2017/08/24/technology-killing-off-corporations-average-lifespan-of-company-under-20-years.html

xvii. Anthonya, S.D., Viguerie S.P., Schwartz, E.I., & Landeghem, J.V. (n.d.). 2018 Corporate Longevity Forecast: Creative Destruction is Accelerating. Retrieved 2020-01-01 from https://www.innosight.com/insight/creative-destruction/

xviii. Anthonya, S.D., Viguerie S.P., Schwartz, E.I., & Landeghem, J.V. (n.d.). 2018 Corporate Longevity Forecast: Creative Destruction is Accelerating. Retrieved 2020-01-01 from https://www.innosight.com/insight/creative-destruction/

xix. YCharts Inc. (2020, January 2). Netflix Inc. *YCharts.* Retrieved 2020-01-01 from https://ycharts.com/companies/NFLX/market_cap

xx. N.a. (n.d.) n.t., retrieved 2020-01-01 from https://s22.q4cdn.com/959853165/files/doc_financials/quarterly_reports/2019/q1/FINAL-Q119-Shareholder-Letter.pdf

xxi. Hilbert, M., & López, P. (2011). The world's technological capacity to store, communicate, and compute information. *science, 332*(6025), 60-65.

xxii. Liu, S. (2019, November 28). *Number of internet of things (IoT) connected devices worldwide in 2018, 2025 and 2030 (in billion). In Statista - The Statistics Portal.* Retrieved 2019-12-28 from https://www.statista.com/statistics/802690/worldwide-connected-devices-by-access-technology/

xxiii. Davenport, T.H. & Patil, D.J. (2012, October). Data Scientist: The Sexiest Job of the 21st Century. *Harvard Business Review.* Retrieved 2020-01-01 from https://hbr.org/2012/10/data-scientist-the-sexiest-job-of-the-21st-century

xxiv. Chuster, M., Johnson, M., & Thorat, N. (2016, November 22). *Zero-Shot Translation with Google's Multilingual Neural Machine Translation System.* Retrieved 2019-12-20 from https://ai.googleblog.com/2016/11/zero-shot-translation-with-googles.html.

xxv. Nvidia Corporation. (2018, May 20). *New AI Technique Helps Robots Work Alongside Humans.* Retrieved 2020-01-01 from https://news.developer.nvidia.com/new-ai-technique-helps-robots-work-alongside-humans/

2 Understanding Data: The Fuel of Digital and Artificial Intelligence Transformation

xxvi. ET Bureau. (2018, May 24). Data is the 21st century's oil, says Siemens CEO Joe Kaeser. *The Economic Times.* Retrieved 2020-01-01 from https://economictimes.indiatimes.com/magazines/panache/data-is-the-21st-centurys-oil-says-siemens-ceo-joe-kaeser/articleshow/64298125.cms

xxvii. Wittgenstein, L. (2013). *Tractatus logico-philosophicus.* Routledge.

xxviii. Rowley, J. (2007). The wisdom hierarchy: representations of the DIKW hierarchy. *Journal of information science*, 33(2), 163-180.

xxix. Lee, S. Y. (2019, July 1). DNA Data Storage Is Closer Than You Think: Life's information-storage system is being adapted to handle massive amounts of information. *Scientific American.* Retrieved 2019-12-28 from https://www.scientificamerican.com/article/dna-data-storage-is-closer-than-you-think/

xxx. The World Bank. *Population (total).* Retrieved 2019-12-23 from https://data.worldbank.org/indicator/SP.POP.TOTL

xxxi. Karl Rupp (2019) – "Moore's Law: Transistors per microprocessor". Published online at OurWorldInData.org. Retrieved 2020-01-01 from: https://ourworldindata.org/grapher/transistors-per-microprocessor?time=1971..2017

xxxii. Hilbert, M., & López, P. (2011). The world's technological capacity to store, communicate, and compute information. *science*, 332(6025), 60-65.

xxxiii. Liu, S. (2019, November 28). *Number of internet of things (IoT) connected devices worldwide in 2018, 2025 and 2030 (in billion). In Statista - The Statistics Portal.* Retrieved 2019-12-28 from https://www.statista.com/statistics/802690/worldwide-connected-devices-by-access-technology/

xxxiv. Dexter, A. (n.d.). How Many Words are in the Bible? *Word Counter.* Retrieved 2020-01-01 from https://wordcounter.io/blog/how-many-words-are-in-the-bible/

xxxv. Panzarino, M. (2012, January 7). Interesting fact: more Tweets posted are 28 characters than any other length [Updated]. *The Next Web.*

Reference List

Retrieved 2020-01-01 from https://smk.co/article/the-average-tweet-length-is-28-characters-long-and-other-interesting-facts

xxxvi. Domo Inc. (2019). *Data Never Sleeps 7.0.* Retrieved 2019-12-18 from https://www.domo.com/learn/data-never-sleeps-7

xxxvii. IBM. (n.d.). *IBM 3380 direct access storage device.* Retrieved 2020-01-01 from https://www.ibm.com/ibm/history/exhibits/storage/storage_3380.html

xxxviii. N.a. (n.d.). N.t. Retrieved 2020-01-01 from https://diskprices.com/?locale=us

xxxix. Conceptcarz.com. (n.d.). Ferrari 308 GTS. Retrieved 2020-01-01 from https://www.conceptcarz.com/vehicle/series.aspx?modelID=1155

xl. Nielsen, J. (2019, September 27). *Nielsen's Law of Internet Bandwidth.* Retrieved 2020-01-01 from https://www.nngroup.com/articles/law-of-bandwidth/

xli. McGarry, C. (2019, December 15). 5G Speed: 5G vs 4G Performance Compared. *Tom's Guide.* Retrieved 2020-01-01 from https://www.tomsguide.com/features/5g-vs-4g

xlii. Karl Rupp (2019) – "Moore's Law: Transistors per microprocessor". Published online at OurWorldInData.org. Retrieved 2020-01-01 from: https://ourworldindata.org/grapher/transistors-per-microprocessor?time=1971..2017

xliii. Nelson, P. (2016, December 7). Just one autonomous car will use 4,000 GB of data/day. *Network World.* Retrieved 2020-01-01 from https://www.networkworld.com/article/3147892/internet/one-autonomous-car-will-use-4000-gb-of-dataday.html

xliv. OICA. (n.d.). *PC World Vehicles in Use.* Retrieved 2020-01-01 from http://www.oica.net/wp-content/uploads//PC_Vehicles-in-use.pdf

xlv. Redcentric. (n.d.). *Byte Size Infographic.* Retrieved 2019-12-28 from https://www.redcentricplc.com/resources/byte-size-infographic/

xlvi. Redcentric. (n.d.). *Byte Size Infographic.* Retrieved 2019-12-28 from https://www.redcentricplc.com/resources/byte-size-infographic/

xlvii. Redcentric. (n.d.). *Byte Size Infographic.* Retrieved 2019-12-28 from https://www.redcentricplc.com/resources/byte-size-infographic/

xlviii. Reber, P. (2010, May 1). What Is the Memory Capacity of the Human Brain? *Scientific American.* Retrieved 2019-12-28 from https://www.scientificamerican.com/article/what-is-the-memory-capacity/

xlix. Boyland, P. (2019, May). *The State of Mobile Network Experience: Benchmarking mobile on the eve of the 5G revolution.* Retrieved 2019-12-28 from https://www.opensignal.com/sites/opensignal-com/files/data/reports/global/data-2019-05/the_state_of_mobile_experience_may_2019_0.pdf

l. Ariely, D. (2013, January 6). N.t. Retrieved 2020-01-01 from https://www.facebook.com/dan.ariely/posts/904383595868
li. Domo Inc. (2015). *Data Never Sleeps 5.0*. Retrieved 2019-12-18 from https://www.domo.com/learn/data-never-sleeps-5?aid=ogsm072517_1&sf100871281=1
lii. Domo Inc. (2019). *Data Never Sleeps 7.0*. Retrieved 2019-12-18 from https://www.domo.com/learn/data-never-sleeps-7

3 Data Storage Technologies

liii. Solid IT gmbh (2019). DB-Engines Ranking. Retrieved 2019-12-19 from *https://db-engines.com/en/ranking*
liv. N.a. (2017, May 8). Deutsche Konzerne bauen Datenplattform auf. *Handelsblatt*. Retrieved 2020-01-01 from https://www.handelsblatt.com/unternehmen/it-medien/allianz-daimler-deutsche-bank-und-co-deutsche-konzerne-bauen-datenplattform-auf/19769198.html?ticket=ST-504379-EYhVBbbNWXAYcYdSgqen-ap1
lv. Indeed.com. (2019, October 9). IoS Jobs. *Indeed*. Retrieved 2020-01-01 from https://www.indeed.com/jobs?q=ios&l=
Indeed.com. (2019, October 9). Ruby Jobs. *Indeed*. Retrieved 2020-01-01 from https://www.indeed.com/jobs?q=ruby&l=
Indeed.com. (2019, October 9). PHP Jobs. *Indeed*. Retrieved 2020-01-01 from https://www.indeed.com/jobs?q=PHP&l=
Indeed.com. (2019, October 9). C# Jobs. *Indeed*. Retrieved 2020-01-01 from https://www.indeed.com/jobs?q=c%23&l=
Indeed.com. (2019, October 9). C++ Jobs. *Indeed*. Retrieved 2020-01-01 from https://www.indeed.com/jobs?q=c%2B%2B&l=
Indeed.com. (2019, October 9). Javascript Jobs. *Indeed*. Retrieved 2020-01-01 from https://www.indeed.com/jobs?q=javascript&l=
Indeed.com. (2019, October 9). Java Jobs. *Indeed*. Retrieved 2020-01-01 from https://www.indeed.com/jobs?q=java&l=
Indeed.com. (2019, October 9). Python Jobs. *Indeed*. Retrieved 2020-01-01 from https://www.indeed.com/jobs?q=python&l=
Indeed.com. (2019, October 9). SQL Jobs. *Indeed*. Retrieved 2020-01-01 from https://www.indeed.com/jobs?q=sql&l=
lvi. Brin, S., & Page, L. (1998). The anatomy of a large-scale hypertextual web search engine. *Computer networks and ISDN systems*, 30(1-7), 107-117.
lvii. Schwartz, B. (2016, November 14). *Google's search knows about over 130 trillion pages*. Retrieved 2019-12-19 from https://searchengineland.

lviii. Porter, J. (2019, April 29). Spotify is first to 100 million paid subscribers. *The Verge.* Retrieved 2019-12-19 from https://www.theverge.com/2019/4/29/18522297/spotify-100-million-users-apple-music-podcasting-free-users-advertising-voice-speakers

lix. Brown, M., & Mishra, K. (2015, January 9). *Personalization at Spotify using Cassandra.* Retrieved 2019-12-19 from https://labs.spotify.com/2015/01/09/personalization-at-spotify-using-cassandra/

lx. Inmon, W. H., Linstedt, D., & Levins, M. (2019). *Data Architecture: A Primer for the Data Scientist: A Primer for the Data Scientist.* Academic Press.

4 Architecting Data: Data Warehouses, Data Lakes and the Cloud

lxi. Liu, S. (2019, August 9*). Total size of the public cloud computing market from 2008 to 2020 (in billion U.S. dollars). In Statista - The Statistics Portal.* Retrieved 2019-12-28 from *https://www.statista.com/statistics/510350/worldwide-public-cloud-computing/*

lxii. Costello, K. (2019, April 2). *Gartner Forecasts Worldwide Public Cloud Revenue to Grow 17.5 Percent in 2019.* Retrieved 2019-12-19 from https://www.gartner.com/en/newsroom/press-releases/2019-04-02-gartner-forecasts-worldwide-public-cloud-revenue-to-g

lxiii. Liu, S. (2019, August 9*). Total size of the public cloud computing market from 2008 to 2020 (in billion U.S. dollars). In Statista - The Statistics Portal.* Retrieved 2019-12-28 from *https://www.statista.com/statistics/510350/worldwide-public-cloud-computing/*

lxiv. Izrailevsky, Y. (2016, February 11). *Completing the Netflix Cloud Migration.* Retrieved 2019-12-19 from https://media.netflix.com/en/company-blog/completing-the-netflix-cloud-migration

lxv. Macaulay, T. (2018, September 10). Ten years on: How Netflix completed a historic cloud migration with AWS. *Computerworld.* Retrieved 2019-12-19 from https://www.computerworld.com/article/3427839/ten-years-on--how-netflix-completed-a-historic-cloud-migration-with-aws.html

lxvi. AWS. (n.d.). *AWS Snowmobile.* Retrieved 2020-01-01 from https://aws.amazon.com/de/snowmobile/

lxvii. Veljovic, I. (2016, October 11). *What does The MoonMail's Technology Stack look like? Serverless? AWS Lambda?.* Retrieved 2019-12-20 from https://blog.moonmail.io/what-is-the-technology-stack-and-architecture-behind-moonmail-4d7d6a113ed6 lxviii. Su, J. (2019, August 2). Amazon Owns Nearly Half of The Public-Cloud Infrastructure Market Worth Over $32 Billion: Report. *Forbes.* Retrieved 2019-12-20 from https://www.forbes.com/sites/jeanbaptiste/2019/08/02/amazon-owns-nearly-half-of-the-public-cloud-infrastructure-market-worth-over-32-billion-report/#6735ea8229e0

lxix. Carey, S. (2019, June 6). AWS vs Azure vs Google: What's the best cloud platform for enterprise?. *Computerworld.* Retrieved 2019-12-20 from https://www.computerworld.com/article/3429365/aws-vs-azure-vs-google-whats-the-best-cloud-platform-for-enterprise.html

lxx. AWS. (n.d.). *Cloud products.* Retrieved 2020-01-01 from https://aws.amazon.com/products/

5 Managing Data in a Company

lxxi. PayScale Inc. *Average Chief Data Office Salary.* Retrieved 2019-12-20 from https://www.payscale.com/research/US/Job=Chief_Data_Officer/Salary

lxxii. Strachnyi, K. (2019, July). *The title CDO started out as a joke.* Retrieved 2019-12-28 from https://www.kdnuggets.com/2019/07/title-cdo-started-as-joke.html

lxxiii. PayScale Inc. *Average Data Architect Salary.* Retrieved 2019-12-20 from https://www.payscale.com/research/US/Job=Data_Architect/Salary

lxxiv. PayScale Inc. *Average Database Administrator Salary.* Retrieved 2019-12-20 from https://www.payscale.com/research/US/Job=Database_Administrator_(DBA)/Salary

lxxv. Association for Computing Machinery, *IBM Dictionary of Computing*, 10th edition, 1993.

lxxvi. European Union. (2000, December 18). *Charter of fundamental rights of the European Union.* Retrieved 2019-12-20 from https://www.europarl.europa.eu/charter/pdf/text_en.pdf

lxxvii. Pfleeger, C. P., & Pfleeger, S. L. (2002). *Security in computing.* Prentice Hall Professional Technical Reference.

lxxviii. Pfleeger, C. P., & Pfleeger, S. L. (2002). *Security in computing.* Prentice Hall Professional Technical Reference.

lxxix. Pfleeger, C. P., & Pfleeger, S. L. (2002). *Security in computing.* Prentice Hall Professional Technical Reference.

lxxx. Armerding, T. (2018, December 20). The 18 biggest data breaches of the 21st century. *CSO.* Retrieved 2019-12-20 from https://www.

Reference List

lxxx. csoonline.com/article/2130877/the-biggest-data-breaches-of-the-21st-century.html

lxxxi. European Commission. *What is personal data?*. Retrieved 2019-12-20 from https://ec.europa.eu/info/law/law-topic/data-protection/reform/what-personal-data_en

lxxxii. European Commission. *What is personal data?*. Retrieved 2019-12-20 from https://ec.europa.eu/info/law/law-topic/data-protection/reform/what-personal-data_en

lxxxiii. Finn, R. L., Wright, D., & Friedewald, M. (2013). Seven types of privacy. In *European data protection: coming of age* (pp. 3-32). Springer, Dordrecht.

lxxxiv. European Union. (2000, December 18). *Charter of fundamental rights of the European Union.* Retrieved 2019-12-20 from https://www.europarl.europa.eu/charter/pdf/text_en.pdf

lxxxv. Baynes, C. (2019, February 22). China blocks 17.5 million plane tickets for people without enough 'social credit'. *The Independent.* Retrieved 2019-12-28 from https://www.independent.co.uk/news/world/asia/china-social-credit-flight-travel-plane-tickets-xi-jinping-blacklist-a8792256.html

lxxxvi. Welford, B. *What is GDPR, the EU's new data protection law?*. Retrieved 2019-12-20 from https://gdpr.eu/what-is-gdpr/?cn-reloaded=1

lxxxvii. Directive, E. U. (1995). 95/46/EC of the European Parliament and of the Council of 24 October 1995 on the protection of individuals with regard to the processing of personal data and on the free movement of such data. *Official Journal of the EC*, *23*(6).

lxxxviii. Voigt, P., & Von dem Bussche, A. (2017). The eu general data protection regulation (gdpr). *A Practical Guide, 1st Ed., Cham: Springer International Publishing*.

lxxxix. European Commission. *EU data protection rules.* Retrieved 2019-12-29 from https://ec.europa.eu/info/priorities/justice-and-fundamental-rights/data-protection/2018-reform-eu-data-protection-rules/eu-data-protection-rules_en

xc. Regulation, G. D. P. (2016). Regulation (EU) 2016/679 of the European Parliament and of the Council of 27 April 2016 on the protection of natural persons with regard to the processing of personal data and on the free movement of such data, and repealing Directive 95/46. *Official Journal of the European Union (OJ)*, *59*(1-88), 294.

xci. European Union. *Data protection under GDPR.* Retrieved 2019-12-29 from https://europa.eu/youreurope/business/dealing-with-customers/data-protection/data-protection-gdpr/index_en.htm xcii. Sinopoli, D., & Purnhargen, K. (2016). Reversed Harmonization or Horizontalization of EU Standards: Does WTO Law Facilitate or Constrain the Brussels Effect. *Wis. Int'l LJ, 34*, 92.

xciii. Brill, J. (2018, May 21). *Microsoft's commitment to GDPR, privacy and putting customers in control of their own data.* Retrieved 2019-12-20 from https://blogs.microsoft.com/on-the-issues/2018/05/21/microsofts-commitment-to-gdpr-privacy-and-putting-customers-in-control-of-their-own-data/

xciv. Regulation, G. D. P. (2016). Regulation (EU) 2016/679 of the European Parliament and of the Council of 27 April 2016 on the protection of natural persons with regard to the processing of personal data and on the free movement of such data, and repealing Directive 95/46. *Official Journal of the European Union (OJ), 59*(1-88), 294.

xcv. Hern, A. & Belam, M. (2018, May 25). LA Times among US-based news sites blocking EU users due to GDPR. *The Guardian.* Retrieved 2019-12-20 from https://www.theguardian.com/technology/2018/may/25/gdpr-us-based-news-websites-eu-internet-users-la-times

xcvi. Gigacalculator.com. (2019). *GDPR Compliance Cost Calculator.* Retrieved 2019-12-20 from https://www.gigacalculator.com/calculators/gdpr-compliance-cost-calculator.php

xcvii. Osborne, C. (2019, January 24). Data security is a major issue in GDPR compliance. *ZDNet.* Retrieved 2019-12-20 from https://www.zdnet.com/article/data-security-is-a-major-issue-in-gdpr-compliance/

6 Understanding Machine Learning as the Key Driver Behind Artificial Intelligence

xcviii. Lynch, S. (2017, March 11). *Andrew Ng: Why AI Is the New Electricity.* Retrieved 2019-12-29 from https://www.gsb.stanford.edu/insights/andrew-ng-why-ai-new-electricity

xcix. Kahn, J. (2002, March 1). It's Alive!. *Wired.* Retrieved 2020-01-01 from https://www.wired.com/2002/03/everywhere/#

c. Welch, C. (2018, May 8). Google just gave a stunning demo of Assistant making an actual phone call. *The Verge.* Retrieved 2019-12-20 from https://www.theverge.com/2018/5/8/17332070/google-assistant-makes-phone-call-demo-duplex-io-2018

ci. Chen, B. & Metz, C. (2019, May 22). Google's Duplex Uses A.I. to Mimic Humans (Sometimes). *New York Times.* Retrieved 2019-12-20 from https://www.nytimes.com/2019/05/22/technology/personaltech/ai-google-duplex.html.

Reference List

cii. Lynch, S. (2017, March 11). *Andrew Ng: Why AI Is the New Electricity*. Retrieved 2019-12-29 from https://www.gsb.stanford.edu/insights/andrew-ng-why-ai-new-electricity

ciii. Choudhury, S. (2019, February 6). In this Chennai restaurant robot waiters serve customers, speak to them in Tamil and English. *India Today*. Retrieved 2019-12-20 from https://www.indiatoday.in/india/story/in-this-chennai-restaurant-robot-waiters-serve-customers-speak-to-them-in-tamil-and-english-1449122-2019-02-06.

civ. Daley, S. (2018, December 19). *19 examples of artificial intelligence shaking up business as usual*. Retrieved 2019-12-20 from https://builtin.com/artificial-intelligence/examples-ai-in-industry.

cv. McCarthy, J., Minsky, M. L., Rochester, N., & Shannon, C. E. (2006). A proposal for the dartmouth summer research project on artificial intelligence, august 31, 1955. *AI magazine*, 27(4), 12-12.

cvi. Russell, S. J., & Norvig, P. (2016). *Artificial intelligence: a modern approach*. Malaysia; Pearson Education Limited,.

cvii. Russell, S. J., & Norvig, P. (2016). *Artificial intelligence: a modern approach*. Malaysia; Pearson Education Limited,.

cviii. Ng, A. (2019, October 19). N.t. Retrieved 2020-01-01 from https://twitter.com/andrewyng/status/788548053745569792?lang=en

cix. Reece, A. G., & Danforth, C. M. (2017). Instagram photos reveal predictive markers of depression. *EPJ Data Science*, 6(1), 15.

cx. AIVA. (n.d.). N.t. Retrieved 2020-01-01 from https://www.aiva.ai/

cxi. Schofield, D., Nagrani, A., Zisserman, A., Hayashi, M., Matsuzawa, T., Biro, D., & Carvalho, S. (2019). Chimpanzee face recognition from videos in the wild using deep learning. *Science Advances*, 5(9), eaaw0736.

cxii. Mercan, E., Mehta, S., Bartlett, J., Shapiro, L. G., Weaver, D. L., & Elmore, J. G. (2019). Assessment of Machine Learning of Breast Pathology Structures for Automated Differentiation of Breast Cancer and High-Risk Proliferative Lesions. *JAMA network open*, 2(8), e198777-e198777.

cxiii. Selvaraj, M. G., Vergara, A., Ruiz, H., Safari, N., Elayabalan, S., Ocimati, W., & Blomme, G. (2019). AI-powered banana diseases and pest detection. *Plant Methods*, 15(1), 92.

cxiv. NYU Langone Health / NYU School of Medicine. (2019, April 22). Artificial intelligence can diagnose PTSD by analyzing voices: Study tests potential telemedicine approach. *Science Daily*. Retrieved 2019-12-15 from www.sciencedaily.com/releases/2019/04/190422082232.htm

cxv. Radiological Society of North America. (2018, November 6). Artificial intelligence predicts Alzheimer's years before diagnosis. *Science Daily.* Retrieved 2019-12-15 from www.sciencedaily.com/releases/2018/11/181106104249.htm

cxvi. Gupta, T., Schwenk, D., Farhadi, A., Hoiem, D., & Kembhavi, A. (2018). Imagine this! scripts to compositions to videos. In *Proceedings of the European Conference on Computer Vision (ECCV)* (pp. 598-613).

cxvii. Wang, Y., & Kosinski, M. (2018). Deep neural networks are more accurate than humans at detecting sexual orientation from facial images. *Journal of personality and social psychology,* 114(2), 246.

cxviii. O'Sullivan, D. (n.d.). What is a deepfake, explained. *CNN Business.* Retrieved 2020-01-01 from https://edition.cnn.com/interactive/2019/01/business/pentagons-race-against-deepfakes/

cxix. Griffin, A. (2017, July 31). Facebook's artificial intelligence robots shut down after they start talking to each other in their own language. *Independent.* Retrieved 2020-01-01 from https://www.independent.co.uk/life-style/gadgets-and-tech/news/facebook-artificial-intelligence-ai-chatbot-new-language-research-openai-google-a7869706.html

cxx. Newton, C. (2016, April 5). Facebook begins using artificial intelligence to describe photos to blind users. *The Verge.* Retrieved 2020-01-01 from https://www.theverge.com/2016/4/5/11364914/facebook-automatic-alt-tags-blind-visually-impared

cxxi. Radford, A., Jozefowicz, R., & Sutskever, I. (2017). Learning to generate reviews and discovering sentiment. *arXiv preprint arXiv:1704.01444.*

cxxii. Games by Angelina. (n.d.). N.t. Retrieved 2020-01-01 from http://www.gamesbyangelina.org/

cxxiii. Quach, K. (2019, January 30). Say what?! An AI system can decode brain signals into speech. *The Register.* https://www.theregister.co.uk/2019/01/30/ai_brain_reader/

cxxiv. Byford, S. (2017, May 25). AlphaGo beats Ke Jie again to wrap up three-part match. *The Verge.* Retrieved 2020-01-01 from https://www.theverge.com/2017/5/25/15689462/alphago-ke-jie-game-2-result-google-deepmind-china

cxxv. Timmer, J. (2019, May 30). Quake III Arena is the latest game to see AI top humans. *ARS Technica.* Retrieved 2020-01-01 from https://arstechnica.com/science/2019/05/googles-ai-group-moves-on-from-go-tackles-quake-iii-arena/

cxxvi. AlphaStar team. (2019, January 24). *AlphaStar: Mastering the Real-Time Strategy Game StarCraft II.* Retrieved 2020-01-01 from https://deepmind.com/blog/article/alphastar-mastering-real-time-strategy-game-starcraft-ii

Reference List

cxxvii. Vincent, J. (2018, June 25). AI bots trained for 180 years a day to beat humans at Dota 2. *The Verge.* Retrieved 2020-01-01 from https://www.theverge.com/2018/6/25/17492918/openai-dota-2-bot-ai-five-5v5-matches

cxxviii. N.a. (2018, May 20). *New AI Technique Helps Robots Work Alongside Humans.* Retrieved 2020-01-01 from https://news.developer.nvidia.com/new-ai-technique-helps-robots-work-alongside-humans/

cxxix. Langley, P. (2011). The changing science of machine learning. *Machine Learning*, 82(3), 275-279.

cxxx. Karpathy, A. (2017, November 11). *Software 2.0.* Retrieved 2019-12-20 from https://medium.com/@karpathy/software-2-0-a64152b37c35

cxxxi. Russell, S. J., & Norvig, P. (2016). *Artificial intelligence: a modern approach.* Malaysia; Pearson Education Limited,.

cxxxii. Chuster, M., Johnson, M., & Thorat, N. (2016, November 22). *Zero-Shot Translation with Google's Multilingual Neural Machine Translation System.* Retrieved 2019-12-20 from https://ai.googleblog.com/2016/11/zero-shot-translation-with-googles.html.

cxxxiii. Whitney, C. R. (1997, August 5). Jeanne Calment, World's Elder, Dies at 122. *The New York Times.* Retrieved 2019-12-20 from https://www.nytimes.com/1997/08/05/world/jeanne-calment-world-s-elder-dies-at-122.html

cxxxiv. Silver, D. & Hassabis, D. (2017, October 18). AlphaGo Zero: *Starting from scratch.* Retrieved 2019-12-21 from https://deepmind.com/blog/article/alphago-zero-starting-scratch

cxxxv. Lee, M. H. (2017, October 19). Go Players Excited About 'More Humanlike' AlphaGo Zero. *Korea Bizwire.* Retrieved 2019-12-21 from http://koreabizwire.com/go-players-excited-about-more-humanlike-alphago-zero/98282

cxxxvi. Irpan, A. (2018, February 14). *Deep Reinforcement Learning Doesn't Work Yet.* Retrieved 2019-12-21 from https://www.alexirpan.com/2018/02/14/rl-hard.html

cxxxvii. Bansal, T., Mordatch, I., Pachoki, J., Sutskever, I., & Sidor, S. (2017, October 11). *Competitive Self-Play.* Retrieved 2019-12-21 from https://openai.com/blog/competitive-self-play/.

cxxxviii. Gregory Piatetsky. (2019). Python leads the 11 top Data Science, Machine Learning platforms: Trends and Analysis. Retrieved 2019-12-21 from *https://www.kdnuggets.com/2019/05/poll-top-data-science-machine-learning-platforms.html*

7 Creating and Testing a ML Model with Supervised Machine Learning

cxxxix.   Coles, N. A., Larsen, J. T., & Lench, H. C. (2019). A meta-analysis of the facial feedback literature: Effects of facial feedback on emotional experience are small and variable. *Psychological bulletin.*

cxl.   Vigen, T. (2015). *Spurious correlations.* Hachette Books.

cxli.   Ng, A. (2013). *Machine Learning and AI bia Brain simulations.* Retrieved 2019-12-21 from https://forum.stanford.edu/events/2011/2011slides/plenary/2011plenaryNg.pdf

cxlii.   Metz, C. (2016, December 12). 7,500 Faceless Coders Paid in Bitcoin Built a Hedge Fund's Brain. *Wired.* Retrieved 2019-12-21 from https://www.wired.com/2016/12/7500-faceless-coders-paid-bitcoin-built-hedge-funds-brain/.

cxliii.   Barreau, P. (2018, April). *How AI could compose a personalized soundtrack to your life.* Retrieved 2019-12-21 from https://www.ted.com/talks/pierre_barreau_how_ai_could_compose_a_personalized_soundtrack_to_your_life?language=en

8 Popular Machine Learning Model Classes for Supervised Machine Learning

cxliv.   Fernández-Delgado, M., Cernadas, E. and Barro, S. (2014), "Do We Need Hundreds of Classifiers to Solve Real World Classification Problems?", *Journal of Machine Learning Research*, Volume 15, Issue 1, pp. 3133–81.

cxlv.   Eindhoven University of Technology. (2018, June 20). New AI method increases the power of artificial neural networks. *Phys Org.* Retrieved 2020-01-01 from https://phys.org/news/2018-06-ai-method-power-artificial-neural.html

cxlvi.   Herculano-Houzel, S. (2009). The human brain in numbers: a linearly scaled-up primate brain. *Frontiers in human neuroscience*, 3, 31.

cxlvii.   Gershgorn, D. (2017, July 26). The data that transformed AI research—and possibly the world. *Quartz.* Retrieved 2020-01-01 from https://qz.com/1034972/the-data-that-changed-the-direction-of-ai-research-and-possibly-the-world/

cxlviii.   Perronnin, F. & Sánchez, J. (2011). *XRCE@ILSVRC2011Compressed Fisher vectors for LSVR.* Retrieved 2020-01-01 from http://image-net.org/challenges/LSVRC/2011/ilsvrc11.pdf

cxlix.   Imagenet. (n.d.). Large Scale Visual Recognition Challenge 2017 (ILSVRC2017). Retrieved 2020-01-01 from http://image-net.org/challenges/LSVRC/2017/results#loc

cl. He, K., Zhang, X., Ren, S., & Sun, J. (2015). Delving deep into rectifiers: Surpassing human-level performance on imagenet classification. In *Proceedings of the IEEE international conference on computer vision* (pp. 1026-1034).

cli. Krizhevsky, A., Sutskever, I., & Hinton, G. E. (2012). Imagenet classification with deep convolutional neural networks. In *Advances in neural information processing systems* (pp. 1097-1105).

clii. Lu, Z., Pu, H., Wang, F., Hu, Z., & Wang, L. (2017). The expressive power of neural networks: A view from the width. In *Advances in neural information processing systems* (pp. 6231-6239).

cliii. Radford, A., Sutskever, I., Jozefowicz, R., Clark, J., & Brockman, G. (2017, April 6). *Unsupervised Sentiment Neuron*. Retrieved 2019-12-22 from https://openai.com/blog/unsupervised-sentiment-neuron/

cliv. Trestman, M. (2013). The Cambrian explosion and the origins of embodied cognition. *Biological Theory, 8*(1), 80-92.

clv. Parker, A. (2003). In the blink of an eye: how vision sparked the big bang of evolution.

clvi. Villanueva, C. (2009, July 30). How Many Atoms Are There in the Universe?, *Universe Today*. Retrieved 2019-12-21 from https://www.universetoday.com/36302/atoms-in-the-universe/

clvii. Guinness World Records. English word with the most meanings. Retrieved 2019-12-21 from https://www.guinnessworldrecords.com/world-records/english-word-with-the-most-meanings/

clviii. Feiner, L. (2019, August 16). Google's assistant is still the smartest, but Amazon Alexa is getting better faster. *CNBC*. Retrieved 2019-12-21 from https://www.cnbc.com/2019/08/16/google-assistant-beats-siri-and-alexa-in-iq-test-as-all-three-improve.html.

clix. Siri Team. (2017, October). *Hey Siri: An On-device DNN-powered Voice Trigger for Apple's Personal Assistant*. Retrieved 2019-12-21 from https://machinelearning.apple.com/2017/10/01/hey-siri.html

clx. Chuster, M., Johnson, M., & Thorat, N. (2016, November 22). *Zero-Shot Translation with Google's Multilingual Neural Machine Translation System*. Retrieved 2019-12-20 from https://ai.googleblog.com/2016/11/zero-shot-translation-with-googles.html.

clxi. Nvidia Drive Labs (2919). *NVIDIA DRIVE Networks*. Retrieved 2019-12-22 from https://developer.nvidia.com/drive/drive-networks

clxii. Nvidia. (2019). Partner Innovation. Retrieved 2019-12-21 from https://www.nvidia.com/en-us/self-driving-cars/partners/

clxiii. Ribeiro, M. T., Singh, S., & Guestrin, C. (2016, August). Why should i trust you?: Explaining the predictions of any classifier. In *Proceedings of the 22nd ACM SIGKDD international conference on knowledge discovery and data mining* (pp. 1135-1144). ACM.

clxiv. Ruder, S. (2017, March 17). *Transfer Learning - Machine Learning's Next Frontier.* Retrieved 2019-12-21 from https://ruder.io/transfer-learning/

clxv. Hof, R. D. (2013, April 23). Deep Learning. *MIT Technology Review.* Retrieved 2019-12-22 from https://www.technologyreview.com/s/513696/deep-learning/

clxvi. Google Trends. (2019, December). "Deep learning (worldwide), 2004 – today" web search. Retrieved 2019-12-22 from https://trends.google.com/trends/explore?date=all&q=deep%20learning

9 Managing Machine Learning in a Company

clxvii. Wirth, R., & Hipp, J. (2000, April). CRISP-DM: Towards a standard process model for data mining. In *Proceedings of the 4th international conference on the practical applications of knowledge discovery and data mining* (pp. 29-39). Citeseer.

clxviii. Davenport, T.H. & Patil, D.J. (2012, October). Data Scientist: The Sexiest Job of the 21st Century. *Harvard Business Review.* Retrieved 2020-01-01 from https://hbr.org/2012/10/data-scientist-the-sexiest-job-of-the-21st-century

clxix. PayScale Inc. *Average Data Scientist Salary.* Retrieved 2019-12-22 from https://www.payscale.com/research/US/Job=Data_scientist/Salary

clxx. PayScale Inc. *Average Data Engineer Salary.* Retrieved 2019-12-22 from https://www.payscale.com/research/US/Job=Data_Engineer/Salary

clxxi. PayScale Inc. *Average Machine Learning Salary.* Retrieved 2019-12-22 from https://www.payscale.com/research/US/Job=Machine_Learning_Engineer/Salary

clxxii. PayScale Inc. *Average Statistician Salary.* Retrieved 2019-12-22 from https://www.payscale.com/research/US/Job=Statistician/Salary

clxxiii. PayScale Inc. *Average Software Engineer Salary.* Retrieved 2019-12-22 from https://www.payscale.com/research/US/Job=Software_Engineer/Salary

clxxiv. PayScale Inc. *Average Software Engineer Salary.* Retrieved 2019-12-22 from https://www.payscale.com/research/US/Job=Business_Analyst%2C_IT/Salary

clxxv. Logan, D., King, J., & Fischer-Wright, H. (2011). *Tribal leadership: Leveraging natural groups to build a thriving organization.* Harper Collins.

clxxvi. Knieberg, H & Ivarsson, A. (2012, October). Scaling Agile @ Spotify with Tribes, Squads, Chapters & Guilds. Retrieved 2019-12-20 from https://blog.crisp.se/wp-content/uploads/2012/11/SpotifyScaling.pdf

clxxvii. Mahadevan, D. (2017, January). ING's agile transformation. *McKinsey Quarterly.* Retrieved 2019-12-30 from https://www.mckinsey.com/industries/financial-services/our-insights/ings-agile-transformation

clxxviii. Mirani, L. (2014, July 9). Car insurance companies want to track your every move—and you're going to let them. *Quartz.* Retrieved 2019-12-23 from https://qz.com/230055/car-insurance-companies-want-to-track-your-every-move-and-youre-going-to-let-them/

clxxix. United States Congress. (2001, October 26). *Uniting and Strengthening America by Providing Appropriate Tools Required to Intercept and Obstruct Terrorism (USA Patriot Act) Act Of 2001.* Retrieved 2019-12-23 from https://www.govinfo.gov/content/pkg/PLAW-107publ56/pdf/PLAW-107publ56.pdf

clxxx. Codella, N. C., Nguyen, Q. B., Pankanti, S., Gutman, D. A., Helba, B., Halpern, A. C., & Smith, J. R. (2017). Deep learning ensembles for melanoma recognition in dermoscopy images. *IBM Journal of Research and Development, 61*(4/5), 5-1.

clxxxi. Vincent, J. (2019, January 25). Gender and racial bias found in Amazon's facial recognition technology (again). *The Verge.* Retrieved 2019-12-23 from https://www.theverge.com/2019/1/25/18197137/amazon-rekognition-facial-recognition-bias-race-gender

clxxxii. Datta, A., Tschantz, M. C., & Datta, A. (2015). Automated experiments on ad privacy settings. *Proceedings on privacy enhancing technologies, 2015*(1), 92-112.

clxxxiii. Dougal, C., Gao, P., Mayew, W. J., & Parsons, C. A. (2019). What's in a (school) name? Racial discrimination in higher education bond markets. *Journal of Financial Economics.*

clxxxiv. Danziger, S., Levav, J., & Avnaim-Pesso, L. (2011). Extraneous factors in judicial decisions. *Proceedings of the National Academy of Sciences, 108*(17), 6889-6892.

10 The Future of Data, Machine Learning and Artificial Intelligence

clxxxv. Martin, N. (2019, June 27). 13 Best Quotes About the Future Of Artificial Intelligence. *Forbes.* Retrieved 2019-12-30 from https://www.forbes.com/sites/nicolemartin1/2019/06/27/13-greatest-quotes-about-the-future-of-artificial-intelligence/#190904363bdf

clxxxvi. Reinsel, D., Gantz, J., & Rydning. (2018, November). *The Digitization of the World: From Edge to Core (An IDC White Paper).* Retrieved 2019-12-23 from https://www.seagate.com/www-content/our-story/trends/files/idc-seagate-dataage-whitepaper.pdf

clxxxvii. *IDC Data Age 2025 Study*, sponsored by Seagate, Nov 2018. Retrieved 2019-12-23 from https://www.seagate.com/www-content/our-story/trends/files/idc-seagate-dataage-whitepaper.pdf

clxxxviii. Yoav Shoham, Raymond Perrault, Erik Brynjolfsson, Jack Clark, James Manyika, Juan Carlos Niebles, Terah Lyons, John Etchemendy, Barbara Grosz and Zoe Bauer, "The AI Index 2018 Annual Report", AI Index Steering Committee, Human-Centered AI Initiative, Stanford University, Stanford, CA, December 2018.

clxxxix. Yoav Shoham, Raymond Perrault, Erik Brynjolfsson, Jack Clark, James Manyika, Juan Carlos Niebles, Terah Lyons, John Etchemendy, Barbara Grosz and Zoe Bauer, "The AI Index 2018 Annual Report", AI Index Steering Committee, Human-Centered AI Initiative, Stanford University, Stanford, CA, December 2018.

cxc. Yoav Shoham, Raymond Perrault, Erik Brynjolfsson, Jack Clark, James Manyika, Juan Carlos Niebles, Terah Lyons, John Etchemendy, Barbara Grosz and Zoe Bauer, "The AI Index 2018 Annual Report", AI Index Steering Committee, Human-Centered AI Initiative, Stanford University, Stanford, CA, December 2018.

cxci. Perlamn, C. (2017, February 26). From Product to Platform: John Deere Revolutionizes Farming. *Harvard Business Review.* Retrieved 2019-12-23 from https://digital.hbs.edu/platform-digit/submission/from-product-to-platform-john-deere-revolutionizes-farming/

cxcii. Brynjolfsson, E., & McAfee, A. (2011). *Race against the machine: How the digital revolution is accelerating innovation, driving productivity, and irreversibly transforming employment and the economy.* Brynjolfsson and McAfee.

cxciii. Brynjolfsson, E., & McAfee, A. (2014). *The second machine age: Work, progress, and prosperity in a time of brilliant technologies.* WW Norton & Company.

Reference List

cxciv. Dreifuss, E. (2017, March 24). Hate to Break It to Steve Mnuchin, But AI's Already Taking Jobs. *Wired*. Retrieved 23.12.2019 from https://www.wired.com/2017/03/hate-break-steve-mnuchin-ais-already-taking-jobs/

cxcv. Johnson, S. (2018, December 6). Global unemployment hits lowest point for 4 decades. *Financial Times*. Retrieved 2019-12-20 from https://www.ft.com/content/1e8f4cf4-f257-11e8-ae55-df4bf40f9d0d

cxcvi. Meulen van der, R. (2017, December 13). *Gartner Says by 2020, Artificial Intelligence Will Create More Jobs Than It Eliminates*. Retrieved 2019-12-23 from https://www.gartner.com/en/newsroom/press-releases/2017-12-13-gartner-says-by-2020-artificial-intelligence-will-create-more-jobs-than-it-eliminates

cxcvii. World Economic Forum. (2016, January). *The Future of Jobs: Employment, Skills and Workforce Strategy for the Fourth Industrial Revolution*. Retrieved 2019-12-23 from http://www3.weforum.org/docs/WEF_FOJ_Executive_Summary_Jobs.pdf

cxcviii. Winick, R. (2018, January 25). Every study we could find on what automation will do to jobs, in one chart. *MIT Technology Review*. Retrieved 2019-12-23 from https://www.technologyreview.com/s/610005/every-study-we-could-find-on-what-automation-will-do-to-jobs-in-one-chart/

cxcix. Manyika, J., Lund, S., Chui, M., Bughin, J., Woetzel, J., Batra, B., Ko, R., & Sanghvi, S. (2017, November). Jobs lost, jobs gained: What the future of work will mean for jobs, skills, and wages. *McKinsey Global Institute*. Retrieved 2019-12-23 from https://www.mckinsey.com/featured-insights/future-of-work/jobs-lost-jobs-gained-what-the-future-of-work-will-mean-for-jobs-skills-and-wages#part2

cc. World Intellectual Property Organisation. (2019). *WIPO Technology Trends 2019: Artificial Intelligence*. Retrieved 2019-12-23 from https://www.wipo.int/edocs/pubdocs/en/wipo_pub_1055.pdf

cci. Forbes Staff. (2018, September 20). *Forbes Releases Digital 100, The Inaugural Ranking of The Top 100 Public Companies Shaping The Digital Economy*. Retrieved 2019-12-23 from https://www.forbes.com/sites/forbespr/2018/09/20/forbes-releases-digital-100-the-inaugural-ranking-of-the-top-100-public-companies-shaping-the-digital-economy/#17a9406e3cf2.

ccii. World Intellectual Property Organisation. (2019). *WIPO Technology Trends 2019: Artificial Intelligence*. Retrieved 2019-12-23 from https://www.wipo.int/edocs/pubdocs/en/wipo_pub_1055.pdf

cciii. World Intellectual Property Organisation. (2019). *WIPO Technology Trends 2019: Artificial Intelligence*. Retrieved 2019-12-23 from https://www.wipo.int/edocs/pubdocs/en/wipo_pub_1055.pdf

cciv. Chui, M. (2018, June). Kai-Fu Lee's perspectives on two global leaders in artificial intelligence: China and the United States. *McKinsey Global Institute*. Retrieved 2019-12-23 from https://www.mckinsey.com/featured-insights/artificial-intelligence/kai-fu-lees-perspectives-on-two-global-leaders-in-artificial-intelligence-china-and-the-united-states

ccv. PricewaterhouseCoopers. (2019). *22nd Annual Global CEO Survey: CEOs' curbed confidence spells caution*. Retrieved 2019-12-23 from https://www.pwc.com/gx/en/ceo-survey/2019/report/pwc-22nd-annual-global-ceo-survey.pdf

ccvi. Harari, Y. N. (2019, January 22). Who Will Win the Race for AI?. *Foreign Policy*. Retrieved 2019-12-23 from https://foreignpolicy.com/gt-essay/who-will-win-the-race-for-ai-united-states-china-data/

ccvii. Grace, K., Salvatier, J., Dafoe, A., Zhang, B., & Evans, O. (2018). When will AI exceed human performance? Evidence from AI experts. *Journal of Artificial Intelligence Research*, *62*, 729-754. Retrieved 2019-12-21 from https://www.jair.org/index.php/jair/article/download/11222/26431/

ccviii. Grace, K., Salvatier, J., Dafoe, A., Zhang, B., & Evans, O. (2018). When will AI exceed human performance? Evidence from AI experts. *Journal of Artificial Intelligence Research*, *62*, 729-754. Retrieved 2019-12-21 from https://www.jair.org/index.php/jair/article/download/11222/26431/

Index

Alphabet 't' after a page number indicates table.

A

Artificial intelligence (AI), 20, 160ff
    AI effect, 161
    AI winter, 165
    General AI, 160, 329ff
    Narrow AI, 160, 330f
    Strong AI, 160, 329ff
    Weak AI, 160, 330f
Access control, 145ff
Advanced analytics, 17f, 28
Agile project management, 296ff
Agent, 194ff
Amazon, 5, 95, 100, 128, 132, 133t, 259, 292, 310, 321, 326
    Amazon Cloud Services (AWS), 16, 110t, 120, 132, 133t, 135t
    Amazon DynamoDB, 83, 133, 95
Apache, 79, 87f, 91, 92t–95t
    Accumulo, 92t
    Cassandra, 87, 92t
    Flume, 92t
    Kafka, 92t
    Hbase, 92t
    Hive, 92t, 114, 293t
    Spark, 92t, 93, 114, 136t, 201, 293t
Authentication, 145t, 146f
Autonomous driving, 20, 35, 164, 171, 182, 194f, 253, 260, 263, 312
Availability, 85ff, 99

B

Batch processing, 47f
Bias, 240, 255, 257, 310, 313

Big data, 14f, 35, 48–51, 73ff, 82, 90, 91t, 92t, 93t, 108, 116f, 160, 201t, 268
Boxplot, 277t, 279
Business analyst, 274, 291, 295, 295t
Business intelligence (BI), 17f, 112, 134t, 115t
Business process, 9, 19f, 27, 29, 56, 89, 98, 100, 104, 109, 271–275, 282–284, 287t, 289, 291, 295t, 296
Business understanding, 271f, 286t

C

CAP theorem, 81ff
Causation, 210ff, 280
Chatbot, 20, 167t
Chief data & analytics officer, 134ff, 303
Churn, customer, 12t
Classification, 180f, 183, 186f, 239, 245t, 246t, 251
Client-server model, 123ff
Cloud (computing), 14f, 16–17, 94t, 118ff
    Enterprise cloud, 119t
    Hybrid cloud, 122–123, 129f
    Private cloud, 16, 119t, 120–122
    Public cloud, 16, 119ff, 128ff
    Virtual private cloud (VPC), 16, 119t, 120ff, 133t
Clustering, 181t, 184, 187ff, 188t, 189–191, 192
Column oriented database, 82, 84, 92t, 94t
Compiler, 197

365

Computer
- Computer cluster, 15, 50f, 76–79, 77t, 79–81, 84ff, 88t, 90, 91, 91t, 92t, 93t, 112f, 132, 135t, 248, 283
- Computer scientist, 68, 73, 200t
- Computer security, 144f
- Computer vision, 20, 164, 182, 207, 250t, 252f, 259–263

Comma separated file (CSV), 42t
Consistency, 38t, 39, 73, 82t, 84ff, 89t, 95t
Conformity, 38t
Continuous deployment, 273, 282ff, 301
Core warehouse, 103t, 103ff, 114
Correlation coefficient, 208ff, 209t
CouchDB, 84, 95, 95t
Curse of dimensionality, 217f, 218t

D

Data
- Data analytics, 17f, 28ff, 89t, 115t, 134t, 302ff
- Data architect, 135f
- Data architecture, 15–16, 96ff, 116–120, 135t, 136, 321
- Data artist, 136, 136t
- Data catalogue, 138t, 139
- Data collection, 30ff, 307f
- Data dictionary, 139ff
- Data democratization, 16, 137
- Data engineer, 288, 291, 293t–294t, 302, 304
- Data ethics, 306ff
- Data exploration, 272, 276ff, 285t, 287t
- Data generating process, 30ff, 38, 307
- Data governance, 16, 99, 134t, 137ff, 156, 302ff, 321
- Data integration, 40, 103ff, 136t, 281t

Data integration expert, 136t
Data, labelled, 182, 183ff, 252
Data lake, 15, 96, 99–111, 111ff, 116–118, 139f
Data mart, 106, 282
Data mining, 17ff, 271
Data model, 57ff, 72–74, 81ff, 89t, 94t, 95t
DataOps, 300ff
Data pipeline, 107ff, 284, 290, 295t
Data preparation, 213t, 271f, 276ff, 299, 302
Data privacy, 127, 139t, 143f, 150t
Data processing, 112, 114f, 154
Data protection, 143–144, 148, 150ff
Data quality, 20f, 36ff, 39ff, 138, 139t, 141f, 286ff
Data security, 143ff, 152, 157
Data science, 17–19, 199t, 290, 305
Data scientist, 19, 140, 198, 240, 274, 291, 292, 293t, 304f, 311, 312, 320
Data source, 31, 40, 46, 103–105, 108, 110, 113, 136t, 139, 276f, 281t
Data staging layer, 104, 105
Data storage, 15f, 52ff, 68, 73ff, 82, 88, 89t, 90ff, 102t, 105f, 108f, 111ff, 117, 135t, 136t
Data, unlabelled, 182ff, 187f, 192
Data visualization, 278ff, 18f, 125
Data visualization expert, 136t
Data warehouse (DWH), 15, 18, 96, 99, 100ff, 115t, 136t
Database, 15, 18, 54–59, 59–76, 81–89, 94t, 96, 99, 100, 104–106, 109, 110, 112, 116, 136, 146
Database administrator, 136t
Database management system (DBMS), 54ff, 61, 68, 73, 91, 94t

Index

Decision tree, 207–208, 225–226, 238t, 239, 245t, 246t
Deep learning, 19, 160, 165, 168t, 169f, 173, 175, 199t, 200t, 249ff, 257ff, 268ff, 294t, 318
Deep neural network, 19, 166t, 194, 241, 244, 248, 249ff, 254f, 256ff, 263ff, 267t, 268ff
Descriptive analytics, 17f
Design thinking, 274, 295t
DevOps, 300ff, 320
Diagnostic analytics, 18, 28
Digitiation, 2ff, 8ff, 76
Digitalization, 2ff, 8ff, 326
Digital transformation, 2ff, 8ff, 13, 319
Distributed file system, 76ff, 91t, 92t, 93t, 111ff
Document database, 82ff
Domain expert, 292, 296

E

Encryption, 145t, 147f, 152, 157
Ensemble learning, 238ff, 245t, 246t
Excel, 31t, 42t, 44, 52ff, 55, 56, 123, 134t
Exploratory data analysis (EDA), 276ff
Extract-load-transform (ELT), 110, 112, 114, 116t
Extract-transform-load (ETL), 103ff, 110f, 114, 116t

F

Feature
 Feature engineering, 203, 213ff, 255ff, 296
 Feature selection, 203, 215ff, 256
Fraud detection, 11t, 47

G

General Data Protection Regulation (GDPR), 152, 153–158, 289
General purpose technology, 9, 164

Generalized linear model (GLM), 244t–245t
Google
 Google File System (GFS), 79
 Google Cloud Platform, 132f
Graph database, 82, 84, 95t

H

Hadoop, 15–16, 79f, 91t, 92t
 Hadoop Distributed File System (HDFS), 79, 91t
Hidden layer, 251, 253ff, 264, 266
Histogram, 278
Hub and spoke model, 304
Human generated data, 31t, 32

I

ImageNet, 251f
Infrastructure as a service (IaaS), 16, 118t, 124t
Insurance, 9t, 11t, 44, 102, 129, 170, 302
Integrity, 38t, 39, 40, 136t
Interface, 54, 93f, 196ff
 Application programming interface (API), 201t
 User interface, 201t
Interpreter, 197f
Internet of things (IoT), 14–15, 32–34

J

JSON, 42, 42t, 83, 88t, 89t, 95t

K

Kanban, 296ff
Keras, 200t–201t
Key-value store, 61t, 82ff, 92t, 95t
Key variable/ attribute, 40, 64ff

L

Label, 182ff, 207
Library, 197, 200t, 201t
Lock in, 128

M

Machine generated data, 31ff
Machine learning (ML), 2t, 17ff, 168ff
- Machine learning engineer, 266, 274, 292, 294t
- Machine learning, reinforcement, 173, 181, 181t, 184, 193ff, 243, 251
- Machine learning, supervised, 172ff, 181ff, 184–186, 203ff, 227ff, 243ff, 251, 294t
- Machine learning, unsupervised, 172, 181, 181t, 183–184, 187–192

Mapreduce, 91t
Marketing, 9t, 12t, 13, 29, 45, 106, 115, 269
Massive Parallel Processing (MPP), 74, 88t, 94t, 109
Master data, 45–46
Mean absolute error (MAE), 230, 232, 233, 236
Microsoft Azure (MS Azure), 110t, 132, 133t, 201t
Mind power, 3t, 8ff, 161t, 162–164, 171
Missing values, 38, 38t, 40, 278, 281
MLlib, 93t, 201t
Model, 205ff
- Model deployment, 272ff, 282ff, 287t, 289ff

MongoDB, 61t, 95t
Moore's law, 34, 317
Muscle power, 8, 10, 161t, 162, 164, 171
MySQL, 61t, 68, 94t

N

Natural language processing (NLP), 20, 160, 164, 167t, 168t, 175, 250, 259ff, 268
Neo4j, 95t
Neural Network, 19, 166t, 169, 170, 194, 200t, 230, 241, 243f, 248, 249ff
Next best action marketing, 12t
Nielsen's law, 34
Noise, 176ff, 216, 234, 235, 239
Node, 77ff, 79ff, 81ff, 89–91, 92t, 94t, 101, 201t, 225, 245t, 249, 250t
NoSQL/ non-relational, 15, 76, 81ff, 95t

O

Observation, 62, 70, 83, 184, 187, 188, 189–191, 205, 210, 221, 225, 248, 265
Operating system, 79, 90, 123–125, 197
Operational system, 104
Oracle, 55, 61t, 68, 94t, 132
Overfitting, 203, 216, 218t, 233–240

P

Package, 197ff, 200t
Partition tolerance, 85–86
Pattern, 11t, 18, 19, 172, 173, 176ff, 183, 185, 188t, 203, 207–209, 220, 233ff, 277t
Personal data, 144, 148ff, 156–157, 307, 308, 313, 319
Platform as a service (PaaS), 16, 118t, 124t, 125, 131
Postgres, 94t
Predictive analytics, 29
Predictive maintenance, 31, 182, 192
Production, 9t, 12t, 32, 38, 41, 104, 182, 275, 284
Programming language, 69, 196–198
Project manager, 296
PySpark, 201t
Python, 93t, 196ff, 199t, 200t, 201t, 293t, 294t

Index

Q
Query, 56, 69ff

R
R, 93t, 196, 198, 199t, 283, 293t, 295t
Random forest, 238t, 239, 246t–247t
Regression, 181, 183, 186–187, 244t, 245t
Relational database system, 15, 59ff, 82, 85–89, 94t, 95t, 96, 100, 101, 108, 109, 112, 114, 117
Relational data model, 59ff, 73, 74, 81, 84, 95t
Retail, 4, 9t, 108
Reward, 184, 194
Robotics, 20, 160, 162, 164, 168t
RStudio, 199t

S
Serverless architecture, 130–132
Scaling, 76, 77f, 77t, 84, 90, 109, 131
    Horizontal scaling/ Scaling out, 77f, 90
    Vertical scaling/ scaling up, 76f
Scatterplot, 209t, 278, 280
Scikit learn, 200t
Schema-on-read, 112
Schema-on-write, 109
Scrum, 296, 298–299
Semi-structured data, 41t–42t
Sensor data, 11t, 12t, 25, 31, 50
Signal, 176ff, 185, 203, 216, 234, 24, 251, 255
Software
    Software as a service (SaaS), 16, 118t, 124t
    Software development, 135t, 173, 175, 199t, 293, 297, 298, 301
    Software engineer, 294t, 295t
Spark (s. Apache Spark)
SparkR, 201t

Statistics, 17ff, 171, 278, 293–295t
Statistician, 291, 294t–295t
Streaming data, 46–47, 92t
Structured data, 18, 41ff, 46, 52, 61, 65, 68, 72, 74, 88t, 89, 108, 113, 115t
Structured Query Language (SQL), 55, 59, 68ff, 73, 89t, 110
Summary statistics, 278

T
Technological unemployment, 6, 31, 323
Tensorflow, 200t–201t
Timeseries, 222
Test set, 219–220, 222, 231ff, 236ff
Training set, 219ff, 233–235, 236t, 239, 240, 246t
Transactional data, 45–46, 104, 106
Transfer learning, 265, 266ff

U
Underfitting, 234ff
Unstructured data, 18, 19, 41ff, 46, 48, 74, 108, 112–114, 115t

V
Validation
    Validation, cross, 237–238
    Validation error, 238
    Validation set, 219ff, 227ff
Variable
    Explanatory, 182t, 207, 213
    Explained, 182t, 207
    Dependent, 182t, 207
    Independent, 182t, 207, 244
    Input, 178, 182t, 185, 188t, 203, 206, 207, 208, 213, 214, 217, 218, 229, 243f, 248, 272, 288
    Key, 40, 64ff
    Label, 182t, 207
    Outcome, 182t, 207

Predicted, 182t, 207
Predictor, 182t, 207
Target, 181ff, 203, 206, 208, 213, 215, 219, 225, 233, 240, 243f, 247–249, 272, 287t

W, X

Weight, 255, 257
XML, 42t, 83

About the Authors

Alexander Thamm is a founder, CEO and pioneer in the field of data and artificial intelligence (AI). His mission is to create value from data and put Germany and Europe back on track to compete at eye level with the AI superpowers, the USA and China. He is a founding member of the German AI Association, a keynote speaker and the author of numerous publications on big data and AI. Alex is also the co-founder of the DATA Festival, where AI experts and visionaries design the data-driven world of tomorrow.

In 2012, he founded Alexander Thamm GmbH (AT), the first data science consultancy in Germany. Today, the company is one of the leading data and AI consultancies in the German-speaking region, with more than 150 experts. AT has successfully implemented more than 600 data science and AI projects and is the trusted partner of medium and large clients across all industries, including 20 corporations of the German DAX-30.

With the Data Journey, Alex developed a coherent system to drive AI adoption and business value for companies, governments and non-profits. He also founded the Data Academy to share knowledge with everyone, in order to create a better world based on new technologies.

Michael Gramlich is a freelance consultant for data science and machine learning. Before that, he worked as a data scientist at Alexander Thamm GmbH consulting for multinational corporations across Europe. He is passionate about implementing data science and machine learning projects end-to-end, from their conception until the deployment of operational data products that generate real value.

The only thing he loves more than getting his hands dirty with data is sharing his expertise and experience, which he has done in many trainings for various international companies and universities. He holds a master's degree in International Economics from the Institut de hautes études internationales et du développement Geneva. You can reach Michael through his website, www.michael-gramlich.com.

Dr. Alexander Borek is a data-analytics executive, evangelist and thought leader. In his current role as Global Head of Data, Analytics & AI, he runs an international unit consisting of data scientists, data engineers and product managers who develop and operate high-end data-analytics products. Before that, he led the data-analytics transformation at Volkswagen Group and worked as a consultant at Gartner and IBM, where he advised Fortune Global 500 executives in multiple industries. Dr. Borek is the author of the books *Total Information Risk Management* and *Marketing with Smart Machines*.

Printed in Poland
by Amazon Fulfillment
Poland Sp. z o.o., Wrocław